LIVES AND TIMES OF DISTINGUISHED ARTISTS

THE MIND OF THE ARTIST

ATTENTION DEFICIT HYPERACTIVITY DISORDER, AUTISM, ASPERGER SYNDROME AND DEPRESSION

LIVES AND TIMES OF DISTINGUISHED ARTISTS

Additional books in this series can be found on Nova's website
under the Series tab.

Additional e-books in this series can be found on Nova's website
under the e-book tab.

LIVES AND TIMES OF DISTINGUISHED ARTISTS

THE MIND OF THE ARTIST

ATTENTION DEFICIT HYPERACTIVITY DISORDER, AUTISM, ASPERGER SYNDROME AND DEPRESSION

MICHAEL FITZGERALD

nova publishers
New York

Library of Congress Cataloging-in-Publication Data

The mind of the artist : attention deficit hyperactivity disorder, autism, asperger syndrome & depression / Editors: Michael Fitzgerald (Trinity College).
pages cm. -- (Lives and times of distinguished artists)
Includes bibliographical references and index.
ISBN 978-1-63463-573-8 (hardcover)
1. Artists with mental disabilities. I. Fitzgerald, Michael, 1946 October 7- editor.
NX164.M45M56 2015
700.1'9--dc23
2014043167

Published by Nova Science Publishers, Inc. † New York

THE MIND OF THE CREATOR

All the world's a stage
And all the men and women merely players:
They have their exits and their entrances;
And one man in his time plays many parts...

As You Like It

William Shakespeare

CONTENTS

SYNOPSIS

The Mind of the Artist (~95,000 words) is a provocative and novel investigation of the psyches of 60 artists, predominantly from the world of film, theatre and television/radio – writers, actors, producers and directors ranging from Shakespeare and Voltaire to major late-twentieth-century figures such as Spike Milligan, Sam Peckinpah and Frank Sinatra, by way of F. Scott Fitzgerald, Orson Welles and Judy Garland. Irish artists featured include Oliver St. John Gogarty, Jimmy O'Dea and Richard Harris.

The chapters, which range from quite brief vignettes to more in-depth studies, examine the background of each individual before considering their personality, social relationships and work. Professor Fitzgerald brings his expertise to bear in elucidating the psychological factors, strengths and frailties that shaped the lives and careers of these prominent creators, many of whom must be regarded as geniuses.

The lives of extraordinary artists are of interest in themselves; when their stories are told from the perspective of expert psychological insight, the results are fascinating and revealing.

ABOUT THE AUTHOR

Michael Fitzgerald is Henry Marsh Professor of Child and Adolescent Psychiatry at Trinity College Dublin. He was the first Professor of Child Psychiatry in Ireland. A Clinical and Research Consultant to the Irish Society for Autism and an Honorary member of the Northern Ireland Institute of Human Relations, he has a doctorate in the area of autism and has been a researcher in this area since 1973. He has clinically diagnosed over 2000 individuals with autism and Asperger syndrome and has served on the Government Task Force on Autism and the Family. He has contributed to national and international journals and is the author of over 120 publications. He has written or co-written 20 books (www.professormichaelfitzgerald.eu/books.html).

ACKNOWLEDGMENTS

Special thanks to my wife Frances, my sons Mark (coincidentally an actor), Owen and Robert, and also to Brendan O'Brien for editorial support.

THE PSYCHOLOGY OF STAGE AND SCREEN

INTRODUCTION

From time immemorial human beings have tried to understand great creators of the stage. More recently, this has extended to the screen. In ancient times it was felt that the gods had the ability to bestow great creativity but nowadays there is a shift towards neurobiology. Scientist Jacob Bronowski (1972) states that "man masters nature not by force but by understanding". To that end, this book attempts to throw light on creative persons associated with stage and screen to gain a greater understanding of their mindset. It will examine their unusual personalities, their brains, and their working methods. Jung (1952) is correct in his assertion that creativity is mysterious. Nevertheless, much progress has been made in understanding creativity since he wrote "creative man is a riddle that we may try to answer in various ways, but always in vain, a truth that has not prevented modern psychology from turning now and again to the question of the artist and his art".

The reductionistic approach to understanding creativity is to reduce it to as simple a formulation as possible. A comment by Einstein is also relevant to a study of stage and screen creativity: "Things should be made as simple as possible, but not simpler" (Heilman, 2005). Psychological tests of creativity have not been of much help in understanding great creativity. However, they may be of more help with low level everyday creativity. Just how complex creativity is can be witnessed in the accounts of creative persons discussed in the book.

Advances in technology in the modern age ushered in film-making as a major art form. Tredell (2002) notes that for the first 25 years of the 20th century major artistic advances were made by the paintings of Picasso, the music of Stravinsky, the poetry of T. S. Elliot, the fiction of James Joyce, and film-making. In reference to film-making, Stam (2000) notes that the characterisation of the cinema as the "seventh art" implicitly gave film artists the same status as writers and painters. Stam (2000) also discusses the "cult of the auteur", whereby the director became a highly creative person and consequently valorised. Indeed French filmmaker Jacques Rivette said that "an auteur is someone who speaks in the first person" (Tredell, 2002). The director as auteur was an artist, according to Tredell, who, like the author of a novel, stamps his distinctive vision and style on his works, for example, Alfred Hitchcock. It was his or her creative vision that could make a film original. And it was a highly inventive and innovative form of expression. Tredell notes French filmmaker Alexandre Astruc's comment that the cinema was becoming a new means of expression "analogous to painting or the novel". In fact, Astruc coined the term "camera-pen", where the director was no longer merely "the servant of a pre-existing text but a creative artist in his/her own right". Of course nowadays, this art form has reached an apotheosis; there is an overemphasis on the director to the detriment of other forms of creativity.

How reality and the objective world are depicted, however, is at the heart of art. According to Bazin (1967), what French filmmaker Jean Mitry argues is not the reality itself but a new appearance correlated to the world of things, what is called "camera perception", and, irrespective of the will of the cameraman, it produces a certain "segregation of space", which is a restructuring of the real so that it can no longer be considered "objective and mediate". Distortion of images is inevitable in art and indeed necessary for great art. In terms of this blurring of fixed positions of subject and object, Tredell (2002) notes that "post-Eisenstein physics offers a conception of representation in which subject and object are no longer caught in fixed positions but caught up in time". Of course, achieving a 100 per cent accurate description of human beings is impossible. When a crime happens, for example, it is very difficult to get different observers to agree on what exactly took place. Obviously, everyone in the audience sees their own unique film in the cinema; no two people have ever seen the same movie from the same subjective point of view.

UNDERSTANDING GREAT CREATORS OVER TIME

Throughout history various hypotheses on creativity have been put forward. Porter (1998) observed different ideas of creativity, including the "divine fire" or "god's touch" idea, and the notion that creativity was the product of the "melancholy humour" and "the muses". The word "genius" does connote innate abilities, which originally, according to the *Oxford Companion to the Mind*, related to the male spirit of the household and subsequently to the spiritual part of each individual (Gregory, 1987). Indeed Mark Twain recognised the importance of the innate when he said "individual differences are what make horse races" (Lykken, 1998).

There is no doubt that persons of genius have a different genetic profile than non-geniuses. The philosopher Immanuel Kant expressed it well when he said that "genius was an incommunicable gift that cannot be taught or handed on, but is mysteriously imparted to certain artists by nature, and dies with the person" (Howe, 1999). English psychologist Francis Galton confused genius and eminence and thought that genius could be passed on. It is very rare but not unheard of to have a genius in the next generation. Genius must not be confused with talent, however, which is a much lower form of creativity (Fitzgerald & O'Brien, 2007).

What you observe in the great artists, according to Ezra Pound, is "the capacity to see ten things where the ordinary man sees one, and where the man of talent sees two or three, plus the ability to register multiple perceptions in the material of his art" (Atkinson, 1993). This ability to register multiple perceptions lends itself to originality, innovation, and novelty. The association of creativity with insanity or eccentricity was evident too from earliest times. Plato saw creativity as a "frenzy of divine madness" (Steptoe, 1998), while in Ancient Rome, Seneca observed that no great genius has ever existed without some touch of madness (Broad, 197a7). Indeed the poet Dryden expressed a similar view: "Great wits are sure to madness near allied and thin partitions do their bounds divide" (Simonton, 1994). The extraordinary talents afforded the eccentric could be enlightening, as Weekes and Ward (1988) quote an eccentric: "Blessed are the cracked, for they shall let in the light."

Great creators can sometimes meet with considerable hostility from the public. They can excite enormous jealousy and envy. This is something that can be difficult for great creators to bear as they are often hypersensitive to criticism. Great creators on stage and screen have to deal with resentful, small-minded attacks from critics on a constant basis. Conflict can be quite complex, given that these creators also rebel against their teachers, against previous artistic work, and have to disturb the status quo. In the face of true genius, Jonathan Swift (Fitzgerald, 2005) recognised that "the dunces are all in confederacy against him" (Roscoe, 1841).

Examining the creativity of filmmaker Ingmar Bergman, Singer (2007) emphasises his "innovative fluidity of openness to change" over time. He claims Bergman's creativity resembled the inventiveness of Picasso, or rather Monet in particular. While Picasso went through many stages, some "parodistic" of what other great artists had achieved, Monet generally remained himself. In essence Bergman used his own personal psyche for his films. According to Singer (2007), Bergman not only went through different periods in his creativity but also developed continuously from beginning to end. Like Picasso his final films constituted "highly advanced resolutions of themes" that preoccupied him in subsequent years (Singer, 2007). For Bergman, art was a way of dealing with his life and personal conflicts. It was art as therapy. Indeed movie-making often constitutes a form of therapy.

METHODOLOGY OF BOOK

There are those who might criticise me for commenting on and "diagnosing" people who are dead and whom I have never met. There is a long academic tradition in this area, however. Some of the most respected academics have written in this fashion, for example, Frith and Houston (2000) in their work *Autism in History* and Sula Wolff (1995) in *Loners: The Life Path of Unusual Children*. I accumulated a great deal of information written about these people by biographers and contemporary writers who had no interest in the conditions I described. There is no basis in fact for claiming the material is biased.

Recording history and the nature of biography are often fraught with controversy. It is absurd to take Henry Ford's view that history is more or less "bunk" (Hyman, 1993); while a cautious approach to history and biography is clearly to be welcomed, Ford presents an extreme viewpoint. I am sympathetic to Monk's (1996) view that the point of biography is to understand its subject and that "you are trying to fit the whole into a comprehensive picture, looking for themes, images, ideas that provide a key to the whole". This is certainly the driving force of this book. It is written with the hindsight of current knowledge (Frith & Houston, 2000) and the fact that I have experience of diagnosing over 1800 of patients with high functioning autism/Asperger syndrome. The persons described in this book are exactly similar.

Asperger syndrome and high functioning autism are often used interchangeably. Science is still trying to separate them. If a difference exists, then it is that persons with Asperger syndrome want to make contact but have poor social know-how, whereas persons with high functioning autism are uninterested. These conditions were first described by Hans Asperger in 1938 and later in 1943 by Leo Kanner, the father of American child psychiatry; he is guilty of not attributing the discovery to Asperger who wrote about them five years previously (Fitzgerald, 2008; Lyons & Fitzgerald, 2007; Rausch et al., 2008). This effectively was plagiarism. These conditions are characterised by poor social reciprocal behaviour, problems reading non-verbal behaviour, being loners with poor capacity to share thoughts and take turns. They often have an unusual tone of voice, have narrow eccentric interests, like to do things repetitively and have preservation of sameness, for example, they like to work with the same people repetitively. They can be very sensitive to touch or sound and have increased sensitivity in many senses, for example, visual and auditory, which can lead to increased creativity.

Many of the great creators in this book show Asperger syndrome or features of it, attention deficit hyperactivity disorder or features of it, as well as depression. Eccentricity would have been an old term applied to them. Certainly, many of the people in this book show a massive capacity for persistence, have massive energy, are workaholics, have huge motivation, and have enormous capacity for observation of detail. Asperger (1944) pointed out that the kind of intelligence he observed in these people was a type of intelligence largely untouched by tradition and culture "unconventional, unorthodox, strongly pure and original, akin to the intelligence of true creativity". This can be clearly observed in many of the people in this book.

School and formal education is frequently problematic for these people. They often show poor school progress. Indeed the father of playwright and poet W. B. Yeats – an unsuccessful painter himself – was told that his son would never amount to anything. Yeats failed to get into Trinity College Dublin but turned out to be a Nobel Prize winning poet, though a lesser playwright (Fitzgerald, 2004). Despite their huge capacity for creativity, these people are bored with the school curriculum and rote learning. A major part of the unwritten curriculum in many schools is undoubtedly to stifle creativity. In the past creative children were certainly seen as a nuisance, eccentric, and needing to be punished accordingly. Most of the people described in this book are not average and are atypical. They are outside the so-called normal range of people. A current concern outlined by Baron-Cohen (2009) is that if we could diagnose these conditions *in utero* – so-called prenatal screening given that mothers of these babies have high testosterone levels *in utero* – this may lead to the elimination of the genes discussed in this book, by that I mean eliminating a section of the population with great creativity associated with high functioning autism/Asperger syndrome, for example, great mathematicians.

The focus of this book is Asperger savants (Fitzgerald, 2004) not autistic savants associated with low IQ. The great creators in this book are successful because they have broken "the grip on [their] imagination of logical-seeming storytelling and retrieve apparently irrational ideas, and put them to constructive use" (Hudson, 1987). This is what persons with high functioning autism/Asperger syndrome so often do. Snyder et al. (2004) note that because autistic individuals have fewer mental models (concepts) of the world, they can be more aware of novelty. Snyder et al., also emphasise the importance of getting a more childlike view of the world to be creative. In a previous study, I have shown that convergers can also be good at the arts (Fitzgerald, 2005) and, in reality, people do not fit into narrow tight categories. Persons with great creativity march to a different drum at a huge psychological price: that is, those with Asperger syndrome are wired differently at a neural level which leads to the odd autistic narrative and their creativity; they are massive observers of tiny social details but poor at seeing the big social picture. For Ludwig Wittgenstein the kind of understanding that exists in "seeing connections", as noted by his biographer Ray Monk (1990), I would use to describe this book; by that I mean linking a person to a type of creative activity. The greatest fallacy in philosophy is in seeing no connection between the author and their philosophical work, the so-called genetic fallacy.

CHARACTERISTICS OF GREAT ART

Great art surprises us and indeed in assessing a work on stage or screen the element of surprise is critical to success. This surprise also comes from the method of presentation of well-known works, as noted by Heilman (2005): "Art historians have repeatedly commented upon Mona Lisa's facial expression, which appears to change, making her appear as if she is alive." Livingstone (2002), quoted in E. H. Gombrich book *The Story of Art*, noticed that when she focused on Mona Lisa's mouth she appeared to have a serious expression but when she focused on another part of the picture, her well-documented smile became apparent (Heilman, 2005). Here you have elements of great art, the element of surprise, and contradiction. You have the condensation of multiple meanings in one picture.

Creativity and change is an endless process. It is creativity that overthrows the dominant ways of presenting material on stage and screen. Great art in any form is not replicative and this is what divides great art from lesser art. Bronowski (1972) is very critical of the notion that art sets out to copy nature:

> Art is not a copy of nature but a recreation of her. We remake nature by the act of discovery … and [great works of scriptwriting] are new to every reader and yet are his own experience because he himself re-creates them. They are the marks of unity in variety; and the instant when the mind seizes this for itself, in art … the heart misses a beat.

Creativity and survival are inherently linked. In evolutionary terms all the greatest artists follow the principle of the survival of the fittest. Only the most innovative and novel great creators enter the pantheon of great creators.

THE PROCESS OF CREATIVE WRITING

The actual process of creativity, often shrouded in mystery, involves a dissociative state. Playwright Neil Simon describes this process as "I slip into a state that is apart from reality" (Andreasen, 2005). Andreasen describes this state as similar to an unconscious state, a place where words, thoughts and ideas float freely, collide, and then "ultimately coalesce". Furthermore, this "dissociative state", as one of the hallmarks of the creative process, is characterised by the capacity to focus intensely to dissociate and to realise an apparently "remote and transcendent place". Simon relates how "my mind wanders – even when I talk" (Andreasen, 2005). Features of attention deficit disorder are very common in great creators; they have less linear thinking and allow all kinds of ideas to float into their mind. Simon (1998) describes all his unformed ideas in the early phase, putting huge emphasis on character and building the play around an event. He says confidence is critical for a writer, emphasising the importance of "a writer's pain" and the need for "some divine inspiration and a slight bit of madness". He describes writer's block as not being able to come up with the correct idea.

By Simon's own admission, he does not write consciously but rather as if "the muse sits on my shoulder" (Andreasen, 2005). Andreasen points out that in general creativity is not a rational, logical process. It emerges from the unconscious and surprises the author. Indeed in Simon's *Rewrites: A Memoir* (1998), he notes that he does not know how the play will end until near the end of the writing process; he simply goes where the creative process takes him. Great artists, whether writers, filmmakers or painters, stop when the work is done. They simply know at that stage, unlike lesser artists, for example in the case of W. B. Yeats's father (Fitzgerald, 2005). The great artist is aware of closure. However, the work may require considerable revision before that point is reached. Simon (1998) remembers doing "twenty-two complete versions" of one play; this demonstrates his massive persistence and search for completeness or closure. Unfortunately, a commercial film is a fixed and finished product, and does not lent itself to endless reshooting and re-editing. Mozart appears to refer to the unconscious when he wrote about his musical ideas: "Whence and how they come, I know not; nor can I force them" (Andreasen, 2005). Tchaikovsky also emphasised the suddenness of the onset of his musical ideas. Similarly, English poet Stephen Spender talks about some poetry given to the poet "by god or by nature, the rest he has to discover himself" (Andreasen, 2005).

Simon explains to Andreasen (2005) that creative people are massive observers, a feature I have written about in previous books (Fitzgerald, 2004; Fitzgerald, 2008). Andreasen (2005) notes that creative people attempt to invalidate Heisenberg's uncertainty principle that there is no observer outside the experiment, but by being "invisible" they can see more. The extent to which they see more is not always under the control of the artist, but what life presents to them and how they engage with it. In this respect, Simon (1998) writes that "life dictates where your pen will move. It starts taking on your inner fears, your responsibilities, your new mature awareness that life isn't just about you". For Simon, good audience reaction was "nourishment" for him. He learned from G. B. Shaw to always make your protagonist and antagonist "equal adversaries", so that the audience was always in doubt as to who was right and who was wrong in a play.

Work patterns also come under scrutiny and are peculiar to the individual artist. Tennessee Williams wrote practically every day of his adult life in order to regulate his self-esteem; Simon's best time of writing was the morning, others again do better in the afternoon or even night. Biological mood rhythms certainly play a large part in these patterns.

Flash of Insight

Rodriguez-Fernandez (1996) suggests that creative thinking is characterised by (1) the ability to gradually structure a vaguely defined problem, (2) extensive background knowledge, and (3) continuing preoccupation with a problem. This then leads to the flash of insight or what he calls the "sudden illumination". He suggests that this may take place in the creative centre of the brain, the prefrontal cortex. This area of the brain is concerned with association or planning of thoughts and actions in line with inner goals. Rodriguez-Fernandez

(1996) gives an example in the case of Gabriel García Márquez's novel *One Hundred Years of Solitude*, in which "the first character of the book suddenly came". Other great creators have had similar experiences, which he cites, for example, Nietzsche, Ibsen, Mozart and Tchaikovsky. This is a kind of *eureka* experience, albeit a less dramatic and quieter one than that of Archimedes. It gives the writer a sense of completeness or harmony rather than ecstasy.

Creativity brings its own rewards for artists. Virgil gets it right when he says "happy is he who is able to know the causes of things". To discover new things is a wonderful sensation, however, creativity of genius proportions in uncommon. For the great creators of stage and screen it is the discovery of new ways of presenting ideas, using new technology creatively and new ways of thinking about old texts that drives them and gives them the creative "buzz".

In the artistic world, chance is also a major factor and a chance observation of a new innovation in art is more likely to occur to the prepared mind of the artist already searching. In this respect, Pasteur is correct in his assertion that "chance favours only the prepared mind". No-one has a better prepared mind than the great artist. Certain milieu can help to lay the groundwork, however. For example, the artistic environment of Renaissance Florence facilitated all of the above. Andreasen (2005) identifies this as the critical mass of creative people. The competition between Michelangelo, Leonardo da Vinci and others pushed them to even greater artistic creativity. They kept moving the "bar" higher and indeed such competitive creativity is not uncommon today.

INTELLIGENCE

Intelligence is a poor guide to identifying great creators. When IQ was used as a guide to potentially identify great creators, it failed and simply eliminated the greatest eccentric creators from the samples being studied. In general IQs of about 120 are necessary and 150 forms of intelligence were posited by American psychologist J. P. Guilford (Heilman, 2005). Great artistic creativity is separate from the intelligence measured by the standard IQ tests. Fluid intelligence, that is, the problem-solving type would appear to be more important in creativity. I do accept Heilman's (2005) point that creativity involves a combination of divergent and convergent thinking. The divergent phase includes tossing around ideas, daydreaming, night-dreaming, reading books, and free association of ideas in groups and individually. The convergent thinking involves creating a plan and putting it into action. It involves focusing on the best ideas and actualising the creative product.

CREATIVE IMAGINATIONS

Nothing is more critical to the artist than imagination. Without it, art is impossible. In discussing imagination, the *Collins English Dictionary* (2000) emphasises "ingenuity", "inspiration", "inventiveness", "originality", "vision", "wit", and "resourcefulness". These are all the critical characteristics of persons mentioned in this book. In addition, Roth (2007) correctly mentions "what if?" thinking and "as if" thinking". An artist associated with the stage or screen is judged by the quality of their imagination. Indeed Einstein declared that "imagination is more important than knowledge. Knowledge is limited. Imagination circles the world" (qtd in Calaprice, 2005; Roth, 2007). Roth (2007) also notes that the imagination is one of the highest prerogatives of man. By this faculty he can unite former images and ideas, independently of the will, thereby creating brilliant and novel results (Darwin, 1995). Without the input of imagination, one has little more than a factual documentary on the screen.

Great imagination is one of the factors that separates us from non-humans, although some animals can demonstrate simple imagination. This relates to the prolific development of the human cortex. Great imagination surprises us and draws us up short; it gives us a new vista. Roth (2007) also notes Isaac Newton's comment on poetry as "a kind of ingenious nonsense" (Abrahms, 1993). Newton was wrong and short-sighted, however, not being able to appreciate poetry and not creative in this fashion. The Romantic Movement at the turn of the 18th century greatly valued imagination, while the Enlightenment and the development of science decried it, despite a scientific hypothesis being a work of the imagination. Of course, behaviouristic psychology dismissed the mind and the imagination in its most extreme form because of their failure to be measured scientifically.

Clear visual imagination is hugely important in film-making. Persons with high functioning autism often have massive imagination, hence their considerable successful at film-making. Some of the greatest visual imagination is shown in science-fiction movies, such as in the work of writer Philip K. Dick. His novel *Do Androids Dream of Electric Sheep?* was the basis for the award-winning 1982 film *Blade Runner.* Massive imagination is largely genetically based but can be enhanced in stimulating environments. Roth (2007) notes that Ian Robertson (2002) provides evidence that promoting people's capacity for mental imagery enhances certain aspects of creativity.

The creative imagination requires free association of ideas, as previously discussed, and Hudson (1987) also notes that in relation to divergent thinking "those who are relatively good at free associating are attracted to the arts". This is partially supported in this book by people who have ADHD, whose thinking can be all "over the place". This allows unusual linkages to be made and is the opposite of linear thinking.

The Perverse Creative Imagination

Many great creators were perverse themselves and engaged in perverse behaviour in private life and used the perverse element of their personality to create great art. One of the most successful writers in the world, Lewis Carroll, demonstrated both scopophilia and voyeurism, particularly of young naked children. He got them to undress and photographed them endlessly. It comes as no surprise that he destroyed most of these photographs at the end of his life. Nevertheless, he had a fantastically imaginative mind which was evident in his children's stories, for example, *Alice in Wonderland* (Fitzgerald, 2005). Filmmaker Alfred Hitchcock too had a dark side. Tredell (2002) notes Hitchcock's voyeurism and fetishist fascination, which can be seen in his 1954 film, *Rear Window*. Of course, the audience also partake in this voyeurism to an extent. Often highly creative personalities have much greater access to this perverse layer than non-creative people. Perversity and violence have always been central to the performing arts, even from Grecian times. Tredell (2002) points out that from that time excess was important on the stage and indeed violence arising from *hubris* (insolent pride or presumption) and *orgia* (drunken or licentious revels), which he notes are "exhilarating and beautiful". Of course, when you examine many great filmmakers they mirror characters portrayed on the screen with excess of all kinds, drug and alcohol abuse, promiscuity and brawls.

This links up with what Julius (2002) calls transgressive art, which he described as "an art that perverts the established art rules; an art that defies the beliefs and sentiments of its audience; an art that challenges and disobeys the rules". Sadomasochistic films would fall into this category and include: *Pursued*, *The Big Heat*, *Brute Force*, *Rope of Sand*, and *Kiss Me Deadly*. For nymphomania/pornography, *The Big Sleep* is one example; perverse sadistic films include *The Secret Life: Jeffrey Dahmer* and *The Silence of the Lambs*. An example of voyeurism is Hitchcock's *Rear Window*, where the character of Jefferies is played by James Stewart, thinking that a man in a room, that he can see from his apartment window, has committed a murder, and sends his lady friend, played by Grace Kelly, to check it out while he watches from the safety of his own window. This is voyeurism. Of course, the audience are also voyeurs, so there is double voyeurism at play in the film. The uncertainty keeps people guessing and is the secret of great film-making in the same way that writers of fiction, who can blur boundaries of fact and fantasy, are more successful. Sabbadini (2003) is correct in saying that we have to use multiple "interpretative approaches" to understand films and creativity; we also need multiple perspectives to understand great artists.

Effects of Great Creativity on the Individual

Writing on the life of German poet, philosopher and playwright Friedrich Schiller, Thomas Carlyle (1825; 1992) deliberated much on the stresses and strains of persons with great creativity in general:

> His fame rarely exerts a favourable influence on his dignity of character, and never on his peace of mind: its glitter is external, for the eyes of others; within, it is but the ailment of unrest, the oil cast upon the ever-gnawing fire of ambition, quickening into fresh vehemence the blaze which it stills for a moment. Moreover, this Man of Letters is not wholly made of spirit, but of clay and spirit mixed: his thinking faculties maybe nobly trained and exercised, but he must have affections as well as thoughts to make him happy, and food and raiment must be given him or he dies.

It would appear that the Man of Letters is in need of support and care. Carlyle goes on to state the degree to which suffering plagues the creative mind: "Far from being the most enviable, his way of life is perhaps, among the many modes by which an ardent mind endeavours to express its activity, the most thickly beset with suffering and degradation." This brings to mind Lord Byron and other persons referred to in this book. Carlyle declares that except for the Newgate Calendar – a monthly bulletin of London executions – this particular kind of suffering is the "most sickening chapter in the history of man" and the personal price of genius:

> The calamities of these people are a fertile topic; and too often their faults and vices have kept pace with their calamities. Nor is it difficult to see how this has happened.

> Talent of any sort is generally accompanied with a peculiar fineness of sensibility; of genius this is the most essential constituent; and life in any shape has sorrows enough for hearts so formed.

The hypersensitivity of creative people is clearly the focus of his discussion, especially those of genius proportions. The actual production of creative works does not always satisfy the Man of Letters, according to Carlyle:

> The most finished efforts of the mind give it little pleasure, frequently they give it pain; for men's aims are ever far beyond their strength. And the outward recompense of these undertakings, the distinction they confer, is of still smaller value; the desire for it is insatiable even when successful; and when baffled, it issues in jealousy and envy, and every pitiful and painful feeling. So keen a temperament with so little to restrain or satisfy, so much to distress or tempt it, produces contradictions which few are adequate to reconcile. Hence the unhappiness of literary men, hence their faults and follies.

Here he is referring to the emotional immaturity and puerile behaviour of great men as well as their massive intellectual creations. He goes on to point out that such men are often not able to withstand the turmoil of life.

> Thus literature is apt to form a dangerous and discontenting occupation even for the amateur. But for him whose rank and worldly comforts depend on it, who does not live to write, but writes to live, its difficulties and perils are fearfully increased. Few spectacles are more afflicting than that of such a man, so gifted and so feted, so jostled and tossed to and fro in the rude bustle of life, the buffetings of which he is so little fitted to endure.

Amid their narcissism and yearning for glory, these men face numerous challenges: having problems dealing with day-to-day life; lacking the ability to manage themselves and others; being unfitted for life; and having a poor income.

Lyotard (1984) states that postmodernism cannot exist without a shattering of belief and without discovery of the "lack of reality" of reality, as well as the invention of other realities. There is nothing new in this for the great artist. This is how it has been for most great artists unless their work is wholly representational or simply documentary. In the arts there is no ultimate reality. Hence identity is not a fixed construct. Neil Jordan films are often about the changes of personal identities due to cultural forces and the formation of new identities sometimes as fictional as their original identities (Pramaggiore, 2008). I see identity in this book in a different way. The great artist starts out with a diffuse identity and his art is an attempt to find something real, an attempt to heal his own identity diffusion. If the great artist started out with a clear personal identity, it would be impossible for him to become a great artist. Carlyle points out this conflict that besets literary geniuses:

> Cherishing, it may be, the loftiest thoughts, and clogged with the meanest wants; of pure and holy purposes, yet ever driven from the straight path by the pressure of necessity, or the impulse of passion; thirsting for glory, and frequently in want of daily bread; hovering between the empyrean of his fancy and the squalid desert of reality; cramped and foiled in his most strenuous exertions; dissatisfied with his best performances, disgusted with his fortune, this Man of Letters too often spends his weary days in conflicts with obscure misery: harassed, chagrined, debased, or maddened; the

> victim at once of tragedy and farce; the last forlorn outpost in the war of Mind against Matter.

This is the best description that has ever been written about literary geniuses. Carlyle describes so well the turbulence of their lives, the moodiness, the highs and lows, and notes that many of these noble souls have perished bitterly, with their tasks unfinished, under these destroying influences. Some in poverty and hunger like Restoration dramatist Thomas Otway, others in mental illness like poet William Cowper and writer Wilkie Collins, or else by suicide like poet Thomas Chatterton. Despite their sad endings, their value to society is nevertheless immense:

> Yet among these men are to be found the brightest specimens and the chief benefactors of mankind. It is they that keep awake the finer parts of our souls; that give us better aims than power or pleasure, and withstand the total sovereignty of Mammon in this earth. They are the vanguard in the march of mind. (Carlyle 1873; 1992)

As we shall see in the book, these persons of creative genius bestow enormous benefits on mankind.

CREATIVITY AND ACTORS

Who were the first actors? Were they our ancestors who danced around the fire in hunter–gatherer society? Does the origin of dance in prehistory give us clues as to the origin of the acting profession? *Homo sapiens* have always wanted to be entertained and indeed groups of *Homo sapiens* have always entertained other groups of *Homo sapiens*. Is the origin of the music performer, with their primitive pipes and flutes, actually based on making music or something else? Was making music something novel? Human beings are essentially novelty-seeking. Throughout the ages actors who can present material in a novel way tend to be more successful. It is likely therefore that many of them possess the novelty-seeking genes DRD4 (Fitzgerald, 2008). Nevertheless, there is another form of novelty-seeking called "Asperger-type novelty seeking", as demonstrated by actor and director Orson Welles. Asperger-type novelty-seeking is shown by the more cerebral method actors who for example play Hamlet successfully.

The actor tries to give us an understanding of society and ourselves as well as entertaining us in a social way. Both are involved in a search for meaning and are trying to do what Gazzaniga and Heatherton (2003) describe as an effort "to consolidate information in coherent stories". Gazzaniga and Heatherton (2003) point out that "people are motivated to make sense of the world". This is one factor in the production of great art. The search after meaning for ourselves and the universe and our place in it is a lifelong quest ending only in death. Actors in their work help us in this quest; they help us and themselves in this endless search for identity and a sense of ourselves. Actors and plays can change the way we think and can change our viewpoint, which we frequently take for granted. Furthermore, they often make us aware of societal injustices. The audience returns to the theatre each time because on previous occasions they have been entertained, frightened, stimulated, or experienced something new. The performance increases our dopamine levels particularly in the nucleus accumbens and gives us pleasure. Of course, the great actor can have a similar buzz at the same time. This is part of the neurochemistry of the gene. The great actor has the capacity to produce new interpretations of a play and communicate these in a novel way. Indeed, the uncertainty of how the actor will interpret a well-known play increases the thrill of expectation and novelty for the audience.

Gazzaniga and Heatherton (2003) point out that "curiosity, play, and creative endeavours all lead to states of arousal". The actors and the audience both seek this state of arousal. Audiences detest being bored and seek plays and actors who produce an optimal level of arousal. People certainly enjoy a good play but, as Gazzaniga and Heatherton (2003) point out, "become frustrated when the plot is so complex that it is impossible to follow". This is not the case for all audiences, however; for example, the psychoanalyst Jacques Lacan gave seminars which were essentially one-man theatrical performances where the audience understood little or nothing, even when he spoke, which was rare. What he said was largely nonsensical albeit most enjoyable to his naïve masochistic audience who found it gave them optimal arousal. The greatest autistic/Asperger "actor" was Adolf Hitler, who sent his audiences into states of mesmeric arousal and ecstasy like a celebrated pop singer (Fitzgerald, 2004).

The successful actor and play gives what Gazzaniga and Heatherton (2003) describe as "novelty, sudden change, incongruity, complexity, and uncertainty", all of which increase arousal to optimum levels. Audiences want to be challenged and stimulated to work on their own free associations in relation to the work of the actor. Then each member of the audience has a unique experience. When this happens in front of a successful actor, the audience's collective mind will not wander and they will remain focused on the play. Great actors have the power to move audiences emotionally and intellectually far more than lesser actors and have the capacity to grasp every nuance or detail of a play. The Asperger-type actor is more successful at plays when the emphasis is on dialogue and language.

The profession of acting is probably the most difficult of all professions with most actors spending many years in the "wilderness", unemployed, working as waiters and so forth. The need for tenacity and persistence is enormous. Persons with Asperger's syndrome often have this persistence and focus; they don't give up after vast numbers of rejections at auditions. They have to have an inner strength to keep them going over the long years of adversity in the doldrums of the acting world.

The play, players and audience are also given time out from everyday concerns in the theatre. It gives distraction and temporary relief and escape from daily concerns – in fact "escapist entertainment" (Gazzaniga and Heatherton 2003) has its place. The profession of acting has to be considered in the context of cultural evolution and possibly sexual selection. Even today actors are very attractive as sexual mates. Ian Cross (2007) points out that "in *The Descent*, Darwin suggests that music arose as a functional component of processes of natural selection" and its goal was to attract mates. You could hypothesise the same for acting or dancing. Social dramas require theory of mind development and the capacity to infer other people's minds. This is less so with science fiction.

Plotkin (2007) points out that "the human capacity for culture is a product of evolution as natural as having bipedal gait". Acting on a stage is part of culture. It can be used for political purposes as in the former Soviet Union where plays had to support the ideas of the regime. In other settings it can play a role in regime change and be a forum for new political ideas. Plotkin (2007) points out that culture is part of "universal Darwinism". He goes on to state that "culture is at once a product of Darwinian evolution, while it itself [is] changing through there same process". Acting on the stage could be seen as part of what Plotkin (2007) calls "niche culture". Human culture is fundamentally far more complex than chimpanzee culture. Plotkin (2007) points out that culture consists of among other phenomena "shared … knowledge, values, beliefs, and customs … that allow an individual to fit into a social group". Writing, acting and attending at plays or movies is part of our culture. The theatre is a social construction. Plotkin (2007) points out that social constructions are "interlocking neural network states in different individuals". Here he is referring to the interaction between two brains.

The activities in the theatre are part of "shared cooperative acting" (Plotkin, 2007). In the theatrical sense this requires what Baron-Cohen (2000) calls theory of mind. The complexity of human culture has evolved over the past 100–150,000 years. The evolution of verbal language was central to the evolution of the complex performing arts, while the FOXP2 gene too played its part. On stage and in the audience issues of empathy and sympathy are vital. It is the audience's capacity to experience these feelings that allows them to react to what is happening on the stage. Issues of imitation and identification, as part of acting, are all very important. Is the actor imitating a character or identifying with a character in his acting? According to Rizzolatti and Fogassi (2007), mirror neurons in the brain only provide "the basis of interpersonal relationships on which more complex social behaviours are built".

Culture and the Theatre

Dunbar and Barrett (2007) notes that Stephen Pinker (1997) in discussing music and literature (and he could have added theatre) stated that this was "mere cheesecake-froth on the evolutionary seascape". This is not true. Theatre has a function in our culture, otherwise we would not put so much effort into it. Dunbar and Barrett (2007) in discussing "high" culture suggest that it may be as important in "creating that sense of groupishness". Once again theatrical language is central. Theatre clearly needs much more study from an evolutionary perspective. The imagination is crucial in theatre and Dunbar and Barrett (2007) note that "the capacity to deal with imagined worlds is not merely cognitively demanding but clearly fundamentally important to many aspects of human social life". The theatre can transmit shared cultural values and ideas or new cultural value and ideas. Furthermore, it can educate and be a force for social change in a positive or negative sense.

Carroll (2007) writes about "consilience", a term used by E. O. Wilson (1998), denoting that "nature forms a unified field of determinate causal relations and that all fields of knowledge are therefore integrally connected". Therefore, ideas from physics, chemistry, biology, and the various human sciences all constrain each other. All these sciences in turn constrain the study of human cultural production, including literature, drama, and the arts. Carroll (2007) notes that adaptationist literary scholars argue that "literary works are produced and consumed to fulfil the needs of human nature, that they depict human nature, and that they are constrained, in their formal organisation, by the species typical dynamics of human social interaction". Clearly theatrical works fit into this frame. The ideas of post-structuralism fits in well with the idea that meaning and the text are indeterminate (i.e., no determinate meaning is possible). This means that all plays "are open to perpetual reinterpretation". This allows each director of a play to re-interpret the play. The theatre that is most successful is subversive of accepted ideas and is anti-establishment, whether political, literary, etc.

Post-structuralism, for Carroll (2007), serves as a means "for deprecating the legitimacy of the dominant social, psychological or sexual norms". In some ways theatrical productions have been doing this since they first came into being. The adaptationist literary perspective described here should be seen as largely hypothetical. Indeed this field of study had been in existence for only about 17 years. Clearly, it is a subjective field of study at present. The theatre is always concerned about a point of view – the director's view of a play. The theatrical enterprise is also about the study of human nature and society in a dramatic way. The notion of adaptationist is that "the human mind has evolved in an adaptive relationship with its environment" (Carroll, 2007).

IMITATION

Dunbar and Barnett (2007) note that the human capacity for imitation is "quite extraordinary by the standards of the more conventional animals". They point out that the imitator has to give up his own interests in order to copy someone else's behaviour. Of course, in the theatre the audience also imitates/identifies with the actor for better or worse.

Imitation on stage is the "process of copying the behaviour of the other person, group or object … intentionally or unintentionally" (APA, 2007). This is replicative uncreative acting. It can of course be very powerful and is probably displayed to a greater extent by actors with Asperger's syndrome. The actor identifies when he or she associates the self closely with other individuals and their characteristics on views (APA, 2007). Many great creators have identity diffusion and maybe more easily able to take on other identifications on stage.

SYMPATHY

It can be important for the audience to sympathise with the character being portrayed on the stage and the actor has to elicit the audience's "capacity to share in and respond to the feelings" aroused by the character (APA, 2007). This relates to the "affinity" between the individuals on stage and the audience (APA, 2007). It is important to contrast this with empathy, which does not "fit self, entail motivation to be of assistance", which is sympathy (APA, 2007).

EMPATHY

Roberts, Hoop and Dunn (2008) describe empathy as "the act of entering into someone else's frame of reference in terms of thoughts, feelings and experiences, to gain an authentic understanding of the other person's experiences imaginatively as one's own". The audience shows empathy when they put themselves in the "shoes" of the character on stage. It is interesting that the word "actor" can mean acting "on behalf of another", as cited in the *Shorter Oxford English Dictionary*. In one way, a group of actors on the stage are a play group in the sense that they are "brought together on a regular basis to play together under supervision" of a director, as the dictionary expounds. Actors therefore need to be in touch with imitation or playful child-like aspects of themselves. Indeed play time can be a time for "play or recreation", according to the dictionary. This is the time that audiences take out from their daily work to attend a play.

All aspects of the theatre and motion picture show extreme human competitiveness in the effort to get our attention and indeed to be a player. Reputation is of huge importance. Indeed the fact endures in Shakespeare's tragedy *Othello*, when Cassio says: "I have lost my reputation! I have lost the immortal part of myself, and what remains is bestial." Of course in Germany prior to and during the Second World War we saw high culture, great artistic productions, and bestiality all at the same time. High culture and the human biology are completely intertwined.

THE GROUP ON STAGE

A group is defined as "two or more independents who influence one another through social interaction", in this case on stage (APA, 2007). Not all actors do this and the best example is Laughton, discussed later. Most actors (except solo performers) need another actor's performance to help them actualise their own performance. The group of actors will affect each individual performance; the group interaction will be critical to an individual actor when they are producing a great performance. He or she cannot do it on their own. Indeed, "it's all for one and one for all" in a great stage performance or movie. The director is essentially the group-centred leader. The director creates the group climate which is the "relative degree of acceptance, tolerance, freedom of expression that characterises the relationships within" an acting troupe (APA, 2007). This then creates a group consciousness which can be "greater than the sum of individual member's awareness" (APA, 2007).

The director of a group of players at the rehearsal stage can, through a strategic intervention, "alter the processing and functioning of a group", according to APA (2007). This usually involves assessing the group's current level of development, helping to clarify its mission and goals, and reviewing its operating procedures. The theatre or movie director has to be aware of the group dynamics and "the changes that occur … which affect patterns of affiliation, communication, conflict, conformity, decision making, influence … and power" (APA, 2007). The director in a way has to be a kind of group psychoanalyst. He or she also has to know which members of the acting group are under stress and require private attention and support. Then the director has to be a kind of individual psychoanalyst, aware of the great individual and temperamental differences between group members. From this can emerge a bond or kinship. Carroll (2007) notes that Coe (2003) argued that in ancestral environments "visual art converged information about kin relations". Certainly a great stage drama is about kin relations and always has been.

IDENTITY DIFFUSION, POSTMODERNISM, AND CREATIVITY

Identity diffusion is and always has been critical to creativity. The artist needs this fluidity of identity to be successful. A less balanced and less integrated brain is necessary for great creativity. This is associated with identity diffusion, of which sexual identity diffusion plays a role. Postmodernism has made us aware of issues of identity diffusion. Discussing postmodernism, Maria Pramaggiore (2008) states that the French theorist Jean-François Lyotard has identified the breakdown of totalising narratives as a central feature of postmodernism. This breakdown of totalising narratives certainly applies to the work of director Neil Jordan.

Stam (2000) points out that theories do not supersede one another in a linear progression:

> Indeed, there are Darwinian survivalist overtones in the view that theories can be "retired", that they can be "eliminated" in competition. It would be silly to adopt a scorched earth policy that suggests that one movement or other got everything wrong. Theories do not usually fall into disuse like old automobiles relegated to a conceptual junkyard. They do not die; they transform themselves, leaving traces and reminiscences".

According to Stam (2000), "theory" became "Theory" in the 1970s. Certainly, psychoanalytic theory developed an enormous capital T during the so-called golden age. However, Stam holds the view that nowadays current theory is more "epistemologically modest and less authoritarian". He believes that Grand Theory has abandoned its totalising ambitions, in favour of a more modest approach to theory, such as that adopted by philosophers like Richard Rorty, who defined philosophy not as "a system-building ... but rather as a civil 'conversation' without any claims to ultimate truth". At best, theories give light and greater understanding but at worst create darkness by freezing thinking.

In postmodernism there is a characteristic fluidity in the meaning of all words. Postmodernism nevertheless greatly exaggerates this fluidity in the meaning of words. Words have not lost all their old meaning; old personal identities do not just diffuse into the air. Indeed in psychiatry we see how enormously difficult it is to bring about real personality change or identity consolidation. Neil Jordan's work is essentially about the exploration of shifting identities. The human protagonist in Jordan's films is cut off from the shore and bobs around in the open sea searching for itself. Indeed this search is part of the human condition for everyone but to a far greater extent in the artist.

Identity diffusion and attempts to clarify identity are one of the motive forces in great creativity. This was put best by Joseph Conrad (Austin, 2003) where he wrote "in your work you have a chance to find yourself, your own reality". This is often a lifelong task for highly creative people yet something they never fully achieve. Even so, it is one of the factors that therefore sustains them. Conrad additionally wrote that one can only find one's own reality and "not others – what no other man will ever know. They can only see the mere show, and never tell what it means".

In terms of identity, artistic work is a form of self-healing. Depression and risk of suicide comes when creative people have an artistic block and cannot express their artistic identity. Another issue characteristic of those with identity diffusion is an easy passage between fact and fiction and back again. This is critical for artistic creativity. These people are often attracted to mystical and esoteric matters, and to the occult and spiritualism, for example, W. B. Yeats and many others. Operating on the edge in these areas appears to be helpful for their creativity.

Great creators are also obsessed with immortality and their identity beyond the grave as well as their artistic legacy. Their artistic work is what remains of them after death and it is hugely important that they are remembered. Like a mountain climber, the great artist is constantly testing his or her own personal limits; they are hugely curious and want to go beyond safety to see "what they are made of", as it is often put. By always having a new creative peak to aim for, it helps them with their search for identity.

GENETICS OF CREATIVITY

In general, I do not believe that genius simply runs in families. Nevertheless, there are exceptions, for example, in music. Creative members of the Bach family extended over eight generations from 1500 to 1800 with Johann Sebastian Bach being the superstar. Andreasen (2005) lists other families such as Bellini, Van Eyck, Titian, Coleridge, Wordsworth, Brontë, Huxley, and James. Andreasen concludes that creativity is "partially genetic" like so many phenomenon. Certainly, I believe that creativity of massive proportions is even more genetic. Other exceptions are described by Pasachoff (2009), who notes that there are at least seven parent–child pairs of Nobel laureates.

> Four of these were in physics: the Thomsons (J.J. in 1906 and George in 1937), Braggs (William and Lawrence together in 1915), Bohrs (Niels in 1922 and his son Aage in 1975) and Siegbahns (Manne in 1924 and his son Kai in 1981). Marie Curie and her daughter Irène Joliot-Curie both won the Nobel Prize in Chemistry (1911 and 1935), after Marie and her husband, Pierre, had won the physics Nobel in 1903. The Kornbergs branched out more (Arthur, physiology or medicine, 1959; Roger, chemistry, 2006), as did Hans von Euler-Chelpin (chemistry, 1929) and his son Ulf von Euler (physiology or medicine, 1970).

Genes have multiple effects and indeed there are some similar genes involved in autism, attention deficit hyperactivity disorder (ADHD), and creativity. Genes are clearly of vital importance when considering the cause of great creativity. The issue here is multiple genes of small effect. Gardner (1997) discusses a principle called "emergenesis" by which traits are passed on by package of genes, but only if the entire package is transmitted. Lykken (1998) has particularly emphasised this aspect, but it is a genetic theory. It does appear now that single gene abnormality can also play a role (Fitzgerald, 2008).

NATURE, NURTURE AND CREATIVITY

Heilman (2005) notes that rodents who were in an enriched environment at a young age could later learn better than the controls not so exposed. Later when the brains from the enriched environments were weighed, they were heavier than the brains of the control subjects and had "larger heads". The brains of persons in the enriched environments made more nerve connections and had an increase in the thickness of their cerebral cortex and an increase in the number of synaptic contacts. Once again, nature and nurture played a role. We can never forget the Thomas Edison statement that creativity is 99 per cent perspiration and 1 per cent inspiration. He underplayed the innate genetic element.

Martindale (1999) notes that for identical twins, Waller et al. (1993) found an intra-class correlation of almost 0.60 for creative personality scales. In simple terms this means that creativity is about as heritable as eye colour or height (Martindale, 1999). I strongly believe that at the extremes of great creativity heritability is much greater than this. Heritability for autism/Asperger syndrome is about 93 per cent, while for ADHD it is 60–90 per cent. This again is a severe blow to the environmental theory of Asperger syndrome. The same can be said for the environmental theory of creativity.

The idea that great creativity is all about practice is simply nonsense. Howe (1999) suggests that people start with a similar basic personality – a kind of level playing field – and then it is practice which makes the difference, but this makes no sense to me. Endless practice will not make a person into another Einstein or Mozart. Huge practice has the capacity to make a person more than an average performer but no more. Howe (1999) also claims that "sophisticated unborn capacity cannot exist". This is absolutely false, even though the philosopher John Stuart Mill claimed that his intellectual capacities were "manufactured" by the environment (Howe, 1999). The environment was not the major factor in his work of genius. Indeed his father was also a prodigy.

In Malcolm Gladwell's (2008) book *Outliers: The Story of Success*, there is a chapter entitled "The 10,000 Hour Rule", in which he claims that greatness requires enormous time. This grossly overinflates the role of environment. There was only one Mozart but vast numbers of children and adolescents have had massive environmental inputs with training and practice and they have not produced one fraction of the work Mozart produced. It is wishful thinking that a mother or father could produce another Mozart. It is unfair to parents to give them the idea that they could produce another Beethoven. There will never be another Mozart or Beethoven, even with 500,000 hours of practice and teaching. One of the key features of innate creativity is that these people learn much faster than those without this innate ability. It is interesting that two of the people Gladwell mentions – Mozart and Bobby Fisher – had developmental disorders. Mozart (Fitzgerald, 2005) had ADHD with Asperger features, whereas Bobby Fisher had Asperger syndrome. Gladwell (2008) states that "practice isn't the thing you do once you're good. It's the thing you do that makes you good". Indeed, it's the other way round. The fact is that no amount of practice will make you a genius unless you have innate talent. One sees this over and over again on stage and screen.

The total environmental explanation of creativity is little more than an effort to turn a sow's ear into a silk purse, which is impossible. This seems to me to be what the environmental theories of creativity are attempting. Persons with great talent tend to show these talents in early life and early education in this area certainly enhances this talent.

Risk Taking, Sensation Seeking, and Attention Deficit Hyperactivity Disorder

Novelty seeking is a major factor in creativity (Fitzgerald, 2008) and in this respect Hamer and Copeland (1998) note that genes seem to account for more than half or more of the person-to-person variation in novelty seeking. In addition, the experience of being creative is enormously exciting and indeed can be exhilarating and a peak experience. It is hardly surprising that great creators become addicted to it. It certainly keeps them going, endlessly trying to catch up with the creative dragon. It is not surprising that if things are not working out that drugs and alcohol can be used as a substitute with catastrophic effects. Indeed in relation to this buzz of creativity, Goethe puts it well when he writes "whatever you can do, or dream you can, begin it. Boldness has genius, power, and magic in it" (Austin, 2003).

The great autistic creator is often sensation seeking and Zuckerman (2007) expressed this very well when he noted that "sensation seeking is a trait defined by the seeking of varied, novel, complex, and intense sensations and experiences, and the willingness to take physical, social, legal and financial risks for the sake of such experience".

All these features are required for many great stage productions and even more so for film productions, which are often highly risky endeavours. These are the people who break the movie mould and are innovative. These are the people who in a stage and film sense "go where no man has gone before". Of course, you still need the accountants to keep some control and not to allow a financial catastrophe. Accountants are more likely to be producers who have to watch the bottom line.

The whole novelty-seeking issue was best summed up by Dr Henry Frankenstein, who in the script of the original 1931 universal film *Frankenstein*, stated:

> Where should we be if nobody tried to find out what lies beyond? Have you never wanted to look beyond the clouds and the stars or know what causes the trees to bud – or what changes dark into light? But, if one talks like that people call you crazy. Well, if I could discover just one of these things – what eternity is, for example – I wouldn't care if they think I was crazy. (Prentky, 1980)

William James stated that it is only by risking our persons from one hour to another that we live at all (Zuckerman, 2007). Of course, many of these traits are also seen in our animal ancestors. Jamison (2004) notes that rhesus and vervet monkeys score particularly high on measures of curiosity, playfulness, and exploration.

Great artists often appear to government officials as reckless. Government officials it must be said are mostly committed to mediocrity and the status quo. If great artists were not reckless, they would not be great artists, which brings to mind Melvin Konner's 1990 book *Why the Reckless Survive*. The genetic predisposition for great creativity and for recklessness overlaps. Of course, the creative process is not linear but is initially rather chaotic. Out of this chaos the creative answer to a problem emerges, given that these people have a "nose" for the creative solution. There would be little great art without risk-takers. This book describes two types of risk-takers: the ADHD type and the autistic or Asperger type.

In ADHD (Fitzgerald, Bellgrove & Gill, 2007), novelty seeking and sensation seeking, where there are overlapping genetic features, make these people more likely to be creative due to their capacity for novelty or new ways of thinking and presenting stage and film scripts (Fitzgerald, 2008). They show poor attention and concentration on matters that fail to interest them and tend to do poorly at school. Nonetheless, they can hyperfocus on what interests them, and tend to possess huge energy and hyperactivity. They also often have associated oppositional defiant problems and depression. These people are essentially rebels, oppositional, defiant and often anti-authority, rejecting current ways of working. They are therefore innovative and likely to make breakthroughs. They show high levels of curiosity as children and retain their immature personalities throughout their life. This helps them to see the world through the eyes of a child, which is critical for great creativity.

From an evolutionary perspective, persons with ADHD could be seen as the "left over hunters" (Hartman, 1999). One of the places in current society that these people can find a "home" is in the arts associated with stage and screen. In that milieu they can enrich society. It would be an incredibly boring world without them, given that they can do wonderfully interesting and novel things on stage. The extent of their sensation seeking reminds one of Oscar Wilde's comment: "I can resist anything but temptation." ADHD undoubtedly had survival value for people in the arts. More than likely these were the people who first moved out of Africa, curious about other lands and in search of food. Jamison (2004) describes these creative people as being "exuberant". The desire to explore new ideas and new ways of staging plays is highly expressed in these people. They have a certain kind of neural connectivity (Fitzgerald, 2008), whereby the neural connections in the frontal lobe work less well due to poorer neurochemical connections between nerve cells.

Lara Honos-Webb (2005) notes that persons with ADHD are great at getting the big picture but poor at details. If you wished for the best of both worlds on a film set, you would have persons with ADHD for the holistic view, for novelty and new sensations, and the persons with Asperger syndrome for issues requiring attention to detail. The ADHD people, according to Honos-Webb, are those capable of "thinking daringly original thoughts and to create new ideas or perspectives [which] requires impulsiveness … to do things that are new and daring that fall outside the boring grind of the everyday humdrum". It is hardly surprising that these people are vital to stage and screen. Persons with ADHD can certainly be good at multitasking (Hartman, 1999) and thrive in high-energy environments where there is a great deal happening. These daring and impulsive features can also become associated with alcohol and drug abuse, accidents, criminality, and depression as the person gets older. These features are common in the persons described in this book.

DEPRESSION

The question of depression allied to creativity is a perennial one. Indeed Raymond Klibansky asked could a happy man have written *Hamlet*? (Murray, 1989). Happiness and great creativity do not go together. I suppose if a person were very happy, why would they bother to express their creativity.

PSYCHOSES

Creativity and psychoses is another area worth scrutinising. When in the throes of a mental illness, like schizophrenia, creativity is impossible. This is exemplified in the life of John Nash, the mathematician and Nobel Prize winner; first, during his creative period he had Asperger syndrome but ceased to produce work of genius proportions when he developed a second condition, schizophrenia (Fitzgerald, 2002). Creativity of genius proportions can often be seen in the relatives of persons with schizophrenia. People on the borderline can demonstrate great creativity.

HIGH FUNCTIONING AUTISM OR ASPERGER SYNDROME

Hollywood has become fascinated with autism, according to Stuart Murray (2008). The 2001 science-fiction film *AI* had a strong autistic structure and narrative. The same could be said for *Star Wars* as well as Stanley Kubrick's *2001: A Space Odyssey*. In films like *Rain Man* and *House of Cards*, the condition is ostensibly central to the narrative (Murray, 2008). In the first half of *A Beautiful Mind*, which depicts the life of mathematician John Nash, the main character demonstrates high functioning autism/Asperger syndrome (Fitzgerald, 2002), and in the second half schizophrenia. During his life Andy Warhol showed signs of Asperger syndrome (Fitzgerald, 2005) and indeed Murray (2008) describes Warhol's movie empire as "a genuine autistic narrative". Similarly, the film *Shine* demonstrates a kind of autistic talent as does *Forrest Gump*. Forrest Gump produces an autistic narrative and tries to understand the world in an autistic fashion. Films about Canadian pianist Glenn Gould, who had Asperger syndrome (Fitzgerald, 2005), also demonstrate autistic creativity. Time will tell if scripting and film production by persons with Asperger syndrome will become a distinct genre in itself.

Other persons associated with stage or screen who had Asperger syndrome include Stanley Kubrick (Lyons & Fitzgerald, 2005), Orson Welles and others described in this book. A certain number of these persons have demonstrated only some traits rather than the full-blown condition. Persons with high functioning autism or Asperger syndrome are often highly visual, for example, Vincent van Gogh and L.S. Lowry (Harpur, Lawlor & Fitzgerald, 2004; Fitzgerald, 2005). Clearly, this is very important to stage and screen work, which by its very nature is highly visual. These people can also have heightened auditory senses, which are important to composers of film scores. Heightened visual sensitivity is associated with Asperger syndrome and cinematographers.

The influence of many movie creators shows the autistic mind in action. This particularly relates to science fiction films, for example, the writer Philip Dick and films that deal with gadgets, computers, and cartoons. In these we see massive autistic creativity. There has never been a better time in Hollywood for persons with Asperger syndrome or high functioning autism. When you examine Hollywood websites by Hollywood reporters there are a huge number of references to autism and Asperger syndrome. Indeed creative people with Asperger syndrome have had a massive effect on Hollywood, pushing it away from social dramas to a preoccupation with gadgets and special effects.

Brain and Creativity

The human brain has 100 billion neurons in the cerebral cortex, according to Andreasen (2005), and each neuron has 5000 connections. The cerebellum has about one trillion neurons and in terms of "neurons subcortical" there are a few billion (Andreasen, 2005). This is the enormously complex organ of creativity. It is in fact the most complex organ in the universe. Zeki (2001) notes that variability is one of the chief determinants of evolution; in terms of Darwin's theory we also see this variability in approach in stage and screen. Zeki (2001) expects neuroaesthetics – the biological and neurobiological foundations of aesthetic experience – to be a major field of study in the future. This is vitally important to creativity on stage and screen.

Creativity has to be studied from a neural point of view, which is basically the neurobiology of creativity. Andreasen (2005) describes the creative process in the brain:

> Multiple association cortices are communicating back and forth, not in order to integrate associations with sensory or motor input [but] in response to one another. The associations are occurring freely. They are running unchecked, not subject to any of the reality principles that normally govern them.

She suggests that in the creative process the "brain begins by disorganising" and then later self-organisation eventually emerges and takes over the brain. Disorganisation for Andreasen means tapping into the unconscious and primary process thinking. The outcome she says is the "creative product". In retrospect, Freud correctly emphasised the importance of the unconscious and creativity in his work.

Some people are extremely strong in the visual area, for example, high functioning autism or Asperger syndrome, for largely genetic reasons. They may have the capacity to see more in a visual image or to see details as well as having a very highly developed aesthetic sense. According to Heilman (2005), during the innovative stage of creativity "the right hemisphere- mediated global attentional systems" are more important, whereas in the second stage of creativity the "verification–production stage of creativity" in the left hemisphere, which focuses more on detail, is probably more important. Atypical cerebral asymmetry appears to be necessary for great creativity. In contrast, a well-integrated brain or indeed personality is not creative.

Changes in the synaptic strength between neurons are critical to learning and memory and therefore creativity (Heilman, 2005). Clearly, there are genetic underpinnings which are mediated by neurochemicals in the brain. Great memory, which is often seen in great creators, is facilitated by the above neurochemical processes. Of course, the brain is capable of both serial and parallel processing (Heilman, 2005) and of the two parallel processing may be more important in great creativity. Phillips (2008) notes that the smallest processing model of neurons in the cortex is called the "minicolumns". These were smaller in successful scientists, which may give "better signal detection and more focussed attention", and in certain artists (Phillips, 2008). One could speculate that this was so in Stanley Kubrick's brain. Phillips (2008) notes Allan Snyder's work who suggests that "savant-like skills arise by shutting down some of the 'rule based' higher-order cognition". This is a special type of talent seen in the film *Rain Man*, which allows the artist to break out of the contemporary paradigm.

My own speculation is that persons with ADHD may have enhanced general connectivity and persons with high functioning autism or Asperger syndrome have enhanced local connectivity. As Shakespeare puts it in *A Midsummer Night's Dream*: "The lunatic, the lover, and the poet are of imagination all compact." The atypical brain is therefore necessary for great creativity. Great creativity occurs best in the border between sanity and madness, at the edge and on the edge.

Neurochemicals

Certain forms of creativity decline with age, for example, the ability to write great lyric poetry. Heilman (2005) notes that the levels of the neurochemical dopamine decline with age in the brain. At the same time there is the hypodopaminergic theory of ADHD. How could this then link with creativity? Creativity can increase dopamine in the brain. One of the factors therefore driving creativity would be the person's unconscious need to increase dopamine and therefore make them feel better. The neurochemical dopamine is also associated with pleasure. Heilman (2005) also notes that brain levels of norepinephrine might influence creativity because they moderate the size of neuronal networks. This is a topic dealt with in *Attention Deficit Hyperactivity Disorder: Creativity, Novelty Seeking and Risk* (Fitzgerald, 2008). Genetic dopamine polymorphisms associated with novelty appear to play a part in some types of great creativity. Clearly these interact with many other genes that we do not know about today.

Male Creator versus Female Creators: Male Brain versus Female Brain

Fitzgerald (2004) showed a link between autism in men and exceptional ability. Other studies too have focused on the male brain versus the female brain. The male brain is particularly good at folk physics, that is, "searching for the physical causes of any other kind of event" (Baron-Cohen, 2000). Indeed Hans Asperger noted that the autistic personality is an extreme variant of male intelligence (Asperger, 1944). Statistically, there are many more males with Asperger syndrome than females, at a ratio of about 10:1. Males are better at systematising (Baron-Cohen, 2000); better at organising data into a system; better mechanically and at engineering. Examples here include Stanley Kubrick, Henry Irving, Orson Welles, and others in this book. These people have a less balanced asymmetrical and integrated brain; there is more lateralisation of functions; they have greater short-range connections of neurons and less good long-range connections than females (Casanova, Switala, Trippe and Fitzgerald, 2007). The males are less verbal and have poorer capacity for empathy and are not as socially skilled as females. They have narrowed interests, for example cars, and engage in a more mathematical-type of film-making.

The female is more verbal, more empathic, better at reading other people and, in human evolutionary terms, more advanced than the male. Female directors should in general be better at making more human interpersonal films, while male directors should be better at making films about ideas, technology, and science fiction. Phillips (2008) points out that women's brains are smaller than men's, even when corrected for body size, yet there is no consistent difference between men's and women's IQs. Heilman (2005) notes the larger corpus callosum found in women's brains:

> Although men have more neurons than do women, the cortex of men and women are equally thick, suggesting that women have a greater number of neuronal connections per neuron. It is this relatively increased connectivity in women that might account for their relatively larger corpus callosum.

This is probably why female evolution in human interpersonal skills is more advanced than in males.

In my view this would link to their reduced nonsocial creativity and increased social and emotional communication skills. Men's brains are probably more modular. In evolution, men were primarily the hunter gatherers, hence "navigation skills were critical for survival" (Heilman, 2005). From an evolutionary point of view rearing children with all the socio-emotional demands and skills that this requires are more highly developed in women. Included in this are increased empathy, verbal skills, and sensitivity to emotional cues. One would expect to see this in the work of female directors.

Hans Eysenck noticed that small differences in the mean score become greatly increased at the extremes of the distribution (Heilman, 2005). Here he was referring to IQ. This might be relevant at the extremes of mathematical intelligence. It appears to me that it is at the extremes of creativity that the gender differences may be more important. Creators of genius are at those extremes.

Andreasen (2005) states that women are as intellectually creative as men, and yet society has as yet produced very few women who are great creative geniuses. I believe that the creativity of women often takes a different form. There are major differences at a neurobiological level between male and female brains. Their talents should be contrasted not compared. The most nonsensical comment ever made about women was uttered by Simone de Beauvoir when she stated "one is not born, but rather becomes, a woman" (Simonton, 1994).

The female actor has had a turbulent history on the stage. They were easily abused and have had a far more complex history on the stage than their male counterparts. Ellen Terry would be a classic example of a female actor. Pullen (2005) points out that the history of females on stage is linked to the idea of "actresses and whores". Prostitution implies sale of sex for money, however, the situation in previous centuries was more complicated. The earlier meaning of the word whore was more akin to "bitch", according to Pullen (2005). Rather than a woman selling sex, the word prostitute also signified "any person that does anything for hire" (Pullen, 2005). Wilson (1958) puts it as follows: "Women without dowries had discovered the possibility of a theatrical career as a springboard to matrimony or 'keeping'". Pullen (2005) claims there were hundreds of lecherous gentlemen eager to seduce an actress as cheaply as possible, where the wise "teased their admirers into some kind of settlement, hoping to live in clover for the rest of their lives". During Restoration England Nell Gwyn is perhaps a more familiar figure of the actress/whore. Of course the public also projected a lot of their own sexual impulses onto these women. Even to the end of the 1800s stage work did not have good reputation.

Take the actress Charlotte Charke, born in 1713, for example. She is called a "whore" by Pullen (2005) but was also regarded as a brilliant actress or "a potential lesbian" (Moore, 1991); as a "disorganised impetuous Moll Flanders" (Charke, 1999); "a cross dressing failure" (Mackie, 1991); "freak" (Moore, 1991); and a "proto-feminist" (Fields, 1991). What is noteworthy about all these labels is that they have parallels with some of the females discussed later in this book. In the 1870s, according to Pullen (2005), there was a link between burlesque performances and prostitution. Of course in the 20th century, the feminist Andrea Dworkin placed marriage on a continuum with prostitution (Pullen, 2005). The public at the time was also interested in the more androgynous actresses who cross-dressed – similar to Greta Garbo. Unlike Garbo, who was a star, most of these women were outsiders and often in major debt. In the past as now audiences were attracted to androgyny in female actors.

The journey to respectability for stage and film performers was a long hard one laced with endless pain, suffering, and prejudice. Indeed the journey for the majority of actors of both sexes even today is an extremely arduous one often with poor irregular rewards.

The Audience in the Theatre and Cinema

Theatre and cinema audiences get perverse satisfaction at second hand. It is perverse behaviour at a distance and in a safe socially sanctioned way. Films allow the audience to take perverse satisfaction vicariously in endless sadistic and violent films. Deep down in every personality there is a perverse level of personality. This is often not visible and it takes special circumstances to bring it to the fore, as can be seen in concentration camp guards depicted in films about Nazi Germany, many of whom were minor civil servants before the Second World War.

The perverse film excites the perverse layer of their personality, which is normally repressed and relatively dormant. Once again the cinema holds the mirror up to reality. Of course what separates humans from non-humans is the appreciation of aesthetic works; to many people films give them enormous aesthetic pleasure. Seeing negative parts of ourselves portrayed on stage increases the authenticity of the film and the sensation for the audience. Sometimes this sensation can be painful for the audience but is better than being unmoved or indifferent to a performance.

Again there is relative safety as the audience is viewing things from the safe distance of their seats. Human beings are fascinated by eccentrics, outsiders and damaged personalities and love to see the pompous (or hubris filled) get their comeuppance. In humans, the powerful, violent and aggressive layer of their personality can have vicarious gratification of violence in the multitude of gratuitously violent films. Great actors are able to portray the nastiest, most violent and most perverse aspects of human personality. They have greater access to this layer of their personality than ordinary individuals. Indeed, it is necessary for actors and directors to be somewhat unbalanced, showing a degree of identity diffusion and poor capacity for relationships. Even for the Greeks the great artist was maimed. In this respect, all great art is to some extent autobiography and reflects people as they are or as they would like to be depicted in fantasy.

The Irish painter Francis Bacon certainly portrays the above features and did express the wish to make a film. Although males would be seen as the prime audience for perverse performances, a not inconsiderable number of women can also get perverse secret pleasure from them.

Understanding Humour on Stage and Screen

According to Lyons and Fitzgerald (2004), quoting Paulos (1980), “humour is such a complex and human phenomenon, any understanding of it will necessarily enrich our understanding of thought in general”. Humour plays a major role in human life: it helps in communicating ideas, feelings and opinions (Brownell & Gardner, 1988); it provides a means of coping with stress (Lefcourt & Martin, 1986); and it is also a core human attribute (Nahemow, 1986).

Researchers agree that one of the main components of both verbal and physical humour is “incongruity” (Fry, 2002; McGhee, 1979; Morreall, 1989; Paulos, 1980; Raskin, 1985; Ruch, McGhee & Hehl, 1990). According to Paulos (1980), “incongruity is intended in a wide sense, comprising the following oppositions: expectation versus surprise, the mechanical versus the spiritual, superiority versus incompetence, balance versus exaggeration, and propriety versus vulgarity”. The major theory of humour, the incongruity-resolution model (Suls, 1972) considers humour appreciation as a problem-solving task in which the punchline, which is incongruous with the body of the text, must be detected and then reconciled with the lead. However, apart from the cognitive processing of humour (incongruity and its resolution), there are also social affective and cultural processes involved. Humour involves reciprocity, that is, the sharing of humour and laughter with others, a common interest in the topic of the laughter and/or the sharing in the laughter of others as an affective state in its own right (Reddy et al., 2002).

To summarise, humour involves a variety of cognitive functions, including problem solving, memory and mental flexibility, abstract reasoning and imagination. In addition to these cognitive functions, real humour appreciation also requires an affective response and needs to be placed within a social context. Humour, as pointed out by Paulos (1980), essentially depends on so many emotional, social and intellectual facets of human beings, and is particularly immune to computer simulation and therefore difficult for persons with autism. Nevertheless, there are comedians who have or have had Asperger syndrome, for example, Kenneth Williams. Superb mimicry is an area of comedy not beyond their reach; in fact mimicking political leaders of countries is often part of the art of many comedians. Persons with Asperger syndrome can be superb at mimicry, despite their identity diffusion. Theory of mind, that is, the reading of other minds, is much less reduced in persons with high functioning autism and Asperger syndrome. These people often have a great deal of aggression that can be expressed through humour. Traits of sadism and perverse traits frequently seen in high functioning autism and Asperger syndrome can also be helpful to humour.

The main neural basis of humour appreciation appears to be the right frontal lobe, given its ability to integrate cognitive and affective information. However, in addition to the strong right hemisphere involvement in humour appreciation, research also indicates contributions of the left hemisphere and diverse neural networks.

Relationship between Giftedness, Autism and Humour

Despite the overwhelming evidence for persons with high functioning autism and Asperger syndrome having difficulties with humour, there are many anecdotal and parental reports of humour in individuals with these conditions at all levels of functioning. Examples range from basic slapstick humour to highly sophisticated humour based on nonsense and logical confusion of language. These accounts seem to contradict the assumptions of our humour understanding in autism/Asperger syndrome and challenge some of the psychological theories with regard to creativity, imagination, reciprocal social interaction, executive functioning and mind reading. It appears that some individuals with autism/Asperger syndrome are highly creative, imaginative and original and their humour can range from "wordplay and sound associations to precisely formulated, truly witty comments" (Asperger, 1944; Frith, 1991). Highly creative and metaphorical language in children with autism has also been reported by Kanner (1946).

Some individuals with autism/Asperger syndrome also seem to master the cognitive processing of humour, that is, incongruity and its resolution and switching of meanings, as portrayed by the production of relatively sophisticated puns and word games. It is obvious that individuals with autism/Asperger syndrome with highly developed linguistic and computational abilities approach humour from a more cognitive/intellectual perspective and are able to grasp the cognitive basis of humour. This is congruent with the abovementioned fMRI evidence of differential systems underlying cognitive and affective humour processing (Goel & Dolan, 2001).

Individuals with high functioning autism, and more so Asperger syndrome with their largely unimpaired linguistic skills, are able to produce and comprehend verbal humour but the quality seems to be more of a cognitive nature, based on linguistic and logical principles and motivated by obsessional characteristics. In many instances this type of humour appears to be learned and does not seem to have the purpose of sharing interaction with others (Lyons & Fitzgerald, 2004). There are fundamentally two types of comedians: one type is preoccupied with themselves on stage and can separate themselves from the audience, whereas the other is more focused on interaction with the audience. In the latter audience reaction is critical, in particular repartee and ad-libbing. The most important ingredients, affective response and reciprocity, are missing in the self-preoccupied performers. For audiences, humour and laughter are principally pleasurable and social experiences (Bergson, 1911; Freud, 1905; Koestler, 1964) that help to create feelings of community and closeness.

Humour is such a universal human ability evident in even very young infants. In the literature of gender differences in humour, it appears that men's humour is more competitive and focused on self-enhancements, whereas women's humour is more supportive and concerned with sharing of experiences (Lampert & Ervin-Tripp, 1998). Finally, the use of humour can reduce anxiety and stress in people. It is very important on stage and screen and central to being human. Its appreciation is one of the phenomena that makes us human. Korn (2007) points out that "the joke was old by the time of the New Comedy"... "as old as the first half-ape who fell out of a tree with the purpose of making his friends laugh, and learnt that a long face was the best accompaniment to a joke". In a general comment about comedians, Tony Jones of the Newbury Festival stated:

> Comics do things you couldn't bear to be seen doing yourself. They say things people think but wouldn't dare to say it. They deal in self-censorship and audiences love the spectacle of a comedian being out of control. Distain is one of the things that drives comedy and shouting about the world is one of the ways that people go about surviving it. (O'Hagan, 2005)

Another general point focuses on the facial features of comedians and suggests that men who have fat feminine faces are far more likely to be hit comedians (Beard, 2006). Beard quotes research psychologist Dr Anthony Little:

> The characteristics of a feminine face imply that the person may be agreeable and cooperative, which can be casual in our first impressions of comedians as being friendly and funny. In the same way that infants are pre-programmed to respond to the warmth and approachability of a mother's face, soft, feminine features encourage us to relax. This is conducive to laughter and enjoyment.

British comedian Ricky Gervais was reportedly shocked by this news: "All these years, I assumed my global success was down to my acute observations and consummate skills as a performer. Turns out it's because I've got a fat, girly face" (Beard, 2006). In relation to the success of the character Borat, as played by Sacha Baron Cohen, the actor's facial traits are masculine, creating a dominant, serious appearance. Little explains that Cohen's atypical comedy face may be the reason why his routine depends on disguise and alter-egos: "Borat's costume, exaggerated accent and feigned slow-wittedness help create a false sense of superiority in his interviewees. The humour lies not in making the respondent laugh, but in convincing them that Borat is serious, if harmless and ill-informed" (Beard, 2006).

The question of unhappiness behind the comedic masks is a familiar one. Rampton (2008) notes that behind-the-scenes despair afflicted such British comedians as Harry Corbett, Wilfred Brambell, Tony Hancock and Hughie Green. Actor and comedian David Walliams in conversation with Rampton (2008) states that the "element of darkness is vital. We are all fascinated by comedians who are deeply unhappy". In his analysis Walliams says that the comedian has to have what is called "funny bones". Comedy was not about "smart one-liners" but rather the ability to be funny without saying a word (Rampton, 2008). Clearly non-verbal communication is critical for the comedian. It is now time to examine individual great creators.

PART I: ACTORS

Chapter 1

HENRY IRVING

Henry Irving (1838–1905) was the greatest actor of his age in both England and America. He was also the most baffling, enigmatic actor of his age: indeed his own generation could not quite fathom him. He had identity diffusion and therefore different people characterised him in different ways depending on which side of his character displayed to them. The intense jealousy that George Bernard Shaw held for him, owing to his close working relationship with the great actress Ellen Terry, gave rise to hypercriticism on the part of the writer. Nevertheless, Terry felt that Shaw was quite perceptive of Irving in some ways.

BACKGROUND

Henry Irving was the stage name of John Brodribb, born in Somerset on 6 February 1838. One of his relatives was described as a rake, another a novelty-seeker and sensation-seeker who was deported to Australia for being involved in poaching and the death of a gamekeeper. In terms of his parents' characteristics, Irving's father was rather ineffectual while his mother was gentle. As a child "he ran wild among the orchards and fields" – essentially he was a brave, novelty-seeking child.[1] Even as a little boy he would treat his audience to a "repertoire of speeches and declamations", which is very typical behaviour of children who later become actors.

As a boy, Irving was remarkably intelligent and often described as eccentric. In conversation he was a very adult child and quite advanced for his years. From an early age Irving was fascinated by acting. He was a contradictory boy in that he loved actors and acting, the height of unconventionality, but at the same time was quite religious. In fact, his mother wanted him to become a pastor. Being oppositional, he went against his parents' wishes by becoming an actor. He moved from the country to London when he was about 11 years old.

Before going on the stage he worked as a clerk, and was regarded as "eccentric but interesting". Early in life he was noted to be "a pale and rather awkward young actor". The awkwardness more than likely stemmed from certain physical features, namely impaired speech and a peculiar gait. The "impediment in his speech", he mastered, much to his great credit. Ellen Terry mentions that he had "peculiarities of diction and gait which hampered his

[1] Except where otherwise indicated, quotes in this chapter are from Irving (1951).

self-expression and were in his power to remedy". Henry James too spoke of Irving's "eccentricity of diction" as though it was a natural and incurable defect; others criticised the action of his legs or his gait like it were a physical or nervous disability that could be cured by willpower or by exercises. During these formative years the bulk of the adverse criticism of Irving concerned these faults, which were styled mannerisms rather than congenital biological defects. Again and again Irving was urged to conquer or control these mannerisms as though they were "habits carelessly acquired". Another physical impediment often seen in creative people is myopia, which Irving certainly demonstrated. He also walked with his head "drooping a little as though in deep thought", which forced passers-by to turn and watch the great actor as he went by.

PERSONALITY

Irving became obsessed with acting – a very narrow focus though extremely strong one – and planned his acting career, in so far as possible, with great care. He had "a fanatical faith in the art he loved" and was "clear of purpose and ruthlessly determined". He was tremendously visual and a massive observer, which aided the process of portraying characters on stage. Given his thirst for the theatre, he was an autodidact and prodigious reader and possessed a massive memory; indeed, it was described as an "elephantine retention of memory". As an artist Irving was likened to French painter Eugène Delacroix: "Both men were almost the last to learn the academic and traditional processes of their craft; on this firm foundation they developed theories and methods of startling originality and later themselves were disconcerted by the work of the ardent disciples whom they had inspired." Both were novelty-seekers in the sense that they ploughed a new furrow and were pioneers. Such was his all-encompassing focus on the theatre that Irving was a workaholic. His life, as a great tragic actor and Shakespearian actor, was his work. In fact, he spent one entire summer holiday studying *Macbeth*. With his extremely obdurate nature and massive energy levels, not surprisingly, he continued to act till the end of his life.

On the street he would practise reciting plays, "oblivious of eccentricity", and certainly passers-by saw this as odd behaviour. Given his very narrow interests in the theatre, he thus began to relate to people associated with it. Getting the money to buy theatre tickets proved difficult at times but he left no stone unturned. He wrote letters with an adult flavour, even as a child. Nevertheless, as an adult there was a child-like element to his personality. He was always rather naïve and innocent, and indeed was described as being "simple".

Irving also showed preservation of sameness in his life; for example, he used watercolours for his make-up, even when greasepaint became available and popular, but he adhered to the practice which he had learned as a youth. Throughout his life he was a highly ritualistic man.

There is much evidence of identity diffusion too. Irving was a self-made man who "fashioned himself" to achieve success. People described him in very different ways: in fact, the different "witnesses" of his character tended to "contradict each other so fiercely". He was a chameleon-like character, which is often said of people with genius. Henry Irving "created, indeed … fashioned himself". Others claimed that he was incapable offstage "of playing anything but himself". It is doubtful if he ever really knew himself, or indeed if anybody else could know him. Sir Max Beerbohm described Irving as the "knight from nowhere". This phrase has echoes of the "man/woman from Mars" analogy often applied to people with autism.

At the age of 27 his somewhat anti-authority character led to his dismissal from a job when he failed to agree with a theatre manager. It is hardly surprising that due to his independent spirit he became "penniless and frustrated" at the age of 27 because of his behaviour. Indeed, at the end of his life he had again exhausted his financial resources. He had little regard for money and bought books incessantly. For him art was all: "his whole life was centred in his art". Nevertheless, exerting control was also characteristic of the man. He always got his own way, particularly as he became famous. Having established himself as the foremost actor of the age, he was massively important to the British stage and getting it taken seriously. He intimidated actress Ellen Terry and many others with his hyper-focused work behaviour. Truth was everything to Irving, and he would never deceive his audience or anyone else. Indeed, like Houdini, he once exposed charlatans engaged in spiritualism. Interestingly, he hated anyone who was "two faced". For him, an actor required "modesty, perseverance, patience, courage and firmness". Irving was extremely egocentric and lived much of his life in a one-person world. He had an autistic sense of duty: "In his life and in his art he was guided solely by his natural instinct for what was right, and by the acute perception which was sharpened by his sensibility."

Irving always had a "lonely inner life" and possessed certain traits that did not always endear him to people: he was aloof, "high-handed and oversensitive" and displayed "caustic humour". He often indulged excessively in alcohol. On a trip to Philadelphia, Irving visited poet Walt Whitman, who had some similar personality traits. Irving did not belong to any "club or coterie". If he did meet a group, he tended to dominate and "stood apart", according to W. L. Courtney in Laurence Irving's biography of Irving. The phrase – "stood apart" – can be seen as an "Asperger phrase". Like many people with Asperger syndrome he loved animals, particularly his dog. Interestingly, Irving paid cab drivers more money if they drove well. He liked to gossip with "cheap-jacks and gipsies" and had no false modesty. He had little interest in financial matters and required just enough money to "keep himself in modest comfort".

As he grew older he became somewhat paranoid and suspicious. J. F. Nisbet in the London *Times* stated that "Irving's personality happens to be peculiarly rich in the elements of the weird, the sinister, the sardonic, the grimly humorous, the keenly intellectual; and any character into which these qualities can be introduced by him remains indelibly stamped upon the mind as a great creation". He also noted that "Irving's Richard is the most Satanic character I have ever seen on the stage". There was a strong sadistic element to Irving's personality, which was seen in his relationship with theatre manager Bram Stoker. Of course Stoker, the author of *Dracula*, in his own life displayed masochistic traits.

Ellen Terry's personality perfectly complemented Irving's: he had the extreme male brain and she the extreme female brain; she was rather inattentive and distracted, while he had the capacity for massive concentration and focus; he was introverted and she was extroverted; she was casual with time-keeping, while he was punctual; he made a huge effort to portray a part accurately, whereas this came to her naturally – her son claimed she simply played herself. She in fact liberated the great actor in Irving. He possessed a strong superego and a very strong ego ideal, particularly in relation to the stage.

SOCIAL RELATIONSHIPS

As a person Irving was extremely puzzling. People found him mysterious and difficult to understand and to get to know. In a way he was a solitary man – something of a loner despite his innumerable acquaintances. He could only relax with the very few people he knew well, most of whom were associated with the theatre. In addition, he was only interested in conversing with likeminded people. For much of his life he had a tremendous professional relationship with Ellen Terry. Commonly seen in people with Asperger's syndrome, Irving had one particular friend, Bram Stoker, the writer and stage manager of the Lyceum Theatre. In conversation, Irving appeared to speak with an autistic narrative and also had dyspraxia. On one occasion, about 10 years after their first meeting, he met Ellen Terry and was uncertain "as to the purpose of his visit" to her. This can be seen in terms of the autistic narrative.

Before meeting Florence O'Callaghan, whom he ultimately married, Irving had a relationship with Nellie Moore, who unfortunately died, yet he kept her photograph in his wallet until his death. Unsympathetic to his profession or failing to understand it, O'Callaghan regarded Irving as a "strange man". When they married, he could not tolerate her henpecking, criticism and temper tantrums. She became pregnant and bore him a son, but the marriage broke down from her incessant nagging. He agreed to pay maintenance but some time later they reconciled and she became pregnant again. However, this time he could not endure her criticism and they separated once more. According to his grandson, Laurence Irving, it was the sense of failure in his human relationships, as a father and a husband, which had embittered the taste of success. In one way the acting company at the Lyceum became his family. He formed Asperger-type relationships with older women: several of whom were much older than himself yet he welcomed their affection and depended a great deal upon their advice on personal matters. He was apathetic "towards his marital obligations" and constantly related better to older women. Ellen Terry's love for Irving was akin to that of a mother "who had borne a son whose genius filled her with wonder and pride – yet whose stubborn and wilful waywardness called upon all her resources of tact and gentle remonstrance to prevent him hurting himself by his rash decisions and ill-considered actions". This mother–son type of relationship is certainly typical of those that men with Asperger syndrome often have with women. Irving similarly was micro-managed by his valet, who became his "fifth limb and his loss at any time would have been crippling … this man was a bantamweight Sancho Panza to his dolorous and much-loved knight." Nevertheless, Irving liked to interact, mainly on an acquaintance level, with people with connections to the stage or other actors. He took few holidays, much like Walt Disney, and was poor at relaxing.

Clearly Irving improved his social skills as he got older similar to philosopher Ludwig Wittgenstein, who had Asperger syndrome. Irving's failure as a father was seen by the fact that when his boys were growing up he rarely saw them, and when he did, they appeared "awkward and embarrassed". This is not unlike Sam Goldwyn, who rarely saw his daughter and failed also as a father. Failure as a parent is not uncommon in great creators.

Work

Irving, as a remarkable and extraordinary man, was capable of inspiring "noble emotions" in an audience, and had massive impact on his audiences. He became the greatest Victorian actor and esteemed manager of the Lyceum Theatre and was acknowledged as such throughout the world. In America, he was greatly admired by the students of Harvard University. Like many actors, however, he suffered "humiliation and despair" initially on stage. He suffered from stage fright at the beginning of his career and later too his performances on first nights were not his greatest. Early in his career he worked in Dublin at the Queen's Theatre, one of the least "reputable" ones.

Irving was one of the most determined actors of all time, and was always "raising the bar", wanting better and better performances. In preparation, he rehearsed in front of his mirror again and again. In the plays he staged at the Lyceum, he had total control: "With infinite patience, though with occasional acerbities, he coached every actor in his part, repeating over and over again word or action until it approximated to the perfection which he aimed. Ellen Terry would watch despairingly Irving's relentless concentration on this often hopeless task."

The whole theatre was organised around Irving's wish for absolute perfection and the execution of his wishes, which to most actors meant the same thing. One actor, Mr E. Booth, stated that Irving was "despotic" on the stage and that at rehearsal his will was absolute law, whether it concerned the entry of a messenger with a letter or the reading of a letter by Ellen Terry: "From the first to last he rules the stage with a will of iron. Over and over again the line is recited or a bit of action done, until it is perfect. At the Lyceum one sees the perfection of stage discipline." This again was very similar to Walt Disney. Much later Irving was interested only in the supremacy of his theatre and the perfection of his art. It is not surprising that he reached the pinnacle of his profession and was painted by John Everett Millais, the esteemed Pre-Raphaelite artist of the day.

As noted above, Irving was extremely single-minded and had no recreation from his work and life in the theatre: for him it was "I work, therefore I exist". He was a hyperkinetic individual: acting at night and rehearsing a new play at the same time as being involved in stage management. All these multiple activities had to do with his single narrow interest. At heart, he was very much a novelty seeker and had an "unorthodox" approach to plays. To this end, he also went to France and observed the French style of "play acting" at the Comédie-Française, which influenced him.

As a producer of plays, Irving was "tireless and stern" in seeking the perfection at which he aimed. He rehearsed his actors to the point of exhaustion – his and theirs – and did not spare himself. The total control extended to Irving keeping his hand on every detail as the components were completed and fell into place for a stage play. His advice to actors was: "First lay down your lines; settle what you want to do and do it; the greater opposition the more persevering and courageous you must be; if you are right and strength and life hold out, you must win." Given his powers of observation, he had a huge capacity to get inside the skin of the men he would portray, for example Cardinal Wolsey. Like Disney, he risked all his financial resources on his productions. He died on 30 October 1905, aged 67, and was buried next to the great actor David Garrick in Westminster Abbey.

Chapter 2

DAVID GARRICK

David Garrick (1717–1779) was the greatest actor-manager of the eighteenth century; his stature is similar to that of Henry Irving in the nineteenth century. They both in different ways created stage performance as we know it today. Garrick became a superstar and celebrity of his time. Like Mozart, Garrick was a genius with immense innate talent, requiring little tuition as is characteristic of geniuses.

BACKGROUND

David Garrick was born on 19 February 1717 in Hereford. A Huguenot, his father was a religious refugee from France and of "amiable disposition" and "agreeable conversation"; his mother was of Irish extraction and "sprightly and engaging".[2] According to Garrick's biographer Thomas Davies, the father became an officer in the army. Both parents were a highly sociable couple, wonderful at entertaining. Such balance is extremely unusual in highly creative families: one wonders if there is more to the story than we are given. (Of course, Garrick comes across as similar to his parents, at least in the accounts we have of him.) When army remuneration was cut by half, the family went into "genteel poverty". This had a profound effect on Garrick's attitude to financial matters for the rest of his life.

Even as a small child he showed "a devastating gift of mimicry" and "a talent to amuse". He was a prodigy and an extremely curious and intelligent child. One of his early mentors was Gilbert Walmesley, the registrar of the ecclesiastical court of Lichfield, whom he used to visit many times each week. This was a tremendous education for Garrick. In Lichfield Grammar School, which Garrick later attended, the philosophy of education focused very much on flogging. Samuel Johnson, his fellow pupil, experienced this flogging far more frequently than Garrick. Garrick showed poor school progress, as people of genius very often do. He may have had elements of attention deficit hyperactivity disorder, and was also novelty-seeking. He was considered an "erratic pupil" and would put off completing the tasks he had been set by his masters until the last moment, "preferring to talk and improvise". Despite all this, he learned a great deal by osmosis, so to speak, because he was so highly

---

[2] Except where otherwise indicated, quotes in this chapter are from Benedetti (2001).

intelligent and "quick-minded". He was also described as being "histrionic" and famous for "jumping over stiles".

From an early age he was hyperfocused on the theatre. As a child he would recite speeches from plays for his peers, who essentially were his first audiences. At the age of 10 he put on a play and took "complete charge of the production, auditioning his friends, designing the sets, and choosing the costumes". This production was far superior to the usual amateur ones on offer. During his early adolescence his mother became "depressed" and housebound. Her physical health deteriorated as a consequence. At this time Garrick's father was overseas and his mother pined for him. Despite dabbling with the idea of becoming a lawyer for a period, it came to nothing when his father died. He was sent to Portugal for a year to his uncle's family, where he continued to perform informally. From his uncle, a vintner, he learned many business skills.

Personality

There were contradictions in Garrick's character: on one hand he was an "extrovert", while on the other he was reflective and "weighed up the possibilities" of any situation. Like many creative people, he suffered from melancholia. Garrick was effectively a workaholic at what interested him and did not wish to waste time. Indeed his time was precious. He was a prodigious reader who greatly valued his privacy and carefully controlled people's access to him.

Social Relationships

The first woman Garrick became emotionally involved with was Irish actress Peg Woffington. She was quite an androgynous lady, though beautiful. She was said to be sexually promiscuous, flirtatious, had a vicious temper and stabbed a rival actress in the wings of Covent Garden. He subsequently married Eva Marie Veigel in 1749. Garrick was childless but got on well with children. At times he was not ungenerous, despite his fear of poverty. Garrick once devastated the Irish playwright Oliver Goldsmith by refusing to put on one of his plays. This arose because Garrick was always calculating the financial risk and could be tyrannical, preferring to stage his own plays. Because of this treatment, Goldsmith refused to give him his masterpiece, *She Stoops to Conquer*.

Success on the stage and superstardom changed Garrick and he became "irritating" to people. He stage-managed every social occasion, allowing him to present himself to maximum effect – he pioneered celebrity culture long before its twenty-first century iteration. Because time was precious to him, he did not waste it with inconsequential or frivolous people. He valued greatly the mind of philosopher Edmund Burke, feeling it worthwhile to spend time with him.

Work

Garrick retained his interest in the theatre, although at this time actors were seen as "drunken profligates dividing their time between wining and wenching". An early mentor was William Hogarth, the painter, who attuned him to the visual arts. At this time Dublin was the cradle of the English theatre because of the number of major actors it supplied. The Irish actor Charles Macklin became Garrick's new mentor, though Macklin had a history of homicide, namely killing a man over a wig at the Theatre Royal, Drury Lane.

Garrick's small stature was a problem because of the practice by theatre managers to pay their actors "by the inch rather than their talent". Nevertheless, he proved himself to be an actor-manager of genius. In relation to his work he had a strong superego and high standards and principles. He became an enormously successful Shakespearian actor. He died on 20 January 1779, aged 61, and is buried in Westminster Abbey. Great actors who followed in his tradition include Ellen Terry, Laurence Olivier, John Gielgud and Michael Redgrave, several of whom are dealt with in this book.

Chapter 3

Orson Welles

Orson Welles (1915–1985) was one of the most famous American actor/directors of the twentieth century. His film *Citizen Kane* (1941) is widely regarded as the greatest of all time, while his radio broadcast of H.G. Wells's *War of the Worlds* (1938) caused mass panic in the USA and made him a household name. He had awesome talent, which appeared early in life, but was also self-destructive – a myth-maker, indulging in excess of all kinds; a man without limits, without boundaries. He had no difficulty in forming superficial relationships and had myriad acquaintances; it was the deep, personal, one-to-one relationships, such as marriage, that he failed to cope with nor had the skills to succeed at.

This chapter presents a brief examination of Welles's psyche. In particular, it proposes that he showed elements of Asperger syndrome, attention deficit hyperactivity disorder (ADHD) and hyperkinetic syndrome (HKS). His genius sprang, perhaps, from the synergy of HKS and Asperger syndrome, which have contradictory features, yet when combined can confer tremendous potential. Simon Callow (1996), in a fine biography that has informed much of the current chapter, notes that "a question mark hovers over practically every aspect of Welles's life and work. This is the more surprising since he is among the most fully documented artists of the twentieth century."[3]

Background

When recalling his early life, Welles tended to be a fantasist and make up stories. Records show he was born George Orson Welles in Kenosha, Wisconsin on 6 May 1915, the younger of two boys – his brother, Richard, had been born in 1905. Their father, also Richard, was a partner in a lamp company. In 1917, at the age of 46, Richard Snr received a large settlement when his company was taken over; he never worked again, preferring to indulge in a life of drinking and womanising. Orson's mother, Beatrice, was a beautiful, intelligent and accomplished woman, with an interest in good works, and who was prominent socially. His brother Richard was regarded as sullen and slow-witted as well as a disappointment to his parents: "No praise for him, no laughter; no plans and no hopes." When Welles arrived, according to Callow, he was "the baby Beatrice and Richard had wanted all along: bright as a

[3] Except where otherwise indicated, quotes in this chapter are from Callow (1996).

button, bonny, iron-lunged and lusty". He evidently was highly intelligent and very verbal from an early age.

The family, now wealthy, moved to the booming city of Chicago in 1918. Here Beatrice was able to find an outlet for her cultural interests, while Richard descended into hopeless alcoholism. The family's doctor in Kenosha, Maurice Bernstein, also moved to Chicago – he was in love with Beatrice and had an affair with her; he was also a great admirer of precocious young Welles, who called him "Dadda", and who now effectively had two fathers.

Beatrice contracted jaundice in 1924 and died on 10 May, four days after Welles's ninth birthday. Bernstein, who was devastated by her death, redoubled the attention and affection he showered on her younger son, seeing him as a living memorial to Beatrice. As his mother had pressurised him, so too did his father and Bernstein, in different directions – his father wanting him to be a journalist or cartoonist; Bernstein pushing him to be a creative genius and literary giant. The picture of the child that emerges from Callow's book is of a mind that was either brilliant or, arguably, meretricious – it certainly lacked rigour. He was a quick learner with a gift for absorbing and regurgitating fragments of language and information, but did not necessarily understand his impressive pronouncements. Other children saw him as an oddity and a loner; this would have been exacerbated by his mother's liking for dressing him up in curious attire such as velvet knee breeches. Later he would describe his childhood as a prison – "a pestilential handicap I determined to cure myself of". At the age of 10 he had a strong and assured personality.

His mother was extremely important to Welles: she was a huge influence on him long after her death (indeed, right up to his own death). She demanded a great deal of him – from a very early age he was expected to converse with her on her own level, and to show a level of mature accomplishment way beyond his years. Naturally, this was impossible, and hence she was disappointed. He describes her deathbed scene in a memoir: she quoted a line from *A Midsummer Night's Dream* referring to a changeling, which later made him wonder what she meant, and whether he was indeed "a changeling". (Interestingly, children with autism have sometimes been described as changelings. As a boy, Hans Christian Andersen said that he was a changeling (Wullschlager, 2000), while William Butler Yeats wrote a poem "The Stolen Child" about a changeling. Both Andersen (Fitzgerald, 2005) and Yeats (Fitzgerald, 2004) are believed to have had Asperger syndrome.) Welles's father died in 1930, possibly from suicide. Both father and mother were larger-than-life figures and indeed Welles showed aspects of both of them throughout his life. He himself was certainly larger than life.

During his school days, Welles had poor relationships with other students, although he and his one friend, Paul Guggenheim, were seen as geniuses, looked upon as VIPs and "carried around on cotton wool". When Welles and "Guggie" were alone together, they discussed "philosophy and poetry; or rather, Orson discussed philosophy and poetry", which seems like a rather "Aspergerish" monologue. Bernstein stated that "Orson really looked up to other children. He didn't know how to behave among them and could not join in their childish pleasures. They mystified him, even scared him", which is typical for a person with Asperger syndrome. At the age of ten he was tested by a psychologist friend of Bernstein, who found "a profound dissociation of ideas" (Noble, 1956). Welles got into journalism at the age of 13, and was thus described by Callow:

> [His writing was] exuberant and opinionated … there are letters of Mozart at the same age which are as bumptious and as callous – but there are few thirteen-year-olds

> who would commit themselves to newsprint in like vein – few who would want to; even fewer who would be asked to.

It is interesting to note Mozart also possibly had Asperger syndrome (Fitzgerald, 2005).

At school, Welles's talent was allowed to develop almost "in isolation" and in all things he got his way. In fact, there is no other way a person with Asperger syndrome can develop. Development has to be within their space, not in interaction with other people. Everything has to be *moi*. Indeed, there is much greater independence of brain modules in persons with Asperger syndrome, which allows them to express and develop their talent more than persons with more integrated brains. Of course, it is also associated with deficits in interpersonal relating, interpersonal skills and the processing of social and emotional features of the human environment. Callow points out, with reference to Welles's teenage years:

> It was an important part of his personal myth, even at this age, that he had no teachers. And, essentially, it is true. He refused what they had to offer, was by nature and conviction an autodidact. He did it his way. He had no intention of playing their game and being judged according to their rules. This again was willed. He knew that criticism was intolerable to him, so he put himself beyond it. He was a one-off, his own sternest critic, and woe betide anyone who attempted to set themselves up in judgement of him.

Many geniuses with Asperger syndrome have been autodidacts. As children, persons with Asperger syndrome can talk easily to adults, almost on an adult-to-adult basis. Indeed, they are often called "little professors" or similar, as was the case with Welles. As a 16-year-old, he could convincingly play the characters of much older men.

His brother Richard also appears to have had Asperger syndrome, misdiagnosed as a mental illness – the diagnosis those with Asperger syndrome were often given until the latter part of the twentieth century (Fitzgerald, 2004). Richard's life and psychiatric treatment amount to a mental health tragedy. He drifted aimlessly through life, wandering the country and working as a casual labourer; he had been expelled from school and was ignored by the family. Even Welles did not really relate to him. In effect, Richard was a kind of black sheep of the family, described as sullen and uncommunicative, and the victim of Richard Welles Snr's cruelty. The latter conspired with Bernstein to have Richard Jnr certified insane and imprisoned in the state sanatorium, despite no evidence of his having harmed anyone or caused any breach of the peace. Nonetheless, Richard Snr's will refers to his elder son's "irresponsibility and ingratitude". Richard Jnr was mistreated in the way persons with Asperger syndrome often are, and was incarcerated for 10 years, between the ages of 25 and 35. On his release, he followed "a slightly erratic career as a social worker, popping up in his brother's life from time to time".

Callow lists the consequences for adults of having alcoholic parents, based on research by Janet Woititz (1983):

> They guess at what normal behaviour is; they have difficulty following a project through from beginning to end ... they judge themselves without mercy; they have difficulty having fun; they take themselves very seriously; they have difficulty with intimate relationships; they overreact to changes over which they have no control; they constantly seek approval and affirmation; they usually feel that they are different to other people; they are super responsible or super irresponsible; they are extremely loyal, even in the face of evidence that loyalty is undeserved; they are impulsive. They tend to lock

themselves into a course of action without giving serious consideration to alternative behaviours or possible consequences. This impulsivity leads to confusion, self-loathing and lack of control over the environment.

This list could apply almost as well to persons with Asperger syndrome. In my opinion, the explanation for his behaviour was that he had Asperger syndrome, not that he was a child of an alcoholic father. Similar mental health tragedies to that of Orson's brother have occurred in many American families – great families such as the Kennedys as well as lesser-known ones. If one child in a family has Asperger syndrome, there is greatly increased risk of a second child having it: heritability for Asperger syndrome has been calculated at about 93 per cent.

PERSONALITY

In an interview with Jean Clay in 1962, Welles summarised several aspects of his psyche well when he said:

> Seventy-five percent of what I say in interviews is false … Introspection is bad for me. I'm a medium, not an orator. Like certain oriental and Christian mystics, I think the "self" is a kind of enemy. My work is what enables me to come out of myself. I like what I do, not what I am … Do you know the best service anyone could render to art? Destroy all biographies. Only art can explain the life of a man – and not the contrary. (Clay, 1962)

His contradictory nature also came to the fore. Welles stated that "everything about me is a contradiction, and so is everything about everybody else. We are made out of oppositions; we live between two poles. There is a philistine and an aesthete in all of us, and a murderer and a saint. You don't reconcile the poles. You just recognise them" (Tynan, 1967). It is certainly true that there were numerous contradictions in Welles's psyche. Callow notes that:

> Throughout his life, Welles maintained an implacable opposition to logical thought, preferring to speak in gnomically resonant phrases that he would refuse to explain. There is a curious tension in this, since his was not a poetic nature, nor was he able or willing to propound any coherent vision. He was in fact, a logical thinker who refused to think logically, in love with the sound of poetry, addicted to paradox and wit, but never with the objective of expressing anything precise … He had the habits of mind of someone who has been expected to talk coherently before he has anything coherent to say.

There is evidence here of an autistic dialogue. Welles showed the pragmatic language deficits that are common in persons with Asperger syndrome – a classic feature is giving the listener too little information to understand what is being said. Welles always had a very close relationship with the press, and was constantly selling them stories about himself. There's no doubt that he was hyperkinetic and novelty-seeking.

Callow notes that melodrama was always close to Welles's heart – it provided opportunities for extravagant displays of acting theatrical effects, with much less emphasis on intimate emotions. It masked his problem with understanding these emotions. John Houseman, a famous stage director, wrote with reference to *The War of the Worlds*: "Welles is at heart a magician whose particular talent lies not so much in his creative imagination … as in his proven ability to stretch the familiar elements of theatrical effect far beyond the normal point of tension. For this reason his productions require more elaborate preparation and more perfect execution than most … Welles's flops are louder than other men's." Callow states that in 1938 Welles began to believe that he could make anything happen as long as the pressure was enough. Not precisely sure of his destination, Welles drove himself and others on, buoyed up by alcohol, amphetamines, food, sex, and almost totally deprived of sleep.

> There seems to have been a need to keep high: the essential motivation of compulsive behaviour. Anything … not to lose the adrenalin … he seems to have indulged in all those stimulants, alcohol, food, drink and sex … he had a massively strong constitution and pushed his body beyond any normal limits. When nothing else worked, he took pills. Throughout the thirties, he chewed amphetamines as if they were candy.

Here is the classic hyperkinetic, novelty-seeking, sensation-seeking person. Welles was always late for things, as hyperkinetic people often are – in fact, he wasted a lot of his own and other people's time. He was very adventurous, needing to hurl himself into the heart of danger and to associate himself with risk and recklessness. Hence he showed an insatiable appetite for new projects. In fact, he went to Ireland at the age of 16, and impulsively decided to disembark at Galway in the West of Ireland. Persons with Asperger syndrome are often impulsive: poor impulse control was a feature of Welles, except when he was hyper-focusing on theatre or film matters.

Welles was also an extraordinary spendthrift. In 1938, Houseman described the scale of his indulgence, detailing "the meals, each one a feast; the nightly consumption of one and two bottles of whiskey or brandy"; the sexual prowess "which was reported in statistical detail … also, apparently, immense". This seems very hyperkinetic. It is hardly surprising then that at the age of 23 he showed "distressing signs of wear and tear". Similarly, his method of working without a plan – of depending on the inspiration of the moment – lacked practicality. This is not unusual in persons with ADHD/HKS. At the Woodstock Festival, Welles's cavalier attitude to money bordered "on the callous, considering it wasn't his own that was at risk". This was also evidence of his lack of empathy and poor reality testing.

His novelty-seeking was well illustrated by the fact that when his first child, Christopher, was born, he was reported to have flirted with the nurse on the maternity ward "because she moved like a dancer". He had married Virginia Nicolson, an actress and his first girlfriend, in 1934; they would be divorced on the grounds of his mental cruelty in Reno in 1940, Virginia explaining that "he's a genius and sometimes works around the clock without sleep. He has no time for marriage and a family." His second wife was the actress Rita Hayworth, who had five husbands in all; his third wife was Paola Mori, a countess.

Geraldine Fitzgerald, an Irish actress with whom he worked, was "struck by … his ability to create intense intimacy on first contact. Maintaining it was more of a problem." She compared his personality to a lighthouse: "when you were caught in its beam, you were bathed in its illumination; when it moved on, you were plunged into darkness".

Welles was described as a very poorly organised man. According to Richard Barr, who worked with him on radio programmes, "Orson did not direct his shows; he conducted them. Standing on a podium in front of a dynamic microphone … he waved his arms, cued every music, sound and speech cue". At this time he was "a screaming and most unstatesman-like autocrat". Paul Stewart, a radio director, said that "There was absolute chaos … every week. Welles is a very destructive man, he has to destroy everything, then put it back together again himself, and there were endless passionate discussions between him, Houseman and me". He certainly was a risk-taker and thrill-seeker.

Micheál Mac Liammóir, actor and co-director of the Gate Theatre, said that Welles's self-possessed air came "from some ageless and superb inner confidence that no one could blow out. It was unquenchable. That was his secret. He knew that he was precisely what he himself would have chosen to be had God consulted him on the subject at his birth." Again, this suggests a "born", i.e., genetic, genius. There is no doubt that the multiple effects of small and interacting genes gave Welles his acting ability – training played a very small role.

He believed that he had a special gift for playing thinking people: not, as he expressed it in an interview with Peter Bogdanovich, "that they're thinking about what they are saying, but that they can think outside of the scene … there are very few actors who can make you believe they think … that's the kind of part I can play". Callow points out that although Welles was unquestionably intelligent, the most striking feature of his acting persona is not intelligence but power. His portrayals of "thinking people" lack intellectual conviction, partly due to a lack of structure in his own thinking: "Welles, instead of actually thinking, acts it." Persons with Asperger syndrome are often great thinkers and intellectually oriented, yet their autistic thinking is a limited form of thinking. Also, it is not always realised that persons with Asperger syndrome can have a massive imagination and be fantasists. They have poor autobiographical memory, a poor sense of their own personal history, and it is therefore easier for them to create a mythical history for themselves. They have the sense of having multiple selves or identity diffusion – something Welles experienced.

Persons with Asperger syndrome and genius are often extraordinary self-publicists: they adore seeing their names "in lights". Callow notes that Welles was unable to resist a fix of publicity; he was "a whirlwind of promotion: self-promotion, particularly … one of the greatest one-man publicity machines ever created". He had to be the greatest – the standard by which everyone else would be measured. The mere sight of a reporter's notebook or tape recorder unleashed his powers of self-invention. He was very egocentric, narcissistic and self-centred, as persons with Asperger syndrome can often be: they have to be number one at all times; other people are regarded as pygmies, and have only a background – almost an invisible – role.

Geraldine Fitzgerald remembered stories of Welles as a young man:

> [He] could be thirty though he was only sixteen, had this stupendous voice and knew every dirty trick in the book and played them on Micheál [Mac Liammóir, whom he directed in *Othello* in 1952] … Welles had no guilt; there was nothing furtive about it. He walked on the end of everybody's lines and moved in front of them and things like that. All the younger actors were awed that someone as young as themselves dared to be so alarming to the brass.

He was trampling on people and nothing mattered except his own personal success and personal acting performance. Of course, because of his Asperger syndrome, he was very often not aware of his tactlessness and lack of empathy.

In a scene from *Citizen Kane*, in Welles's own words, "Kane's monomania finally exerts itself: his enraged conviction that no one exists but himself, his refusal to admit the existence of other people with whom one must compromise, whose feelings one must take into account". Callow points out that there is some sense here of an overlap between Kane and Welles. Callow draws attention to the similarity between Welles and Oscar Wilde: as well as having the same initials and both being flamboyant, they "set out to conquer the world by seeking to master the instruments of publicity; both became its servants – perhaps, if it is not too melodramatic a phrase, its victims".

Welles was a compulsive chameleon, merging into whatever situation he found himself in, "always able to become part of a different clan with ease: to identify with them, to join in, to be one of them". This ability to merge with the environment is paradoxical in persons with Asperger syndrome, as one would expect them always to be very conspicuous, but it does sometimes occur. Similarly, Herman Melville, author of *Moby-Dick*, had Asperger syndrome and also had this ability; it saved him from lashings on the whaling ships of the South Seas (Fitzgerald, 2005).

Welles was a kind of empty shell – a hollow man with identity diffusion, like a vessel waiting to be filled, and "a way of invading you that was nothing to do with the sheer size of him, but to do rather with a knack of immediate intimacy that was one of his greatest assets". One often has a sense of being psychologically invaded by persons with Asperger syndrome. They don't have a sense of normal distance from another individual; they also lack normal ego boundaries, a "core" and a sense of self. If they had a clear sense of themselves, they would not invade another person in this way. In this situation the other person generally feels anxious, uncomfortable and invaded, and wants to push the person with Asperger syndrome away.

Callow says that theatre provided for Welles (as for others who made their lives in it) "a focus and a release for all the many conflicting and sometimes intolerable aspects of his personality. It is both liberation and affirmation; one is no longer trapped inside one's murky self, because one offers it to other people". It is particularly a liberation and affirmation for persons with Asperger syndrome. Since these persons often have an "empty self" or a sense of emptiness, they are fully available to be "filled up" by parts in plays. Their "prison of personal emptiness", or very diffuse sense of self, gives them a sense of not knowing who they are – a most distressing feeling. Acting gives them a release from this. Callow points out that "the urge to impersonate, in its most literal sense, is surely the essence of the actor: to become somebody else. This is not an attractive idea to Welles, who had worked so hard to become what he was".

Callow notes that Welles's power as an actor, "while undeniable, seems assumed, put on – like a false nose – and thus vulnerable". He goes on to state that "the notion of acting – great acting – as a burden he'd been born to, willy-nilly, is a common one with Welles … Welles tried to make himself a great actor simply by playing leading parts one after another. That is not the way to do it." This again suggests identity diffusion and lack of a central cohesive self. Perhaps actors are better if they don't have a strong sense of themselves and therefore can take on other roles to make up this deficiency within themselves; still, Callow makes the valid point that study and practice are necessary as well as instinct and enthusiasm.

Welles had a high ego-ideal for acting: he longed to be a great actor, but his notion of great acting was so exalted that no one could possibly fulfil it. He was obsessed with the Great Actor – "the superhuman, lordly figure, whom one aspires to be". Indeed he wanted to be recognised as a theatrical god. Welles directed Christopher Marlowe's *The Tragical*

History of Doctor Faustus in 1937, and played the title role. Apparently, he felt a special relationship to the character of Faustus, according to Houseman (1972):

> There was a deep personal identification which, across a gulf of three and a half centuries, led him to the heart of the work and to its vivid re-creation on the American stage.... The truth is that the legend of the man who sells his soul to the Devil in exchange for knowledge and power and who must finally pay ... with the agonies of eternal damnation was uncomfortably close to Welles's own personal myth.

As Callow points out, there was a "chilling resonance" for Welles in the lines from the Prologue which compare Faust to Icarus:

> Till swoll'n with cunning, of a self-conceit,
> His waxen wings did mount about his reach
> And melting, heavens conspired his overthrow!

Later in life Welles complained that "nobody reviews my films; they review me". Here he was producing crocodile tears because all he ever wanted reviewed was himself. Nevertheless, he had a Faustian relationship with the press, concomitant with his philosophy of "no limits" and an addiction to sensation-seeking and novelty-seeking.

Welles suffered a great deal from boredom, and had episodes of deep depression – this was a factor in his alcohol abuse, although, as with Stanley Kubrick, work also served as an antidepressant: "His lack of proper preparation, either in rehearsal or before the performance, condemned him to insecurity and made it impossible for his work to grow, thus denying himself the real satisfaction of the job". The hyperkinetic part of his personality interfered with proper planning and organisation.

Callow notes that Welles was no theorist but "a pragmatic operator". Persons with Asperger syndrome often are atheoretical or anti-theory. Callow also points out that his relation to acting was paradoxical: he was immersed in its lore and usually well equipped, physically, to practise it, but he never allowed himself to discover its deep rewards. Like someone who confines himself to casual uninvolved sex and never experiences a real act of love, Welles's acting was statistically impressive, but deeply fulfilling neither for himself nor for his audience. Once the immediate sensual thrill was over, nothing was left for either partner. His lack of communion both with himself and with the character he was playing made this inevitable. His idea of acting was purely cerebral; when that is the case, the god can never enter in. This type of cerebral acting is "Aspergerish", in that persons with Asperger syndrome can be over-intellectual. While superficially impressive, it ultimately shows itself to be somewhat limited, except when the character being portrayed has Asperger syndrome too.

The manager of a company he acted with, Gertrude Macy, stated Welles was "flamboyant, exciting, hammy ... he gave an excellent performance. He should have been slight and delicate; yet he was enormous and clumsy". The clumsiness would go hand-in-hand with Asperger syndrome.

Welles seems to have had a rather autistic superego: "his various guilts merged, as they often do, into one nameless guilt; whatever its source, it never left him. He scarcely knew an untroubled night until the day he died (Houseman, 1972). Houseman wrote that "Orson really believed in the Devil ... this was not a whimsy but a very real obsession. At twenty-one

Orson was sure he was doomed … he was rarely free from a sense of sin and fear of retribution so intense and immediate that it drove him through long nights of panic to seek refuge in debauchery or in work" (Houseman, 1972). As a teenager he was fascinated by mythology, as persons with Asperger syndrome often are.

Asperger syndrome is largely "hard-wired" into the brain, so one would not expect dramatic changes over a short period. In relation to his art he had extremely high standards and aspirations. In psychoanalytical terms this would equate with a very demanding ego ideal. In addition, in this area it was associated with a very harsh conscience or superego. He was also hypersensitive to criticism, as persons with Asperger syndrome very often are.

Callow says that, according to Welles, "the actor controls the audience totally, that's what so great about it. Equally, he is saying that actors are born, not made, and that there is no system of work on oneself or one's art that can produce great acting". Welles was very controlling and dominating – in fact, persons with Asperger syndrome want absolute control. An unwillingness to learn from others, and arrogance and contempt for others, also feature in Asperger syndrome, and these were central to Welles. Even as an 11-year-old he had an adult presence. In his teens, he said "Why should I waste my time going to college and teaching those goddam professors what I know?" Here he was presenting himself as a kind of god born with complete knowledge, owing nothing to anyone and having nothing to learn from anyone. Welles was "all for father-figures, until they told him what to do. Then he was off". He was "pathologically resistant to authority imposed from above", and insisted on imprinting his own personality on his work. He was anti-authority and oppositional.

Even at school, "being directed by him was a fairly terrifying experience, in which democratic consultation was unknown, and ordinary politeness a luxury". One of the actors recalled that he never said anything about "interpretation": "If you had a lead, you did exactly as you were told. He choreographed everything: that's your mark. Don't move. Don't wriggle. He was a martinet." The result, however, was extraordinary theatre: "His vitality swept you away. He drilled us and we became a magnificently choreographed company."

Paula Laurence, an actress with whom he worked, said that "Orson designed everything you saw on that stage. Everything originated in Orson's head; it was the duty of everybody to fill it out – it was presented with such clarity." Callow says that the phrase "hands-on" might have been invented for Welles, and that it gave his rehearsals an unusual excitement. Callow also points out that questions of originality and authorship were to plague Welles throughout his career, largely because of his insistence on sole responsibility for his own work and his increasing need to appear as an original genius, "a quite unnecessary and largely unsustainable claim".

He was compulsive about achievement in the acting world. Because of his autistic extreme control, he would not allow others to be critical of him. Everything had to come from within himself and he was self-critical only in a very narrow autistic area. Persons with Asperger syndrome tend to be compulsive and have a very narrow focus. Nonetheless, Houseman (1972) wrote that he revealed a surprising capacity for collaboration: "For all the mass of his own ego, he was able to apprehend other people's weakness and strength, and to make creative use of them." There is a contradiction here in his personality – it was probably a secret of his success that he could be totally dominating but could also collaborate. The collaboration, presumably, would have had to be on Welles's terms. The lighting designer Jean Rosenthal wrote that "I do not think Orson made the utmost use of his collaborators' talent, although he often inspired their achievements. He did make the utmost use of his talents at the beginning, but perhaps his lack of respect for others accounts in some measure for the ultimate dissipation of his multiple talents".

Rosenthal recalled that at the Mercury Theatre, nobody else had any identity for Welles at all:

> You were production material. If he liked you, the association could be pleasant. If not, it was injurious. As a director, he approached other talents as he did his gargantuan meals – with a voracious appetite. Your contributions to his feast he either spat out or set aside untouched, or he ate them up, assimilated them, with a gusto which was extraordinarily flattering. (Rosenthal & Wertenbaker, 1972).

She said that Welles was one of the first directors to dominate every single aspect of a production.

There is also the matter of the actor's mask. For Welles, the mask is the face: "It mustn't be questioned. You can hide parts of the mask, but you can't go beyond the mask, much less take it off. This refusal to go beyond the public front denies the possibility of the actor being taken over by the character. 'It is through illumination that you create a true thing'". The notion of the mask is also very important in the life of W. B. Yeats: I have written elsewhere that the mask or anti-self is a manifestation of Yeats's autistic persona, and indicates the cognitive intellectual approach typical in Asperger syndrome (Fitzgerald, 2005).

The question of whether or not Welles was satisfied in his various roles emerges. Callow notes that, as Virgil Thompson had observed, Welles "never gave his mind, let alone his heart, to his work as an actor. Did he want to be one at all? He still seemed unsure forty years later." Welles himself confessed that he had an idea that wanted to be known as a director and "that was that". The role of director was more appealing and more controlling: "The idea of being a director – the big boss – somehow struck him as having more weight. Welles was constantly trying to give himself weight, solidity. He succeeded beyond his wildest ambitions, and not at all: always feeling small, despite girth and glory."

His behaviour also had echoes of Winston Churchill with his generals and civil servants during the Second World War. "He dictated the pace and regularity of his work according to his personal mood", said his stage manager Howard Teichmann. "When he felt like rehearsing, we rehearsed. When he felt like sleeping, we didn't rehearse … when he was tired he would say 'All right, children'. Now mind you, he was younger than most of the people but we were his children." Teichmann also said that Welles played people off against each other and created stress for the people who worked with him, and was often only "a throw away from bullying". Callow notes that Welles's instinctive sense of how to release an actor and a scene in physical movement was the equal of his English contemporary, Tyrone Guthrie, with whom he shared a revulsion for dealing with the inner life of the character, or indeed, of the actor. This is the Asperger style.

Callow points out that throughout his career, on film and on stage, Welles was never entirely in command of his texts and hence given to improvisation: "He was not a quick study and rarely had the time or the inclination to ensure that the words were so securely lodged in his memory that they would spring spontaneously to his lips at the appropriate moment. Fortunately, he had considerable powers of … improvisation." Despite his massive wish to control, Welles was frequently out of control and his projects lacked an overarching plan: "He created an atmosphere where everything seemed possible. No one was tolerated who expressed caution or anxiety; neither time nor money were held to be acceptable limitations. But there was no master-plan". This sort of behaviour is characteristic of persons with HKS/ADHD.

While directing the comedy play *Too Much Johnson* in 1938, Welles discovered a new enduring passion, editing, which never lost its absolute fascination for him:

> Editing … he sat surrounded by thousands of feet of film … He had discovered the Frankenstein element of film-making … it is really possible to assemble your own creature and give life to it. The sense of power is intoxicating: a slow scene can be made fast, a funny one sad, a bad performance can be made good, and actors can be expunged from the film as if they had never been. To shoot is human; to edit, divine".

Certainly, this element of control is rather "Aspergerish".

Welles was a very visual artist and "often moved by what he sees" in terms of natural scenery. It is not uncommon for persons with Asperger syndrome to be highly visual and good at drawing. Welles had "a very lively talent for sketching; his line drawings are sharp, witty and evocative, especially effective in capturing the essential character in a face … his gift was for illustration."

It was clear to those around him that Welles evidently had no fear, "which people as well as dogs can spot in an instant". Persons with Asperger syndrome either have no fear or are flooded with anxiety and too fearful. This extreme variation in the clinical picture is a feature of the syndrome. Those with a lack of fear are extremely courageous and will take massive risks – this was Welles.

Welles's physical appearance was odd-looking and he demonstrated an unusual gait. The radio actor Dwight Weist described him as follows:

> I saw this very strange guy dressed in a strange ill-fitting suit and he walked very funny. He never moved his shoulders, arms hanging limply by his side and sort of getting off in a corner by himself. And he was a strange-looking man. He looked like a Eurasian with a head that seemed to be too big for his shoulders, a mouth almost too small for his face which was sort of round, rosy cheeks.

Welles had a "shuffling, flat-footed gait" – indeed his flat feet kept him out of the army during the Second World War.

According to Callow, Welles was not interested in psychology. His approach was "anecdotal", in that its impact was cerebral rather than visceral. The audience would feel they got the point of the character and not that they had experienced him in all his richness: "Welles's real concern was not with the essence of the character but his tempo, pitch and rhythm: his texture." This was as true of his own performances as those of his fellow actors and they rarely touch "a human core". Welles was drawn to the work of the actress Agnes Moorehead, who appeared in *Citizen Kane*; however, "he could neither touch his own centre in the way she touched hers, nor bring it out in other actors" because of his Asperger syndrome. The film *Citizen Kane* was certainly striking for its cerebral tone. According to Callow, there is no more "linear performance" in the history of film than that of Welles in *Citizen Kane*. "And what is wrong with that? Nothing; except that what comes only from the mind, reaches only to the mind. Nothing more is stirred". Again, this would be typical of someone with Asperger syndrome.

Citizen Kane was described by a critic, Bosley Crowther, as failing to provide a clear picture of the character and motives behind the central character – "at the end, Kubla Kane is still an enigma – a very confusing one". The emptiness at the centre – the undefined nature of Kane – was felt by a number of critics. They detected "this hollowness in the film, the void at the centre". Welles himself noted that the film had "a curious iciness at its heart" and had moments when the whole picture seemed "to echo a bit" for him. The film was also described as "a labyrinth without a centre … endlessly enigmatic". Indeed the *Citizen Kane* that Welles produced had considerable similarities to himself.

To make a film based on a living newspaper tycoon – William Randolph Hearst – who could and did damage the film after its release may have shown a certain naivety. It was not a commercial success, however.

> Driven from within to achieve even more, his work in all the areas in which he was employed had been amazingly accomplished for one so young; it did not, however, contain the seeds of future development. The same may be said of his personality, equally completely formed at an uncommonly early age. In fact, the work is the personality, the personality the work to an alarming degree. His creations have no autonomy; they are but his creatures.

Social Relationships

There were two sides to Welles: his public side, according to Mac Liammóir, was not attractive, but with theatre people he was at his best: "Good nature bubbling irresistibly out of him sweet as wild honey in a young bear's paw. He was charming … and full of generosity, giving little parties for us all and suddenly asking for advice like a penitent child who has been fractious when there were strangers in the house." It is often falsely believed that persons with Asperger syndrome are characterless. In fact, they can perform well, and often superbly, in front of large and small groups of people – it's in the one-to-one intimate relationships that they have huge difficulties.

There is no doubt that he did use people, including Houseman. All great artists are users to some extent. Houseman describes working with Welles when he was thirty-four and Welles was nineteen, being exposed "to the strange combination in Welles of seductively submissive, rather female charm with other, very masculine attributes: mastery, bending to his will, recreating, re-shaping". An actress who worked with him, Brenda Forbes, described him early in his career as "gauche and tiresome". He was always talking about plans for his own theatre or else wanting to take over any group he joined. Persons with Asperger syndrome typically want to control and take over groups that they come into contact with. It is hardly surprising that he was found to be tactless and boring early in his career.

Welles talked a great deal about men being attracted to him when he was a teenager. At that time he was, of course, emotionally immature; whether he ever matured emotionally is questionable. He was always "looking for affirmation and approval specifically from men". This was his search for a clear, definite male identity, which he did not have because of his very significant identity diffusion.

According to Callow, Welles was capable of expressing himself lovingly and had an overwhelming need for affection and affirmation, however, love was also a complicated thing, "a source of guilt, disappointment, and fearful vulnerability". Often he would seem to need "to kill the love that he had provoked". Because of his immaturity and his Asperger syndrome, he was always looking for, and finding, someone to look after him. Persons with Asperger syndrome frequently seek a partner to mother them and to pander to their child-like personality. It is interesting that Welles's teacher and friend, Roger Hill, said that he could play Jew Süss but not a normal 16-year-old boy. Given his Asperger syndrome, it is hardly surprising that he was not a normal 16-year-old boy. Persons with the condition very often do not appear their age and as adults come across as immature and childlike; even children can give an adult-like appearance and behaviour.

In common with many with Asperger syndrome, Welles had traits of the loner too, despite his lofty aspirations: "by temperament and conviction, as well as by sheer youth, [he] embraced the contrary idea of the actor as a law into himself, anarchic, antinomian, born for the exception, not the rule". Clearly, he saw himself as a kind of god, who was not subject to the normal rules of society and for whose uniqueness an allowance must always be made. At the same time he had insight into his behaviour, but he rarely acted on this insight, or had the capacity to act upon it, because of his Asperger syndrome. He wrote in a letter: "About twice a year I wake up and find myself a sinner … I see my boots are roughshod and that I've been galloping in them over people's sensibilities – I see that I have been assertive and brutal and irreverent."

Callow notes that Welles always had to present himself as the "passive and innocent recipient of love or hate", while it was equally important for him to believe that his career had simply happened to him as "a series of happy accidents". However, in those crucial relationships, he was a very active partner and "their trajectories are often identical to those of intense love affairs". If Welles had been capable of good reciprocal social interaction with other theatrical people, he perhaps would have been much more successful in the long run – but then he would not have been Orson Welles.

WORK

Orson was a workaholic who was "frightened to death of being thought ordinary in any way". Opinions on his acting ability vary and many caveats expressed, but he is generally regarded as having been an exceptional actor to the extent that he was prepared to take advice. The only training he ever received was during his time at the Gate Theatre in Dublin, where he showed up as a 16-year-old in 1931. It seems clear that he was a born genius – a born actor. According to Callow, his first performance was "one of those occasions … when a newcomer creates an excitement verging on hysteria that the greatest artists at their height cannot create, and that they themselves can never duplicate". Orson at this time had a "crude lust for applause" and was "ruthlessly vainglorious". Emotionally, he was very immature.

Welles had a massive physical impact. Mac Liammóir recalled that "the voice, with its brazen transatlantic sonority, was already that of a preacher, a leader, a man of power; it bloomed and boomed its way through the dusty air". Unusual prosody is a feature of person's with Asperger syndrome and they often speak in a high-pitched tone of voice. No matter which voice Welles assumed, it was "always unmistakably him". He also had a good command of accents and, while he could vary the pitch of his voice, its timbre was said to give him away every time. A reviewer noted his "eccentric phrasing" and indeed eccentricity of all sorts is associated with persons with Asperger syndrome.

Welles's use of language was highly original. It was "sweeping, rhetorical, perfectly adapted to his own cadences, knowing, lofty, echoing with other men's phrases, infectiously exhilarating". His brilliance was clearly displayed on radio, a medium that suited him well because of its immediacy, the flexibility of its language, and the circumstances of its creation: "a whole world summoned up in a few days' rehearsal, the cycle of theatrical creation speeded up to engender maximum adrenalin". It was a medium that might have been invented for him. Houseman said that Welles could make an impromptu speech to fit any occasion and had a beautiful voice: "The power of the speaking voice is widely underestimated. Welles's was … a siren voice to which Houseman succumbed completely".

Even as a teenager, Welles was able to work frenetically on several things at a time. At the age of 19, he was heavily involved in organising the Woodstock Theatre Festival in the USA. Callow notes Welles's "uncontrollable overacting", that he was "fatally drawn to roles in which he could experience the rush of adrenalin that comes from eating up the stage", and that for a teenager to both act in and direct a play is not necessarily a good idea: "One thing at a time. This was a lesson Welles would never learn, or, more to the point, a proposition he would never accept." All of this again suggests risk-taking, hyperkinesis, and sensation-seeking.

In his assessment of Welles, Brooks Atkinson, theatre critic of *The New York Times*, stated that:

> He is an intuitive showman. His theatrical ideas are creative and inventive. And his theatrical imagination is so wide in its scope that he can give the theatre enormous fluency and power. Ingenious lighting, stylised grouping, strange sounds and bizarre show effects are the instruments he uses for playing his macabre theatrical tunes. Plays have to give way to his whims, and actors have to subordinate their art when he gets under way, for The Shadow is monarch of all he surveys. It is no secret that his wilfulness and impulsiveness may also wreck the Mercury Theatre, for he is a thorough egotist in the grand manner of the old-style tragedian. (Atkinson, 1938)

Even early in his working life, the public profile Welles presented was of a remarkable, actor extraordinaire. His "precocity, direct succession to the great ones of the past, possession of special insights gained from foreign wanderings. His curriculum vitae thus presented bears a striking resemblance to that of Jesus Christ." Of course, he regarded himself as an artist god and that he was born a fully formed great actor and a great man. It would seem that many of the colourful stories about Welles originated with Welles himself. Nonetheless, Welles's acting prowess was hugely instinctive and not nurtured or learned through experience. Houseman writes that "what amazed and awed me in Orson was his astounding and, apparently, innate dramatic instinct … I had the sense of hearing a man initiated, at birth, into the most secret rites of a mystery – the theatre – of which he felt himself, at all times, the rightful and undisputed master". This again suggests the importance of genetic factors.

Welles's megalomaniacal ambition often brought success – "who dares wins" – and while organising the Woodstock Theatre Festival, he decreed that the festival's publicity "should have a great deal about me in it".

The pinnacle of Welles's career was the 1941 film *Citizen Kane* and subsequent projects never surpassed the critical acclaim he received for it. Callow describes the 45 years of Welles's post-Kane life as:

> A sort of sustained falling apart in which, Lear-like, as his world crumbled further and further around him, and as his own behaviour became more and more extravagant, he was vouchsafed extraordinary insights … Still reluctant to go within, to examine himself, he produced, in more and more original forms, a body of wildly uneven work that could never have been predicted from his early efforts. His engagement with his own personality led to the complete abolition of the dividing wall between himself and his creations; but he came increasingly … to display himself as a phenomenon. He became a figure of pity and terror. He had no castle, no baronial mansion: the world was his Xanadu; he roamed its corridors, looking for money with which to make films, but also, beyond that, for the chances which he had lost.

Welles, then, was a hugely fascinating character, which is reflected in the number of books, articles and websites dedicated to him and out of all proportion to the volume (whatever about the quality) of his work. There appears to be no diminution in the flow of new biographies of him reaching the bookshop shelves – quite the opposite, in fact. His psyche was complex and mercurial: viewing it through the prism of his possible Asperger syndrome may offer some new angles and illuminate some hitherto dark recesses.

Orson Welles died in Los Angeles on 10 October 1985, at the age of 70.

Chapter 4

John Gielgud

John Gielgud (1904–2000) came from an enormously artistic family: it could be said that there was tremendous familial loading onto his artistic ability. He showed it very early in childhood and continued it throughout his life. Given his theatrical lineage, he was multiply talented in acting, playwriting, stage design, directing, etc. He was often described as the greatest actor of the twentieth century.

Background

John Gielgud was born in London on 14 April 1904. He was "a demanding baby, absorbing much of his mother's time" and a delicate, spoilt, overprotected child.[4] His father was a fine musician and interested in theatre, though distant from his son. His mother, Kate, was "shy, rather lacking in humour" and preferred to "lose herself in a book" rather than go to house parties and fancy dress balls. Possessed of a good memory, she was acutely observant of life around her and greatly interested in art, history and literature. She became the dominant figure in his life.

The young Gielgud, known as Jack, was described as being "self-conscious", "conceited" and somewhat shy. He was a highly imaginative child and quite musical. At the age of seven, when given a toy theatre for Christmas, his life as an actor, director, and designer began in earnest. He played endlessly with this toy, making up dramas, designing sets, and so forth. A great-aunt on his mother's side was the famous Victorian actress Ellen Terry and there were many other famous actors in the family. His brother Lewis became a playwright and a translator of Latin verse. Another sibling, Val, became a novelist and playwright. His grandmother Kate Terry, herself a famous actress, introduced him to the theatre in London. In his early childhood, his intense involvement with the theatre, "both imaginary and real", had a powerful effect on him. Caught up in "a fantasy life", he had little contact with other children outside the family circle.

At school he showed features of attention deficit hyperactivity disorder (ADHD) and was described as being "clever but slapdash and ill-regulated". Nevertheless, he could hyper-focus on what interested him. He was bullied at school and expressed no interest in games. The

[4] Except where otherwise indicated, quotes in this chapter are from Croall (2001).

library was his haven: he was a great reader, as is typical of children with Asperger traits. He was also sensation-seeking and enjoyed the bombing raids from Zeppelins during the First World War. As he got older his grades fell, which is not uncommon in children with ADHD. Indeed, he himself said: "I tried to avoid learning anything that did not come easy to me." This is also typical of persons with Asperger syndrome. When he attended Westminster School, he "sat through lessons in a half dream" – again, suggestive of ADHD – and was obsessed with drawing. He was a restless child and tended to wander, and indeed played truant. His obsession with the theatre continued and remained with him all his life.

In late adolescence, Gielgud walked with "slightly bent knees", was not at all athletic, "his movement was generally poor" and he had a tendency to "gabble". This awkward gait is very characteristic of persons with Asperger syndrome. At school, hating physical exercise, he tried to shirk the fencing and dancing lessons: "Likewise Henry Irving, a notoriously poor mover, used to draw a leg when walking on the stage." Indeed both actors showed signs of dyspraxia. He was quite emotional, easily moved to tears, androgynous and showed sexual identity diffusion: his effeminacy was a problem in the early years. Nevertheless, this feminine side of him was critical to acting success.

PERSONALITY

Gielgud had a "slender build, melodious voice, and highly strung sensibility". He was much loved and had a phenomenal memory. As far as his work was concerned, there was an element of the superego: "what he valued was accuracy, truth, and fairness". His restless nature "made concentration hard" and during the long rehearsals he shifted from foot to foot. He was told that he needed "physical culture and rougher and firmer movement, and a tightening up of all his limbs". Laxity of the musculoskeletal system is certainly common in Asperger syndrome. Gielgud tended to focus on what interested him and ignored the rest. He may have been more right-brained than left-brained: it is impossible to know if he had atypical cerebral asymmetry, but he may well have had.

When he saw himself on film he was horrified by his "vulturine grimaces", and the "violent and affected mannerisms" of his walk and gestures. These are not uncommon in Asperger syndrome. He often grew bored by doing the same scene over and over again in movies. This is unsurprising, as people with novelty-seeking and sensation-seeking want new experiences and certainly have no wish to repeat the past.

SOCIAL RELATIONSHIPS

At school, his greatest problems were his shyness and acute self-consciousness. Nevertheless, he must have improved greatly in terms of socialising to have ended up as head boy of the school. This would suggest some interpersonal talent; the alternative explanation was that he had leadership talent. He learned massively from other great actors of his time. Despite being somewhat tactless and arrogant, he was popular with his fellow actors and disliked confrontation.

WORK

In adolescence his style of acting was "mannered, effeminate, and conceited". A brief year spent at the Royal Academy of Dramatic Arts (RADA) in late adolescence was far from distinguished but his technique did improve. His progress in mastering his art took many years and was laboriously achieved despite his innate talent. His grandmother Kate Terry advised him: "Be kind and affable to all your co-mates, but if possible be intimate with none of them." He prepared intensively for each new role and was a great observer. Harold Hobson, the critic, referred to "the electric, febrile energy of the lithe, active, slim young man … I felt myself instantly in the presence of a great actor."

He was a man of massive energy and stamina and "thrived on the work, and the speed with which the productions were staged". Always a hyperkinetic worker, he had multiple projects going on at the same time. The producer Harcourt Williams stated that "his keenness, his modesty, his infinite capacity for work, spread their influence through the company". Work was Gielgud's antidepressant. When he worked he lived, outside of working he existed. His work rate was truly phenomenal, indeed he was a workaholic. In the theatre, over a period of 67 years, he played more than 130 roles in over 200 productions; his screen work consisted of 60 television plays and 70 films.

Every great actor has a deep flaw, and to understand the actor's greatness and creativity one must understand this flaw. Gielgud probably had multiple genes of small effect for ADHD, Asperger syndrome and creativity. He died in England on 21 May 2000, at the age of 96.

Chapter 5

Rudolph Valentino

To generalise on women is dangerous. To specialise in them is infinitely worse.

Rudolph Valentino (Botham, 2002)

In his day Rudolph Valentino (1895–1926) was as big a star as, if not bigger than, George Clooney is today. Filmmaker D. W. Griffith had predicted that "the girls would never like him", but nothing could have been further from the truth. He displayed all the positive features and deficits of a great actor. His best-known films include *The Four Horsemen of the Apocalypse*, *The Sheik* and *Blood and Sand*. As will be seen, Valentino had a peculiar mixture of traits of attention deficit hyperactivity disorder and Asperger syndrome. These can be complementary and often occur together but can also be contradictory. Nevertheless, they are critical for great creativity.

Background

Rudolph Valentino was born Rodolfo D'Antonguolla on 6 May 1895 in Italy. His mother, Marie, was artistic, with considerable linguistic talent, and a born storyteller. His father, Giovanni, was a vet who engaged in scientific experiments in the infectious disease area, became infected and subsequently died. Valentino's paternal grandfather was an engineer. As a child Rodolfo was hyperkinetic and impatient, restless and reckless. He had phenomenal energy and imagination and was an impulsive and fearless novelty-seeker, a sensation-seeker and daydreamer. His legs "moved with panther-like nimbleness, he got into scraps and injured himself regularly".[5] In his formative years he had problems with attention and concentration, showed poor school progress, and played truant. His hyperkinesia extended to climbing excessively and having difficulty remaining seated. Not surprisingly, he was accident prone. He also showed evidence of oppositional defiant disorder and was a disruptive schoolboy. His nickname at this time was "Mercury". Indeed, as he grew up people felt he was going to be either a genius or a criminal. Shortly after moving from Italy to America he earned money as a dancer: in fact, women paid to dance with him in certain

[5] Except where otherwise indicated, quotes in this chapter are from Leider (2004).

clubs, and he was thus described as a gigolo. Then he became a movie extra, which was his entrée into the film industry.

PERSONALITY

Valentino had a tremendous capacity to hyper-focus on what interested him and was fascinated by plays and the stage. Being a fantasist and highly imaginative, he tended to move between fact and fiction. The notion of the afterlife was very important to him. He turned to spiritualism and other occult ideas, but was naive in his use of a palm reader. His engagement in odd behaviour, such as automatic writing and attendance at séances, was similar to W. B. Yeats, who also had Asperger syndrome (Fitzgerald, 2004).

Valentino was childlike, immature and poor at negotiating with studios. For example, he was rather naive in the way he asked film producers for jobs initially. In appearance, he was dandyish and called a "green fig eater", a term denoting a person with impractical ideas. Because of his identity diffusion he identified with characters that he played on the screen, and indeed took on some of their characteristics. He also liked to be seen with famous people. There was a range of other occupations that fuelled his imagination or his career: he loved animals and riding horses, and wanted to be a cavalry officer; he was a gambler; he was a pianist, a reasonable singer and a spectacular dancer, which fed his natural exhibitionism; he trained as a pilot; he liked sport and fast cars in particular and drove them recklessly. There is widespread evidence of his immaturity: his carelessness and incompetence with money, his self-destructive behaviour, narcissism and emotional lability. Moreover, he was like a small boy who wanted all the candy in the store.

SOCIAL RELATIONSHIPS

Valentino was "in love with love" and idealised women. He had a very old-fashioned view of what a wife should be and what she should do; he wanted a perfect wife, basically a domestic goddess, who would be completely devoted to him, always put herself second, have children, and look after him completely. In fact, he loved being mothered by older women. He developed a good relationship with June Mathis, a screenwriter, who looked after him for a period, mothered him, and greatly advanced his career. She in fact trained him to be an actor. He began to be seen as a modern Don Juan and women began to adore him. His nickname was "the Great Lover", but this was far from the truth in real life. His personal life was always something of a shambles. Initially, his thoughts of marriage related to furthering his career. He married actress Jean Acker somewhat impulsively, as did she; they did not consummate the marriage and separated on their wedding night. She felt that he was dictatorial, though their marriage was a pretence on her part, as she was a lesbian. Valentino found it hard to believe that his wife was not heterosexual. Certainly, he appeared to have poor theory of mind skills in relation to women and indeed men as well. He remarried before his divorce was settled – further evidence of his impulsiveness and naivety – and was charged with bigamy. He was jailed but a court dismissed the charge against him. His second wife was set designer Natacha Rambova, who soon noticed a loneliness in him and that he was emotionally immature. Personality contradictions are the nodal points of creativity and indeed great art requires this kind of naive personality. In the course of his marriage break-up to Natacha, amid rumours of infidelity and her controlling nature, he tried to shoot himself but was stopped. He suffered great grief and depression over this. Harold Grieve, who worked with him, said that "marrying one lesbian was a foolish accident. Marrying a second was really dumb" (Botham, 2002). This is what males with sexual identity diffusion often do: Valentino was not particularly interested in the sexual side of relationships, notwithstanding his screen image. Indeed, privately he was uncertain about his masculinity and following the break-up of his second marriage had a relationship with a bisexual actress named Pola Negri.

WORK

Valentino was initially cast as a villain in movies, and showed considerable narcissism in the time spent getting ready for a scene. It was easy for studios to exploit him. He had a row with the Famous Players-Lasky Corporation, which kept him out of movies for a period, yet he was naive in how he handled the situation. Always anti-authority, he felt that he was not being appreciated enough. Leider notes that Valentino had a massive capacity "to move, arouse and commune with his audience, men as well as women, both straight and gay". Again, this was due to his identity diffusion. He had a sphinx-like mysteriousness: his eyes were striking and the secret of his success. It is very hard for anyone to cope with the sort of massive success and adoration that Valentino achieved. Filmgoers saw him as possessing a "sexual menace and air of Oriental mystery" – he was the *homme fatale* of the age. He became a movie superstar and sex symbol with all that entailed. Nevertheless, he was seen as a somewhat effeminate man, particularly by men – the *Chicago Tribune* described him as a "pink powder puff". In essence, he was a highly complex figure whose androgyny challenged the notion of the alpha male. This was also where his creativity lay.

When he developed abdominal pain due to a perforated ulcer he refused to let the surgeons operate until it was too late. His suspicion of hospitals and the medical profession remind one of Andy Warhol, who met quite a similar death. There were also similarities with Harry Houdini's death. The reaction to his untimely death from peritonitis in New York on 23 August 1926, aged just 31, was extraordinary; comparisons can be made with the tragic death of Princess Diana in 1997. There was a massive outpouring of grief and mass hysteria across the USA with some fans committing suicide. All his possessions were sold off, at lower prices than they were worth, and many women claimed to be his true soulmate. In one sense, he was a tragic figure at the end, which is often the price of greatness. Rudolph Valentino remains a fascinating figure even today.

Chapter 6

MICHAEL REDGRAVE

Michael Redgrave (1908–1985) was a major actor of the twentieth century, and an extremely complex personality. His great movies were *The Lady Vanishes*, *The Dam Busters*, and *The Go-Between*. He had traits associated with ADHD and Asperger syndrome.

BACKGROUND

Michael Redgrave was born in Bristol on 20 March 1908. His background, like himself, is quite complex and multifaceted. There was a strong history of theatrical activities in his family, which in time would continue in his children. There would appear to be many genes of small effect, not yet identified, that played a part in this creativity. His great-grandfather Cornelius was a novelty-seeker, a sensation-seeker, a risk-taker and "less than prudent with money".[6] Cornelius's son George, a great-uncle of Michael Redgrave, was "a typical Redgrave – volatile, agile, sensitive, impetuous and supremely kindly". George, for his part, was noted for having a poetic and artistic temperament. Michael's father, Roy, achieved recognition as a stage and silent film actor. In addition, Roy was agile and had excellent motor skills, but was "recklessly heedless of injury". In his life he showed signs of hypochondria, as Michael would later. There were many unfavourable facets to his character: he was financially irresponsible; somewhat promiscuous; abused alcohol; and had a callous, unemotional, slightly sadistic streak. There was also evidence of emotional immaturity as well fecklessness and being a hyperkinetic wanderer.

Roy had the ability to merge almost totally with his stage characters. He soon abandoned his wife and son, then aged six months, in order to pursue an acting career in Australia, and once there remarried, most likely guilty of bigamy. He died in Australia in 1922. After Roy's disappearance, his wife, whose name was Daisy Scudamore, subsequently married Captain James ("Andy") Anderson, who became Michael's stepfather. Daisy was also an actress as well as a talented singer. An intelligent woman, she was also "highly strung", somewhat eccentric and interested in séances. In his early years Redgrave was reared by various relatives and had a fairly nomadic childhood.

[6] Except where otherwise indicated, quotes in this chapter are from Strachan (2005).

PERSONALITY

Redgrave had a number of features of Asperger syndrome. He had the "piercing eyes" as well as the unusual tone of voice. He was a reserved man who read widely and had a tremendous memory and massive observational skills. He showed poor school progress, however. He did not excel at sports and was easily bored with things that did not interest him: he had poor concentration, restlessness and hyperkinesia, common Asperger traits. He essentially had an immature personality. There were features of novelty-seeking and sensation-seeking, but also a tremendous capacity to hyperfocus on what interested him. He was also a risk-taker, and this was particularly evident with regard to his promiscuous homosexual behaviour. He took the stimulant Benzedrine, later used as a treatment for ADHD, of which he also showed signs.

After a Cambridge education and brief period as a schoolmaster, Redgrave began acting and described himself as an "acteur". Throughout his life he suffered a good deal of anxiety and torment because of his acting-out lifestyle. He received psychiatric treatment and also suffered from stomach ulcers. As an intellectual, he took an interest in the work of Sigmund Freud, and once edited the *Cambridge Review*, yet he had a very negative thinking or attributional style.

SOCIAL RELATIONSHIPS

Bisexuality was central to Redgrave's life. He was "effeminate" in secondary school and engaged in homosexual acts from his teenage years. Before marrying the actress Rachel Kempson, he confided in her about the difficulties in his nature and she agreed to go ahead with their marriage. This sexual identity diffusion is very common in creative actors. It was similar to Oscar Wilde, who engaged in homosexuality, was married, and considered himself an aesthete. Throughout his life Redgrave had affairs with men and women simultaneously. He was in a way polymorphously perverse, which is another characteristic associated with creativity. Paradoxically, he had a strict conscience: he was courageous, a man of honour, and joined the armed forces during the Second World War. According to Strachan, Redgrave's wife "never pretended that the dissonance at the centre of Michael's personality did not on occasion cause her acute unhappiness and suffering". Strachan also mentions that Jung claimed that a human being is born with a limited store of energy but creativeness usually absorbs the energy in the artist at the expense of some sort of deficit in life's other areas. Jung was certainly correct in that assertion.

WORK

Redgrave's biographer Alan Strachan quotes William Hazlitt to the effect that actors "can show us all that we are, all that we wish to be and all that we dread to be", and that "actors are the only honest hypocrites. Their life is a voluntary dream." He also quotes the actor Ralph Richardson as saying that "the actor must dream … constantly". Throughout his life Redgrave did indeed keep a "dream diary". He suffered from anxiety, however, often experienced on first nights where his performances were not as polished as later. Nevertheless, his delivery was outstanding. In the pantheon of great English actors, he was widely ranked with *Gielgud*, Olivier and Richardson when he died in England on 21 March 1985, aged 77.

Chapter 7

Charles Laughton

Charles Laughton (1899–1962) was a major film actor of the twentieth century. Many of his performances were unforgettable, for example in *The Hunchback of Notre Dame* (1939). Simon Callow describes him as a difficult actor.[7] He was enigmatic and had identity diffusion, which was one of the reasons why he was so hard to "pin down" or get to know. This chapter makes the case that he showed traits of Asperger syndrome.

Background

Laughton was born on 1 July 1899 in Yorkshire. The family business was in hotel-keeping and he worked in that trade for quite a while. His mother, Elizabeth, of Irish ancestry, was rather critical and distant. Callow states that "the absence of intimate relationship with parents is notorious for the encouragement of two species, actors and homosexuals". This is debatable, as genetic factors are also influential. Millions of people have experienced what Callow describes without becoming either actors or homosexuals.

Laughton displayed poor eye contact, typical of persons with Asperger syndrome. As a child he was extremely interested in nature, flowers and botany, and read voraciously. He was also a keen observer from an early age. His wife, Elsa Lanchester, in later years, stated that he was the kind of boy "one longed to take a good kick at". He had a somewhat naive, immature personality all his life; this childlike element was critical to his creative success. He was generally mediocre, as well as oppositional and defiant, at school. He also showed evidence of poor hygiene, common in persons with Asperger syndrome, which I believe Laughton displayed. Laughton also had a peculiar gait and displayed various motor aspects of Asperger syndrome. It was noted how he was one of the "oddities" of human nature: "that pale puffy face, curious manner of walking, his shoulders hunched up, one a little higher than the other, that jerky step". During the First World War, he served in the trenches and was gassed. As a result, he suffered post-traumatic stress disorder, like many other soldiers, including the actor James Stewart; this took some time to manifest itself when he returned from the war. He was somewhat haunted by his wartime experiences, typically for someone with post-traumatic stress disorder. These memories were again brought to the fore by the Second World War.

---

[7] Except where otherwise indicated, quotes in this chapter are from Callow (1988).

Personality

The creative process for Laughton was painful; nevertheless, he achieved it through contact with his perverse personality, through his Asperger syndrome, and through a massive internal effort. He was an autodidact to an extraordinary degree – again, a common Asperger trait. To teach himself was a way of healing his psyche. He had the capacity to drill down into the deepest part of his personality and to use that for creative purposes. In preparing for future roles he would meticulously study everything he could get his hands on. He eventually burned himself out in his acting career with the enormous efforts that this demanded. Needless to say, he was rather hyperkinetic and had boundless energy in addition to being a novelty-seeker and sensation-seeker, which was largely expressed through his acting. Being highly visual and possessing a remarkable memory, he appreciated the visual arts and was a significant collector.

Laughton had identity diffusion common to great actors. This allowed him to take on many parts convincingly. According to Callow, "there are no straight lines with him: everything is composed of a myriad of tiny arrows, each pointing in a different direction. Hence the illusion of life itself." He was a man in search of a sense of self indeed in search of the creation of a whole identity for himself rather than the splintered identity that he had. His life was an attempt to heal his psyche, which he never achieved. Nevertheless, he remained intensely interested in emotional conflict and in the psyche.

Laughton was also quite a controlling figure. He was an obsessional man, narcissistic and egocentric. His lifestyle was pared-down in one sense, given how self-preoccupied and inward-looking he was, living in a one person world. There was also a malevolent side to his personality. He was very masochistic and allowed directors to bully him, which in turn fed his masochism.

Social Relationships

For most people he was mysterious, enigmatic and very hard to understand. Like many with Asperger syndrome, he found cocktail parties and small talk very difficult and avoided them if possible. Instead of relating to people socially he liked to give grand speeches. Socially, he was rather clumsy and suffered much depression and unhappiness. A few sessions of psychoanalysis with Ernest Jones came to nothing because he simply stopped going. He was a sadomasochistic figure, who was caught and brought before a court because of his homosexuality. Despite his homosexuality, he married the actress Elsa Lanchester, as Hollywood couples sometimes did, but their relationship with sadomasochistic. For Laughton his sexual orientation was wracked with deep inner guilt for most of his life.

Work

Laughton began acting at school, where he excelled in the school play. He had a wonderful face for acting and for expressing feelings. At drama school, according to Kenneth Barnes, other students would take time to drink coffee and chatter, but Laughton used the time alone creating: "He was a student of infinite curiosity, always searching for a new and meaningful approach to whatever character he was studying." Early in his career in London he was lucky to work with Theodore Komisarjevsky, a brilliant director, from whom he learned how to infuse characters with depth and an intensity of feeling. Because Laughton was so oppositional, however, directors found him difficult to work with. He was a rather odd, eccentric actor, and perfectionistic.

Callow points out that Laughton had the capacity of acknowledging his "inner self, summoning repressed and shapeless desires and instincts out of the shadows and onto the stage". He was an intellectual actor, who found it very difficult to be a "relating" performer, unlike, for example, the actor Clark Gable, who was very much a relating performer. He did not relate well to his fellow actors, as Callow notes:

> Laughton's performances were in the nature of solo efforts, devised during long and tortured hours of self-communion without the participation of his fellow players, and delivered more to the audience than to them. It is possible that is what the lonely, obsessed man did. The kind of relaxation that makes team-playing possible would have been hard for him to come by.

Again, this can be seen as reflecting his Asperger syndrome. It is interesting to note that Lawrence Olivier advised actors "not to lose yourself in the other actors". Laughton's self-contained performances made it hard for the other actors, as he was essentially acting within his autistic world with little or no connection to them. He was brilliant at playing monsters and nasty or perverse characters, never questioning their rationale, according to a *Theatre World* critic:

> He was, then and later, uninterested in psychology ... he was not interested (either for himself or for his characters) in the why of human action; only the what concerned him. He wanted to show what human beings were, to offer the raw material: not to explain it.

This can be a feature of Asperger syndrome, though of course the actor's job is to show not to give a lecture in psychology.

Laughton also worked with director George Cukor, keen for him to work on his movies. Cukor felt that Laughton was using method acting, going to great lengths to immerse himself in a role, even if comic. Callow points out that Laughton was "not at all comic". He dazzled his audience rather than making a connection with them, which is an autistic style of acting. Later in his acting career, recognising this fact, Laughton began to make more of an effort to connect meaningfully with his audience.

Laughton loved playing the emperor Nero in *The Sign of the Cross* (1932). He also played the H. G. Wells's character Dr Moreau, a gentleman and monster, in *Island of Lost Souls* (1932). Naturally, he was able to portray this perverted character brilliantly. There is no doubt that he was an actor of genius and wanted his characters to be real. He delivered a magnificent performance as Captain Bligh in *Mutiny on the Bounty* (1935), but was less successful in Shakespearian roles. He found verse very difficult to handle. Nevertheless, he was willing to try and courageous in that sense. According to Callow, he simply was "not at home in verse" and records from his later years suggest that he never really came to terms with it. This was probably because of his Asperger syndrome.

Laughton relished the roles of downtrodden figures. In *Les Misérables* (1935), he played Inspector Javert, whose character was so close to Laughton it was almost a self-portrait – "obsessed, repressed, fanatical, conscience-ridden". According to Callow, "Laughton was highly sensitive to pain, and disliked physical discomfort. Perhaps pain was the quickest route to feeling; and feeling was the basis of his art. Quite clearly, he was haunted by guilt." In effect, he was the "tortured spirit" of Javert.

Laughton's working relationships with several directors were often fraught and troubled. Callow points out that Laughton was temperamentally incapable of standing up to the harsh dictatorial style of Josef von Sternberg, so he adopted a defensive posture: "He retreated into babyhood." Alfred Hitchcock, who had a similar personality, also encountered difficulties with Laughton, claiming: "Charles never became a craft professional. He was always an artist and a genius, and he worked that way, so it became a disordered lack of control." Similarly, the director William Dieterle observed that Laughton was not able to play his part until "it was ripe within himself". This certainly gives a sense of how an actor develops a part, how he creates it within himself, and how he brings his unconscious to nourish the part.

The Hunchback of Notre Dame (1939) was reputedly Laughton's last great part: after that he became more superficial, according to Callow, and made less effort because of the monumental demands of drilling down to the depths of his personality. This suggests that he could not continue to return to the well, or that the well became empty, or that he burned out. Subsequently, he focused more on teaching, public reading, directing, and having love affairs. His identity diffusion continued to play a part in his creativity, however. In a stage production of *Life of Galileo* (1945), he collaborated with Bertolt Brecht for a period, causing the director to observe: "The actor appears on stage in a double role, as Laughton and as Galileo." Indeed Laughton said of himself: "I just can't get myself down on paper." Effectively, he created many identities for himself in his acting, which became separate compartments of the mind, so to speak. Despite his Asperger syndrome he did need other people at times to help him in his creativity, for example Brecht. The same could be said of Ludwig Wittgenstein in his work.

Charles Laughton died in Hollywood on 15 December 1962, aged 63. He will not be forgotten: his face is imprinted on the mind of every filmgoer that ever saw him.

Chapter 8

FRANK SINATRA

Frank Sinatra (1915–1988) was one of the major singers of the twentieth century and, through his recordings, into the twenty-first century. He was also a minor film actor and a highly complex individual with an unusual background.

BACKGROUND

Francis Sinatra was born in New Jersey to an Italian immigrant family on 12 December 1915. He was like his mother, Natalie, a woman who recognised no limits and lived her life "in search of power and excitement".[8] She sold alcohol during prohibition and had trouble with the law because of the abortions she performed, though she was never incarcerated. Sinatra found his parents somewhat distant. At school he showed poor progress and dropped out, which prompted his father, Antonio, to call him a "quitter". He was a disruptive student rather like the musician John Lennon. In addition, he was hyperkinetic, restless, impulsive and oppositionally defiant. Not surprisingly, his mother administered frequent corporal punishment to him. He later was attracted to people on the wrong side of the law, finding them exciting and believing it was good for business to be involved with people who owned big casinos. Maureen Paton (2004) quotes Sinatra's daughters as saying that he was connected to the mafia because "they employed him for 20 years of his life", and that the mafia owed the clubs and also Las Vegas.

PERSONALITY

Throughout his life Sinatra was not someone to be crossed. He was egocentric, narcissistic, energetic, intense, novelty-seeking and sensation-seeking. He certainly did what he wanted to do, totally in the grip of his passions and desires, and lived a life of excess. He lived only for today, in the here and now, with a low tolerance of boredom. In a way he was a street kid and liked the excitement of the street – life on the edge – and was well able to use his fists and survive on the street. He became an unpredictable, loud-mouthed tough guy.

[8] Except where otherwise indicated, quotes in this chapter are from Taraborrelli (1998).

As his biographer Taraborrelli points out, “Frank Sinatra is like that diamond – brilliant on the surface, flawed beneath. Of course, it is those flaws, those hidden complexities, that make him human and reflect his story.” Like many creative geniuses, he had identity diffusion and showed multiple selves. He was often quite different from one day to the next. For example, he had genuine concerns about young people and delinquency and often spoke at high school auditoriums and youth centres. He was sensitive to people in poverty. Tina Sinatra (Sinatra & Coplon, 2006) describes her father as generous, and mentions the time that he bought an expensive doll for a girl whose mother could not afford it. He was a spendthrift and “a grandiose tipper: 100 dollars for a round of drinks”. Sinatra also had courage and tried to get into the army but was rejected because of ear problems. There was a split in him between the great authentic artist and the perverse social personality: he was a Jekyll and Hyde figure.

His success allowed him to express the deeper, perverse layer of his personality. As well as having an incredible memory and being an avid reader, he hyper-focused on what interested him and was very determined and persistent. Indeed, there was an obsessive-compulsive element to him, which was shown for example in his extreme cleanliness and addiction to alcohol. Summers and Swan (2005) wrote that Sinatra made a number of suicide attempts during his life: taking an overdose, cutting himself, etc., which is not rare in sensitive, creative persons.

Social Relationships

Sinatra lacked the capacity to be alone and hence adored and needed the adulation of the audience. Tom Galvin (2005) describes him as “a lonely soul” and a man in search of “mothering”. He was extremely charismatic, particularly to women, and could also move men. Indeed his effect on women was not unlike that of Errol Flynn. In social relationships he could be quite unpleasant, similar to Richard Burton. Initially, Sinatra used sex to boost his ego, at other times he could be charming and helpful to women. More often than not he was a user and heartless with women, not unlike Picasso in that sense; he was a transgressor and could be quite perverse. He became a sex addict and not surprisingly suffered from venereal disease. He had amorous encounters with at least one of the same women as John F. Kennedy had.

He used his first wife, Nancy Barbato, to support his career in its early stages, and she proved critical in that role. This is not unlike W. B. Yeats in his later life (Fitzgerald, 2004). Sinatra left his first marriage to be with actress Lana Turner and followed that up with marriage to Ava Gardner and then a brief one to Mia Farrow. In total he had four marriages. Even in adulthood Sinatra was quite dependent on his mother and suffered major grief when she died at the age of 82. She was a dominating figure all his life.

Sinatra would metaphorically walk on people to get ahead, and in so doing was very impulsive and aggressive. Brian Morton (2005) states that he was also capable of “brutish violence, direct, or by other hands”. He was also hypersensitive to criticism and used to beat up “skinny defenceless reporters” in Hollywood because of what they wrote about him. Brown (2005) points out that Sinatra once had a man beaten up resulting in skull fractures so bad that he lapsed into a coma. In his extremely controlling and dominating way, it wasn't the only person that Sinatra had beaten up.

WORK

Sinatra had massive singing talent, which showed itself very early in his life. He had a gut instinct for music and knew everything about recording. He also had huge "intelligence as a singer", with tremendous breath control and sense of phrasing. He improved his breath control with heavy swimming sessions. Though physically a rather small man, he had a tremendous presence at the microphone. He worked with the Tommy Dorsey Band initially and then went solo and enjoyed a phenomenal international career that lasted six decades. Even on his last tours in London at the Royal Festival Hall, with his voice sadly deteriorated, audiences still came to pay homage to his previous greatness. He felt he would die if he stopped working. Despite being on antidepressants and suffering from dementia, he worked to the very end, and eventually collapsed on stage while singing. He died in hospital in Los Angeles on 14 May 1998, aged 82.

Chapter 9

RICHARD BURTON

Richard Burton (1925–1984) was one of the major actors of the twentieth century. He was a highly complex individual: a man with identity diffusion, a man of multiple selves who had attention deficit hyperactivity disorder yet had the capacity to hyper-focus on what interested him. He was perverse and sadomasochistic, a novelty-seeker and a sensation-seeker. Such was his fame that he earned vast amounts of money during his career. Among his most famous movies are *The Night of the Iguana*, *The Spy Who Came in from the Cold* and *Who's Afraid of Virginia Woolf?*

BACKGROUND

Burton was born Richard Walter Jenkins on 10 November 1925 in Wales, the twelfth of 13 children in a working-class family. His mother, Edith, died when he was two years old, and his eldest sister Liz – a strong solid woman – took over the mothering role. His father, Richard Jenkins, a coalminer, was an alcoholic and gambler but still a powerful father figure. In fact, he was a rather feckless type, a King Lear of the Welsh coalfields. Father and son had a row when Burton was about 15 years of age, causing him to leave home.

As a child Burton showed oppositional defiant disorder and his school progress was poor. He was a behaviourally disordered, hyperkinetic and restless adolescent who was disruptive, had a bad temper and dropped out of school. He displayed many features of ADHD. Such was his challenging behaviour that one teacher at his school said "he had the devil in him".[9] Biographer Melvyn Bragg describes him as "a misfit, troublesome, confused" and a "young tearaway" who liked street culture when growing up. He was highly independent, often used repetitive language and showed a depressive personality.

When out of control in his teens, Philip Burton, a former teacher of his, began to mentor him. Philip took him over, gave him his surname, and brought about a transformation in Richard; he began to act and his innate talent was seen immediately. Philip was described as "a father figure who selflessly dedicated his life to forwarding his young protégé's career". Burton returned to school and later went to Oxford aided by Philip Burton. He showed courage and great leadership potential there. Burton joined the Royal Air Force (RAF) and

---

[9] Except where otherwise indicated, quotes in this chapter are from Bragg (1988).

served as a navigator, but too late to see any wartime action. Upon leaving the RAF his desire was to do as he wished and make the world bend to his wishes.

PERSONALITY

Bragg notes how Burton was "a man of multitudes, of vast qualities, immense flaws, wonderful ambitions, crippling melancholy and illnesses, something of a scholar, a fighter, and a reckless warrior who lived the life of a legend". In addition, he was an intelligent man and a sportsman and indeed a "man's man". Like many people with ADHD, he was a poor sleeper, which was later aggravated by alcoholism.

Bragg describes Burton as "a crossword fiend, an acrostic fanatic, an inveterate amateur etymologist, and a Berlitz Blitzer on new tongues". This suggests Asperger-type traits or the kind of traits often seen in creative people. Given his intellectual and literary bent, Burton was fascinated by writers and scholars and obsessed with language. He was an avid reader and fanatical about the correct meaning of words. With his great memory, he could memorise and recite massive amounts of poetry and Shakespeare.

Burton also had multiple identities, one of which entailed returning to Wales and relating well to the local people. In this respect, Bragg describes Richard as "a maker of his own myths, Celtic, Faustian, an Icarus and a Don Juan, coming out from his beloved Wales like a mystical warrior to rove the world for conquests, forever unsettled, forever daring". He was also likened to a natural aristocrat who was born to command.

SOCIAL RELATIONSHIPS

Burton married the first of his four wives, Sybil Williams, at the age of 23. He was highly promiscuous and during his marriage had a sexual relationship with Rosemary Kingsland aged 14, which terminated when she was 15. According to her, during sex he wanted her to wear her school uniform and that he liked young and boyish-looking women (Thomas, 2003). Men with identity diffusion often seem attracted to women of this type. Furthermore, Kingsland claimed that the actor had an earlier sexual relationship with Philip Burton and who referred to his mentor as "a bloody arse-bandit" (Thomas, 2003). While Burton's later alcoholism and other behaviour had genetic components, the environmental abuse which he suffered greatly enhanced his negative genetic potentiality. Of course sexual abuse of females and males as they climb the actor's ladder is quite common – a price extracted by many film directors and producers. In some cases it's the price of fame.

Burton was always in search of a mother to replace the one that died in his childhood. Perhaps this was why he had five marriages to four women, the most celebrated one with actress Elizabeth Taylor. He never found the perfect mother in any woman. While obsessed with sex, he had sensory integration issues: he hated to be touched and had a physical aloofness. The sexual abuse he experienced may have been a factor in this. Sex for him was robotic and mechanical and indeed he was more excited by the chase than by the catch. Despite all the hellraising and alcohol abuse, there was also a "reserved" element to his character common in great actors. He could be quite withdrawn and showed evidence of detachment and melancholy.

WORK

Burton had massive presence, whether on stage or screen. He came across as a man of substance, a man to be reckoned with. He had a wonderful voice and timing. Fairly quickly in his acting career Burton became the "heir apparent to Gielgud and Olivier". Because of his identity diffusion he could sink into a part with total conviction. He was successful in Hollywood and at his best when capturing "dispirited men at the end of their tether", cynical world-weary men such as Alec Leamas in John le Carré's *The Spy Who Came in from the Cold* and George in Edward Albee's *Who's Afraid of Virginia Woolf?* (Estrin & McCarthy, 1997). Richard Burton died in Switzerland of a brain haemorrhage on 5 August 1984, at the age of 58.

Chapter 10

James Stewart

James "Jimmy" Stewart (1908–1997) was a celebrated film star and a courageous bomber pilot during the Second World War. He made films from 1935 to 1981, working with great directors, such as Frank Capra in *It's a Wonderful Life*, George Cukor in *The Philadelphia Story* and Alfred Hitchcock in *Rear Window* and *Vertigo*. It is quite possible that he had Asperger syndrome.

Background

James Stewart was born in Pennsylvania on 20 May 1908. He was a shy and introverted boy who did poorly at school and in group games. He preferred to be by himself and pursue his own interests, one of which was animals; in fact he was rather a lonely child. Mechanically minded, he loved to build model airplanes as a child and once made a plane that he could sit in, which he attempted to fly. Not surprisingly, it was unsuccessful but it certainly showed the novelty-seeking, risk-taking and sensation-seeking aspects of his personality.

His mother, Elizabeth, was artistic in temperament; however, Stewart bore some similarity to his father, Alexander, who was a scientific and single-minded workaholic in the family hardware store: "imperious, distant, and at times completely absent".[10] Like Michael Yeats, son of poet W. B. Yeats, Stewart saw his father as a "deity" and "god-like". Alexander Stewart most likely also had Asperger syndrome. Following in his mother's footsteps, an accomplished pianist, Stewart took up a musical instrument – the accordion. This was in some way a defence between himself and other people; he found it easier to relate if he could hide behind the accordion. Control was of critical importance to his parents and indeed Alexander only bestowed approval on his son's work late in life. Stewart studied architecture at Princeton but his university performance took second place to its music and drama clubs, which became the springboard to his acting career.

During the Second World War, Stewart initially failed tests to enlist in the Air Corps because of his poor physique but later got in having acquired the extra weight. He became a bomber pilot and won medals for his bravery in the war but hated being used as a celebrity in

[10] Except where otherwise indicated, quotes in this chapter are from Eliot (2007).

the forces. By war's end, following many bombing missions in Germany, he spent several weeks in hospital suffering from post-traumatic stress disorder.

PERSONALITY

Determined and persistent, Stewart was rather autodidactic and a tremendous observer of detail. He was considered "withdrawn" and "a wanderer", which are typical features of Asperger syndrome. Associated features were his high-pitched voice, his idiosyncratic behaviour and a "physical tic". In terms of his voice, he spoke rather autistic language and was a very slow, soft speaker; his voice had an unusual tone, that is, a slow, familiar drawl. The *New York Times* described it as "laconic with a hesitant nasal drawl". It was also one of the most easily recognisable voices on screen. He had the piercing eyes so common in persons with Asperger syndrome and certainly dramatic eyes are critical for success as an actor. He also had sensory integration issues and was highly sensitive to smell.

Awkwardness and clumsiness also characterised this somewhat tall, gangly man. Like the actor Henry Irving, he had dyspraxic "automatic mannerisms". Many people imitated these mannerisms, as they did with the philosopher Ludwig Wittgenstein (Fitzgerald, 2004). Stewart had an Asperger (autistic) superego and believed completely in the "moral righteousness of western Christian ideology". However, he failed to understand context or the big picture and showed weak central coherence. There was also evidence of success neurosis and moral doubt in this giant of the silver screen. Like the director John Schlesinger, he showed his controlling nature by putting on theatrical productions at home.

SOCIAL RELATIONSHIPS

Stewart showed major intimacy problems and had a fear of intimacy; however, in acting he could hide behind the role he was playing. At the end of adolescence he had no steady female relationship; indeed he was somewhat socially phobic. He also presented a "non-sexual on-screen persona" because of his Asperger syndrome and indeed there were concerns about his sexual orientation. According to biographer Marc Eliot, his notions of the emotional, non-physical complexities of love were "not very sophisticated" and he had problems with "lightening up". Indeed the feeling of love for Stewart was "the hardest of all to emote". This is hardly surprising given that he had Asperger syndrome. Stewart's identity diffusion and sexual ambivalence were critical to his type of creativity. Persons with Asperger syndrome tend to bring out the mothering instinct in women; hence his relationship with many women was of a mother–son type. The same went for female members of his film audiences. In a way he was searching for an "Asperger mother" relationship.

Stewart did have a number of sexual relationships before he married, however. Because of his autistic superego, he suffered huge guilt from these relationships and initially was fearful of being morally damaged by women. Ginger Rogers left him because he was too naive for her, whereas Marlene Dietrich got him to impregnate her. The latter regarded him as a "dundering, humourless fool, in real life exactly the young confused fellow he played to perfection on the screen". Barbara Stanwyck called him a "problem child" and "crazy". His relationships with women were very passive, which is an Asperger position in intimate relationships, where the other person has to take the lead. At the age of 41, however, he married Gloria Hatrick McLean, whom he described as being "like my mother" and their union lasted 45 years until her death in 1994.

The death of his son during the Vietnam War affected him greatly and he suffered a good deal of grief and major depression. Work was normally his antidepressant.

WORK

In the early phases of his career, Stewart was "gawky, shuffling, stuttering" and a far cry from the Hollywood legend he would become, being no more than an "overlooked contract player". *Collier's* magazine said that he had an "alert, kiddish, eagle-beaked appearance". He nonetheless became transfixed by acting and studied other actors in detail, for example, Gary Cooper, segmenting their performances. In one way, this was how he learned his craft: by merging with people and taking on their acting persona. People with Asperger syndrome and weak central coherence approach roles in this manner. Indeed, in early plays he was often seen as being robotic. At this time, he did a good deal of radio work – radio, of course, being the classic autistic medium. Enthralled by films, he was attracted to characters with personalities similar to his own. Aviator Charles Lindbergh, whom he played in *The Spirit of St Louis*, was another that had Asperger syndrome (Fitzgerald & O'Brien, 2007).

Stewart was described as "naturally gifted" – an instinctual actor whose talent came from "forces deep within him". Indeed many of these forces are genetic and part of his temperament. He also had the ability to express "the emotional ambivalence of the action hero", according to film historian Andrew Sarris. Stewart's identity diffusion also meant that he was more flexible and therefore able to take on a greater variety of parts than an actor with a more definitive personal persona. He was somewhat chameleon-like in that respect.

Clearly his stature as an actor was consummate and unrivalled. Film lobbyist Jack Valenti said that he was a "shy, modest man who belonged to cinema nobility". Yet his multi-layered character appealed to certain Hollywood directors like Capra, Mann, Ford and Hitchcock. According to Hitchcock historian Dan Auiler, "the Hitchcock male was complex: the hero, yet reluctant; lover, yet confused and restrained; the innocent, yet menaced as if guilty. They were men drawn reluctantly to women." This is essentially what characterises the Asperger male, and one of the reasons that Hitchcock (who also displayed Asperger traits) instinctively chose to cast Stewart in his films. Biographer Donald Spoto (1983) claimed that Stewart was closer to a representation of Hitchcock himself than any presence and his image reshaped by Hitchcock to conform to much of that was in his own psyche. In *Vertigo*, according to Eliot, Stewart's style of acting reflected his real-life personality as well as "his familiar cinematic persona – the ordinary man adrift, perhaps trapped in an abnormal world, longing to find his rightful physical, emotional and spiritual place in it". Frank Capra saw Stewart as "the perfect old-American innocent on whom he could attach the cross of decency and democracy". By all accounts Steward used Capra as a father figure and was highly dependent upon him.

James Stewart died on 2 July 1997 in California, aged 89. He was an actor of the highest rank and will not be forgotten.

Chapter 11

ALEC GUINNESS

Alec Guinness (1914–2000) was an enigmatic stage, film and television actor. Some of his best-known roles were in Ealing Comedies, for example, *Kind Hearts and Coronets* (in which he played eight parts), *The Bridge on the River Kwai* (for which he won an Academy Award in 1957), and Star Wars.

BACKGROUND

Alec Guinness was born in London on 2 April 1914 to a woman named Agnes Cuff. His mother failed to reveal the identity of his father but used the surname "Guinness" for him. She may have had a relationship with a member of the Anglo-Irish Guinness brewing family, although biographer Piers Paul Read maintains that a banker named Andrew Geddes from Scotland was a more likely candidate for fatherhood.[11] Geddes gave financial support to Agnes and generously helped with her son's education. Guinness's childhood was somewhat traumatic: Agnes was financially devious, stole things and got in trouble with the law. She had an unsuccessful marriage to a retired army officer, whom Guinness described as a violent eccentric that made his life miserable for three years. A lot of anger was directed against his mother, who abused alcohol, was a frequenter of taverns and once abandoned him in a church while on an alcoholic escapade.

At boarding school he learned proper social behaviour, but agonised over the terrible secrets of his upbringing: "his illegitimacy, his tipsy, scrounging mother, and the grandmother who smoked a clay pipe and lived in a hovel with a packed-earth floor". Psychoanalytic understandings of trauma are relevant in this context and these experiences clearly marked him for life. At school he had trouble with Latin and mathematics but liked history and drama. Described as "aloof", he was intellectually curious and read massively, as solitary boys often do. Despite being somewhat hyperkinetic as a child and tending to run rather than walk, he was not sporty. He showed an interest in acting from early in life, though his headmaster told him he would never make an actor. After leaving school, he worked as an advertising copywriter but devoted himself to acting and pursued it assiduously, often playing

[11] Except where otherwise indicated, quotes in this chapter are from Read (2005).

Shakespearian roles. His acting career was interrupted during the Second World War when he served in the Royal Navy.

PERSONALITY

It is not easy to get an understanding of Guinness's personality. He was similar to T. S. Eliot and Michael Redgrave in being shy and somewhat withdrawn, with narrow intellectual and bookish interests and the paranoid traits so common in persons of great creativity. He felt he had an unattractive personality that somehow repulsed people. His behaviour was rather paternalistic in his early career and he had a strong feminine identity, which appears not to have been expressed in reality but only in fantasy, and which troubled him greatly. He had sexual identity diffusion, important to the creative actor, and this feminine side of himself was key to his acting success. He had elements of the schizoid intellectual and was also rather a faceless figure. In fact, he had the capacity to be invisible, and was often not recognised in the street.

English director Tyrone Guthrie believed that actors' very talent comes from a psychological flaw. Guinness was a somewhat tortured individual, with significant obsessive compulsive traits and very strong defences against his sexual and aggressive impulses. He had a harsh superego or conscience, which meant he suffered a lot of guilt and was very self-critical; what caused him most guilt was his criticism of others. Indeed he had a "reserved and brittle personality and could quickly take offence".

Guinness's search for meaning and identity also found expression in religion. At the age of 16 he was confirmed in the Anglican faith, though he secretly claimed to be an atheist, but retained an interest in religion nevertheless. He once considered becoming an Anglican clergyman, however, playing the character of Father Brown in 1954 led to a growing interest in the Catholic Church. When his son Matthew developed poliomyelitis he sought refuge in religion and converted to Catholicism upon Matthew's complete recovery. This was part of his search for meaning and identity in life. In fact, he was often troubled by his sins and probably obsessional sexual thoughts. Like T. S. Eliot, he was fascinated by Catholic saints and also suffered much depression like the esteemed poet, who also showed signs of Asperger syndrome.

SOCIAL RELATIONSHIPS

Guinness cut a rather a lonely figure, who was "shy and bumbling", and got on better with older women. He seemed happiest "chatting on the telephone", which is a most attractive form of communication for persons with Asperger syndrome. Read also notes his sharp tongue, bitchiness and irascibility. There was a great deal of anger buried in him, particularly towards his mother and mother figures, and this was behind some of his misogynistic traits. He was probably a latent homosexual, or, to put it another way, he was bisexual but expressed only the heterosexual side of his nature in external action. He was sexually attracted to women to a mild degree and certainly was not convincing playing this role in films. Michael Billington points out that sexuality became a kind of metaphor or clue to his art: "Some actors' art is based on a naked, breast-baring self-revelation; but his art was an act of mimetic skill and behaviourist detail which meant the cancellation of himself."

Guinness married the artist and actor Merula Salaman in 1938, despite having panicked the day after they got engaged and wanted to call it off. She was a tomboy and possibly had some sexual identity diffusion like him. She said: "I never thought of myself as a girl, I was a sort of nothing. I certainly didn't want to be a girl, or a boy either, I was just me." During their marriage Guinness was very critical of his wife and threatened to leave her if she continued acting, which showed a rather sadistic, brutal side to him. He was excessively controlling and dominating of people in his close circle but reserved particular control, domination and high-handedness for Merula and a lack of empathy. As a parent, he was excessively harsh and called his son, Matthew, "the fat arse of Chiswick". Indeed he lacked the capacity for an easy, warm father–son relationship. The actor Corin Redgrave reported that Matthew had to ask permission to play with his train set, "chiefly because it was such an expensive train set and Alec liked to play with it by himself".

WORK

Guinness showed tremendous persistence in pursuing an acting career and prepared meticulously for his parts. As a young man, he managed to get drama training in London and before a scholarship audition asked John Gielgud for lessons. This was extraordinary, as Gielgud was a major star at the time. Gielgud nonetheless suggested a tutor who turned out to be very good; hence Guinness began to get small parts and turned in noteworthy performances. In Gielgud's 1936 production of *Hamlet*, the emerging actor played the part of Osric, and his career began in earnest. Despite being mentor to Guinness, Gielgud bullied him somewhat as well. Guinness also learned a great deal from watching other great actors of the time. Actor and director Michel Saint-Denis coached Guinness for a period and was another major influence. Merula Guinness noted that Saint-Denis stripped people down "mentally and, more or less, physically, so that he could build [them] up into actors and actresses to his own moulding". However, the method presented problems given that sometimes it was not always possible to put the person back together. This kind of training is theory based, utilised often more for the director's sadistic pleasure than the actor's benefit. The training did not sit comfortably with Guinness, who saw the method as "a rape of unformed talent". Nevertheless, Saint-Denis' emphasis on mime was important later for Guinness. Theatre director Theodore Komisarjevsky was the next major influence on Guinness, who revealed:

> I need no longer worry whether I was moving gracefully or looking handsome … instead I must try to create a character utterly different from myself, and then behave as I imagined the creature would behave whose odd appearance I suddenly saw in the looking glass.

Yet another major influence was Tyrone Guthrie, who directed Guinness in the lead role in *Hamlet* in 1939. Guthrie wrote:

> I have had plenty of time to wonder why people take up the theatre as a profession … some, it is perfectly true, want to show off, but it is my belief that these are a minority.

> Far more people go on the stage as a hiding place, as an escape from the real world, which they find unsatisfactory and feel powerless to change, into a world of make-believe where they can be someone else, an assumed character over whose nature and environment they have some control.

This certainly could sum up Guinness's motivation for acting. In Guinness, Guthrie found a "rare intelligence, humour, and pathos". It was noted that after playing Hamlet in the 1938 production that he had the quality of being able to "stand still and yet arrest attention". Guinness was described as "a man of a thousand faces". Read notes that he combined a mixture of kindliness, impudence, and pathos in a single smile so that his talent was to be convincing "not as men as we imagine them to be but as men as they are – shy, uncertain, ambiguous". Of course this ambiguity also shows the idea of an unclear identity.

Guinness was a hugely introspective, self-critical, cerebral actor. Michael Redgrave – an actor with a similar personality – very much appreciated his style of acting and noted Garrick's famous statement: "You can fool the town in tragedy, but comedy will find you out". Alec Guinness died in England on 5 August 2000, aged 86.

Chapter 12

JAMES MASON

James Mason (1909–1984) was a major character actor. His movies included *The Wicked Lady, A Star Is Born, 20,000 Leagues Under the Sea*, and *North by Northwest*. He was enigmatic, quirky and somewhat of an oddity – an intriguing and unpredictable actor. He wrote an autistic autobiography in which he was "remote even from himself"[12] – it contained little sense of himself and he seemed something of an alien in this world. He was one of the most intriguing and unpredictable of actors – a "craftsman actor". This chapter makes the case that James Mason had Asperger syndrome.

BACKGROUND

James Mason was born on 15 May 1909 in Huddersfield, Yorkshire to Mabel and John Mason. His father was a successful businessman, who educated his son at Marlborough College and later at Cambridge University. While studying architecture at Cambridge, Mason developed an interest in acting and pursued it after graduation.

PERSONALITY

Mason had highly focused narrow interests; outside the acting profession, his interests were in architecture and photography. This is unsurprising since he was tremendously visual and loved drawing and sketching, and often carried sketching paper with him. Another of his great interests in life was cats, of which there were many. Indeed persons with Asperger syndrome are particularly interested in cats and other animals as well as in drawing. Like many with Asperger syndrome, he too had an unusual tone of voice. It was described as "very nasal and self-limiting", or "monotonous and a trifle nasal", while the critic, David Fairweather, noted the "very curious intonations that sometimes mar his diction".

Mason was a loner who liked solitude and introversion, but was attracted to powerful, controlling women. His deeply reserved nature, setting him apart from others, often attracted comment. Diana de Rosso, opera singer and half-sister of his first wife – described him as

---

[12] Except where otherwise indicated, quotes in this chapter are from Morley (1990).

"one of the most withdrawn men I've ever met", while director Leslie Arliss remarked that he had an "intellectual, impersonal, academic reserve". Actor Stuart Whitman described him as a quiet man, very low-key, and always seemed to be reading: "He kept his distance from cast and crew … very reserved around people."

Contradictions and ambiguities were central to his nature and marked his identity diffusion. The actor Alan Todd stated that there was something electric and at the same time very dangerous about Mason. Furthermore, he showed "that sense of otherness, a sense that he'd really have been perfectly happy, as he once said to me, living as a guide in the Swiss mountains, or being an architect, or a painter, or even a gardener in Mexico". He was a man in search of self, remarking that at Cambridge he had time and space in which to read and think about his circumstances and "to figure out just who I was to be". This was the big question in his life that was never fully resolved. He was often moody, morbid and indecisive, and felt himself to be an empty shell.

His enigmatic nature hid a deeply divided man, this empty shell. Diana de Rosso said that "he was totally cardboard, because he never showed anger or passion of any kind. That dark and stormy-looking man wasn't really dark or stormy at all: he was nervous, diffident, constantly in doubt about his own work and his own life." Director Joseph Mankiewicz always said that Mason was one of the great genuine eccentrics because "he never knew quite how eccentric he was. He always wished to be some place else but could never quite decide where that some place was, or why he wanted to be there. He felt desperately unfulfilled by everything." This bears striking similarities with Ludwig Wittgenstein, who also had Asperger syndrome (Fitzgerald, 2004). Indeed you say Mason was something of an autistic wanderer. For his part, Mason confessed: "I seem to have become a sort of grease-paint gypsy, roaming the known world in search of work on film locations. It is not too bad a life, really; at least, I am sure there are worse."

His fellow actors made some revealing comments about Mason, the misfit who could fuse with the characters he played. The actress Vera Miles said that a camera can recognise "a kind of private coldness, a low degree of sexuality and a rather cynical, almost academic interest in women. He was never quite a rebel, but nor did he ever fit in easily anywhere." Shelley Winters remarked that he had a curious ability to become the men he played, so that "all through the shooting he remained in character". It would appear that Mason merged with his characters, wholly inhabiting them. This was easier to do because of his own lack of clear identity.

There was a paranoid undercurrent to his narcissistic personality as well. Recognition was important to him and he was obsessed with control, domination and independence. He received a lot of bad press for his conscientious objection to serving in the Second World War and was never sure whether this policy was right or wrong in the long term.

Social Relationships

Mason was described as a shy and retiring man. He was melancholic and restless and rubbed people up the wrong way, particularly the media. He was always "very wary of people" and a huge amount of repressed anger and hostility lay within him. In fact, he did admit that he was an angry man. A very poor mixer, he had little capacity for social interaction. He had the Asperger trait of wishing to relate more to people but found it very difficult to do so. Martin Landau, the actor, observed in him an odd mixture of loneliness and yet a desperate desire for friendship, "as though he wanted to be alone a lot and somehow couldn't quite bear it when he was".

Mason married twice, first to Pamela Ostrer, who bore him two children, and then Clarissa Kaye. His first wife Pamela revealed: "James is a strange man, you know, very moody. One night when we had some guests he just got up from the table, poured himself a glass of prune juice and went to bed, turning off all the lights, totally forgetting there was anyone else in the room. He just tuned us all out, so you can see it wasn't the easiest of marriages." He lived for long periods with a third person involved with himself and his wife. This may have reduced the tension between the couple and made marriage more tolerable. His second marriage, to Clarissa Kaye, was a happier one. He may have learned some marital know-how or may have chosen a woman who could manage his Asperger syndrome better. Nevertheless, those with Asperger syndrome are fairly fixed and rigid.

WORK

Mason dabbled in acting at Cambridge, while studying architecture, and gradually became more attracted to being an actor. At this time he was "a very nice, inexperienced, shy young man". He did reasonably well at the Gate Theatre in Dublin early in his career, and appeared in many second-rate films as well as some excellent ones. He played the villain quite convincingly in several films and was thrice nominated for an Academy Award. According to his biographer Sheridan Morley, "he had that curious quality of a man with an eternal secret; like Charles Laughton on screen, he could seem to be thinking about two quite different things at once; he was always on a double track, and that was what was so arresting and incredible about him." This is more of the identity diffusion displayed in his personality.

In the late 1940s Mason left England for America in search of greater fame. It was a catastrophic decision. He got into legal trouble in Hollywood by not fulfilling a letter of commitment he had given, attracting a lot of bad publicity in the process. This was largely due to his tactlessness and lack of empathy and social know-how. While in America he attacked British filmmaking in a classic case of the man biting the hand that fed him. His hamfistedness was considered "breathtaking", though not a major setback to his career. He certainly managed his career poorly because of his social skills deficits.

Many of his memorable roles included menacing villains, corrupt men and the morally preserve. His "man you love to hate" roles indicated, if not outright sexual or sensual perversions, then at least the possibility that sex and violence were intermingled with the strongest and most aristocratic love affairs. Appearing in Stanley Kubrick's *Lolita* brought a certain notoriety in 1962. Of his performance, Mason said: "After *Lolita*, I became a sinister foreigner who molested little girls. The truth is that I am just a character actor." For Mason there had always been ups and downs in his life, though on balance "the downs did seem to have been more frequent than the ups". James Mason died in Switzerland on 27 July 1984, at the age of 75.

Chapter 13

MICHEÁL MAC LIAMMÓIR

The English-born Micheál Mac Liammóir (1899–1978) was one of the greatest actors on the Irish stage. The key to understanding him is his identity diffusion or multiple selves.

BACKGROUND

Micheál Mac Liammóir was born Alfred Willmore in London on 25 October 1899 into an English theatrical family. He did not do well at school and was bullied, which traumatised him for life. He was clearly very talented from early childhood and had a successful career as a child actor; a teacher who ran a drama group however described him as "highly strung".[13] He played in *Oliver Twist* and in *Peter Pan* for a number of years, working with Noël Coward, and "had an unquenchable thirst for sightseeing". He subsequently studied art and drawing, at which he was also talented, at the Slade School of Art. He maintained his interest in painting throughout his life and initially worked as an illustrator. In 1917 he moved to Ireland designing theatre sets and took up an acting career. He was clearly very intelligent and proficient in languages; he learned the Irish language and spoke it well and wrote in Irish.

PERSONALITY

Mac Liammóir was a man of great charisma and charm, sometimes seen in persons with Asperger syndrome. There was also a child-like aspect to his character that he retained all his life. He was a dreamer and a fantasist and defended a fantasy identity to the end of his days. The most remarkable aspect of his personality was his identity diffusion and how he reinvented himself. Micheál Ó hAodha's (1990) biography of Mac Liammóir concerns itself with his identity diffusion, about multiple selves, about the difficulty of knowing him, his difficulty in knowing himself. Ó hAodha refers to Oscar Wilde's comment that "the first duty in life is to assume a pose", and clearly Mac Liammóir lived by this code. According to Ó hAodha (1990), Mac Liammóir once said that he "could be natural" but that it was "a very difficult pose to keep up". The dramatic moment was far more important to him than anything

[13] Except where otherwise indicated, quotes in this chapter are from Fitz-Simon (1994).

factual and combined with a tendency to exhibitionism. People with identity diffusion often move between fact and fiction very easily. This gives them their strength and indeed is a source of creativity. Mac Liammóir was a myth-maker and told myths about himself and his childhood in particular. Even though he was English, he identified wholly with Ireland and created a totally Irish identity for himself. In his twenties he changed his name from Alfred Willmore to "Micheál Mac Liammóir", an Irish transliteration, but used the English pronunciation of Michael. He also claimed to be a native of Cork city and born into a Catholic family, a far cry from the reality of his English Protestant upbringing. Mac Liammóir also used to claim that he was a *seanchaí*, a storyteller, according to Ó hAodha (1990). His greatest creation was his own mask – his persona or character that he showed to the world. Indeed this is how great actors often attempt to deal with their identity diffusion and it can be a tremendous emotive force for them. Conscience was certainly not something that troubled him much. But perhaps the strain of keeping a constant pose precipitated his one-time "nervous breakdown" (Ó hAodha, 1990). The search for an authentic sense of self in a way he never achieved. It can explain why he travelled a lot and was a bit of an autistic wanderer.

Mac Liammóir was quite narcissistic and required much adoration; he absolutely needed the sound of applause to feel well. Growing old gracefully was something he found particularly difficult: his narcissism was shown in his efforts to thwart the ageing process. To the end of his life he was preoccupied with retaining a youthful countenance and always wore a hairpiece in later life, which was another kind of mask. His eyesight deteriorated in later life almost to the point of blindness, yet he still insisted on appearing on stage.

Social Relationships

At school he was more interested in the female than the male sex. As he grew up and left child acting behind, however, he became aware of his homosexuality. His conduct at times "bordered on the promiscuous", according to Ó hAodha (1990), despite his long-term relationship with Hilton Edwards, co-founder of the Gate Theatre. Mac Liammóir largely cut himself off from his parents, which was rather cruel, perhaps because they belonged to his English identity on which he had turned his back. He showed little reaction to his father's death and failed to attend his mother's funeral when she died. On the other hand, he suffered huge grief when friends of his died and certainly had the ability to experience grief. When Edward Longford, benefactor of the Gate Theatre, died in 1961, Mac Liammóir said that "the death of an enemy seems more distressing than the death of a friend".

Work

Mac Liammóir's acting career in Ireland began through his association with Anew McMaster, the great actor-manager whose company toured the country with plays ranging from Shakespeare to Sophocles. Anew McMaster happened to be his brother-in-law, married to his sister Marjorie, so he joined his company, where he met fellow actor Hilton Edwards. The theatre became Mac Liammóir's all-encompassing focus, his narrow interest. With his deep love of Irish culture and literature, in 1928 he was involved in producing the inaugural play, *Diarmuid agus Gráinne*, for An Taidhbhearc, an Irish-language theatre in Galway. Of course, he is linked forever with the Gate Theatre in Dublin, which he founded with his partner, Hilton Edwards, also in 1928. In addition to writing plays, doing various adaptations and also appearing in some films, he also designed innovative costumes and sets for the Gate. According to biographer Christopher Fitz-Simon, the cultural background to which Mac Liammóir played was "an unusually censorious political regime" – de Valera's narrow, introverted Ireland and a "pharisaical church". John Charles McQuaid, later Archbishop of Dublin, said that "the Gate was brilliant – but dangerous" (Ó hAodha, 1990). Indeed the Gate and Abbey Theatres were often described as "Sodom and Begorrah" (Ó hAodha, 1990). Mac Liammóir is particularly remembered for his successful one-man show *The Importance of Being Oscar*, a celebration of Oscar Wilde. Actor and director Orson Welles also worked with Mac Liammóir at the Gate Theatre and invited him to do theatre in America; he subsequently played Iago in Welles's film version of Othello in 1952, furthering his international reputation.

Micheál Mac Liammóir died on 6 March 1978, aged 78.

Chapter 14

HARRY HOUDINI

The American escapologist Harry Houdini (1874–1926) was one of the earliest celebrities, a unique, eccentric artist of the stage and screen, and a massive novelty-seeker and sensation-seeker. Risk-taking utterly defined him. Highly intelligent, innovative and possessing a massive memory, he also showed signs of Asperger syndrome.

BACKGROUND

Harry Houdini was born Erik Weisz in Budapest on 24 March 1874 to Jewish parents. The family moved to the United States when he was four and settled in Wisconsin and later in New York. As a child, he showed great resourcefulness and was a talented athlete and trapeze artist. He was fascinated by locks, especially picking and opening them. At the age of 12, he left home, worked as a messenger boy and became an amateur boxer. The area of magic interested him greatly and he read voraciously on the subject, finally deciding that his life's work would be as a magician and escape artist. He wanted to be the greatest, to be immortal, and he largely achieved this ambition in life. Once he became a professional magician he changed his name to "Harry Houdini".

PERSONALITY

Houdini was very curious, even as a child, and had a tremendous capacity to hyper-focus. Like Isaac Newton, he could hyper-focus to such an extent that he would forget to eat. In terms of physical make-up, he had piercing eyes, common in those with Asperger syndrome. The *Omaha Daily News* reported that he had "the physique of a young lion. His muscles are like steel. He has a nervous, artistic temperament." There was also a naive, childlike and immature element to his personality, described as a "quirky sensibility".[14] Displaying a hyperkinetic quality, he was an incessant talker, restless, and always on the go. He wrote letters obsessively and was an inveterate collector of books and art; indeed his personal

[14] Except where otherwise indicated, quotes in this chapter are from Kalush and Sloman (2007).

scrapbooks alone amounted to more than 17,000 pages. He was also a savant and calendrical calculator and mechanically minded.

Houdini's life was a search for an authentic sense of self, often seen in Asperger syndrome. This identity diffusion was quite pronounced and evident from an early age when he used to write about himself in the third person. He travelled the world, always on the lookout for new mountains to conquer, new demands and new challenges. His range of identities was astonishing: an escapologist, illusionist, collector, actor, businessman, author, philanthropist, aviator, secret service agent. Rather bizarrely, he was recruited by the secret service in the USA and spent some time in England, Germany and Russia, echoing the work of Mata Hari, and was a consultant to the German police. Later during the First World War, Houdini put huge energy into the war effort and entertaining military personnel. In respect of these activities, biographers Kalush and Sloman (2007) remark that "all his identities suddenly paled in comparison with his new version of himself: Houdini the Patriot". Another identity was that of a scriptwriter and for a period films became a novelty with him. It resulted in him setting up his own film laboratory company but it was a financial disaster. Houdini became obsessed with flying while in its infancy and flew many times in Australia setting an aviation record there. The drive to be number one at whatever he did was ever-constant, especially if it concerned novelty-seeking and sensation-seeking.

Clearly, Houdini was courageous but ultimately self-destructive and masochistic. There was always some insecurity driving him to greater heights and he put his reputation on the line in each performance. His relentless self-promotion could be seen as an effort to define himself as superhuman. There was much aggression in him also and he used "to lash out against his perceived enemies". In fact, he was extremely dominating and controlling and it was not sufficient for him to succeed but others had to fail. He also had an autistic superego and was obsessed with exposing fake spiritualists. Eventually, the spiritualists began to take legal action against him.

As usual with great artists, he suffered periods of depression and wrote on one occasion that "life is but an empty dream". In Monte Carlo he was fascinated by suicide, precipitated by his gambling losses. Death intrigued him and he often diced with it, insisting on "pushing the envelope" whenever he could. He drove himself relentlessly and it is hardly surprising that he died in the end through overwork and taking on excessive challenges. He never knew when to stop, as do few great creators. In a way he was a tragic figure, and the price he paid was monumental. Having boasted that he could withstand any blow to his abdomen, two university students took up the challenge one day in his dressing room. One of them punched him in the stomach several times causing a ruptured appendix, Houdini not having braced himself for the onslaught. Despite in great pain Houdini continued to perform and refused to go to hospital for several days, though by now his condition had deteriorated to peritonitis, which proved fatal. Like Andy Warhol, he had refused emergency care until it was too late. Before he died, Houdini said: "Doctor, you know, I always wanted to be a surgeon, but I never could. I have always regretted it." He also said at the very end: "I, in almost ever respect, am a fake".

SOCIAL RELATIONSHIPS

Throughout his life Houdini remained dependent on his mother and grieved deeply when she died. So much so that he desperately sought to contact her in the afterlife. As a very young man, in 1894, he married Bess Rahner, who also worked in vaudeville shows, and his wife became his stage assistant thereafter. The marriage was successful but produced no children, though he had a good relationship with children, given his childlike personality. Like Picasso, Houdini was a kind of Minotaur and made massive demands on those around him: he was highly litigious and paranoid and his good name mattered incredibly to him. He often threatened to sue imitators and loved confrontation, even sending people to break up rivals' acts.

WORK

Houdini was highly entrepreneurial, a great self-publicist and a huge celebrity of his day. He would get the police to lock him into cells and escape as a publicity stunt for his tours. In his acts he was a master of timing, always defying death and challenging fate. That was the source of the thrill for him. Endlessly persistent, he was a constant learner and always tried to improve his acts, preparing meticulously though never satisfied – he was "superegoish" in that respect and had extremely high standards. He was intensely competitive and always sought greatness, believing himself invisible and wanting to be almost god-like. He was totally addicted to what he did and suffered a great deal, despite his high pain threshold. Sometimes his escape from chains or handcuffs was excruciatingly painful. On one occasion, after performing some feat, he ruptured a blood vessel in one of his kidneys. His medical adviser told him to give up his type of work but he flatly refused. There was no possibility of giving it up. However, he was also rather fatalistic and knew the glory would not last forever. Harry Houdini died in Detroit on 31 October 1926, at the age of 52.

Chapter 15

Richard Harris

Richard Harris (1930–2002) was a gifted Irish actor with an uneven career, who never won an Oscar, although nominated twice. He played out in life the archetypal wild, drunken Irishman – a figure that is both pitiable and self-destructive. Among his best-known films are *This Sporting Life*, *Camelot* (for which he won a Golden Globe Award) and *The Field*.

Background

Richard Harris was born on 1 October 1930 in Limerick, Ireland, where his father, Ivan, had a successful flour business. In school there was evidence of poor progress because of his attention deficit hyperactivity disorder. He had poor concentration, was restless, bored by school, and once "fell asleep" during an exam.[15] At secondary school he was one of the "eleven hopeless cases", a group of rebel boys isolated from the rest of the class. Of course, it is generally from such groups that significant artists of various hues emerge. The Jesuit order that ran the secondary school were certainly not proud of him and made that clear in no uncertain terms. In childhood Harris showed oppositional defiant disorder and as an adult too remained oppositional and defiant: he even organised a workers' strike against his own father. In truth, he never outgrew his adolescence and was a rebel without a cause, somewhat like the actor James Dean.

Personality

Harris has variously been described as never being relaxed, extremely tense, "out of control" and dyslexic. These features are commonly associated with attention deficit hyperactivity disorder and oppositional defiant disorder. In addition, he had obsessive compulsive traits and was a hoarder. Indeed Harris shared some of the same personality traits as Frank Sinatra, specifically the "bad boy" image. Biographer Cliff Goodwin describes Harris as having a history of drunken adventures, near-fatal accidents and illnesses, a string of dreadful B-movies, abandoned wives and necessary lovers, careless friends, and curious years

[15] Except where otherwise indicated, quotes in this chapter are from Goodwin (2004).

of self-imposed retirement. Filmmaker Jim Sheridan recalls how unpredictable Harris was and emphasises his “controlling presence and immense charm … like royalty, he commanded people and space and he didn’t seem to care.”

There is also evidence of identity diffusion. In this respect, he was a fantasist and myth-maker who told endless “fibs” about his life. He was chameleon-like: a man with identity diffusion and multiple selves. So ingrained were these lies that he began to believe his own myths as he got older. He never really found his true authentic self and hence abused drugs and alcohol to deal with his problems.

Harris once had ambitions to be a great poet and heroic rugby player but achieved neither of these; admittedly he did publish some poetry and his rugby career was thwarted by illness. Rugby was one of his enduring passions and he nursed hopes of playing for Ireland. He certainly showed massive aggression and determination on the field. However, a bout of tuberculosis put an end to that ambition. He was always a novelty-seeker, a risk-taker, sensation-seeking and accident-prone.

Social Relationships

Harris was a multifaceted character, who could be sadistic and aggressive as well as charismatic and affectionate. These were his quite different selves. He used and took advantage of people but remained loyal to his two ex-wives, Elizabeth Rees-Williams and Ann Turkel. Jim Sheridan also notes that despite the popular hellraising image, Harris was a family man and cared for his three sons. He looked after wives and lovers and ex-lovers and children.

Work

As a youth, Harris was fascinated by films and by Shakespeare. He identified with Vincent van Gogh, who, like himself, was a tortured, self-destructive, masochistic figure. Both had very high artistic ideals. Harris’s artistic ego ideal was powerful and there were echoes of Clark Gable in him too. He tried to resolve his identity diffusion and to heal his conflicted self through acting. In his twenties he moved to London and enrolled at the London Academy of Music and Dramatic Art and soon began to make a name for himself on the West End. His film career was extensive and endured over many decades. Despite very high personal standards as an actor he failed to live up to them on occasion. While he had tremendous innate acting talent, because of his oppositionality he was unwilling to learn, which limited his progress. By nature he was musical and as a singer found success with the song “MacArthur Park” and the musical *Camelot*. Work, however, was his antidepressant and gave him a reason to live. Richard Harris died in London on 25 October 2002, aged 72.

Chapter 16

DAVID NIVEN

David Niven (1910–1983) was a popular middle-ranking film star who won an Academy Award in 1958 for *Separate Tables*. Biographer Graham Lord describes him as a "hilarious, utterly charming, delightfully engaging fantasist and fibber".[16] He loved making up stories about himself and others, but there was also a hidden depressive layer to his personality.

BACKGROUND

David Niven was born in London on 1 March 1910. There are some doubts as to whether William Niven or Sir Thomas Comyn-Platt was his father. His mother, *née* Henriette Degacher, was married to Niven, a "rich son of a newspaper executive" and a gambler, who was killed at the Dardanelles in the First World War. There were many successful army officers on both sides of his family. The widowed Henriette married Comyn-Platt, whom the London *Times* described as "austere and aloof", when Niven was seven years of age. Niven found him very controlling and critical, disliked him intensely, and claimed he inflicted a lot of corporal punishment on him. Comyn-Platt was also something of a fantasist, like Niven.

His mother, on the other hand, was a social butterfly and had multiple sexual liaisons. Niven felt rejected by her and was brought up mainly by governesses and sent off to boarding schools. At school, he was the class and school clown: disruptive and a notorious prankster, who was expelled for "exposing his buttocks to the public gaze" in his tenth year. He was also the victim of institutionalised bullying, a then feature of the British public school system. Niven said that in general his teachers were "sadistic perverts", again common behaviour in the education system at the time. It is hardly surprising that he was sent to a special school for "difficult boys". This did not stop the beatings he incurred, however. Though a mediocre sportsman at school, Niven's other talents did emerge. He began acting and could sing and was talented at drawing, particularly "cartoons" which he would pass around in school in his role of class clown. Later a very gifted headmaster, John Ferguson Roxburgh at Stowe School, was able to see deeper into him: Roxburgh had a great intuitive understanding of boys like Niven and managed to transform him into something of a gentleman. Although he

[16] Except where otherwise indicated, quotes in this chapter are from Lord (2004).

continued to have "incidents" in school, this was a key turning point in his life after a long list of authority figures, including parents, had let him down.

After Stowe, Niven entered the Royal Military College of Sandhurst and eventually joined the Highland Light Infantry as a lieutenant. At first, Niven enjoyed what excitement there was in military life but soon found the routine intolerably boring. He was not good at obeying rules and often in trouble. Indeed his poor attention in class had been noted in military college. Restless for new opportunities, he resigned from the Highland Light Infantry in 1933, travelled to the United States, ending up in Hollywood where he enjoyed several minor film roles, such as in *Mutiny on the Bounty* in 1935. The outbreak of the Second World War interrupted his acting career and he rejoined the army. He certainly showed courage in joining the armed forces, although he was not placed in particularly dangerous situations during the war.

PERSONALITY

Niven clearly had attention deficit hyperactivity disorder (ADHD) and oppositional defiant disorder (ODD) as a child. Indeed, he described himself as the "most poisonous little bastard that God ever put breath into". He was very impulsive, attention-seeking, oppositional and disruptive in school, and bullied a lot by the more senior boys. The many beatings he received at the hands of teachers are not surprising given that ADHD and ODD boys are very provocative and irritating for teachers and peers. The impulsivity and provocation continued into adult life. His commanding officer in the army said he was very unbalanced and irresponsible. At a time when he had little money, Niven sold his body to a London medical school for use when he died.

Niven displayed a keen intelligence, was extremely verbal and had good linguistic skills. He had some identity diffusion and moved easily between fact and fiction: he was not an accurate storyteller, but used whatever material suited his purpose. For him, the effect on the audience was far more important than the facts of a story. He certainly had a false façade and was an excellent mimic right from the beginning. A contemporary, General Sir Charles Harrington, said that "Niven lived a Walter Mitty life at Sandhurst and would make things up, as he did all his life". He was also somewhat enigmatic. It is very common for boys with ADHD to have one or two minor Asperger traits: in Niven's case it was to be a "self-contained, even solitary figure whom it was hard to know".

SOCIAL RELATIONSHIPS

Niven was a Don Juan, highly promiscuous and a sex addict. He had endless relationships with women, both married and single, and got into trouble with army officers because of his relationships with their wives. He claimed his first sexual relationship was with a prostitute which endured for some time, however, it is likely that this was untrue. Later he engaged prostitutes with the actor Douglas Fairbanks Jr. In 1940, he married Primula Rollo and she bore him two sons, but died tragically in an accident in 1946 that left Niven grief-stricken. His second marriage was to Swedish model, Hjördis Tersmeden, in 1948, and they adopted two little girls. His womanising continued as ever. Hjördis said that he was a "very insecure, sad, melancholy man" and indeed losing his youthful looks depressed him. At times he was extremely controlling and described as a control freak, so much so his nickname was "J.C., short for Jesus Christ". In later life he became rather paranoid and felt that "everyone was either useless or trying to cheat him". This suggests that he also suffered from depression.

WORK

Success came rather quickly in Hollywood for Niven, where he displayed "ruthless determination" in terms of his acting career. With his good looks and charm he rapidly progressed from movie extra to minor role to leading man. He was brilliant at social networking, which helped greatly in Hollywood: he had contact with Douglas Fairbanks Sr, a hugely influential figure in the film business, and similarly film producer Samuel Goldwyn was also very important to him. In all Niven made over 90 movies, most notably, *A Matter of Life and Death*, *Around the World in 80 Days*, and *The Pink Panther*. In 1958, he was awarded an Academy Award for Best Actor for his performance in *Separate Tables*. Writing in *The Film Greats* in 1985, critic Barry Norman that he was "less an actor than a great screen personality, most of the time he simply played himself". David Niven developed motor neuron disease in 1980, and died in Switzerland on 29 July 1983, aged 73.

Chapter 17

ELLEN TERRY

Ellen Terry (1847–1928) was one of the most successful English actors of the nineteenth century. She wrote a memoir that gives a far better description of her stage partner Henry Irving than it does of herself. She starts by quoting poet Walt Whitman from *Leaves of Grass*:

> When I read the book, the biography famous,
> And is this, then, (said I,) what the author calls a man's life?
> And so will some one, when I am dead and gone, write my life?
> (As if any man really knew aught of my life!
> Why even I myself, I often think, know little or nothing of my real life;
> Only a few hints – a few diffused faint clues and indirections,
> I seek, for my own use, to trace out here.)

BACKGROUND

Ellen Terry was born in Coventry, England on 27 February 1847 into a family of itinerant actors. Her mother, Sarah Ballard – whose father was a builder and Wesleyan preacher – eloped with Benjamin Terry, the son of an Irish innkeeper. At the time Benjamin played the drums in theatre and worked as a stage hand, but had trained himself to be a competent supporting actor. He was also hyperkinetic, restless and impulsive. Sarah, as well as being an actor, also worked as a stage hand. It was a tough life for a young married pair, whose family grew to eleven children, though Sarah's mother did support them. Terry was a contented child who had her father's "impulsive temperament".[17] She quoted Shakespeare from her earliest years and his words became imprinted on her brain like a first language, which flowed out of her spontaneously in later life. As a child she was a prodigy, endowed with innate talent, and the stage was her natural environment. Several of her siblings were also actors, notably Kate, grandmother to John Gielgud. Terry claimed she had no formal schooling and could not sit still as a child, in fact she was hyperkinetic.

---

[17] Except where otherwise indicated, quotes in this chapter are from Holroyd (2008).

Personality

In her memoirs, Terry wrote that "a child's earliest impressions mould its character perhaps more than either heredity or education" Terry (1982). She underestimates heredity here, however, even in her own family. Terry had the identity diffusion so necessary for great creativity. A flavour of this feature is found in her memoirs, in which she quotes Keats: "The poet lives not in one, but in a thousand worlds, and the actor has not one, but a hundred natures." It is clear that Ellen Terry was no ordinary woman as she rose to become a celebrated actress. Dramatist Charles Reade best captured her extraordinary complexity, describing her as "paradoxical", "egotistical", "extremely changeable in her desires", a "flirt", "so calculating", "false as hell", "fascinating", "hysterical", "impulsive", "an enigma", "charming" and "innocent" (Holroyd, 2008). This complexity of character is often necessary to be a great artist.

Commenting on her career, Terry said that for the stage one needs "imagination, industry, and intelligence" (Terry, 1982), which she had in abundance. In fact, she was quite hyperkinetic and high-spirited and had to learn to curb this on stage. Indeed when actor Henry Irving first worked with her he thought she was "on the hoydenish side" and a critic described her as a "spoilt child". During her affair with Edward Godwin she was able to detach herself totally from her previous life on stage. She had a massive capacity to compartmentalise her life, only returning to the stage because of debts and having two children to rear.

Terry's nature was given to extremes. She once described herself as a lunatic, while her first husband described her as restless and impetuous, with "sensational and exaggerated, not to say intolerable fantasies" and "insane excitability". His solicitor concluded that she was mad. For her part she admitted to "hysterical fits" and apparently was given to making paranoid accusations. Some of these features are not rare in actors. Of course, she had mellowed and matured by the time she wrote her memoirs. There was a degree of self-censorship to Terry, mindful of her legacy; she burnt a lot of her diaries early in her life and later regretted it. Furthermore, she omitted from her memoirs much of the excitement and recklessness of her life.

Social Relationships

Terry was an extremely poor judge of suitable marriage partners in her life. In her early adolescence, her mother was a careful chaperone. This was rather necessary as Terry was a novelty-seeker and a sensation-seeker, attracted to reckless and undependable men. Holroyd describes her as a "notorious flirt" and a seductress. With her tremendous imagination she was full of romantic fantasies and impulsive. At the age of 15, she was painted by George Frederick Watts, "England's Michelangelo", who was an odd, eccentric, talented painter. He was looking for a muse – "a child–wife–model" – to stimulate his work and considered "adopting" Terry. A highly inappropriate marriage was then contracted to take place. Just short of her seventeenth birthday, she married Watts, then aged 46, and abandoned the stage. At this time she was emotionally immature, a child bride, and not ready for marriage in any sense. She expected adoration and complete happiness from Watts, which did not materialise.

They separated after less than a year and Terry became depressed. Watts paid her father substantial sums of money for a dozen years after the separation.

The short period of her marriage, however, did allow her to mix with famous people such as Tennyson, Disraeli and Gladstone. She soon returned to acting and went to live with a feckless architect-designer named Edward William Godwin, and had two children by him, Edith and Edward Gordon. Charles Reade accurately described him as "a blackguard", and he was exciting and dangerous, which is what Terry desired. She found him rather enigmatic in a different way to Watts. However, after six years the relationship had run its course and she was greatly upset when he left her and married another woman, not least because of conflict over the custody of the children. Her daughter Edith said that Terry was not an easy person to live with and had episodes of depression. Her next marriage was to Charles Kelly, another needy man and an actor, given to bouts of drunkenness. Her son Edward claimed that Terry was "not a marriageable person" and was a "mad woman". The marriage to Kelly also broke down within a few short years. The third and last man she married was American actor James Carew, some 30 years her junior. Sadly, that marriage too ended in divorce within a short period. It is interesting to note that her daughter Edith produced numerous suffragist and anti-war plays. Edward, her son by Godwin, fathered 13 children by eight women and had a tempestuous relationship with the dancer Isadora Duncan.

WORK

At the age of six years Terry joined the actor-manager Charles Kean's theatrical group. Kean worked them to the point of exhaustion, particularly during the rehearsal of a new play. Nevertheless, she adored what she was doing from the beginning, and the stage work fitted her perfectly. She was less happy with the theatre as she moved through puberty and became more aware of the interpersonal stresses of the theatrical group. She had to grow up quickly when her maternal grandmother, who had supported the family, died. Despite all her early experience she still had stage fright, as many great actors experience.

In her early life she played second fiddle to her sister Kate who was the star on stage. But through persistent hard work over the course of her lifetime she perfected her craft and eclipsed her sister. The influence of Henry Irving on her career was groundbreaking and together they transformed the theatrical profession. In 1878, at the age of 30, she joined Irving's company at the Lyceum Theatre as its leading lady, playing Ophelia to Irving's Hamlet. Fame and fortune followed. Soon she was hailed as the leading Shakespearean actress in Britain and toured America several times. The partnership with Irving endured for over 20 years and ensured their place in the pantheon of great English actors. For all her detractors, she nevertheless had legions of admirers, including George Bernard Shaw.

Ellen Terry suffered a stroke in later life and died in Kent on 21 July 1928, aged 81; her ashes lie in St Paul's Cathedral.

Chapter 18

GRETA GARBO

Greta Garbo (1905–1990) was one of the most mysterious and enigmatic actresses of the twentieth century. Her best-known films include *Grand Hotel*, *Camille*, *Anna Karenina* and *Ninotchka*. Females with Asperger syndrome are often difficult to diagnose, however, the condition offers an explanation for her inscrutable and puzzling personality, nicknamed the Swedish sphinx.

BACKGROUND

Greta Garbo was born Greta Gustafsson in Stockholm, Sweden on 18 September 1905. Her father, Karl Gustafsson, was a "quiet, reticent person"[18] – an unskilled labourer who became an alcoholic. Her mother, Anna, was equally uneducated and had a noticeably large head. They had three children, of whom Garbo was the youngest. Anna shared some of Garbo's traits, being something of a loner, whereas Garbo was Karl's favourite and he spoiled her within his very limited means – psychoanalysts would emphasise an almost Oedipal triumph over her mother. In fact, she became extremely hostile to her mother and their relationship was so toxic that Garbo once said that "children should have no mothers".

Garbo showed poor school progress. Clearly, school bored her, though she was fascinated by works of fiction, of which she read a great many. She was also very much an autodidact.

Her father died in 1920, when she was 14, forcing her to leave school and go to work. Her first job was in a barber shop followed by the millinery department of a large department store, from which to progressed to fashion modelling, not surprisingly given her angular beauty and mesmeric eyes. The newspaper commercials she appeared in caught the attention of director Erik Arthur Petschler and he began to give her parts in his films.

PERSONALITY

Garbo was a shy, introverted, sensitive girl, with a vivid imagination and given to daydreaming. In common with many with Asperger syndrome, she said very little and

[18] Except where otherwise indicated, quotes in this chapter are from Gronowicz (1990).

engaged in somewhat challenging behaviour. Her local pastor said she was "impatient and arrogant" and referred to her "sharp tongue – although you do not speak much – and your rude behaviour".

Garbo was essentially very serious and a fantasist, and had identity diffusion. Hence she was enigmatic and sphinx-like, having only a partial and very negative female identity and not much self-knowledge. She defined herself by the way other people – reporters, photographers and the public – reacted to her, and liked to toy with them at a distance. She maintained the mysterious façade to the end of her life, constantly searching for an authentic sense of self and never achieving it. Mysterious masks became a substitute for a real personality. On retirement, she continued to create myths about herself by her withdrawn behaviour. Despite rarely speaking, she observed a great deal and became something of an art connoisseur, amassing an impressive and valuable collection of paintings.

Garbo also displayed sexual identity diffusion. When she was young, her mother was having sexual relations with the local pastor and Garbo began to feel "disgust about sexual intercourse". She became aware of her bisexuality and that she "had similar sexual feelings for both boys and girls". She began to engage in some sexual play with a girl and also to think of adult men and women in a sexual way: in her dreams she saw a female body with male organs or a male body with female ones. This sexual identity diffusion never left her. In mid-adolescence she began masturbating to images of famous actors that she looked at in magazines. Her mother thought this necessitated medical intervention and inflicted heavy corporal punishment on her. Later as an adult, Garbo was androgynous, wore trousers, and loved talking about "the boys' room".

Film critic Richard Schickel described her as a "singular screen presence" and "into control" – indeed the latter is how persons with Asperger syndrome are often described. Notoriously secretive, she guarded and controlled any references to her private life for obvious good reasons. She certainly displayed preservation of sameness and insisted on the same persons working with her on many films.

Garbo was fundamentally narcissistic and egocentric and thought of little else but herself and how she was viewed by other people. Once her film career ended, she had a rather pointless egocentric life with the idle rich and famous and gave no thought to society at all during that time. Many people with Asperger syndrome are excessively concerned with health, death and growing old, as was Garbo. Always wanting to be remembered as she had been, Garbo was loath to show herself ageing. What concerned her most was her long-term legacy as a star.

SOCIAL RELATIONSHIPS

There was a lonely element to Garbo's personality, often to be seen in great actors. The phrase "I want to be alone", famously delivered by her in the 1932 film *Grand Hotel*, came to be associated with her, and indeed she was a loner, only mixing with people when it suited her. She especially liked taking long walks in the rain by herself. Schickel noticed her "silence and withdrawal", her "lack of resonance", and "air of removal from the contexts in which she was presented" – again, this may have been due to Asperger syndrome. Despite the

"I want to be alone" image, she was an Asperger (autistic) wanderer. She exchanged frivolities with celebrities and accepted their hospitality but was not adverse to using people.

In adult life, Garbo lived alone, never married and had no children. There were sexual relationships with several men and women, including co-stars, over a number of years. She had a very confused sexual psyche, and reputedly had affairs with some male homosexuals. According to biographer Antoni Gronowicz "her manner was touched with masculine shadows". The sexual identity diffusion confused people and indeed herself as well.

WORK

Encouraged by her appearances in newspaper commercials, Garbo hyper-focused on becoming an actress. At the age of 17, she won a scholarship to study at the acting school of the Stockholm Royal Dramatic Theatre. She was spotted by director Mauritz Stiller, a major figure in Swedish films at the time, who cast her in the epic *The Legend of Gösta Berling*. He became her mentor and lover and gave her the screen name "Greta Garbo"; his tuition was superb and Garbo kept their relationship as long as he was useful to her. When Metro-Goldwyn-Mayer offered Stiller a film contract, he brought Garbo with him to Hollywood, where she made her American debut in the 1926's silent movie *The Torrent.* It was successful and launched her career and by 1930 she had started to appear in sound films, the 'talkies'. With her husky voice and thick accent, combined with a magnetic screen presence, she became a sensation. The 1930s were her heyday with films such as *Anna Christie*, *Grand Hotel*, *Camille*, *Anna Karenina* and *Ninotchka*; she received numerous awards and was nominated for three Academy Awards, though never won due to the stiff competition of the day.

Much of her popularity was linked to her sex appeal on screen. She had no well-defined sense of her own or other people's sexual identity, seeing everyone, including herself, as a confused mix of male and female. This was critical to how she portrayed herself on screen, and led to males and females in the audience being very attracted to her, with each performance akin to a sexual performance. Because of this there could never be another Garbo – never such a uniquely confused sexual person. It was the well from which she drew her acting ability. In 1941, she retired from the screen at the age of 35 after appearing in 28 films. She declined all subsequent offers to return to the screen but was honoured with an honorary Academy Award in 1954. Her premature retirement was highly narcissistic – what could be more tantalising than her withdrawal from public view? Greta Garbo died in New York on 15 April 1990, aged 84.

Chapter 19

LENI RIEFENSTAHL

Helene (Leni) Riefenstahl (1902–2003) was a highly talented and opportunistic German film director. She wholeheartedly embraced Nazi ideology, as did another opportunist, architect Albert Speer, and was one of the most successful propagandists for Hitler, Goebbels and their party. After the Second World War, like Speer, she became a myth-maker about her Nazi work. She was multiply talented as a dancer, actress, film director and photographer. Like Speer and thousands of others, she seized the opportunity and made a Faustian bargain with the Nazis. Throughout her life she showed many traits of Asperger syndrome.

BACKGROUND

Helene Riefenstahl was born in Berlin on 22 August 1902. Her father, a successful businessman, was controlling and dominating, and quite volatile: he had empathy deficits and administered corporal punishment to his daughter, showing her almost no love. During adolescence Riefenstahl confronted him more and more and "locked horns" with him.[19] It was an unhappy father–daughter relationship and indeed there was major marital disharmony between her parents. The family included a younger brother Heinz, who was a loner.

There was a family history of interest in the arts and of some talent in that area. Her mother had to repress her own artistic talents, but Riefenstahl inherited them and received encouragement from her mother. In fact, her mother nourished Riefenstahl's creative side, painting and writing poetry from an early age and, later, dancing. Riefenstahl probably also inherited some artistic potential from her father, who, in his early life, was interested in the performing arts at a minor level.

Solitude was extremely important to Riefenstahl and she very much appreciated nature and the outdoors. She often seemed quite detached, in a world of her own, and almost unaware of men during her adolescence. An intellectual and extremely curious, she could hyper-focus on her interests at school, but found it difficult to focus in class. She certainly was an autodidact throughout her life in the fashion of persons with Asperger syndrome. Riefenstahl showed hyperkinetic tendencies in her childhood. In addition, she was a sensation-seeker, a novelty-seeker and a fantasist. Even in childhood and adolescence she had

---

[19] Except where otherwise indicated, quotes in this chapter are from Trimborn (2008).

a massive capacity to deny unpleasant reality. You could say she inhabited a kind of autistic mindset. She appears to have had good motor skills and was attracted to individualistic sports such as swimming and gymnastics, and indeed athleticism would feature highly in her artistic oeuvre. From an early age she was quite narcissistic and wanted her talents to be publicly appreciated. Indeed she became obsessed with the performing arts. In sum, Riefenstahl was an extremely driven person, with extraordinary self-belief.

Personality

Riefenstahl had identity diffusion and was chameleon-like. As she grew older she began to believe her own lies about her life, not unlike Albert Speer. She became as domineering, controlling and unempathic as her father and would walk on anyone to get to the top. As a Nazi propagandist, she was ruthlessly professional and had traits of the stormtroopers, overcoming any obstacle, no matter how insurmountable. During the war she witnessed the killing of Jews and, possibly, as a Nazi sympathiser knew all about the Final Solution. She was not adverse to using forced labour during the war either, as extras in her films. Trimborn (2008) points out that Riefenstahl had the power "to have people released from concentration camps but could also arrange to have them sent there". He states that she had no moral scruples and disregarded human life.

Her egocentrism was legendary. The only issue for her was to show how brilliant she was and to be the brightest star. In her work, she was meticulous and perfectionistic and therefore a slow worker. Her identity diffusion continued throughout life. Her greatest life challenge was to justify herself after the end of the war, and as usual she had a great deal of success in this area. Always an extremely persuasive person, she often convinced naïve western observers that she knew almost nothing about the Holocaust, just like Albert Speer did. She did nevertheless help a few people when it suited her. In fact, she wasn't much worse than thousands of professionals, such as lawyers, who cooperated and greatly helped the Nazis to their own benefit. During this time she had to submit to denazification, which was considered a joke for most people, and placed under house arrest for three years. Vast numbers of former Nazis became mainstream in society in a relatively short time and began to prosper again. Riefenstahl also rehabilitated herself by engaging in lawsuits against journalists to protect her name. She also suffered major depression after the war and was treated in a psychiatric hospital. Nevertheless, Riefenstahl reinvented herself as a still photographer in the 1960s. She took many photographs and even in her sixties remained a novelty-seeker and sensation-seeker. Indeed, she outlived almost all the other famous Nazis, remaining extremely exhibitionistic to the very end. Rarely ignored except for relatively short periods after the war, she always wanted to be in the public eye.

Social Relationships

Riefenstahl considered the issue of men as a logical problem to be appreciated in a mechanical fashion. She completely lacked the social skills to interact with men on an intimate basis, though she had several lovers. She was often naïve and a user of people when it suited her. She effectively used men and then rejected them. Great artists tend to have a poor capacity for marriage and Riefenstahl was no different. During the war she engaged in an impulsive, poorly thought-out marriage to a military man, Major Peter Jacob. The marriage broke up after the war and indeed she lacked the social skills for an intimate marital relationship of long duration.

Hitler was Riefenstahl's obsession and she studied his writings in great detail. She adored him from the beginning and succeeded in making face-to-face contact with him quite quickly, before he came to power. She invited him to her home, to which he came, and got to know his inner circle. Hitler was her greatest ally and regularly intervened on her behalf. When she went to America, she was described as "Herr Hitler's emissary-in-skirts" (Birdwell, 1999). Indeed she became Hitler's special filmmaker.

WORK

In dance, Riefenstahl choreographed her own routines. As one would expect from a person with Asperger syndrome, she pursued a solo dancing career for a period and performed all over Europe. Again, she was hyperkinetic and totally driven. She recognised no limits, physically or otherwise, and pushed herself until her body gave up. A leg injury, however, forced her dancing career into early retirement. Her acting career was equally driven, and she appeared in many mountain films of the 1920s and 1930s. She was intensely visual and, like many people with Asperger syndrome, got great satisfaction from looking at the physical structure of the environment. With the arrival of the talking films, she had a problem with the pitch of her voice, which is common in Asperger syndrome.

After a successful period as an actress she became obsessed with becoming a director. She learned a vast amount about film from Arnold Fanck's film-making and editing, but grossly downplayed this later and minimised his input. This was essentially the myth of the self-creator, who was extraordinarily egocentric. Riefenstahl showed great determination and self-belief in directing her first film, *The Blue Light*, setting up her own company and investing her own capital. She was never one for half measures. Her work was marked by utter meticulousness, with great attention to detail, and enormous courage in a very risky business. She was successful with the film but refused to pay the man who helped her, and sent the Nazis after him in a vicious and unscrupulous manner.

Riefenstahl was intimately involved with the Nazi project, which allowed her to fulfil her artistic vision. Hitler gave her work a massive boost and she was deeply enmeshed with the Nazi top brass and loved it. It gave her tremendous access, power and control. She became a solo operator with Hitler as her protector and financier. There is no doubt that she had a high level of talent and was critical to Hitler, as Speer had been, as a propagandist. Her major documentaries for the Nazis were *Triumph of the Will* and *Olympia*. Hitler gave her the means for a major career and she grabbed it with both hands before and during the Second World War. She was a true artist; her art was everything to her. There were no limits and she was willing to sacrifice everything for her art.

Nevertheless, for such a high-profile person associated with the Nazis, it took time to restart her career after the war. In the 1960s Riefenstahl became fascinated with Africa and went in search of the Nuba people. Living with this tribe in southern Sudan for long periods made it a kind of second home. She published several books and achieved success in this area.

Leni Riefenstahl died in Germany on 8 September 2003, aged 101.

Chapter 20

JUDY GARLAND

Judy Garland (1922–1969) was a huge film star, best known for her role as Dorothy in *The Wizard of Oz* (1939). She was a woman with a massive talent and an immature, child-like personality. She had no secure identity or authentic solid core.

BACKGROUND

Judy Garland was born Frances Gumm on 10 June 1922 in Grand Rapids, Minnesota. There was artistic talent on both sides of her family – parents and grandparents. Her parents, Frank and Ethel, were involved in vaudeville and were talented musicians who played professionally. Her stage career commenced when she was just two years old. Initially, she sang with her two older sisters, but fairly quickly became the star. Garland was a child prodigy in relation to singing: "Audiences were indeed amazed to discover a woman's voice coming from a child's body."[20] She was a natural performer. Whereas most child stars burn out, this was not to be the case for the girl who became Judy Garland.

Garland had a traumatic childhood, whereby her mother was the central destructive figure in her life, exposing her to a great deal of marital disharmony, including physical violence. Ethel Gumm was quite a disturbed woman and had a huge effect on her daughter's life. She was the classic showbiz mother who drove her child relentlessly and ultimately to self-destruction, being pushy, bossy and overbearing. Clarke describes Ethel as being like a bulldozer. She regarded Garland as simply an extension of herself, whereby the child had to do everything that she wanted. Hence the young girl was pushed relentlessly from one agent and one studio to the next; in effect a prisoner of her mother in childhood. This inhibited her development of a sense of self and ability to look after herself. Garland always had a great deal of anxiety, including separation anxiety in childhood. There was a lack of separation from her mother – what psychoanalysts call "lack of self–object differentiation". Garland herself said "mother and I, we're almost one person". Ethel was grossly unempathetic, and, according to Clarke, there was a "stoniness" in her heart. Her callousness was shown when she remarried on the fourth anniversary of her husband's death – he had died on 17 November 1935. Ethel also began to give Garland stimulants and sleeping tablets that set her up for later

[20] Except where otherwise indicated, quotes in this chapter are from Clarke (2003).

drug addiction. This was highly reckless and irresponsible, as stimulants often cause insomnia and can sometimes require sedatives to get the person to sleep at night, particularly if given too late in the evening.

Garland's hyperkinesis came from both sides of the family. When Ethel became pregnant with Garland, she did everything in her power to abort her but was unsuccessful. Not surprisingly, Judy was a rather weak child, subject to various illnesses. That led to some very early overprotection. Even at the age of two, Judy was "uncontrollable" and very excitable.

Her father was a bisexual, artistic man who sexually abused boys and was driven out of places as a result. Nevertheless, he had a winning personality and was liked by everyone until the sexual abuse came to the fore. He was a good singer and something of a wanderer. Her father invested massively in her and continued to adore her throughout his life. At the age of fifteen, she was devastated when he died from meningitis. Despite their good relationship, it was not sufficient to save her from the traumas of her mother. If there is a good relationship with one parent, a child will often survive reasonably well. One could say that her mother was sadistic while her father was masochistic and a sexual abuser.

PERSONALITY

Like many people of genius, Garland had a massive memory. She retained an immature personality and had the "child-like" demeanour critical in persons of genius. An executive in Columbia Pictures described her as being like "a little Huckleberry Finn". This was a good description of her. At the same time, she was a very complicated, contradictory figure and, according to Clarke, was often shy and uncertain. She had very little sense of herself as a person: her identity was that of a singer: "I sing, therefore I am." Garland had great confidence in her singing and her work on the stage, something that she found quite difficult to hold onto later in life. She clearly had a very advanced voice but was behind in emotional development.

Vulnerable self-esteem was certainly one of the factors in her ultimate downfall. She became obsessed with her appearance and felt unattractive, which tormented her greatly. You could say she was the classic chronic neurotic actress. She always had a tendency to overeat and be overweight. In fact, in adolescence her weight was a great stress, which she tried to curtail. As a result, she was often very fearful and anxious going on stage.

There were no limits to her behaviour. She had novelty-seeking and sensation-seeking genes and was addicted to drugs. She earned a massive amount of money and wasted just as much, and indeed could not manage money. Drug and alcohol addiction were a major part of her life, started by her mother dosing her with drugs in childhood. There was certainly a strong perverse self-destructive element to her personality. She had periods of psychoanalysis without great benefit. One of her analysts, Ernst Simmel, tried to overcontrol her. In adult life she had borderline personality disorder with multiple suicide attempts and drug addiction; her death was by an accidental barbiturate overdose.

Garland tried to make up for the deprivations in her childhood by endless promiscuity. Louis B. Mayer of MGM was very influential with her for a good deal of her career; however, he was "one of the worst of the sexual predators". Garland in fact was used by men sexually for at least the latter half of her adolescence. There is little doubt that the phrase "genius – gift or curse?" applies to her, and both are true.

SOCIAL RELATIONSHIPS

Garland was often the life and soul of the party, not unlike her father. People tended to interact with her as if she were a submissive victim and, indeed, she seemed unconsciously to encourage people to victimise her in a not dissimilar way to how her mother victimised her. Even her servants did not see her as fully grown-up, but as a rather immature little girl who needed to be controlled. Garland was often "aggressive sexually". She was massively emotionally labile: high when in love and seriously depressed when the love ended. She pursued men in whom she was interested in the same way that her mother relentlessly pushed her career. There could be no limits and there could be no waiting. The man had to pay complete attention to her now, even if he was married. When she failed to get a particular man, she "started banging her head against the wall" and became suicidal. As an adult, she often behaved like a child in a temper tantrum who shouted and screamed to get what she wanted.

She married several completely inappropriate men: men who were the least likely to give her what her father had given and to be sensitive and caring of her. Her relationships were often sadomasochistic. Her emotional life was in a way a search for the care and love that she missed in childhood. At the same time, there was massive acting-out, novelty-seeking, sensation-seeking and thrill-seeking in her relationships. This, of course, was not a good sign in terms of stability. Quite a number of Judy's partners in later life were also bisexual. She was attracted to this bisexual type of man based on her father as a model. She was very much in search of father figures and could also be attracted to men with the extreme form of the male brain, that is, Asperger syndrome. These would be very strong, rather robotic men more interested in mechanical things than in her. She was in some ways an extreme form of the female brain herself. This combination was of course doomed to disaster.

Garland appeared to need a man to merge with her before she could feel complete. She was attracted to Tyrone Power, a great actor, who was also bisexual. This relationship didn't work out because she was too impatient. She also experienced some sexual relationships with women but these were really novelty-seeking or sensation-seeking – just a new thrill rather than being any big part of her life.

In a way she wanted her men to have the sensitivity of a female or, indeed, of a mother with a child. Initially, she would idealise men. Emotionally, she was extremely confused and contradictory. Her search was for the perfect man who would make her happy for evermore. When a man tried to put her on the straight and narrow, she experienced him as being like her overcontrolling mother and rebelled.

WORK

Garland was endlessly used and abused by the film studios, and of course she abused them in turn. This was a disastrous interaction. An example of her great talent was seen in

The Wizard of Oz in 1939. If she had stuck to live performances she perhaps might not have damaged herself, or needed to damage herself, so much. There is very little feedback in the endless making of films, but feedback is instant with live performances and she hungered for applause. This could possibly have steadied her vulnerable self-esteem.

Judy Garland died in London on 22 June 1969 from a drug overdose, aged 47.

Chapter 21

MATA HARI

Mata Hari (1876–1917) was a Dutch exotic dancer and celebrity of her time, executed by the French at the age of 41 for alleged espionage during the First World War. She is probably more famous as a dancer than Nijinsky and unlikely ever to be forgotten. Her execution by firing squad has contributed greatly to her renown as are the two films made about her life.

BACKGROUND

Mata Hari was born Margaretha Geertruida ("Grietje") Zelle in Leeuwarden, the Netherlands on 7 August 1876, into an affluent family. She had a very traumatic childhood, however. She was initially loved by her very narcissistic father – Adam, a businessman – who later abandoned her. He was reckless and irresponsible, as she would later become. In the early stage of her life she knew she was special and was overindulged as a child, although she had three brothers. Her father's business went bankrupt in 1889 and resulted in the separation of her father and mother, Antje. Two years later Antje Zelle died, while her daughter was in early adolescence. The family was broken up, with the young girl sent to relatives in the nearby city of Sneek, and her father forming a new liaison in another country. It is hardly surprising that this was wounding, traumatic and devastating for her. At the age of eighteen, she impulsively married Rudolf MacLeod attached to the Dutch Colonial Army and went to live in the Dutch East Indies. The marriage proved unsuccessful, forcing Zelle to eventually earn a living as a dancer.

PERSONALITY

Zelle was novelty-seeking, a sensation-seeker and an extremely restless child. The dark-skinned beauty was extraordinary and exotic, leading one schoolfriend to call her "an orchid in a field of dandelions". She was extraordinarily impulsive and had an immature personality. Her promiscuous career started at the age of 16, when she flirted with the local headmaster, and was very much a courtesan in adult life. She was essentially lost, had identity diffusion, and changed her name a few times. Finally, she began to reinvent herself with a mythical story of her life and became a dancer.

Social Relationships

Zelle essentially searched for her lost father for much of her life through relationships with many different men. She formed a relationship with a much older man, Rudolf MacLeod, in response to a newspaper advertisement he placed looking for a wife. Following the marriage she went to the East Indies where she bore him a son and a daughter. Her husband wrote that she was only interested in her own pleasure and scandalously negligent of their children. Their son Norman died at the age of two, possibly of congenital syphilis or due to treatment of syphilis, while their daughter Jeanne-Louise also fell ill. Zelle was grief-stricken at her son's death. Furthermore, her husband described Zelle as a floozy, a debauched woman, vain and egotistical, and "a bitch".[21] For her part, Zelle claimed that her husband was violent and hit her with his cat-o-nine-tails. Most likely his accusations that she was a spendthrift were probably true. He lived extravagantly, drinking and gambling, and entertained thoughts of self-destruction, while certainly having murderous thoughts about her. Many years later the family's general practitioner defended Zelle's behaviour at the time, pointing the finger of blame at her husband. Nevertheless, both were probably at fault. She left him and developed an interest in Indonesian dance and culture.

Shipman (2007) suggests that what really upset Mata Hari was that "she bored her husband. He did not find her sexually attractive anymore. Her vanity … and fragile sense of self were deeply wounded." A court battle ensued over the marital breakdown and the recriminations on both sides were severe. For a while Mata Hari drifted into high-class prostitution and her ex-husband got custody of Jeanne-Louise. Sadly, their daughter would die tragically at the age of 21, possibly for reasons related to syphilis.

Work

Zelle developed dances with an oriental flavour and took on her final name, Mata Hari, the Malay for "sun". Her first exotic dance performance as Mata Hari took place at the Musée Guimet, a museum of oriental art in Paris in 1905. She was immediately successful at this work and became a celebrity in Paris and performed in Vienna in 1906/1907, "vanquishing her dance rivals, Isadora Duncan and Maud Allan". Her acting skills were also in demand, and she performed in a play called *The Crusaders*. Her dancing career brought her in touch with rich men who could indulge her extravagant tastes. Her exotic stage performances were highly appreciated: she was a natural exhibitionist, with revealing costumes and tremendous dramatic presence.

Despite the money she was earning, she developed huge debts, and lived then "like a butterfly in the sun". As the years passed, money became more and more of a problem, especially now that younger dancers were in vogue. She began to perform in less salubrious venues and seduced government and military men for money. As the First World War started her financial situation was desperate and she returned to neutral Netherlands but found life uninspiring there; she needed excitement and novel experiences to feel alive and well. She was given 20,000 francs by the German Consul, Karl Kroemer, to spy for Germany at a time

[21] Except where otherwise indicated, quotes in this chapter are from Shipman (2007).

when she was bored and had little or no luxuries. She took the money but stated that she never actually spied. She was subsequently recruited by head of French counterespionage, George Ladoux, to spy for the Germans. Her career as a so-called double agent came to an end when she was captured and arrested in Paris by French military in February 1917. Captain Pierre Bouchardon, who later interrogated her, wrote: “Feline, supple and artificial, used to gambling everything and anything without scruple, without pity, always ready to devour fortunes, leaving her ruined lovers to blow their brains out, she was a *born spy*.”

DEATH

Following her arrest in 1917 she spent time in Saint-Lazare prison. Her trial interrogators strongly felt that she was a German agent and her sexual behaviour counted against her. Naively, she had admitted that she had “taken money from Kroemer, the German Consul, who wanted her to spy for Germany”. She was tried in what was effectively a kangaroo court. In many ways she was a rather harmless woman who behaved in a silly way. The war was going badly and the French needed a scapegoat – a spy. It was easy and politically convenient to convict her because of public opinion as much as anything else.

Julia Keay (1987) states that Mata Hari was portrayed at the trial as a “sinister Salomé who had been responsible for the deaths of more than 50,000 French soldiers” and the “incarnation of evil”. Keay also points out that her trial was a travesty of justice: “Mata Hari had been sacrificed to official expediency”. Shipman notes that “addicted to excitement and seriously short of money, she blundered naively into the murky world of espionage, and it destroyed her”. Most likely, the man who had enlisted her as a spy, George Ladoux, was a double agent.

It was her exhibitionism and naivety that put her at risk: “It was not enough that she was sentenced to death, but her possessions were to be sold to pay the French state for the cost of prosecuting and convicting her … The evocation of a biblical seductress who killed heartlessly only heightened public feeling against Mata Hari. She was condemned twice over, once for her sexuality – which was undisputed – and once for her dubiously proven espionage.” Her appeal to have her conviction quashed by President Raymond Poincaré was in vain. There were echoes of Oscar Wilde in her: “She had done nothing wrong in her view … she had only loved men and let them love her.” On 15 October 1917, at the age of 41, he was taken out into muddy fields to be shot:

> She refused to be tied to the stake, and so she stood, lonely but regal, in the desolate field on her own. When the senior officer offered her a blindfold she declined with a dignified movement of her head … Pitifully, no one came to claim her body. Her head was sent to the Institute of Anatomy Museum in Paris for study with those of other criminals.

According to Shipman, “the iconic female spy – beautiful, seductive, utterly duplicitous – owes much to Mata Hari”. She was an extreme novelty-seeker and sensation-seeker for whom ordinary life was intolerable, and for this she paid with her life. Shipman concludes by saying that “butterflies who live in the sun must die young”.

Chapter 22

GROUCHO MARX

Groucho Marx (1890–1977) was a great comedian, whose witty one-liners, like those of Oscar Wilde, will never be forgotten. A much-loved favourite is "please accept my resignation. I don't want to belong to any clubs that will accept me as a member" (Marx, 2008). Groucho was in truth a comic genius. His fame was associated with three of his siblings, the Marx Brothers, namely "Chico, the pianist with an individual technique", "Harpo the dumb clown and harp maestro", and Zippo.

BACKGROUND

Julius Henry Marx was born on 2 October 1890 in New York City, into a Jewish family with vaudeville connections, who "became Groucho because of his serious demeanour".[22] His grandfather was a magician and ventriloquist, while his grandmother yodelled and played the harp. A maternal uncle, Al Schoenberg, whose stage name was Al Shean, was a successful vaudevillian. There was considerable talent in the family also. Groucho's French-born father, Sam Marx, was a tailor, who by all accounts was a great cook but an incompetent tailor: "The only tailor I ever heard of who refused to use a tape measure" (Marx, 2008). He was also a fantasist. Groucho's German-born mother, Minnie, was a harpist, who dedicated herself totally to her sons' careers. It is unlikely they would have reached the top of show business without her drive and determination. She went to endless pains initially getting them gigs. Groucho's brother Adolph (Harpo) described her as having "the stamina of a brewery horse, the drive of a salmon fighting his way up a waterfall, the cunning of a fox, and a devotion to her brood as fierce as any she-lion". Minnie was certainly a feminist before her time and had the heart of a show woman.

Marx showed poor school progress and regarded school as an "unspeakable bore" (Marx, 2008). His fascination was with the theatre, although he did initially consider studying medicine. His brother Leonard (Chico) was a savant and "had a brain as fast and as accurate as a calculating machine. He could solve mathematical problems in his head faster than I could do with pencil, paper, and an abacus" (Marx, 2008). Indeed musical talent and

---

[22] Except where otherwise indicated, quotes in this chapter are from Chandler (2007).

mathematical talent often go together (Fitzgerald & James, 2007). Chico was also a gambler, who like his mother, adored playing cards for money.

PERSONALITY

Marx's language was pared down or restricted in that he often spoke in single short sentences, like those with Asperger syndrome. You could say the title of his 1959 autobiography, *Groucho and Me*, was Aspergerish in that he referred to himself in the third person. His humour was described as "aggressive" and certainly persons with Asperger's syndrome tend to be verbally aggressive. Many people regarded him as showing "scant sympathy". He was a massive reader of books and an untutored intellectual, prepared not to accept religious dogma, though always asking questions. Indeed he was an avid Bible reader and somewhat mystical. Because of his intellectuality he loved the company of writers. The famous figure from the past he would most liked to have been was British prime minister, Benjamin Disraeli.

Throughout his life Marx was hyperkinetic, in "perpetual motion" and constantly needed novelty and new sensations or else he got bored. These traits are common in great comedians and highly creative people. In common with many great artists, he had "extreme self-control and self-discipline". So much so that he was dictatorial in his home, and obsessed with "punctuality, order, and discipline". In fact, he was a Jekyll and Hyde figure. Interestingly, he confessed that it was almost impossible to write a "truthful autobiography" (Marx, 2008).

He adored food, which was hardly surprising as his father was a brilliant cook, and ate leisurely, keeping each item of food separate. This is a trait often seen in those with Asperger syndrome. At times he would eat in complete silence. Like Andy Warhol and Rudolf Valentino he had a phobia about hospitals and indeed the ageing process upset him greatly. Chandler (2007) states that Groucho never answered his own telephone "because he couldn't see the reaction of the other person". He had come to rely on people's faces from his vaudeville days when he tried out his material on audiences. The practical side of show business bored him. By the time his mother died in September 1939 he had lost all his money in the Wall Street Crash.

SOCIAL RELATIONSHIPS

Marx was essentially "a reserved, private individual", who showed "little emotion". He did not enjoy the cocktail party circuit and, if he organised a gathering, he had to have piano music to drown out conversation. He loved women but found them perplexing. He wrote that the female of the species had "always baffled me" and that he regarded them "as a race apart" (Marx, 2008), going so far as to say that "men are fooled by women". His initial period of promiscuity was with black chambermaids in hotels, where he claimed he had sex eight times in one night. Groucho wed three times and all his marriages ended in divorce; his first marriage produced two children and his second one child. All of his wives were considerably younger than himself. It is interesting that persons with Asperger syndrome sometimes choose very young wives; the immaturity of the former makes them more at ease with this age group. The downside to divorce was that Marx paid a great deal of maintenance to his ex-wives, leading him to remark: “Paying alimony is like feeding hay to a dead horse.” Indeed the producer Bert Granet said he abandoned his wives “intellectually and emotionally”. Marx was unable to decipher what his wives needed emotionally; he was unempathic to them and could not read their minds emotionally. However, he did love women who were more intellectual. His later non-marital relationship was with such a woman.

WORK

Groucho Marx is known for his razor sharp, wisecracking films – 26 in total, 13 of which also starred his brothers Chico and Harpo – and for being a radio comic and show host. He once remarked that the mystery of comedy is “ephemeral”, which, as noted by Chandler, Marx sensed could be dissipated by “excessive scrutiny”. Regarding his comedic talent, Marx remarked:

> I am not sure how I got to be a comedian or a comic. Perhaps I am not a comic. It is not worth arguing about. At any rate, I have been making a good living for many years masquerading as one. As a lad, I don’t remember knocking anyone over with my wit. I am a pretty wary fellow, and I have neither the desire nor the equipment to analyse what makes one man funny to another man. I have read many books by alleged experts, explaining the basis of humour and attempting to describe what is funny and what isn’t. I doubt if any comedian can honestly say why he is funny and why his next door neighbour is not. I believe all comedians arrive by trial and error. (Marx, 2008)

It is interesting to note that Thompson (2002) described Marx’s disconnection from the audience in comparison to Charlie Chaplin or Buster Keaton. According to Thompson (2002), Groucho in his performance knows how “alien” his brothers are and concedes that his own greasepaint moustache and collapsible walk “have not fully admitted him to their company”. Thompson notes that “the Marx Brothers are not interested in us. Chaplin hypnotizes us, Keaton calls us through his utter deadpan but the Marx Brothers are as fiercely preoccupied … [with] spinning non-existent webs”. This disconnection is achieved by Groucho’s persona of “confessional confidence trickster”, using “barbs”, “donnish jokes” and the “sharp answer”, serving only to retreat into “surreal anonymity” (Thompson, 2002 The wisecracks sometimes bear uncomfortable truths. Groucho said that no one was completely unhappy at the failure of his best friend (Marx, 2008), and that people adore bad reviews about other people.

The true worth of comedians was underestimated by audiences, according to Marx. He reckoned there were not one hundred top-flight professional comedians, male and female, in the whole world: “They are a much rarer and far more valuable commodity than all the gold and precious stones in the world. But because we are laughed at, I don’t think people really understand how essential we are to their sanity” (Marx, 2008). Comedic actors were a rarer breed again, to judge by Marx quoting playwright S. N. Behrman:

> Any playwright who has been up against the agony of casting plays will tell you that the actor who can play comedy is the fellow to shoot for. The comic intuition gets to the heart of a human situation with a precision and a velocity unattainable in any other way.

> A great comic actor will do it for you with an inflection of voice as adroit as the flick of the wrist of a virtuoso fencer. (Marx, 2008)

However, Groucho believed there was hardly a comedian alive who was not capable of doing "a first-rate job in a dramatic role" (Marx, 2008). Later in life, the honorary Academy Award he received in 1974 brought him great pleasure.

Groucho Marx had a stroke in 1971 and died in Los Angeles on 19 August 1977, aged 86.

Chapter 23

Peter Sellers

Peter Sellers (1925–1980) was a great comic actor – among his best-known films are *Dr Strangelove*, the *Pink Panther* series and *Being There*. He had huge identity diffusion with very little idea of who he was and therefore could be anybody and could play any role in the comedy canon. The chaos and confusion of his mind were necessary for the greatness of his art; however he suffered a great deal psychologically.

Background

Richard Henry (Peter) Sellers was born in Portsmouth on the south coast of England on 8 September 1925. There was a history of the performing arts in his family. His father Bill was a variety entertainer as was his mother Agnes; she was "highly strung" like her only son and "pampered and protected" him.[23] In fact, she suffocated him and his mind, saying "I do all the thinking for him". Sellars as a small child lived off stage in various theatres while his parents toured the country. The young boy was grossly overindulged by Agnes, who regarded him as an omnipotent, all-knowing and perfect prince, and wanted him always to have preferential treatment. He became at this very early time in his life a kind of "child-king", whose every whim had to be obeyed. His father Bill was a more shadowy figure in his life and appeared to be a somewhat submissive "loner" type. This weak unassertive father let Sellars down as well, especially when he separated from Agnes in 1929, when Sellars was just four years old.

Travelling around from theatre to theatre, Sellars lacked the experience of peer relationships, which was a great loss to his development. He certainly did not have the opportunity to share with peers. His childhood days were marked by challenging behaviour: he was oppositional, defiant and behaviourally disordered. He became a tyrannical child who was cruel to animals and indeed to adults as well. There were also obsessive–compulsive traits, for example "switching lights on and off six times" – this kind of behaviour is common in children with obsessive–compulsive disorder and Asperger syndrome traits. While he showed poor school progress, he was intelligent but a huge fantasist. His early life was that of a wanderer, and indeed his later life was much the same – a kind of rolling stone.

[23] Except where otherwise indicated, quotes in this chapter are from Lewis (2004).

As he grew up he was not given the opportunity to separate psychologically from his mother and develop his own autonomous identity. In fact, Agnes was equally overprotective and interfering in his young adult life. She moved heaven and earth in an effort to have him exempted from military service in 1943 but in vain. Indeed she did everything in her power to prevent him growing up. She and Sellars interacted as peers rather than having a normal adult–child relationship, similar to Kenneth Williams's relationship with his mother. It was a pathologically close mother–son relationship. In psychoanalytic terms, Sellars certainly triumphed over his father – an Oedipal triumph – and Agnes was insanely jealous of any relationship with women that Sellars might have. During the Second World War, having joined the Royal Air Force (RAF), he was moved overseas in the military and finally joined the entertainments section, where he excelled at drumming and mimicry. Indeed he was fascinated by drum playing but not by other musical instruments.

PERSONALITY

Blessed with a prodigious memory, Sellars was a massive novelty-seeker and sensation-seeker. In common with many with Asperger syndrome he had unusual voice qualities. The tone of his voice was very difficult to pin down and changed as much as his identity did. Identity diffusion, however, characterised him to an extraordinary degree. His mood and his thoughts were extraordinarily labile and he often confused fact and fiction. The disconnected thinking and lack of a central core identity were critical for his artistic success, however. He was a very immature personality and retained a child-like view of the world throughout his life. Sellers himself put it very precisely when he revealed:

> I have no personality of my own … I have no concrete image of myself. I look in the mirror and what I see is someone who has never grown up … when I'm doing a role I feel it's the role doing the role … when I finish a picture I feel a horrible loss of identity.

No comedian has ever described the source of their creativity better, the key to which is profound identity diffusion. He was chameleon-like and had a different personality from one day to the next. He tended to take on the personalities of people he met – he was almost like an empty vessel ready to be filled up. Indeed, he was dimly aware of this. There was a hypersensitive quality to his personality too and he was very emotionally labile, easily aroused to temper tantrums and often showed paranoid traits. After the Second World War, before becoming established as a comedic actor, Sellars began to struggle with his identity diffusion and, as noted by his biographer Roger Lewis, he was "a man divided against himself". Lewis also notes that he had no moral sense, no judgement and was never sure how to behave or gauge appropriate courses of action. Psychologically, he was a little boy lost, even as an adult. While on a film set, one way of holding onto his film persona was to eat alone. His life was hallmarked by hyperkinesis and restlessness, never really feeling at home anywhere. Just like the disgraced tycoon Robert Maxwell, he restlessly travelled around the world in search of himself in an effort to deal with all the pain. He used workaholism as an attempt to cure it and indeed as an identity creation mechanism. In terms of possessions, he never knew exactly what he wanted because he did not know himself. Often when he acquired a new possession he got bored with it quickly and disposed of it just as quick. His obsession with buying cars was particularly pronounced; once bored with one model he had to have newer one immediately.

Regarding his work, he had very high personal standards and was equally demanding of other people such as cast and crew. He could become extremely jealous and angry if anyone upstaged him. In fact, he was autocratic, dictatorial and controlling, and people had to obey him instantly. There could be only one voice – his. He was utterly egocentric and self-centred, and oblivious to what others might be suffering. This also found expression in very perverse and sadomasochistic behaviour, and he was much given to domestic violence. Sellars had a sense of not being like other people in some way and, in this regard, Lewis notes his solipsism. He was rather schizotypal in personality, which can overlap somewhat with Asperger syndrome and other personality disorders. Nevertheless, he could "act and convey abstractions like nobody else".

Lewis points out that Sellers had aversions to certain colours and an obsession with omens and oracles. He was often searching for the meaning of life. Like many people with identity diffusion, he was fascinated with mysticism and spiritualism and thought they might answer some questions about who he was. Among his great interests were the occult, mediums, séances, psychics and reincarnation, and he tended to treat astrologers as learned men. He was also extremely superstitious. This lack of reality testing and inability to clearly separate fact from fiction is characteristic of great comedians like Sellers.

At one level Sellars felt himself to be a god and invincible but also had a great deal of death anxiety, like the actor Micheál Mac Liammóir. He was very distressed when the ageing process became evident, which damaged his narcissism. In his life he suffered a great deal of depression. Despite the success and adulation, he was uncertain about himself and his true worth. The description of him as a "Peter Pan" by Lewis is a fitting one and indeed he was a tragicomic figure, as many comedians are. The tragic and the comic are closely allied and central to the comedic trade. Ultimately, Sellars was destroyed by his behaviour and by too much adulation. Adulation is incredibly destructive to people with identity diffusion; they became self-destructive and masochistic, and certainly this applies to Sellers. He was massively overindulged as he got older and once given a Rolls-Royce to read a script, according to Lewis.

It is hardly surprising that people found it hard to know him. It was beyond even his understanding; he did not and could not know himself because of his multiple selves. His whole life was a search for an authentic identity, which he never achieved. Indeed he got some relief from his inner confusion when given an acting part that he could step into and be taken over by.

Social Relationships

There was a pronounced "loner-type" aspect to Sellars' personality. He had a huge number of acquaintances but almost no intimates. The kinds of people attractive to him were outsiders and unusual and odd people, yet he would show a massive lack of empathy towards them as indeed to those all around him. He used people, especially women, and became very promiscuous. Being extremely narcissistic and wanting special dispensation from normal social behaviour, he failed to consider how his behaviour would impact on other people.

There was major anxiety in his close personal relationships and poor social reciprocity. Three of his four marriages ended in divorce and family life was difficult for his three children. For Sellars, family life was repetitive, intolerable and painfully boring. It is hardly surprising that he liked to change wives and female partners for novelty's sake and to relieve boredom. Some of the domestic violence that he engaged in was also to relieve painful boredom. Of course it was also perverse and sadistic. He also failed dismally at the parental role, being a rather cruel and abusive father. Because of the weak and very indistinct boundaries between himself and other people, he lost himself in other people. Some of his aggression in this situation was an effort on his part to find himself. An obituary for his son Michael in the *Daily Telegraph* in 2006 recounted how Michael had painted his father as a "spiteful and neglectful parent" in his own memoirs of the great actor. Michael revealed that his father once disturbed him in the middle of the night to ask: "Do you think your mother and I should get divorced?" The extreme viciousness towards Michael and his other two children was evident when Sellars cut them out of his will for no good reason.

Sellars comes across as one of the nastiest fathers that ever lived. Of course he was also a genius, but he failed as a human being. The best description of Peter Sellers is by himself: "Sometimes he bores me, sometimes he frightens me. Frequently he frightens me. Frequently he bewilders me. Occasionally he astonishes me, and sometimes I think he is mad."

WORK

Sellars appeared in over 60 films, most notably, *Dr Strangelove*, the *Pink Panther* series and *Being There* – and in his lifetime was nominated for an Academy Award three times. As Lewis notes in his epic biography, Sellars' genius was for "creating an atmosphere, vibrating and fluttering between gaiety and sorrow". This ability to mix up gaiety and sadness is critical for the great comedian. The same confusion was part of his mind, where he could merge with a part more than any other comedian. Film work suited his personality far more than stage work. Stage performances, which are inevitably repetitive, were intolerable to him psychologically. He preferred television and films, where there was constant change, and indeed there was a robotic side to him, in that he wanted other actors on the set as "automata". In practice, he was extremely competitive and wanted everyone to treat him with extreme sensitivity, while allowed to be as brutal with other people as he liked. Not surprisingly, he often was very difficult to work with because of his temper tantrums and at times guilty of malingering. He showed his sadism, aggression, and contempt for other workers on the set in this way. Certainly, he behaved in a very thuggish way to many people and was violent and destructive of property.

Peter Sellers died in London on 24 July 1980 from a heart attack, aged 54.

Chapter 24

TONY HANCOCK

Tony Hancock (1924–1968) was a giant among British comedians in the mid-twentieth century. His life story mirrors what the public regards as the typical life story of a comedian – ultimately tragic.

BACKGROUND

Anthony Hancock was born in Birmingham, England on 12 May 1924 and grew up in Bournemouth on the south coast. His father, John, was a shipping clerk, a hotelier and a radio entertainer; he had a tremendous capacity to imitate people and was very funny. His mother, Lucie, also had a keen sense of humour and was a pianist, as Hancock later became. As a boy Hancock lived in his parents' hotel for a period. His father was rather casual about his parenting duties, despite Hancock being temperamentally a very difficult child. In fact, there was a host of childhood issues: he had speech and language difficulties, preservation of sameness, hated change, liked to be by himself, was emotionally labile, found it hard to go to sleep, and was a selective or faddy eater – so much so he contracted rickets due to vitamin D deficiency.

At school Hancock was probably average at best but could hyper-focus on what interested him. He loved films and would watch the same film repeatedly. He always had a great capacity to observe detail, wanting to know about things and what made people tick. At secondary school his untidy appearance did not go unnoticed; in fact, it remained with him for the rest of his life. It made it easy for him to behave as a class clown.

Hancock was a rather lonely boy, who considered becoming a train driver when older. In adolescence, he became oppositional and defiant. The death of his brother in action during the Second World War affected him, and he coped by becoming very active himself. He joined the Royal Air Force (RAF) at the age of 18, where he developed his lifelong taste for alcohol. In a stage performance at this time he was noted to be "like a penguin … one foot pointed to one wing and the other to the opposite wing".[24]

[24] Except where otherwise indicated, quotes in this chapter are from Goodwin (2000).

PERSONALITY

Hancock possessed several artistic traits, such as being finely attuned to music and very good at drawing. He was highly innovative, a novelty-seeker and a sensation-seeker, and not surprisingly impulsive and extremely restless. In terms of language, he was fascinated by words and relished odd sounds and often spoke with a high-pitched voice. He had a lot of aggressive humour and a penetrating gaze, and was also insular, morose and introverted. Hancock chiefly displayed identity diffusion and multiple selves, and indeed self-doubt was never too far away. At heart he was very insecure and had low self-esteem. He was always searching to find his true, authentic identity, which constantly evaded him. It came with a fragmented sense of bodily self, leaving him obsessed with the great philosophical questions such as the meaning of life. His private study of philosophy led to an interest in Spinoza and a love for the writings of Bertrand Russell and H. G. Wells, all of whom had Asperger syndrome (Fitzgerald, 2005; Lyons & Fitzgerald, 2005; Fitzgerald & O'Brien, 2007). In keeping with his identity diffusion, he was fascinated with mysticism and spiritualism, and had odd beliefs, for example a "belief in ghosts; and if not ghosts, then the power of the dead to inhabit and manipulate physical objects". Actor Kenneth Williams remarked that he was "almost mediumistic". All of this is not rare in Asperger syndrome.

Emotionally, he was naive, immature, very controlling and wanted to do everything on his own terms. His work became his total focus, hence he was driven, persistent and a compulsive worker. Being emotionally labile, temper tantrums were not rare with him and he suffered too from performance anxiety and was easily moved to guilt. Hancock was perverse too, which is a trait often necessary for high creativity. He was a poor financial manager and lived in fear of penury. Disloyalty was a trait never too far away and on occasions he would bite the hand that fed him, such as that of his agent, Phyllis Rounce. She described him as a "wonderful, lovable, hideous, vile, hateful, glorious and an idiotic genius". Agents found him as impossible to manage as comedian Spike Milligan.

SOCIAL RELATIONSHIPS

Hancock tended to be suspicious of people, was tacitly defensive and had major empathy deficits. In conversation he was quite abrupt and could recommence a previous conversation without niceties. With his low boredom threshold, he positively disliked the cocktail party circuit. His tendency to use people was quite brazen and gave rise to much conflict. He broke up a creative acting relationship with comedian Sid James and lost a great deal of money as a result. He abandoned scriptwriters in the same way, wanting to prove he could do it all himself, yet he could not. Indeed his treatment and dismissal of colleagues could only be described as sadistic. His disloyalty could be extreme on occasions, for example, when he embarked on an affair with the wife of his friend John Le Mesurier that proved utterly destructive.

Though women tended to mother him, Hancock was rather misogynistic and saw women as inferior to men. The unhealthily close relationship with his mother, like those of Kenneth Williams and Peter Sellers, had a lasting effect on him. Both of his marriages were troubled and ended in divorce, not helped by his alcoholism and depression. He often beat up his first wife Cicely while second wife Freddie was a victim too of his physical violence, once breaking her nose. His wives turned to either alcohol or parasuicide in despair. Hancock also abused drugs, which would finally prove his undoing. His self-destructiveness had an uncanny similarity to that of Peter Sellers, and J. B. Priestley noted rather insightfully:

> He was like a man in a leaky lifeboat, throwing away one pair of oars after another. Most of us are divided men, but in him the lack of any possible integration was appalling. He could be Tony Jekyll in the afternoon and Hyde Hancock at night.

Work

Hancock is best remembered for *Hancock's Half Hour*, which was a successful and long-running BBC radio comedy series, and later television comedy, of the 1950s and 1960s that was written by Ray Galton and Alan Simpson. Actor Richard Briers said that Hancock had a great sense of timing and a "musical ear". Much like a psychoanalyst, Hancock was forever speculating on what made people the way they were and, being such a massive observer of people, he was able to create very good comedy situations. Hancock declared frequently that "comedy was pain, a ceaseless probing for the truth", and while he was decidedly rough on those who worked with him, he was hardest on himself, according to biographer Philip Oakes (1975).

Like Peter Sellers, Hancock found theatre very repetitive. In fact, there is no stage job more difficult than that of the stand-up comedian. He was always in search of novelty and showed tremendous innovation as a television comedian. He had extremely high comic standards, though intimidated by other comics, and felt he had a duty to his audience. For him, there was an ambivalent about fame, but as his fame grew he gained a sense of omnipotence and wanted to be a bigger and bigger star. Ultimately, he could not cope with it and ruined it with alcoholism. "He had the temperament, the ego of a great star. He was a born warrior. Anything – or anyone – which stood between him and his so-far-unimagined goal had to be removed" (Oakes, 1975).

According to the actor Richard Briers, Hancock was a working-class hero, battered by life and bamboozled by his friends. He was self-destructive in a very similar way to comedian Frankie Howerd: going solo, thinking he could do it all by himself, and forcing himself to go back to where it all started. Once he found his comic "winning formula", he wanted to change it in a completely destructive, masochistic way – dismissing the writers and agents who had done so much for him – an "extended act of professional suicide" (Oakes, 1975) – late in his career.

Tony Hancock committed suicide with drugs and alcohol in Sydney, Australia on 24 June 1968, aged 44.

Chapter 25

KENNETH WILLIAMS

Kenneth Williams (1926–1988) was a major British comic actor of the twentieth-century, appearing in numerous *Carry On* films and in radio and television shows. He later became famous on the chat show circuit. During his life he displayed identity diffusion and Asperger syndrome.

BACKGROUND

Kenneth Williams was born in London on 22 February 1926 to Louisa and Charlie Williams. His "outspoken" father, Charlie, was a barber who died in 1962 after taking poison, possibly accidentally.[25] Possessing a naive and immature personality, Williams was clingy towards his mother and retained a close relationship with her all his life. From an early age he was marked as a loner: his parents' most frequent comments about him were "he is up in his room" and "he likes to be on his own" (Williams, 1985). Williams himself confessed: "I was solitary, apart from the odd encounter with my sister's boyfriends" (Williams, 1987). Despite his desire to be alone, he displayed an exhibitionistic side. On this aspect of his character, he wrote: "My exhibitionism concealed a sense of inadequacy. The real self was a vulnerable, quivering thing which I did not want to reveal; showing off, affectation and play-acting I used like a hedgehog uses his spines. The façade was not to be penetrated. My parents respected this privacy" (Williams, 1985).

At school he showed poor progress but was fascinated by poetry. He realised early that he was very good at recitation: "Poetry and performing fused for me. It had nothing to do with careful perusal or imagination … it was instinctive, involuntary and authentic … I was inwardly exultant. I felt like someone had the door of a treasure house. Words would supply the keys to open it" (Williams, 1985). Upon leaving school, given his excellence at drawing, he was apprenticed as a litho draughtsman to a mapmaker, and in 1944 at 18 years of age, he enlisted in the Royal Engineers and served in Bombay. It also gave him an opportunity to perform on stage in the army entertainment services, which furthered his desire to be a performer. After the war he worked as a draughtsman, while pursuing an acting career.

---

[25] Except where otherwise indicated, quotes in this chapter are from Davies (1993).

PERSONALITY

Dyspraxia and sensory integration issues were evident in Williams from an early age. Clearly, he was an autodidact, with wide intellectual interests and a massive memory, as people with Asperger syndrome often have, and similarly engaged in a great deal of self-talk and fantasising. In his diaries, he said that in his fantasising "artistes were heroes and the imagination was king" (Williams, 1985).

Persons with Asperger syndrome often write a great deal (Fitzgerald, 2004), and Williams wrote more than four million words, keeping diaries for almost his entire adolescent and adult life. He was often inconsistent in his writing about people, in keeping with his identity diffusion. Indeed, his diary was almost alive to him and his "mentor"; however, it did not criticise him and was always the same. He also displayed traits of preservation of sameness, which is one of the reasons why he did not pursue a career in America when given the opportunity by Orson Welles. He preferred familiar places and was a "home bird", prompting Welles to remark he was "boring".

Williams had a massively contradictory personality, with identity diffusion and multiple selves. He essentially lacked a solid authentic core and had a very fragile personality, which disintegrated in his final days. It is no surprise that he was interested in the "pessimism of Schopenhauer" and in the novels of Thomas Mann. Given his personality, reading was his antidepressant. In fact, he was an acute critic of fiction and was novelty-seeking.

With his harsh autistic-type (Asperger) superego, he was intensely masochistic and massively self-critical. In fact, he was more critical of himself than his greatest enemy could ever be. He lacerated himself psychologically, though always brutally honest. His controlling nature reached fever pitch at times, to judge by biographer Russell Davies:

> Williams sometimes revealed an uncontrollably demanding personality, issuing insults, corrections and high-pitched protests in a terrible crescendo which might momentarily endanger the playfulness of the game. But if his rage were punctured by a remark he perceived to be witty, he could subside into a comical, even touching, contrition. One knew it was all performance – even if it wasn't, it could be safely taken as one.

Williams was also obsessed with his health and his bowel movements. Control and domination also came to the fore here, especially regarding hygiene matters, as recounted by Davies:

> Many rumours circulated, in and around show business, about his mode of living. The best-known, and most widely corroborated, concerned his reluctance to make his lavatory available to visitors, who were directed to a nearby public convenience instead. At one point it was whispered that he kept his kitchen stove wrapped in cellophane; this was true. Again, Williams did not go out of his way to disguise these obsessive tendencies.

As he got older, fundamental problems in his personality became evident, in particular his self-destructiveness, similar to Tony Hancock, Peter Sellers and W. C. Fields. As far back as 1947 Williams described himself as a "suicidalist", who did not believe in existence at all. Indeed this was a theme that recurred frequently in his diaries. On several occasions he considered putting an end to his suffering – "only to be saved by a failure of nerve, or a realisation that all necessary dispositions had not been made, or by dramatic improvement in circumstances". Davies remarks that the last words of his diary – "Oh, what's the bloody point?" suggest depths of exhaustion and resignation hitherto unexperienced. The "hoard" of barbiturates washed down with alcohol would be his undoing, though it was not certain that he intended to kill himself.

Social Relationships

Williams had a massive fear of intimacy and felt guilty about not making greater efforts to mix socially. Life in the military services during the Second World War was difficult for him and he was "appalled by the subsequent invasion of privacy" (Williams, 1985). His poor behaviour in social relationships was to a considerable extent innate and not deliberate. Drinking even a small amount of alcohol could make him obnoxious, however. Hence people labelled him as "nasty" and very difficult to get on with. With the exception of Maggie Smith and Siobhán McKenna, he clashed with many an actress and indeed looked down on them as inferior and inexperienced compared to himself. He got on far better with children, as is common with persons with Asperger syndrome. That said, his work groups, such as the cast of the *Carry On* films, were really his "family". His relationship with his mother was almost like that of a married couple and her ageing troubled him greatly. Indeed the likely loss of her and the prospect of loneliness played a part in exacerbating his problems.

Williams was homosexual, but his sexuality had a "tortured history" and he proclaimed his celibacy, mindful that homosexual relations were a crime given the legal climate of the time. In any event, he had major difficulties in reciprocal relationships and thus incapable of a long-term partnership with men. His fear of intimacy was also shown by his not indulging in full sexual relations and choosing masturbation as a safer option for his sexual outlet. In his diaries he reveals that his masturbatory fantasies were "sadomasochistic". He was extremely narcissistic, and Davies points out that "the synonym for masturbation is self-love", whereby he was also "captivated by his own image in the mirror".

Work

One might think that it was contradictory for an intellectual such as Williams to be involved with what was almost slapstick humour. Indeed it was contradictory, but then Tony Hancock was the very same. Williams rose to national fame in Britain during the 1960s and 1970s with his *Carry On* films that revelled in double entendre humour. His manner of speaking and facial expressions were unique and quite celebrated. His autistic/Asperger-type language was fascinating, often remarked upon and very important to his career. He was told that "your consonants are overdone and the vowels are too clipped", while theatrical agent Peter Eade advised him that "there is a great danger in such mannered speech … the form gets in the way of the content, you see. The audience stop listening to what is being said and starts thinking about how it's being said. You will have to watch it" (Williams, 1985). In an early film, his voice was dubbed because it was unsatisfactory; however, that situation did not last long, as his voice became more and more iconic: it "suggested unreconciled duality, swooping as it did, often within a single phrase, from a sort of professorial waffle, patronising and/or vain, to an acidulous, jeering Cockney".

In the chat show appearances that were the starring roles of his late middle age, he became his own material. According to Davies, his foibles were part of what he had to sell; so he was as candid as the airwaves allowed about "his solitariness, his celibacy, and his bouts of despair, though the briskness required of the entertainment format obliged him to make light of his problems".

He died on 15 April 1988, apparently of a drug overdose, aged 62. His diary revealed that he was calm on the day, which is not uncommon in those who have completed their plan for suicide. Comedic talent comes at a very heavy price.

Chapter 26

W. C. Fields

W. C. Fields (1880–1946) was a colossus in the comedy hall of fame, best known for the 1941 comic masterpiece *Never Give a Sucker an Even Break.* He possessed all the positive and negative traits the public attributes to comedians: there were tremendous high and lows in his life, which was turbulent, conflicted and often depressing. He had the sadomasochism common in great comedians as well as having Asperger syndrome and attention deficit hyperactivity disorder. The genes for these disorders overlap with the genes for creativity and most likely for comedy.

Background

W. C. Fields was born William Claude Dukenfield in Darby, Pennsylvania on 29 January 1880. Described as having "low cunning",[26] his mother Kate stole, abused alcohol and was stingy with money. When she died she had "$40,000 in her accordion". (This has echoes of Robert Hooke, the great scientist with Asperger syndrome, who had a vast sum of money in his room upon his death.) Kate was a woman who bent the rules, whom Fields saw as "ineffectual and Scottish", by which he meant that she was stupid and alcoholic. His father, James, of English heritage, was similarly an alcoholic in addition to being novelty-seeking and sensation-seeking – highly temperamental, oppositional and defiant, with frequent temper bouts. Like his son, he was emotionally labile and poisoned the family atmosphere with his aggression. He was once dismissed from his job for stealing. Fields hated his father for many reasons, one of which was the severe corporal punishment he administered. It is not uncommon for two disturbed, chaotic parents – as here – to produce a genius, and indeed Fields had a combination of his parents' traits.

As a boy, Fields identified with "Huck Finn" from *The Adventures of Huckleberry Finn.* (Interestingly, Twain's fictional character shows traits of attention deficit hyperactivity disorder and is oppositional and defiant). Although highly intelligent, Fields was disruptive at school and went from oppositional defiant disorder to conduct disorder and truanting. Not surprisingly given these conditions and attention deficit hyperactivity disorder, he found

---

[26] Except where otherwise indicated, quotes in this chapter are from Curtis (2004).

school extremely boring and performed poorly. From the age of nine years he began running away from home, with episodes of sleeping rough and minor theft.

His first fascination, at the age of 15, was with juggling and he spent endless hours practising, showing enormous persistence and determination in learning juggling tricks. He was a perfectionist, hyper-focused on this area, and learned quickly on the street from people he met. He set himself extremely high standards and there was no doubt as to his talent. He had tremendous fine motor skills, employed in both juggling and stealing, whereas clumsiness is more often associated with Asperger syndrome. From fairground juggler he moved on to vaudeville and thus began the long arduous struggle to stardom.

PERSONALITY

Fields was a massive observer of detail, especially society, and very good at drawing. From his earliest years he was an autodidact, with a remarkable capacity to learn by experience on the stage, i.e., from observing what worked and indeed what "mistakes" should be continued because of the effect on the audience. He had a "famously bad memory", which is typical of those with ADHD. Furthermore, a lifelong fascination with language and words and an avid reader gave rise to huge improvisational powers and tremendous capacity to play with words.

Fields was also a novelty-seeker and a sensation-seeker with poor impulse control. He grew bored and impatient easily and was constantly on the go – in fact, he was a wanderer and toured much of the world. Like many people with ADHD, he rose late in the day and was best at night.

Odd tones of voice are common in persons with Asperger syndrome, and Fields was no exception. When not performing he had a rather monotonous voice or an "English accent" and it was said that his voice had the range and distinction of an "antique pipe organ". Biographer James Curtis notes that his private speech was "devoid of volume and flourishes, which made him one of the most imitated of personalities". This suggests that there were some pragmatic language difficulties, which of course he turned to his benefit. He showed some evidence of sensory problems, as demonstrated by his excessive reaction to touch, and being upset by noise.

Fields showed identity diffusion, lacked a core sense of self, and indeed had multiple selves. His identity diffusion is highlighted in his own comment that he "wanted to be a definite personality". Had he achieved this, it is highly doubtful that he would have been a comedian. In describing Fields' personality, John Cleese remarked he was "generous yet stingy and both a dream and a nightmare to work with … [he] could be warm or distant". This reflects his multiple façades. It was not uncommon for him to move between fact and fiction in conversation and sometimes he made not much distinction between them. He even had a capacity to tell lies when it suited him. Not surprisingly, people found him enigmatic and baffling – it was hard to know just what made him tick. There was also a schizoid element in his personality, whereby he "had the courage to cast himself as the decidedly unfavourable light of a bully and a con-man", which was his masochistic side.

Fields was always persistent, stubborn and difficult. Never satisfied with his act, he always wanted to change and improve it. Given his low self-esteem, he needed applause to feel any form of contentment and hence was unforgiving and hypersensitive to rejection and failure. He was a highly conflicted person, with massive emotional lability and poor ego control. Of course, this caused huge problems in interpersonal relationships but was vital for his work on the stage. Being such a moody individual, he often got depressed. There was a thuggish element to him too in the extent to which he was controlling and unempathic. In fact, he often showed a murderous rage. On one occasion he beat a man within an inch of his life because he made a "rude comment" on the street. For such violent altercations he found himself behind bars a few times. There was also evidence of paranoid tendencies, which can occur in those with Asperger syndrome. Certainly, he could be quite litigious, especially about people plagiarising him. Fields has been described as "solipsistic" – he was undoubtedly obsessed with his own view and extremely egocentric and somewhat narcissistic. His entry in *Chambers Biographical Dictionary* (1990) states that "a bulbous nose and gravelly voice enhanced his creation of a bibulous, child-hating misanthrope, continually at odds with the world, an image that was said to be not unlike his own personality". There were also rather perverse and sadomasochistic elements to his character. Indeed, he alternated between sadism and masochism. In the end he was extremely self-destructive and masochistic, abusing alcohol, which ultimately killed him.

Social Relationships

During adolescence Fields was a timid outsider, a disconnected loner, who was awkward around girls. In his early vaudeville days he teamed up with a chorus girl, Harriet Hughes, of Irish extraction, and married her. There was a huge amount of disharmony in the marriage, which produced one son Claude. Harriet found Fields temperamental and restless, while he tended to be morbidly jealous of her. Indeed his wife described him as a bully and separated from him several years later. He had not always been faithful to his wife and it was said that he "changed women every seven years". In his later years, he lived with Carlotta Monti, who bore him a son out of wedlock. Fields certainly used women, not uncommon with great artists, and moved on to new relationships out of boredom and a desire for novelty. As a parent, Fields failed in his duties to his offspring, forcing Claude to "earn his way through school". His miserly side was also demonstrated in his will, in which he left one of his sons a "single dollar". Like many people of genius, children were just a nuisance. They held little or no interest for him, which is another element of his lack of empathy.

Work

Field's work ranged from vaudeville and Broadway musical comedies to silent film, sound films and radio broadcasts. He began quite an extensive film-making career with director D. W. Griffith, enjoying a highly successful period in silent movies. He adapted well to the talking movies, but had huge dips in his career, like many comedians. He is best remembered for *The Bank Dick*, *The Man on the Flying Trapeze*, and *Never Give a Sucker an Even Break*.

W. C. Fields died in California on Christmas Day 1946, at the age of 66.

Chapter 27

SPIKE MILLIGAN

Terence "Spike" Milligan (1918–2002) was one of the great comedians of the twentieth century. (My personal contact with him was in a queue in a Dublin Airport café where he asked for "low-fat sugar".) He was an extraordinarily multifaceted figure. Biographer Norma Farnes described him as "lovable, hateful, endearing, despicable, loyal, traitorous, challenging, sometimes all of these things in a single day, but always original and never boring".[27] This was partly the key to his success as a comic.

BACKGROUND

Terence Alan Milligan was born in Ahmednagar, India on 16 April 1918. He had artistic inputs from both sides of his autodidactic family. His English mother, Florence, was musical and artistic, while his Irish father, Leo, was an army captain and often absent, though musical and artistic as well. Leo in fact was a semi-professional actor, obsessed with cowboys (Carpenter, 2003), who had a massive imagination and was stubborn and persistent. Milligan was a temperamental, difficult child, who, according to his father, "never stopped bloody screaming" as a baby. Milligan was educated in India and Rangoon and excelled at the trumpet, which he played professionally before being drafted into the Royal Artillery during the Second World War.

PERSONALITY

In some ways Milligan was a one-off, completely unique and enigmatic. He had massive imagination and capacity for improvisation, augmented by novelty-seeking and sensation-seeking. He hyper-focused on very narrow interests and was a workaholic and, with his autodidactic genes, taught himself how to play guitar, drums and trumpet. Not surprisingly he was hyperactive and talked on the telephone endlessly.

The *Daily Mail* described Milligan as a "Jekyll and Hyde personality", while others depicted him as impossible, fascinating, original, insensitive, sensitive, hypersensitive,

---

[27] Except where otherwise indicated, quotes in this chapter are from Farnes (2004).

controlling and dominating. He was undeniably childlike, but this immaturity was critical to his success. It allowed him to see life through the eyes of a child to the end of his life. He drifted between fact and fiction in his conversation, often mixing the two up. In fact, he was a great liar. Carpenter (2003) notes that he "was virtually incapable of thinking that he might possibly be in the wrong". Milligan was certainly a contradictory figure, who lived his life "according to Victorian values".

Throughout his life, he had sensory integration issues, including being highly sensitive to noise and having low sensitivity to temperature, which are not uncommon in highly creative people. His obsessive–compulsive traits were well documented. For example, when flying, he had to have a certain seat in the first class section of the aircraft and insisted on taking along "his emergency survival kit", which consisted of a packet of Elastoplast, penknife and "not one but two watches". Like many creative minds, he was a poor financial manager.

Milligan had volcanic emotions and, indeed, engaged in volcanic emotional storms. His mood disorder was his primary problem – or at least what caused him the most difficulty. He had major mood swings, sometimes very rapid, for which he was treated in hospital. He also suffered a great deal from insomnia and post-traumatic stress disorder from his time in combat during the Second World War. To cope with his psychic conflict and turmoil he would lock himself away for periods. In terms of medication, he self-medicated, like many artists, and used uppers, downers and mood stabilisers in addition to abusing alcohol. His depressive illness, for which he received electroconvulsive therapy, led to him writing a book with psychiatrist Anthony Clare entitled *Depression and How to Survive It*. His advice was to "remember life is one long Hell" but "don't let the bastards grind you down". He also rejected the stereotype of "it's all been worth it for my art" (Carpenter, 2003). There also existed a paranoid side to his personality, as can occur with manic-depressive illness and creativity. However, it was his work that saved him and kept him from completing suicide.

Social Relationships

Milligan had somewhat poor life management skills and had to be looked after. Hence, he was good at getting people to do this for him, in particular women. In his relationships with women, Milligan was rather promiscuous: he married three times and had numerous affairs. Fidelity in marriage was certainly not one of his traits and marriage for him was highly turbulent and conflictual. In essence, he had a kind of "harem", whose members knew each other and tolerated it, which is quite common in men of genius, as indeed with tribal leaders. In his dealings with people, Milligan could be unpredictable: unempathic or "brutal" or generous. On the other hand, he found it very easy to empathise with children, of which he had six from his marriages and various affairs.

Work

Milligan was fascinated by eccentricities – of course he was highly eccentric himself – and loved practical jokes. He famously worked with Peter Sellers and others on the BBC radio comedy *The Goon Show*, as creator and main writer, which brought him to national prominence. He was also a noted writer and poet, famous for his memoirs, Adolf Hitler: My Part in His Downfall. Being an “idealist”, he was a campaigner for good causes and occasionally a crank letter writer, who used to make anti-Semitic remarks, which showed a perverse side of his personality. In effect, Milligan was an archetypical comic genius, whose work lives on. He had many of the traits associated with the other creative people in this book.

Spike Milligan died at his home in East Sussex on 27 February 2002, at the age of 83.

Chapter 28

JIMMY O'DEA

Jimmy O'Dea (1899–1965) was one of Ireland's greatest comedians. He was naturally talented and also a magnificent stage actor.

BACKGROUND

James Augustine O'Dea was born on 26 April 1899 in the Liberties area of Dublin, near where Jonathan Swift had been Dean of St Patrick's Cathedral. His mother owned a toyshop and his father was an ironmonger. He served mass at the local John's Lane Catholic Church and attended Belvedere College. Having served an apprenticeship in Scotland, he became an optician initially and opened a practice in Dublin. When he told his father about his theatrical ambitions, his father replied: "I would rather see you in your coffin first".[28]

PERSONALITY

O'Dea was shy but perfectionistic, and naïve and immature in personality. He retained a child-like view of the world as he grew up. During the Irish Civil War, as a young man, he sided with the Republicans who opposed the new Free State government. In fact, O'Dea could be quite dictatorial and may explain why he sided with such a dictatorial politician as Éamonn de Valera. O'Dea lived for comedy and had no interest in money as such. However, he was contradictory in relation to money to, and once lost a job in England because he looked for too much. He was also highly ritualistic in his lifestyle, starting each morning with a visit to the bookies. There was also an element of preservation of sameness in that he always took up the same position in the pub he frequented, Neary's in Dublin, at each visit.

[28] Except where otherwise indicated, quotes in this chapter are from Ryan (1990).

SOCIAL RELATIONSHIPS

There was a large "loner" component to O'Dea's personality, whereby he liked long solitary walks. Biographer Philip Ryan notes that many comedians tend to allow their private lives to become extensions of their stage performance. Not so, with Jimmy, who was quietly married. He liked to be with a few regular friends in the pub and was a massive observer of the social environment, being more a listener than a talker, unlike many comedians who like to be the centre of attention. He showed no empathy deficits as such and was rather sympathetic to those in poverty and did a huge amount of charity work.

WORK

O'Dea was a massive talent, even coming close to Charlie Chaplin: "Jimmy had a knack of turning laughter into tears and many compared him in that respect to Chaplin". Had O'Dea been more adventurous he could have had a bigger international career, but he was happiest touring Ireland and England. He toured endlessly around these regions and used to enjoy meeting actors from other companies at Crewe station, a rail transport hub in England. With extremely high personal standards, he was very controlling and dominating in his work, and a "cranky producer", according to the actor/director Séamus De Búrca. He was often quite self-righteous. His word was the law and he had an eagle eye as far as the development of a production was concerned.

He worked with many of the greats of Irish comedy, including Maureen Potter, Cyril Cusack, Vernon Hayden and Noel Purcell, and had a very large following. He thought deeply about comedy and was something of an intellectual where it was concerned. Comedy for him had to be real, authentic, believable. He once confessed: "You cannot make up comedy. You must live it. It must be real. It must be based on real people and real situations – a slice of life." Like Tony Hancock and Kenneth Williams, he was a superb radio performer, but also performed quite a lot on television towards the end of his life.

Despite his brilliance on radio, his real "comedy home" was on a theatre stage. There he lived more intensely than anywhere else. He was extremely sensitive to the feedback from the audience, whereas other actors worked within themselves, paying little attention to the audience: "Jimmy favoured some thought and meaning or purpose behind his comedy rather than the mere empty routine of cracking jokes."

His delight in language and verbal dexterity made him a perfect comedian. The theatre critic of *The Crystal* stated: "It is hard to believe that Jimmy O'Dea's gift for nonsense and laughter-making absurdity would not make a fortune abroad. His sense of fun is as spontaneous as a six-year-old child's, and he has something of a child's pathos, as those who have been moved by his sobs and tears know well."

Actor Noel Purcell declared that, with the exception of Laurence Olivier, there was never English spoken like Jimmy spoke it: "each word was given its full value in enunciation and clarity". This can certainly happen in persons with Asperger syndrome. "Jimmy can press into one glance three minutes of legitimate acting to say nothing of ten lines of dialogue."

Jimmy O'Dea died in Dublin on 7 January 1965, aged 65.

PART II: DIRECTORS

Chapter 29

CECIL B. DEMILLE

Cecil B. DeMille (1881–1959) was one of the great directors of the cinema, famous for biblical epics, such as *Samson and Delilah* and *The Ten Commandments,* and the circus drama, *The Greatest Show on Earth*. He was an enigmatic, contradictory figure, who displayed a perverse sexuality. There is evidence to show that he had Asperger syndrome.

BACKGROUND

DeMille was born on 12 August 1881 in Ashfield, Massachusetts, into a theatrical family. His mother and father were playwrights and teachers. His mother, Beatrice, had a rather "dramatic" personality and as a teacher was highly regimented and ritualistic. She was controlling, dominating and obsessional in her behaviour. She described playwriting as "a germ", which was ineradicable, contagious and hereditary.[29] His father, Henry, in appearance "effete looking" and short-sighted, was moralistic and perfectionistic – he was also a lay reader in the Episcopal Church. When DeMille was 12 years of age his father died of typhoid and his younger sister, Agnes, died two years later. Like his father, DeMille too was obsessional and perfectionistic. An imaginative child, he often went for long walks in the woods and, given the family theatrical tradition, he too became an actor.

PERSONALITY

DeMille, as a person, was highly impatient, and "a doer, not a talker". Indeed those with Asperger syndrome sometimes use limited talk in their daily lives. Given that he was hyperkinetic, a workaholic, and had massive energy, he required very little sleep. In essence, he was a sensation-seeker, a novelty-seeker, daring to become a pilot and pioneer in aviation. Not surprisingly, he had a lifelong fascination for the circus and ultimately made a film about it.

DeMille was a man who mixed fact and fiction, which is highly important in the creative domain. He was tremendously imaginative and immature in some aspects of his personality

[29] Except where otherwise indicated, quotes in this chapter are from Louvish (2008).

all his life, and retained this child-like view of things. This, paradoxically, is also the secret of success. And like many great creators he liked to mythologise himself and claim that he developed his talent without outside influences. He regarded himself as a pioneer and as a man of originality: "Like any mortal, Cecil DeMille excelled either in what he knew or in those imagined realms that best expressed his inner muse or demons." Of course, a confusion of fact and fiction is the key to the great artist.

In fact, he was a Jekyll and Hyde figure, often described as "imperious", and certainly control and domination were critical to him. The Jesuit writer Daniel A. Lord noted that:

> [He was] a strange and fascinating blend of absolute monarch and charming gentleman, of excellent host and exacting taskmaster, of ruthless drive on the set and a complete letdown the moment that the day's shooting had come to an end; a renaissance prince who had the instincts of a Barnum and a magnified Belasco.

Gloria Swanson, one of his most famous actresses, described him as "almighty God", who wanted everything to be in its proper place. He was also described as an "emperor" and as "the monarch of all he surveyed". The director shared some traits with filmmaker William Hearst, who built his own castle on a hill. DeMille had an isolated ranch in California where he was complete master and expected people to fit into his routines. The ranch contained a "mint collection of European erotica", and everyone had to dress up as he desired. There was an element of preservation of sameness about his own clothing. His repetitive dress was "field boots and riding breeches and coat, a French, narrow-wale corduroy". The kind of control he exerted certainly has echoes of Hearst. DeMille's universe was essentially a "separate island, adrift from the main".

Clearly, DeMille had identity diffusion and multiple selves. One was the promiscuous man; another the actor, while another again was the man who made films about stories from the Bible. Switching from one self to another was highly creative and innovative. It was impossible then to pigeonhole him as this kind or that kind of director.

Throughout his life, he was a great collector, if not a hoarder, and "kept voluminous paperwork". However, it was all carefully ordered and ritualistic. The writer Mayme Peak stated that DeMille's methodical neatness and thoroughness are indicated "by the neat piles of carefully assorted mail, reference books with markers, his open engagement calendar".

DeMille was not above humiliating people in public, especially if they voiced any criticism. Those who fell foul of him included his niece Agnes de Mille: "Cecil's pronouncements were given with total certainty [and] with less hesitancy than I have ever heard from professors, critics, or historians … Differing views were unthought-of at his table" (de Mille, 1973). No one wanted to be on the receiving end of a major rant from him, she wrote, and he could be "as unpleasant in his wrath as he was supportive to those who obeyed him." In fact, DeMille could never resist a grand gesture, "on or off screen".

With his heritage steeped in biblical study, he engaged in a search for "spiritual meaning" and showed "extreme eccentricity" throughout his life. Always civic-minded, he took an interest in politics and supported the Republican Party. His political journey brought him "from soft left to hard right, becoming the scourge of left-wing unions and the communist menace". During his time as host of the Lux Radio Theatre, the radio union demanded a one-dollar assessment for political activity from each member. He refused and it spawned his hostility to unions, like Walt Disney. He said "we have in America a weapon as powerful as the Gestapo or the Soviet Secret Police. That weapon is the closed union shop controlling the right to work." He also got caught up in the anti-communist sweep through Hollywood. His film *This Day and Age* was banned in The Netherlands because of strong fascist tendencies. Indeed he had double standards in relation to poverty and was in trouble with the Inland Revenue over back taxes.

Social Relationships

Agnes de Mille stated that her uncle did not socialise with the glitterati but kept absolutely to his own circles, priding himself on being a "profound biblical scholar". It is very common to have a perverse personality with an external false image at the same time. This was the major split in his personality. DeMille married a woman eight years older than himself, Constance Adams; they had one biological child and three adopted children. Within his family he was totally controlling and dominating, if somewhat sadistic. After the wedding he became promiscuous and it was said that he had a "harem" of mistresses. Clearly, he was a user of men and women, and had a perverse sexual identity.

In his depiction of women DeMille show a lack of empathy. He declared that "a really good woman … is the broad, wise, pure, understanding woman, who with every right weapon she can grasp tries to kill the beast in man … helping him to overcome the Adam inheritance of lust and dust that eventually lead to ruin". There is no sense of empathy for the woman here, and no sense of her needs. The ideal woman will allow herself to be abused and be masochistic. Man has to be allowed to do what he wants to do with other women and the wife has to cater for every whim. The idea of intimacy with a woman, the idea of respect for a woman and the idea of marital reciprocity were completely unknown to him. His idea of a human relationship was a sadomasochistic one, which is often reflected in his films. The religious themes were a cover for his voyeurism and sadism, but were also a split-off side of his personality.

Work

DeMille was highly visual and this was seen in his "expressive use of light and shadow", which became one of his trademarks. He is credited with inventing several film stereotypes: "the swaggering director, with his desert puttees and rough-hewn casual get-up, the snapping generalissimo with his megaphone and his dedicated chair-boy, who always has the boss's chair ready for him to sit on wherever and whenever, without looking around." And, as mentioned, his films comprised the arena on which he played and replayed his ideas, emotions, and peculiarities in matters of male and female sexuality and mores, according to biographer Simon Louvish.

At all times DeMille was highly innovative and a quick learner. He always wanted to make better pictures and was constantly setting the bar higher and pushing his body to the limit. In some ways he was quite "superegoish", i.e., a harsh self-critic. In effect, he became a physical machine, as noted by Jeanette Meehan: "Emotionally he becomes a slave driver for a vast army of workers. He doesn't request, he demands absolute and unfailing efficiency from every member of his staff … no stone within a mile of him gathers any moss." The public address system was used so he could rant and shout. For him "each extra must be an actor" and he would focus in on individuals in crowd scenes. He was described as the great field marshal of Hollywood, and not surprisingly was a great collector of pistols and the like. His special attention to extras on a film was highly original. In his major epic *The Ten Commandments*, he used his signature method of controlling a crowd by setting myriad individual tasks for the extras to carry out, "whether it is to rein in a goat, collect a child's doll, pull a donkey, witness a new birth in a cart, haul bundles".

In his work, as in family matters, he was very autocratic, controlling, and domineering. He was *the* boss. He once declared "I am the only one who gets mad on a DeMille picture". He certainly did not talk to his actors about "motivation"; like Hitchcock, he more interested in the structure of the film and had a fascination for detail, of which he was a great observer. Indeed Asperger-type directors have little interest in motivation.

For all his eccentricities and controlling nature, he nonetheless was surrounded by loyal workers who stayed with him for very long periods. He often browbeat and scolded his writers. One of his mistresses, Jeanie Macpherson, was an excellent writer and his primary mistress, remaining close to him until her death in 1946. She too was a rather masochistic figure who complemented his sadism. Dominance–submission partnerships were common motifs in his films and fitted his sadomasochism. He loved to watch men being whipped, for example in *The Ten Commandments*. Indeed he got a great deal of perverse sexual satisfaction from voyeurism. All his biblical epics reflect this to lesser or greater degrees. Louvish notes that elements of "vulgarity, sexuality, lewdness, piety, spectacle, violent action, sadistic whipping, the presentation of wild animals and divine miracles" are present in *Samson and Delilah*. DeMille was into "the parabola of the sadistic lash, as a great chief might weigh the condiments for one of his sauces".

Similarly, his picture, *The Godless Girl*, contained a great deal of sadism. It was "sensationalist, unusually brutal in places and with moments of high melodrama tinged with religious hysteria … among his strangest and arguably most DeMillean films". It is hardly surprising that he was attracted to the Emperor Nero. The producer Jesse Lasky stated that his fetishes were a passionate hatred of "red nail polish on actresses" and a penchant for small, well-shaped feet.

In an age of image and consumerism, DeMille films often set trends in fashion and design. His audiences could see the close attention paid to every aspect of set design, decorations, props, furniture, and costumes, "which not only mirrored the new fashions but often anticipated them". There were repetitive themes in his work, some of which were moral issues, such as a conflict between spiritual values and commercialisation. One of his big themes was reversal of fortune, while some of his films are "dream-like", with Freudian elements. He was also very much into "daydream images" and people noticed its novelty at the time. Clearly, he confused fact and fiction to an enormous degree and it contributed to his legacy: "The fantastic, the outlandish, and often the bizarre would be major tools in his arsenal, his box of cinematic tricks that would continue to dazzle and confuse those who thought they could pin DeMille down." This is further evidence of his identity diffusion.

DeMille was highly conscious of his legacy and of how history would judge him. He wrote that "a man is no better than what he leaves behind him". He certainly was a complex figure, being "a savant, sinner, malcontent and artist". Many, like Louvish, have remarked that in some ways he was a nineteenth-century figure, and indeed this is often said of persons with Asperger syndrome.

Cecil B. DeMille died in California on 21 January 1959, aged 77.

Chapter 30

CONSTANTIN STANISLAVSKI

Constantin Stanislavski (1863–1938) was a Russian actor, director and theoretician of acting. His ideas on the process of acting continue to be influential to this day. Lee Strasberg stated that the work of Stanislavski and his disciples "changed not only my life, but that of the entire 20th-century theatre. Just as our understanding of human behaviour and modern physics is still turning on the revelations of Freud and Einstein, so our contemporary knowledge of the actor's craft is still heavily indebted to Stanislavski's 100-year-old discoveries."[30] I believe that he had Asperger syndrome.

BACKGROUND

Stanislavski was born Constantin Sergeyevich Alexeyev on 17 January 1863 to a wealthy family. ("Stanislavski" was the stage name he adopted.) His father, Sergei, a rich industrialist, was paternalistic and engaged in good works for people, while his mother, Elisaveta, was quite strict. She was against him becoming an actor, then deemed a very inferior occupation in society. She also was rather hypochondriacal and held odd ideas; for example, that the fumes of horse manure were beneficial to human health. However, odd ideas are not rare in mothers of great creators; take, for example, Andy Warhol. Stanislavski was initially taught at home and as a child suffered much ill-health: he had difficulty supporting his head and had weak muscle tone. In fact, such physical symptoms are common in persons with Asperger syndrome.

He also had speech problems as a child, particularly with the sounds "l" and "r". When he eventually attended school as a boy, he hated rote learning and was bored; it is hardly surprising then that he showed poor school performance and failed his exams; in fact, his academic failure haunted him all his life. His schooling difficulties were further compounded by his persistent and stubborn nature and wanting to do his own thing in the most oppositional and defiant way.

His family was intrigued by the stage and could afford to create a theatre in their own home. This gave the adolescent Stanislavski the much-needed opportunity to indulge his love of theatre. When the time came he was delighted to get away from school and went into the

---

[30] Except where otherwise indicated, quotes in this chapter are from Benedetti (1990).

family business and also began his preoccupation with the theatre, with which he was soon obsessed. The idea of actors spending hours at the theatre getting into a part captivated him in particular. Even in his early life Stanislavski kept a notebook to "analyse his performance". Notebooks became his companions for the rest of his life and indeed persons with Asperger's syndrome are fascinated by them.

Even at the age of 14, he was highly self-critical and a perfectionist, and could analyse the technique of a leading character actor. Like Cecil B. DeMille, Stanislavski loved the circus and was fascinated by colour, as is often the case with persons with Asperger syndrome. Music was another of his passions and he had a deep love for opera all his life.

There was also a narcissistic element to his character, in that he felt it was tremendously important for him to leave his mark for posterity and on Russian society, given his abundant talents. He once declared: "I have a duty to do something for the theatre … my name must go down in history."

PERSONALITY

Stanislavski was naturally a shy person and could be withdrawn on occasions. Like many creative geniuses, he had identity diffusion and a divided sense of self: "He needed the protection of another individual's identity and the mask of make-up". As a person, it was said that he was "never good at playing himself". Referring to his acting days in his earlier life, he once confessed that when deprived of the typical characteristics of a role he felt "completely naked on stage" and that it was pure embarrassment for him to stand in front of an audience as himself, "so shamelessly exposed". Nevertheless, in his young days he had tremendous potential as a character actor. He researched his parts in great detail and, if they related to some aspect of contemporary life, he got close to it to understand what it was like to inhabit the situation. He essentially engaged in a search for "theatrical truth", which he saw as a moral issue.

He once said that an actor should always look for the opposite traits of a person. In so doing, Stanislavski was always trying to look for the evil in the good. This was a deep psychological insight, because positive and negative traits always go together. Despite his knowledge, he had difficulty in truly portraying a part on stage himself and was a rather superficial performer. He was well aware of the uniqueness of the actor, and said that they have to be "a little different. That is their charm and their misfortune". This again was a profound observation, and indeed Stanislavski was a massive observer of society.

Throughout his life he was an autodidact and a novelty-seeker, interested in originality and in new theatrical ideas right to the very end. He undoubtedly was a genius and a creative force, but also a workaholic who constantly worked himself to the edge of nervous breakdown. Stanislavski was obsessed with detail and rehearsed endlessly. His high standards were legendary – if somewhat Aspergerish – and he was a rather puritanical figure in this regard, who smoked excessively but did not take alcohol.

It is hardly surprising that he suffered episodes of depression. However, work was his antidepressant in effect. He said "spiritual happiness is only given to a chosen few. They listen intently to the minute rustling of a growing blade of grass and turn their eyes on the mystical contours of worlds unknown".

Like many people with Asperger syndrome, Stanislavski was naive in relation to politics, especially the Russian Revolution and its aftermath. Lenin, before he died, was quite interested in Stanislavski's work and his plays. Stanislavski remained highly regarded even during Stalin's time and because he was naive, it was easy for Stalin and the communists to take advantage of him. Eventually, he wanted a pared-down lifestyle where nothing interfered with his theatrical work on behalf of the audience. This is very similar to the Asperger lifestyle that Ludwig Wittgenstein also led (Fitzgerald, 2004). Autobiography was extremely difficult for him, given his identity diffusion, and he was resistant to it, as many with Asperger syndrome are. Nevertheless, he did write *My Life in Art*, and also a book called *Work on Oneself: A Pupil's Notes*.

Social Relationships

Stanislavski was naturally a shy person and could be withdrawn on occasions. As a child he had just one close friend – again, this is typical of Asperger syndrome. He did not relate well to people his own age and later in life never had a friend who was his contemporary. In 1889, in his mid-twenties, he married the actress Maria Liliana. After marriage he followed his own interests and desires and was usually absent from his wife. This brought considerable stress and strain on her, and was typical autistic-type behaviour, like that seen in Chekov. The marriage produced three children, the first of whom died as a baby.

Stanislavski had a very strong autistic superego, and was obsessed with the truth. According to Benedetti, he was "normally reticent in all personal matters". He refused to have a sexual relationship with Isadora Duncan, even though she desired it greatly, preferring instead to keep the relationship on a professional footing. In fact, he forged excellent working relationships with certain individuals, most notably the playwright Vladimir Nemirovich-Danchenko, who co-founded with him the Moscow Art Theatre in 1989. His first meeting with Nemirovich-Danchenko was like that between Freud and Jung, kindred spirits, and went on for 18 hours. They needed each other and enhanced each other's work. Nemirovich-Danchenko was better at organising matters and running a theatre: hence the practical aspects of the theatre were left to him. He found Stanislavski interpersonally clumsy, immature, extremely stubborn, determined and difficult. An immature or child-like view of the world is critical for the great artist. Likewise, Stanislavski, worked with Anton Chekhov, and staged a number of his plays, including *The Seagull*, *Uncle Vanya* and *The Three Sisters*. This was a hugely important relationship to him and he was extremely upset when Chekhov died.

Work

Despite his early acting career, Stanislavski is best-known as a theatre director and acting theoretician. His style of acting became known as the Stanislavski method, or simply "method acting". He became the preeminent theatre director in Russia, even during Stalin's time, and also had massive impact abroad, for example, on Max Reinhardt's theatre work in Vienna.

In 1885, he set out 13 aspects of acting that needed to be considered, ranging from the temperament of the role to the outward appearance of the role, as well as the author's intention, the physiological aspect of the role, the psychic aspect of the role, and so forth. He developed a systematic "grammar of acting" and emphasised improvisation and stimulating the actor's imagination. This essentially involved expanding the script. Persons with Asperger syndrome are massive systematisers and therefore it is not surprising that Stanislavski developed such a complex system.

Living a part was Stanislavski's major concern: "It seemed to him that the test of the truth of characterisation was the ability to maintain it in real life." Even at the age of 22, he had spent hours in front of a mirror practising a part, not unlike Henry Irving. For him, Shakespeare was "simple" and understandable and should not be overanalysed. He claimed that excessive analysis destroys Shakespeare's plays and makes them only a dry academic work. In fact, Stanislavski wanted himself and his colleagues to break the mould of acting and stage presentation and to allow "imagination and creative ability" to burst forth.

Stanislavski possessed a penetrating intellect and was greatly influenced by many Russian writers and dramatists. For example, he met Tolstoy, who impressed him with his essay "What is Art?" According to Benedetti, for Tolstoy art had to be intelligible and of moral use to simple, unsophisticated minds, without the need for commentary or explanation. It had to be "self-evident". Tolstoy also stated that "in art, subtlety and the power to influence are almost always diametrically opposed". Therefore, Stanislavski wanted his productions to be absolutely accurate in every way and saw plays as a way of educating the public. He was aware that the Russian dramatist Gogol had once described the theatre as a platform with which to give "a living lesson to the masses", which was a point the authorities readily understood.

Stanislavski wanted theatre to be a true reflection of man and rebelled against anything artificial and false. He rejected the notion that acting, which for him was essentially a mysterious and poetic process, could be reduced to a set of individual operations; later described by him as "a crude, manufactured, artificial surrogate". For Stanislavski, man in his animal nature was brutish, cruel and vain.

His work with the dancer Isadora Duncan was important in the development of his system. Stanislavski said: "I am the only one who is doing any thinking, I have to galvanize the will of every single actor. I am living for everyone, sitting here behind my table." You could say that this is an autistic, narcissistic statement. He once met a man who by chance remarked: "You know that an artist's experience and creativity are based on affective emotion and memory?" This comment went straight into his notebook and thus began his work and research on the idea.

Like Sigmund Freud, Stanislavski got a lot of his ideas from self-analysis. The ethics of acting was extremely important to him considering he was a highly ethical man. As an actor he was able "to give genuine life to the dreams and ideals expressed in the script, to make them vital rather than rhetorical". He liked to have a living model on which to base his interpretation of a character or of a play and in this sense he was a concrete thinker. Although he never read Freud's works, he put huge emphasis in his theatrical work on the Freudian idea of getting in touch with the "superconscious", by which he meant areas of the mind outside conscious awareness. He felt this was "no more than a substitute for the intuitive creation" of a player of genius. In effect, he wanted a holistic type of acting, meaning that the actor, in each performance, had to understand the part fully and recreate anew the complete part – conscious and unconscious. This naturally took time before each performance.

In practice, Stanislavski was controlling and dominating and wanted actors to apply his method to their acting unequivocally. Hence the interpersonal process between directors and actor was highly important for him in the bringing of new characters to life on the stage. He wanted to break down the acting process into sections or units, which has echoes of car manufacture. The visual and non-verbal were also very critical in this endeavour, and indeed, he once said that he had been called a photographer. Putting together a part was like putting together a jigsaw. It sounded mechanistic, yet it contained "emotion, memory ... personal experience" and conscious and unconscious components. Stanislavski put huge emphasis on the psychological aspects of a role but also emphasised the physical action and the importance of stimulating unconscious creative processes. The system or method was not doctrinal, as it was always in the process of change. He was always searching, according to Benedetti, for some "unattainable theatrical truth".

Stanislavski worked right up to his death, just like Ludwig Wittgenstein. He once remarked "you can die on stage, but you can't miss an entrance". Constantin Stanislavski died in Moscow on 7 August 1938, aged 75.

Chapter 31

FEDERICO FELLINI

Federico Fellini (1920–1993) was one of the great Italian film directors. His films include *La Strada*, *8½*, *I Vitelloni*, and *La Dolce Vita*. He was a complex, contradictory and creative character.

BACKGROUND

Federico Fellini was born in Rimini on 20 January 1920 to a middle-class family. It had been a difficult birth for his mother, Ida, who was a harsh parent and suffered from depression, being "private and austere" and very religious.[31] In contrast, his father, Urbano, was easy-going. Fellini was a difficult, destructive child yet showed evidence of considerable intelligence, but poor school progress and school attendance. He was a solitary and reflective child, a naturally good drawer and a mimic.

He was also extremely imaginative, tending to confuse fact and fiction. He experienced delusions and fantasies and "between dream state and wakefulness he had paranormal experiences", imagining he was "flying like an eagle or transported into an alternate universe". Indeed the poet William Blake, who had Asperger syndrome, had similar experiences. Fellini also used to talk about himself in the third person, as those with Asperger syndrome often do. As a child Fellini wanted to be a puppeteer and loved his toy theatre and "messing around with crayons and paint".

An avid reader, he loved adventure stories but showed no interest in sport, and was always an insomniac. Later, he dropped out of university but managed to avoid being conscripted at the outbreak of the Second World War, when aged 19. During the war he was rounded up by the Nazis and escaped by pretending to know a German soldier. Certainly, he was a risk-taker.

Early in his life Fellini, with his innate drawing skills, excelled at caricature and painted portraits for a while, but used to get distracted by the zoological peculiarities he tended to perceive in people's faces: "He ends up producing something closer to a bestiary than a portrait gallery, drawing giraffes, elephants, rhinoceroses, and other animals. Often his clients refused to pay for the final product." With such abundant talent, he wanted to be a cartoonist,

---

[31] Except where otherwise indicated, quotes in this chapter are from Kezich (2006).

though wasn't interested in film at this time. He once confessed: "We spend the second half of our lives making up for the mistakes that we made in the first part of our lives as the result of our upbringing".

PERSONALITY

Fellini was tremendously curious, as are all great creative people, and was a massive observer of detail. According to Kezich, he lived inside of things with indomitable curiosity and unflappable openness. Clearly, he had the capacity to hyperfocus and was a workaholic where films were concerned. From early on Fellini demonstrated identity diffusion and therefore lacked a road map for what to do with his life. He didn't like the idea that any of the characters in his films represented any aspect of himself, which of course they did. The search for identity meant Fellini was recasting himself anew each time. Italian screenwriter Cesare Zavattini made an interesting point when he said that cinema is a collaboration where everybody tries to erase everybody else's work. However, it was the opposite with Fellini, he says, who took pains to erase his own work. He also had "an uncanny self-confidence" and was able to take failures on the chin. Interestingly, like many people of genius, he liked to give the impression that he arrived as a fully formed genius without influence from outside, which is something that Picasso also did.

Fellini also took amphetamines, which was one of the standard treatments for attention deficit hyperactivity disorder, which he clearly displayed at that time. He was very easily distracted, unpunctual, impatient, disorganised and repetitive – a novelty-seeker and risk-taker who spent his life searching for a solution to his identity diffusion. He essentially abandoned himself to what Dostoevsky called "the river of life" and was a hyperkinetic, restless man who always wanted to be someplace else. It is hardly surprising then, with his immature personality, that he was bored a lot and told rather naive lies. The financial aspects of filmmaking held no interest for him too and he was a rather poor financial manager.

Nonetheless, being highly visual, Fellini was fascinated by outsiders and by strange, eccentric people. He also took an interest in the male–female relationship, as in *La Strada*, and in the violence of urban landscapes as well as the bleakness of rural landscapes. *La Strada* is about "the brutal male and the humiliated, submissive woman". At times some of his films seemed deliberately obscure, though he was "anti-intellectual" and did not accept the culture of the status quo, according to Kezich. In fact, he rejected ideology and was practically apolitical. That made him almost a man from another planet in the context of Italian wartime politics and the aftermath of the Second World War.

SOCIAL RELATIONSHIPS

Fellini was highly contradictory; some people described him as outgoing and others as solitary. He tended to compartmentalise people and to socialise intensely with one person at a time. He was attracted to powerful women who would "mother" him and so married the actress Giulietta Masina in 1943, when he was 23 years of age. Wanting to escape the humdrum in life, however, Fellini used filmmaking "to avoid familial and social obligations while expressing himself". Nevertheless, Giulietta was the anchor in his life and their marriage lasted half a century, right up to his death, although he had frequent affairs. He often used the women with whom he had affairs, and certainly exchanged them for a new one when the occasion demanded. There was one long-term relationship outside his marriage, with Anna Giovannini, which effectively was his "secret life". At the same time, however, Fellini found his wife Giulietta mysterious and this retained his interest in her; she remained novel and stimulating to him.

Outside of personal relationships, Fellini also used colleagues and collaborators. At the end of their working relationship, comedian Aldo Fabrizi was left with the bitter taste of what he considered a friendship betrayed, which was a rather common impression among Fellini's former companions, according to biographer Tullio Kezich. But there is nothing new in that feature: the great geniuses of all time have always used people only to later discard them. Music was not one of Fellini's strengths but he was very lucky to have a long-term partnership with the composer Nino Rota. Rota was able to mould himself totally to suit Fellini and understood his "twofold aesthetic of a cheer and melancholy". They were capable of perfect attunement to each other.

The director Roberto Rossellini would play a major role in Fellini's career and was a key figure in Fellini's evolution. However, Fellini made contradictory statements about him, claiming on the one hand, that he learned "everything from Rossellini", and on the other, that Rossellini "didn't teach him anything". Paradoxically, as biographer Tullio Kezich notes, the two statements do not exactly cancel each other out.

Having become stressed and an insomniac in 1954 from excessive work, Fellini saw a psychoanalyst but only attended a couple of sessions: "He's ultimately embarrassed by the relationship between patient and analyst. The chiming of the clock that marks the end of each session is like a bureaucratic ordinance (talk now, stop talking now) and when he is on the couch he feels claustrophobic, like he is suffocating." In the early 1960s, however, Fellini returned to psychoanalysis. This time it was with esteemed Ernst Bernhard, who was a rather humane, non-doctrinaire analyst, and it lasted four years. It was in relation to Bernhard that he began his "Dream Book" and indeed the dream world became enormously important to his future filmmaking. He was also attracted to Carl Jung, the founder of analytical psychology, and they shared an interest in the interface between dream and reality. Jung confused fact and fiction, like Fellini, and also had Asperger syndrome. Fellini loved the "fantastical and marginal" and furthermore was interested in the link between fact and fiction and between film and dream. He once declared: "I believe in everything; there is no limit to my capacity for surprise" and that he would "get lost when experiencing the magical aspects of reality".

Work

For Fellini, with his massive energy, filmmaking was a vocation that totally possessed him and totally drove him. He appeared to fuse with his films when making them and was capable of total dedication. Gradually, he turned into "a real movie animal", quite capable of being creative and modifying things while the film was in progress. The guiding lights for a true artist, according to him, were "fantasy, sincerity, and inspiration". In the early 1940s Fellini contributed to a radio series, *Terziglio*, created by Cesar Cavallotti. In Fellini's early writing for these radio plays, according to Cavallotti, there was no proper plot, rather a series of sensations, "expressed and born all in the same moment". This in effect is a kind of autistic narrative. Cavallotti described Fellini's work in radio plays as showing a "child-like interest in noises and onomatopoeic sounds" and that he "finds irritation in simple things".

Similarly, in the film, *I Vitelloni*, instead of narrative, the author moves from the description of a situation into an articulation of significant episodes over a year, from the end of one summer to the beginning of the next. His films, as time passes, show "less attention to the facts and a greater focus on setting, environment, and emotions". Early in his career he had worked as a gag writer with the comedian Aldo Fabrizi, who felt that "Fellini was a madman" in that he lost his grip on reality at times and extreme fantasy took over.

Kezich remarks that you need a certain kind of personality to direct a film, one that has boundless patience, unshakeable decisiveness, and incredible stamina. Fellini was "a master of emergencies" because they suited his novelty-seeking and sensation-seeking. In films he liked to be "a life guard, a problem solver" and felt at home in this setting, much like the director John Ford, who coincidentally fascinated Fellini. Fellini undoubtedly liked the controlling nature of being a director too.

Film producer Clemente Fracassi, who knew him well, noted that he was Machiavellian in the best sense of the word and that he understood the pragmatism of cinema. He was an incomparable follower of the "rule of results" and that the film itself was far more important than anything else. In fact, according to Fracassi, Fellini thought that the cinema called for clear ideas, hard work, and the ability not to care about anything else.

Fellini was rather voyeuristic; however, this is probably necessary to be a cutting-edge director. The film *8½* is often regarded as his best work: "It is important to remember that in *8½*, objectivity and autobiography coincide, and that truth and lies are two sides of the same coin." In a review, Alberto Moravia stated that Fellini's character was obsessed by eroticism, that he was a sadist, a masochist, a self-mythologizer, "who was scared of life and wanted to go back into the mother's womb", before adding, "he is a clown, a liar, and a cheater". If nothing, the film reflected Fellini's identity diffusion.

Federico Fellini died on 31 October 1993, at the age of 73. He is buried in Rimini, where the city airport is named in his honour.

Chapter 32

TYRONE GUTHRIE

Tyrone Guthrie (1900–1971) was one of the major international theatre directors of the 20th century. He founded a theatre in Minneapolis, Minnesota, a writers centre at his family home in County Monaghan, Ireland, and also helped to found the Stratford Shakespeare Festival in Ontario, Canada. I believe that he had Asperger syndrome.

BACKGROUND

Tyrone Guthrie was born in Tunbridge Wells, England on 2 July 1900. His father, Thomas, was a medical man, while his mother, Norah, came from a military Anglo-Irish family. With a history of acting in his family, his mother fostered in him a great love of theatre in childhood. He was a highly intelligent child who became fascinated with "ritual street theatre" and was hyper-focused on theatre from the age of eight years. A shy boy, he displayed a huge capacity for observation of detail and was highly visual; in fact he was fascinated by landscape and also by funerals and processions, much like the Irish writer Brendan Behan.

The First World War years were spent being educated at Wellington College in Berkshire. There, the "botanically minded boy" showed great "zest" but had problems in "pulling himself together", according to one of his teachers.[32] Despite his military leanings, the war ended before he could enlist, and he subsequently attended St John's College, Oxford and read history.

PERSONALITY

Guthrie was rebellious and enigmatic and a rather tyrannical figure, but also a workaholic, a careful financial manager and a massive reader. Needless to say, he was hyperkinetic and impatient, loved multitasking, worked very fast and got bored if in one place for too long. The massive energy he exuded often infected other people. There was an immature, child-like element to his personality and he was "clever, often to a foolish degree".

---

[32] Except where otherwise indicated, quotes in this chapter are from Forsyth (1976).

This also found expression in his fun-loving personality and his unusual sense of humour, with a penchant for pranks, as persons with Asperger syndrome often have (Lyons & Fitzgerald, 2005). Guthrie also had considerable sensitivity to the spoken word and later became a professor of speech and drama in the USA. Indeed he was great raconteur and had "the gift of the gab". In his work he had to think and visualise his way "in cerebral flashes". He would snort and then rattle statements off like "telegraphese", while a cigarette was stuck in his tight lips. This, in fact, is Asperger-type language.

Persons with Asperger syndrome are usually oppositional and Guthrie was no different. The oppositional and novelty-seeking aspects of his personality were expressed in his being an anti-Establishment figure. Forsyth points out that he was anti-Broadway, anti-West End, in fact anti-everything that was implied in the term "legitimate theatre". He was essentially an innovator and trailblazer and certainly not interested in long-term planning, but was a man for the moment, getting the show on the road as of *now*, dealing with crisis *now*. This was novelty to him, and long-term plans were deadly boring: "He was in his element as *enfant terrible*".

His anti-Establishment and oppositional nature invaded many areas of his life; when made Chancellor of Queen's University Belfast in 1963, he made a speech urging rapprochement between Catholics and Protestants in Northern Ireland. However, he was almost dismissed from the job.

At Guthrie's memorial service, Alec Guinness – whom Guthrie once sacked from a play – said that he "never cut his cloth, or trimmed his sails, to suit other personalities, but gave wholly of himself. A man of the greatest integrity." On the subject of cloth, Guthrie carried very few clothes with him when he travelled, not unlike the mathematician Paul Erdős, who also had Asperger syndrome (Fitzgerald & O'Brien, 2007). In fact, Guthrie kept a heavy overcoat for an incredibly long time during his life, showing preservation of sameness – this was similar to the composer Glenn Gould who also had Asperger syndrome. Guthrie was also known to greet visitors "inappropriately dressed", much like Thomas Jefferson had.

Guthrie was enamoured of psychoanalysis. However, he allowed the Freudian analyst Ernest Jones, whom he called "the oracle", to lead him astray with psychoanalytic nonsense.

Social Relationships

Forsyth describes Guthrie as a formidable, remote, giant of a public figure, and a rather shy, boyish, private Irishman. He also paints a picture of him as a "social eccentric". Guthrie was in effect a shy man and an autistic wanderer, who was "at his happiest as a theatrical nomad". In fact, Forsyth notes that he was "a highly emotional, ambitious, and awkwardly tall young man, whose public zest was often a cloak for real shyness and a tendency to private tears". Guthrie did display a compassionate side of his personality, however, in that he always had a wish to help poor people. And indeed when a friend was dying of cancer he looked after him with great care.

He had a good relationship with the actress Flora Robertson for quite some time; however, the letters he wrote to her were cold and "frightened her". The relationship ended but later he married Judy Bretherton, but the marriage produced no children. He appears to have had a very low sex drive: "He was personally just not interested in sex and it continued to be so throughout most of his life". On this matter, he confessed: "I have always been rather prim and shy about sexual matters". Forsyth claims that his "tendency to tyranny" was "part of the product of a sexual frustration". You could say that this tendency was just part of his genetic and hormonal make-up. In fact, he was quite dominating and "loved organizing". Indeed control was enormously important to him – particularly self-control.

Work

Forsyth describes Guthrie as "the electrifying professional figure of an indefatigable worker in theatre". Initially he worked at the BBC and had a very successful career there, writing and producing radio plays. However, he excelled as a theatre director, with his modern, experimental approach to traditional theatre, notably Shakespeare. It reflected his novelty-seeking behaviour and love for new adventures, new jobs, and to discover new things in the theatre. Furthermore, he achieved fame for his association with several institutions: the Old Vic Theatre in London, the Guthrie Theater in Minneapolis; and the Tyrone Guthrie Centre in County Monaghan. His greatest success was perhaps in Canada, where he and others successfully launched the Stratford Shakespeare Festival in Ontario in 1953.

Guthrie loved pushing the limits and devising new ways of presenting plays. Though he was one of the first to write radio plays, he was not a first-rate playwright as such – indeed you can't write plays in a hyperkinetic fashion unless you are Shakespeare. His play *Top of the Ladder* showed the emotional underdevelopment of his personality. His directing talents also extended to the big screen; in 1957 he directed *Oedipus Rex*, remarkable for the stylised masks the actors wore, emulating the Greek actors in Sophocles' time.

Guthrie was often controlling and dominating and even tyrannical at his work and could be quite tactless. He claimed that much of the process of playwriting was subconscious and that the first thing a producer should do was to decide what the play was about, and that "the last person to consult should be the author". He had an authoritative capacity to treat all players like "temperamental children, all longing to be loved and corrected too". In fact, he could be brutal at times, for example, when he told the great actress Edith Evans, she was "too old". Forsyth describes his auditions as a "sort of slave market". He demanded much from his actors, and once declared: "We must know – they must feel". He worked with Lilian Baylis, the great producer and manager of the Old Vic and Sadler's Wells theatres in London, who was indeed far more tyrannical than he ever was. Nevertheless, they did manage to work together successfully. Indeed work was his antidepressant and his source of happiness. He was knighted in 1961.

Tyrone Guthrie died on 15 May 1971, at the age of 70.

Chapter 33

ALFRED HITCHCOCK

Alfred Hitchcock (1899–1980) was one of the most famous film directors of the 20th century. He had a unique style of filmmaking, was one of the greatest technical directors and the master of suspense. His most famous films include *Spellbound*, *Rear Window*, Psycho and *The Birds*. He also displayed the characteristics of a person with Asperger syndrome.

BACKGROUND

Alfred Hitchcock was born in London on 13 August 1899. His father, William, was a greengrocer and his mother, Emma, who was of Irish extraction, had obsessive–compulsive traits. Hitchcock as a child was always rather clingy to her and dependent on her. Indeed it is not uncommon for great artistic creators to be "mummy's boys". As a child he was fascinated by the traffic, in particular "horse-drawn vehicles"[33], and certainly had no interest in what other children were interested in. Even as a child, his appearance was odd and he was described as "funny-looking", not helped by his obesity. He was a lonely child who lived in the internal world of his imagination, which he could control. Because of his Asperger syndrome and the difficulties that it brought about in social relationships, he suffered a great deal of stress in childhood. Like many persons with Asperger syndrome in childhood, he loved to draw and did so prolifically.

PERSONALITY

Clearly Hitchcock was highly visual from an early age. He once declared: "My mind works more like a baby's mind does, thinking in pictures. I have vague memories of my infancy, all visual, none verbal. I can't be certain, but I believe they are true memories." Persons with high functioning autism think in pictures and Hitchcock certainly was no different. In adult life he adored the visual arts and became a major collector and it was said that his drawings bore a certain resemblance to those of Paul Klee.

[33] Except where otherwise indicated, quotes in this chapter are from Chandler (2005).

There was also an immature aspect to his personality that remained with him throughout life. Indeed, it was one of the keys to his creativity: always able to see things through the eyes of a child. This gave him a unique vista on the world and allowed him to be a massive observer of detail. It was noted by his biographer Charlotte Chandler that he "didn't make eye contact with people".

Despite having no verbal memories in childhood, Hitchcock loved language and playing with words. Because of his difficulty with understanding narrative, he paid great attention to it. This is shown by his comment that "languages are a great deal more than words … they are full of idiomatic expressions with subtle shades of meaning that takes years of living in the language to understand and, even more important, to feel". This is reminiscent of Ludwig Wittgenstein, who struggled with understanding language in the same way that Hitchcock did. Both had Asperger syndrome.

Hitchcock also displayed identity diffusion, which was important to his creativity. He found the image of himself in the mirror that of "a stranger" and presented many false selves to the public. He was an aesthete and his identity merged at times with his films. Like many with Asperger syndrome, he moved easily between fact and fiction, necessarily so for a great filmmaker. He had little interest in the "motivation" of characters – he was more superficial in that it was what they did that interested him. Actress Janet Leigh once said that he was "an imp, a mischievous pixie, and a genius". In a way actors for him were like carbon cut-outs who did as he wished; he was the puppeteer that moved them. In fact, not only was he adept at manipulating actors but also audiences.

In essence, Hitchcock was a novelty-seeker and sensation-seeker, which found expression in his films. He had preservation of sameness also, evidenced by his working with the same people repeatedly in many of his films, for example, Cary Grant, Gregory Peck, Ingrid Bergman, James Stewart, Janet Leigh and Grace Kelly. He also dressed in the same type of suits repetitively. He was fascinated by perversity and sadism, like Cecil B. DeMille, and indeed was voyeuristic in watching sadistic acts. Edgar Allan Poe, who wrote much about perverse behaviour, fascinated him greatly. There was certainly a good deal of hidden aggression in Hitchcock and a number of individuals were on the receiving end. He sometimes traumatised women in his films by what he put them through. For example, actress Tippi Hedren recalled that in the film *The Birds*, "all those birds started pecking at me. He hadn't told me about that. I could have been blinded. But I was very young, I did what I was told. I shouldn't have been put through that."

Hitchcock had exquisite taste bud sensitivity and was obsessed by food, often eating the same gourmet meal. He imported his favourite food, such as oysters, from England, and was also a connoisseur of wine. Existing for him was eating and making films.

Social Relationships

Like many with Asperger syndrome, Hitchcock had no capacity for small talk and "didn't waste time on pleasantries". He was not interested in chitchat with actors and did not want their input. In his dealings with people, he could be hypersensitive and unforgiving, and once declared: "I would like to have been a hanging judge".

Hitchcock also had problems with reciprocal social relationships. It is interesting that he approached his future wife Alma Reville first "by telephone" and their initial relationship was based solely on professional interests. While Hitchcock was a visual thinker, Alma was an auditory thinker; actor Norman Lloyd said that "she was the ear" and "he was the eye". With a shared fascination for films, Alma was a film editor and they complemented each other professionally. Moreover, she was critical to his creativity by becoming a stable anchor in his life and providing a home life that was very routine-bound, which suited him. Later she revealed that he "never bored me". Their marriage produced one daughter, Patricia.

Hitchcock had difficulties with intimacy with people, but Alma had similar obsessive–compulsive traits to his own. Those with Asperger syndrome are often attracted to and can cope with people like themselves. There may also be some element of repressed sexuality in his character, having once declared that "repressed sex is more constructive for the creative person".

WORK

Hitchcock's early choice of career was in engineering and navigation. Following his time in engineering, he applied the skills he had learned to the film business. Initially, he was a jack-of-all-trades on the set and turned his hands to various jobs – then and always a workaholic. Fairly quickly he began his directorial career, hyper-focusing on this work for the rest of his life.

His trademark was to focus more on objects and the structure of a scene than on the actors. Chandler points out that Hitchcock seemed to be more interested in things than in people: "He treated props like actors." For example, he was far more absorbed in the knife in a murder scene than the actors. This behaviour is typically autistic. He reportedly said "actors are cattle" and on another occasion used the word "children". For him they were like chess pieces to be moved around at his will. The actors were there to do his bidding, to be controlled and dominated by him, to be used as he saw fit. He certainly did not want actors challenging him; the only word he wanted to hear was "yes". In fact, looking after actors generally bored him, only wishing they would get on with the job. However, he was fascinated by eccentric and odd people, and these kinds of characters figured in his films.

Before he ever started shooting, the film in question was completely planned in his head. His style was unique and unorthodox but highly successful – he made over 50 films and worked with many of the greatest actors of his time.

Alfred Hitchcock died in California on 29 April 1980, aged 80.

Chapter 34

LUIS BUÑUEL

Luis Buñuel (1900–1983) was a highly original and influential Spanish filmmaker who broke the mould of filmmaking during his era. He was fascinated by transgressive and perverse behaviour, which was central to his filmmaking. He himself was a rebel and an anti-authority type. He demonstrates the link between transgression and creativity and I believe that he had Asperger syndrome.

BACKGROUND

Luis Buñuel was born on 22 February 1900 in Calanda, Spain to a wealthy family. His father, Leonardo, had run away from home at the age of 14 to join the army as a bugle boy. However, when boredom set in, "he signed up with four friends to fight in Cuba in the Spanish/American war."[34] Clearly, he was a novelty-seeker, like his son. Many great creators have poor relationships with their fathers and Buñuel was no exception. He was not close to his father, who was fascinated by insects – a feature common with persons with Asperger syndrome. Buñuel's mother, Maria, was of the dominatrix type.

Buñuel had a rather lonely childhood and was a mediocre student at various Catholic schools, including a Jesuit one, although he did excel at history. He adored putting on masks of one sort or another and was a novelty-seeker. As a child, he had perverse fantasies about women and indeed such fantasies were central to his creativity throughout life. He had a schoolboy relish for sacrilege and scatology, according to biographer John Baxter.

While studying engineering at the University of Madrid, he expected to transfer quickly to agronomy and into the world of insects – an interest he shared with his father. A burgeoning interest in philosophy, however, led him to switch to the arts and he gained a degree in philosophy. At this stage he saw the world from a "mechanistic and entomological" perspective, having studied Darwin's ideas. Team sports did not interest him, according to Baxter, and indeed persons with Asperger syndrome are not team players and rarely enjoy sports. However, Buñuel did excel at boxing.

---

[34] Except where otherwise indicated, quotes in this chapter are from Baxter (1994).

PERSONALITY

Buñuel was a highly complex, contradictory figure, as all great creative people are. One common feature of Asperger syndrome he displayed was "piercing eyes". He certainly looked odd and eccentric and talked to himself, as persons with Asperger syndrome often do. The fact that he had problems with writing could suggest some underlying language difficulties. Undoubtedly, he had problems with the language of reciprocity, which suggests some pragmatic language deficits. He also had dyspraxia or clumsiness, which showed in his dancing.

In some ways Buñuel had a rather child-like, immature personality, but was an intellectual and highly intelligent. He always moved easily between fact and fiction, indicative of identity diffusion, and this was important for his creative work. Unusual perceptual experiences occur not uncommonly in persons with this profile: Buñuel experienced a pseudo-hallucination when his father died, i.e., that his father was standing alive, which had a major impact on him.

Buñuel embraced Surrealism with Salvador Dalí in the late 1910s and revealed the outcome of that encounter: "I discovered a world of extraordinary subversion, one that included everything: from insects to social customs, sex, theology ... In short, I was utterly dazzled." He was fascinated to the end of his life with the Surrealist art movement, which mixed dreams and reality, fact and fiction. Surrealism is a somewhat perverse art form; yet one he felt completely at home in.

Baxter compares him to the writer Graham Greene, who was also "remote, ascetic, and misanthropic". They were both interested in "lonely men drifting along the edges of empire, troubled by moral doubts, losing themselves in casual infidelities but obsessed always with the lack of meaning in their lives". These are men with identity diffusion and lack a core sense of self. Nevertheless, this sense of unintegrated personality is associated with creativity. Some psychological torment is helpful for creativity, which can be an attempt to heal it.

Buñuel was an eternal rebel, particularly against the middle classes, and indeed great creators are almost required to be rebels. He relished attacking and perverting middle-class values and relationships, like a child wanting to smash up his parents' house or the local school. Chaos was thrilling for him. He loved to behave like a naughty boy in provoking people, stirring things up. However, there was also an element of preservation of sameness about his behaviour; he liked home routines and working with the same people.

Regarding chaos and order, he wrote: "I was torn between my intellectual (and emotional) attraction to anarchy and my fundamental need for order and peace." This again shows his inner conflict between order and chaos. He partly dealt with this by intellectualisation and by having more faith in thinking than in feeling. For example, he was not bothered by the brutalisation of animals, but was "squeamish about killing them himself". At the same time he had a scientific, systematising frame of mind, contradicted by his belief in the "primacy of dreams and the subconscious" – the Surrealists' position.

Buñuel's sexuality was often perverse. Despite his great fear of being watched in a sexual act, at the same time he adored watching other people engaged in sexual acts. He enjoyed cross-dressing, voyeurism and frottage and, for him, sex and death were in some way united. Indeed he had a morbid fascination with rotted corpses and the primitive autopsies that he saw. According to Baxter, he had a "necrophiliac attraction to a beautiful but inanimate woman, an image that was fast becoming his sexual ideal." Moreover, Buñuel always believed that he had the power to hypnotise women and to read and influence their minds. His sexual fetishism was connected with "feet, calves, and high-heeled shoes". Like his fantasies of drugged and hypnotised women, it was "a means of displacing his taste for sexual violence". Buñuel was greatly influenced by the Marquis de Sade. According to Baxter, de Sade was the first philosopher to articulate a "rational vision of man" and his atheism and materialism echoed Buñuel's mechanistic and entomological view of life.

The Cuban writer G. Cabrera Infante described Buñuel as a "sublimated sadist", evident in his film *Belle de Jour*: "If you think of it, he was much closer to the masochists than to the sadist. *Belle de Jour* is the exact portrait of a masochistic woman, and very precise." In fact, Buñuel was a sadomasochistic person who damaged himself in early filmmaking by having conflicts with the director, not being able to collaborate or take instruction. Jacques Lacan, who was a somewhat perverse psychoanalyst and paranoid person himself, used Buñuel's film *Él* in his classes as a classic example of paranoia.

Buñuel had many obsessive–compulsive traits. For example, he used rolls of film very sparingly and exerted tight budgetary control in filmmaking. Given his love for shooting, he built up a collection of guns, and could be quite impulsive, shooting and checking his accuracy. Another obsession of Buñuel's was "boxes" – boxes often appear in his films, yet no revelation of their contents is given to curious audiences. Obsessional repetition was the order of the day. On one occasion after he briefly left a film set his cameraman changed his camera position by 10 cm. When Buñuel returned, he noticed and demanded it be replaced. Only a man with weak central coherence and Asperger syndrome would have noticed this detail.

Having rejected his Catholic upbringing, Buñuel had a perverse relationship with the Catholic Church for the remainder of his life. He loved the Surrealists' violence and anti-clericalism, as well as their "penchant for subversion, betrayal and delusion". Like Ludwig Wittgenstein, the philosopher with Asperger syndrome, he was fascinated by Catholic rituals. Orson Welles described him as a deeply Christian man who hates God as only a Christian can. For Buñuel, "Surrealism replaced the church he had rejected". There was a kind of religious asceticism in his make-up, although he always drank a great deal of alcohol and smoked heavily.

Like many great creators, he had a lot of death anxiety. When he was dying, as a final thrill, a final perversion, he – the virulent anti-Catholic – had a priest listen to him. His behaviour was controlling to the end and he would not allow the priest to "convert" him. Of course, Buñuel was a fascinating character to be with; persons of genius tend to be captivating because they perceive life in a different way and therefore often make interesting, unusual comments.

Social Relationships

Buñuel lacked the capacity for small talk so necessary at social gatherings. He also had some empathy or theory of mind difficulties. Indeed, he was a man for whom systematising the world came easy. Of course, this does not help in social relationships. Social reciprocity was not part of Buñuel's make-up and he inhabited a "one-person world". He was always something of a loner, a man who stood apart, and liked to sit in cafés alone, like Samuel Beckett and Henrik Ibsen, watching the passing parade of humanity. Buñuel set his own standards of behaviour and created an "order" for people he had relationships with, most notably his wife. Of course, he was the dominant one in this order, the lawgiver, and controlled it.

His relationships with people were often fraught with intense emotion. He and Salvador Dalí had a great hatred for each other after some early filmmaking. Indeed, they were very similar in personality. While Buñuel could be hostile to homosexuals, he loved El Greco's homoerotic crucifixions and scenes of martyrdom which made explicit the Spanish Church's "preoccupation with the flesh and its mortification".

In 1934, possibly on impulse, he married Jeanne Rucar Lefebvre, a gymnast who had won an Olympic bronze medal. His paranoid traits and extremely controlling behaviour came to the fore, especially when he insisted that their wedding was to take place entirely on his terms: "It would be a civil ceremony, without guests or reception, and must remain a secret even from her parents." This kind of behaviour can occur in Asperger syndrome.

Rather bizarrely, Buñuel thought of killing his wife because of the possibility of her having an extramarital relationship. This is certainly a form of morbid jealousy. In contrast, Buñuel himself had periods of sexual promiscuity during their marriage. He was autocratic and dictatorial in the marriage from the start. Given his cruelty to Jeanne, it is hardly surprising that she found it hard to love him, insisting on one occasion that she have an abortion. She confessed that he was "brutal". She had to tolerate his "long absences and sexual eccentricities" and, at Buñuel's insistence, they had separate bedrooms throughout their marriage. Jeanne stayed at home at night and looked after the children while he went out. In a way their marriage was a sadomasochistic one. Following his death, she wrote an autobiography called *Memoirs of a Woman Without a Piano* (2010) – detailing how he had rather perversely stopped her from playing the piano.

Baxter states that Buñuel, inhibited since childhood by a fear of women, often fantasised about using drugs or hypnotism to render them helpless. Hence his relationship to Jeanne was on a part–object basis, whereby she was less than an independent human being. Nevertheless, she was his anchor in life and he would not have achieved as much without her. She tolerated his domination while he covertly showed his dependence on her. When dying of cancer he was entirely dependent on her.

Work

Buñuel did some acting himself, but clearly the role of director attracted him and fired his creative energies. Like Alfred Hitchcock, he was a meticulous planner of his films and very controlling on a film set; indeed he always pulled the strings, whether on set or at home. He also shared with Hitchcock a systematising approach to filmmaking. He was interested in the fundamentals, for example, "the blind instinct of insects" and indeed actors were little more than "experimental animals" for him. He told actors what physical movements he required, but otherwise gave them little direction. This in fact is an autistic style of direction. In relation to actors, Catherine Deneuve said: "I wouldn't say he loved them. That's why he worked with the same people. He didn't like to get involved." This kind of behaviour also demonstrates a degree of preservation of sameness.

Buñuel made over 30 films in his 50-year career. Always a Surrealist at heart, he liked to portray perverse activity on the screen and loved actors with a similar perverse core to their personality. It is hardly surprising then that the Marquis de Sade and Gilles de Rais – two of the most perverse individuals in history – were his heroes. His movie *Viridiana* was described as "sacrilegious and blasphemous" by a Spanish Dominican monk named Fierro.

Luis Buñuel died in Mexico City on 29 July 1983, at the age of 83.

Chapter 35

WALT DISNEY

Walt Disney (1901–1966) was a massively successful animation filmmaker who created a unique worldview, that of Disney World. A legend and giant in the filmmaking industry, he is one of the most famous and recognisable names of the 20th and 21st centuries. I believe that he had Asperger syndrome.

BACKGROUND

Walter Elias Disney was born in Chicago on 5 December 1901, to a family of mixed Irish, Canadian, English and German heritage, and spent his childhood in Chicago, Missouri and Kansas City. His father, Elias, was a strict, taciturn and self-important man – hyperkinetic and something of an autistic wanderer, a failed farmer and failed businessman. According to biographer Neal Gabler, Disney found his father "so unapproachable and obdurate" that he scarcely talked to him.[35] A friend of Walt's, Walt Pfeiffer, remarked that "the whole Disney family seemed to me aloof and unbending". Here Pfeiffer was describing a high functioning autistic family and indeed most of the Disney family would appear to have had some autistic traits.

Nevertheless, Disney had a reasonably happy childhood and later showed his massive autistic memory by remembering "every detail of Marceline, Missouri". He drew incessantly as a child – in fact, persons with Asperger syndrome often have savant skills in drawing, as Disney had. He also liked playacting and acting the clown. He found that he could act well and adored the praise derived from such activities. Indeed, he was somewhat starved of praise during his childhood. In school he played Peter Pan – a role you could say he was born for. However, he showed poor school progress and evidence of attention deficit disorder. In fact, he was a daydreamer, easily distracted, his imagination constantly in flight, and was fascinated by magic. By all accounts he was a rather fearless child who failed to think through the consequences of his actions.

Evidence of his sexual identity diffusion came to the fore at school, where he took an interest in "domestic science … homemaking with the girls, carrying a little blue bag with his supplies". Walt Pfeiffer recalled that the kids used to make fun of him carrying this bag

---

[35] Except where otherwise indicated, quotes in this chapter are from Gabler (2007).

around. Even in the classroom, he continued to draw endless pictures; this gave him the kind of attention that he craved. Disney was essentially a boy who drifted between fact and fantasy; indeed this was so throughout his life and one of the sources of his great creativity. He could hyper-focus on drawing and not be distracted, compared to being hugely distracted in mainstream school and faring badly. The school magazine, *The Voice*, stated that he was “extremely shy and reserved”, “unusually diffident” and “unable to loosen up”. While he did have a kind of girlfriend, his idea of a relationship was “sharing ghost stories”. This is all fairly typical of high functioning autism or Asperger syndrome. In high school Disney became a cartoonist for the school magazine and immensely enjoyed this kind of work.

Disney endured a very difficult period from the age of 10 as a newspaper boy. His father purchased a newspaper delivery route for The Kansas City Star and Disney was completely controlled by his father and customers, when delivering a huge number of newspapers early every morning and evening. The stress of this control and work gave him posttraumatic stress disorder for a time.

Disney had a pronounced superego and was intensely keen to join the American forces in the First World War – he feared being criticised later in his life for not fighting, although under-age at the time. He dropped out of high school and joined the Red Cross and went to France, but did not see action before the Armistice. Nevertheless, joining up showed that he was brave and courageous. On this return he took up work in an ad agency where he created adverts for newspapers, magazines and cinemas.

Personality

Disney had a narrow range of interests and spoke almost only of studio work. He spoke with an autistic narrative too, using the minimum number of words to communicate. Disney became obsessed with animation and motion and studied everything that was known about it at this time. It took over his life and became a fixation. He once said that “the trick of making things move on film is what got me”. Persons with high functioning autism are often fascinated by movement. Disney hyper-focused on it and began to experiment – something he did throughout his life, which was also linked to his autistic novelty-seeking. He engaged in tremendous intellectual or cognitive work and there was massive activity in his internal world – the world of his imagination. According to Gabler, “the kind of men who were attracted to animation were likely to be emotionally stunted and loners, lost in their own heads”.

People could neither fathom nor understand Disney because he was hidden behind an Asperger façade – a chameleon with multiple identities. He did not present the same persona from one day to the next and indeed his brother Roy said there were “40 different Walts”. With great flair, he created myths of his own life, mixing fact and fiction. This easy movement between fact and fiction is part of high functioning autism. Disney was a massive self-publicist too, despite also appearing unprepossessing – another contradiction. He also claimed he had no interest in being admired as a great man.

Critical to Disney’s success were his Asperger syndrome and his identity diffusion, however. His multiple selves made him “at once a nostalgist and a futurist, a conservative and visionary”. Like a chameleon, he had a “knack for splicing many disparate and even contradictory strands together”. He also had an emotionally immature personality that allowed him to see the world through the eyes of a child and be in touch with children's wishes and fantasies throughout his life. This was much like Lewis Carroll (Fitzgerald, 2004) and Jonathan Swift (Fitzgerald, 2005), who also had Asperger syndrome. Disney always retained the wishes, desires and fantasies of a child but this was critical to his genius and great works.

Despite being egocentric and compulsive, he was also "naive, unselfconscious and innocent". He created his own perfect childlike world of the imagination in his films and his theme parks. Because they were his own creation, he had total control of them. Absolute control is critical to persons with Asperger syndrome, and not surprisingly Disney reacted negatively to the control exerted by his father and his customers when he worked as a newspaper boy.

Disney also showed the negative aspects of Asperger syndrome – autistic psychopathy, having very low levels of empathy, and indeed being a "callous man, oblivious to patterns inherent in nature, art, literature" (Carpenter, 1968). Carpenter (1968) also stated that "he had a magic touch, but it turned things into gold, not art. He lacked perception and sensitivity for genuine artistic creativity, and his compulsion to control made him no respecter of the integrity of the works of others."

Disney was quite paranoid and mistrustful of his workers. He saw things in black and white: people were either for him or against him. Nevertheless, he could be extremely naive in his business dealings: his poor theory of mind capacity let him down and he admitted on occasion to problems in reading people's characters. Another tremendous fear was of failing artistically – of not producing something new. According to Gabler, Disney said that if he quit growing mentally and artistically, then he would begin to die.

Despite all the success, Disney harboured feelings of low self-worth. This could only be dealt with by making better and better films that were applauded by the critics. As he made more films he operated as a dictator rather than a director, striving to be the fount of all wisdom. He was always setting the quality bar higher and drove people to work relentlessly, like General Montgomery of Alamein, another martinet with Asperger syndrome (Fitzgerald & O'Brien, 2007). Indeed Disney was described by Gabler as "overbearing, mercurial, ungrateful, and impossible to please".

His novelty-seeking meant that he was highly innovative at times. He built a new film studio and was fascinated from an architectural point of view with its functionalism. You could say that functionalism is the Asperger way. The philosopher Ludwig Wittgenstein had a similar flair for architecture – and also had Asperger syndrome – and placed a large emphasis on functionalism.

Disney could be quite apolitical. He was initially largely oblivious to the Second World War – typical of someone with Asperger syndrome – but later got drawn into it and had to produce works for the US government. He tried to "insulate himself from reality". Money too was not a driving force for him, but just the means to an end. Like most people with Asperger syndrome, Disney was obsessed with nature and animals. In one way he was an early campaigner for a greener world and his environmentalism the extent of his engagement with the real world. He had certain food fads too, notably his favourite meal was "canned beans", which is a typical Asperger diet.

Social Relationships

Disney had a vast number of acquaintances but was very poor at intimate relationships. In fact, he feared marriage. When his future wife, Lillian Bounds, met him, "there was no attraction, much less romance". The central issue in Disney's life was control and this also extended to his wife; for example, he would select a hat for her without consulting her. During their marriage she experienced a number of miscarriages before giving birth to a daughter, Diane, which pleased him greatly, and later they adopted a child, Sharon Mae. The marriage was often a lonely one for his wife as Disney spent most of his time away working, which is common in an Asperger-type marriage.

Disney formed a relationship with the animator and cartoonist Ub Iwerks, with whom he shared some traits, not least tremendous talents in drawing. Appearing to display some features of high functioning autism, Iwerks was "painfully shy, even withdrawn, doleful, and forlorn; he seldom spoke". Indeed it is not uncommon for persons with high functioning autism to link up. Iwerks and Disney started their own commercial art business together and in time he became the co-creator of one of the most famous cartoon figures in history: Mickey Mouse.

Disney did not mix much outside of work and felt that work and sleep were more important than socialising. The animator Walt Kimball said that "Walt was a hard guy to get close to", while another employee said that "he didn't appear to accept close friendships". This is typical of Asperger syndrome. The motivation to interact with other people served only to bring his creative ideas to fruition. He was "self-absorbed, so fully within his own mind and ideas that he emerged only to share them and to have them executed".

In this respect, one of his production managers recalled that Disney seemed to have trouble fully relating to his employees. "He kept his guard up, his employees at arm's length, and was touchy." Moreover, he seldom engaged in small talk and it was often tense being around him. In his dealings with others, he was a great user of people for his own benefit: he weeded out "marginal people" or got rid of "dead wood", according to Ben Sharpsten, one of his long-time producers. On one occasion during a conference, someone was fired because he announced that it was noon and they should break for lunch. Nonetheless, Disney created in work an artificial family where he was the controlling, dominant one. This was a substitute family – the kind of family in which he could be happy.

Work

In filmmaking, Disney was a novelty-seeker, a sensation-seeker, a massive experimentalist who was fascinated by colour, as many people with Asperger syndrome are. Aside from his major contribution to the American animation industry, he is acknowledged as creating or spawning other disciplines such as theme park design. Gabler points out that critic Robert Hughes even credited Disney with inventing Pop Art. Gabler also notes that Disney's detractors called his effect "Disneyfication", which meant the substitution of a synthetic world for a real one. In my view, Walt Disney created an autistic world, whether in his cartoons or theme parks, which had its own internal logic. He took us into his psychological world – his imaginative world – and millions of people, particularly children but also adults, adored this world. People preferred it to the drab, dangerous world of everyday life, from which human beings wanted to escape. It signified order and harmony. Rather significantly, the cultural historian Warren Susman stated that "the Disney world is a world of order".

Disney's first major creation was the cartoon figure Mickey Mouse. Palaeontologist Stephen Jay Gould noted features of juvenility (quoting zoologist Konrad Lorenz) in Mickey Mouse: "a relatively large head, predominance of the brain capsule, large and low-lying eyes, bulging cheek region, short and thick extremities, a springy elastic consistency, and clumsy movements" (Gould, 1979). Interestingly, the large head is a feature of high functioning autism or Asperger syndrome. The attraction and appeal of the cartoon figure was derived from its slapstick humour, however. Maurice Sendak believed that Mickey Mouse "stole screen slapstick from its live practitioners and then extended it because his elasticity exceeded theirs, and that it was slapstick that made the cartoons appealing".

Psychoanalysts saw the cartoons as a place where wish fulfilment could take place. *Time* magazine said in 1933: "[Mickey] can break all natural laws (he never breaks moral laws) and always win." In fact, Mickey Mouse represented aspects of Disney's personality, particularly the child-like aspects. His wife Lillian once said that her husband and Mickey were "so simpatico … they almost seemed like they had the same identity". Indeed people with Asperger syndrome often love animals and in some ways Mickey became Disney's alter ego.

Next came Donald Duck who was given a different identity: he was more aggressive and naughty. Because Disney had identity diffusion, he was more easily able to take on other people's ideas by "osmosis". According to Gabler, Snow White was the story of Walt Disney's personal growth, "the story of what he had to surmount and what he had achieved". He could incubate cartoons in his mind, which of course is typical of the great creator.

In his work Disney was obsessive and compulsive and it formed his identity – "I work, therefore I exist". Known for always pushing the limits, he worked for years without a holiday and pushed himself into a nervous breakdown. Disney was larger than life and he achieved the work of 20 men in his lifetime. A deep hatred of industry unions, however, meant that he was callous and vicious to them, to his own detriment. He wanted total control of his employees; he wanted them to only have the rights he bestowed on them. The unionisation of his workers was totally mishandled by him and the idea of them negotiating with him or having any rights was anathema. His idea was that everyone should take the salary he gave them, do as he wanted, and shut up.

Disney was therefore extremely paternalistic and everything had to be for the greater glory of Walt Disney. When an animator approached Disney with the idea of giving awards for the best animation, Disney replied: "If there is going to be any awards made, I am going to get them." He certainly was a genius at "using someone else's genius". New employees were there to be moulded as he wanted. It essentially was a kind of part–object relationship in that they had to do his bidding almost to the point of being an extension of him. He demanded immediate and total obedience from everyone; there could only be one voice and that was his. This modus operandi was made possible by creating his own fairy-tale world and setting himself up as the ultimate boss. According to Gabler, this will to power also explained why animation was his preferred medium. "In animation one took the inanimate and brought it to life, or the illusion of life. In animation one could exercise the power of a God." Because of his films and theme parks, it was never necessary for him to grow up.

His autocratic, insensitive and imperious manner was further compounded by a vindictive and unforgiving nature, and indeed he could be a very nasty character. Like the poet William

Blake (who had Asperger syndrome), he was a systematiser echoed in the epic poem *Jerusalem*:

> I must create a system
> or be enslaved by another man's;
> I will not reason and compare:
> my business is to create.

Walt Disney died in California on 15 December 1966, at the age of 65.

Chapter 36

OTTO PREMINGER

Otto Preminger (1905–1986) was a prominent and successful Hollywood film director and actor, who showed a combination of traits of attention deficit hyperactivity disorder and Asperger syndrome.

BACKGROUND

Otto Preminger was born on 5 December 1905 into a prominent Jewish family in Wisnitz, then part of Austria–Hungary, now in Ukraine. His father, Markus, was an Attorney-General and described as a very intelligent man who was "a shrewd debater and forceful advocate in court".[36] Preminger had a good relationship with both his father and his mother, Josefa.

He was a rebel from an early age and found public school "frightful" (Preminger, 1977). Not surprisingly, since he was often bullied and beaten up at school. As a child he was fascinated by "famous plays" and would truant with other boys and read them in the library. Indeed he began to perform with a private group from about 11 years of age. His first real trainer and mentor was the Viennese director Max Reinhardt, who facilitated his involvement with a theatre in Vienna. At his father's request, he completed a law degree at the University of Vienna but continued to pursue an acting career, which culminated in his move to Hollywood in 1935.

PERSONALITY

Preminger was a perfectionist who could hyper-focus on what interested him. He was highly independent: a gambler, a novelty-seeker, a sensation-seeker and a rebel. He essentially had an immature personality, which may reflect some identity diffusion, giving rise to the contradictory, enigmatic figure. Even as a young man he was described as being arrogant and remote. An anonymous friend said of him: "He is vicious, sadistic, cynical, ruthless and heartless – but he is charming". This shows the multiple selves so necessary for

[36] Except where otherwise indicated, quotes in this chapter are from Frischauer (1973).

great creativity. Reflecting on his charisma, Billy Wilder declared: "I always suspected that behind this charisma there was an enigma and that within the enigma there was a web of perplexing riddles challenging the curiosity of the sceptic". This is characteristic of the creative person with unempathetic Asperger traits.

Preminger did display some features of attention deficit hyperactivity disorder. Features that are sometimes seen in association with this condition include being "an extrovert, youthfully brash, volatile, sociable, a public rather than a private man, doer rather than thinker, propelled by instinct as much as by theory". He clearly had a tendency to rage, to engage in endless temper tantrums, but generally calmed down fairly quickly. In fact, his nickname was "Ottocrat". Preminger was always rather hyperkinetic and wanted to move fast. He was described as a man of "perpetual motion and incessant telephoning", involved in "multifarious activities". Producer Nat Rudich, who worked with him for a long time, said that "something has to happen all the time. It is a 24 hour job" being with him and working for him. This is the hyperkinetic part of the ADHD novelty-seeking spectrum. Indeed studio executive Darryl F. Zanuck once remarked that "nobody gave Otto Preminger a start; he gave himself a start!" Not surprisingly, he was a great publicist who showed "egocentricity, megalomania, hang-ups, prejudices, constricted view of the world and indifference to things non-Hollywood".

Preminger certainly was the life and soul of the party and lived a high life, relishing the most expensive hotels. He was a collector of art and amassed a great collection. He loved to find an unknown person and make them a star, as it made him feel extraordinarily powerful. Certainly, he often failed at this.

Preminger had a perverse personality, which is often associated with great creativity. He was an exhibitionist and sadist, and had a "pathological fear of animals". His autobiography, *Preminger: An Autobiography*, (Preminger, 1977) is full of facts with little feeling and giving little sense of himself.

Social Relationships

Preminger was sexually precocious. He was a womaniser who "hated being alone", yet showed characteristics of a loner. He was married three times but each marriage was marred by continual infidelity on his part. According to his third wife, Hope, he enjoyed the image of the "big blustering bully", and he knew all about human emotions and about women. The novelty-seeking and sensation-seeking aspects of his personality found expression in promiscuity and he was particularly fascinated by black women. He had a son, Erik, by the burlesque performer Gypsy Rose Lee, who made contact with him in later life and to his credit Preminger accepted him fully both publicly and privately.

Preminger was noted for being quite sadistic, particularly with children – when they failed to cry on demand in a film he told them their parents wouldn't come back. Where his friends were concerned, he had many a redeeming feature to judge by biographer Willi Frischauer:

> He was loyal to old cronies to the point of sentimentality, extravagantly generous, singularly unpompous, instantly accessible and as free with his time as with his money, never, apparently, operating in compartments and mixing associates from different

spheres of his life, which suggests an honest man who need not adjust to the company he keeps.

He also rescued a few actors in the twilight of their careers and gave them parts when nobody else would.

Work

Likely many a creative talent, Preminger had a shaky start. He turned down a film at the beginning of his career and, not surprisingly, was out of work for quite a while. During this time he was told that he was "signing his professional death warrant". Nevertheless, he was highly persistent and determined. Preminger became a major filmmaker best known for *Anatomy of a Murder*, *Advise & Consent*, *Fallen Angel* and *Bonjour Tristesse*. His career was interspersed by acting roles, but controversial to the end. He was described by the media as "the most hated man in the movie history". He loved to shock and did so superbly in his enthusiastic acting of Nazi figures in various films. The more distasteful a subject to the public, the more he was attracted by it. In fact, he was "totally lacking in political judgement". He loved controversy, high emotion and sensation-seeking, and he created these endlessly both on and off screen.

He had filmmaking talent in no small measure and best remembered as a mould-breaker and taboo-breaker in being the first to depict drug addiction in *The Man with the Golden Arm*; homosexuality in *Advise & Consent*; and rape in *Anatomy of a Murder*.

Like many celebrated directors, he was dictatorial and often paranoid in his work. His working philosophy was "I am the king here. Whoever eats my bread, sings my song." With his law training, he was quite litigious and crossed swords with unions and wanted "a no-strike clause", and was not above mistreating actors either. According to Frischauer, he was a stern puppet master, "vigorously pulling the strings, storming his way through production after production, losing his temper, terrifying one moment, all sweetness the next as if there had never been an unholy row." In the trade he was known as a teaser, a taunter, and a tester of other people's endurance. Actor Michael Caine said of him that he loved to embarrass actors in front of other people "to tear down their egos". He was only happy if everybody else was miserable: "Still, if you can keep his paranoia from beating you down, you can learn a lot from this guy."

Otto Preminger died in New York on 23 April 1986, aged 80.

Chapter 37

SERGEI EISENSTEIN

Sergei Eisenstein (1898–1948) was Russia's most famous film director and film theorist. He has been described "as much a theorist of the cinema as a director".[37] His best-known films include *Battleship Potemkin* (1925), *October: Ten Days that Shook the World* (1928) and *Alexander Nevsky* (1938). I believe that he had Asperger syndrome.

BACKGROUND

Sergei Mikhailovich Eisenstein was born on 23 January 1898 in Riga, Latvia, into a middle-class family. His father, Mikhail, was an architect, who was described as "pedantic", "preposterous" and a "bully". Like many great artists, Eisenstein had a fantasy that his father was not his real father (another example is Richard Wagner). Eisenstein said that his mother, Julia, was eccentric and that he himself was eccentric too. As a child he was overprotected by her and had a hostile relationship with his father. This is frequently a typical background for a great creator. Family life was uneasy and Eisenstein remembered the repeated beatings he received as a child. His parents separated during his childhood and his mother brought him to live in St Petersburg. In fact, his mother was quite a courageous, independent-minded woman. Interestingly, she and Eisenstein had "big" heads in common. At his death Eisenstein's brain weighed 1,700 grams, as against an average of 1,400 grams. About half of those with Asperger syndrome have large heads.

Eisenstein loved to draw as a child and was fascinated with reading, devouring many a book. He often in fact found books more companionable than peers. Another fascination was footwear. In school he was a lonely, highly intelligent boy – isolated and not a good mixer. He was also rather hyperkinetic. A classmate, Erwin Mednis, referred to his "rather feminine" appearance and said that "he often looked more like a girl than a boy". This would manifest itself as identity diffusion throughout his life.

Early in life Eisenstein became fascinated with the theatre. He had a systematising brain and, not surprisingly, loved theorising. Initially he studied engineering, like Alfred Hitchcock. According to biographer Ronald Bergan, the "earnest and logical" side to Eisenstein was one of the few positive traits that he inherited from his father – the engineer's quality of

---

[37] Except where otherwise indicated, quotes in this chapter are from Bergan (1999).

preparedness, the belief in the need for pre-planning, and the merits of construction. He developed intricate, detailed blueprints for each project, as his scripts and sketches testify. In 1918, he joined the Red Army and supported the October Revolution.

PERSONALITY

Eisenstein was described as having the classic Asperger features of piercing eyes and a "strange, semi-sarcastic smile". He had an unusual tone of voice, as is characteristic of persons with Asperger syndrome too; Bergan describes it as a "quirky timbre" and having an "unpleasant squeaky quality". With a great capacity to hyper-focus, Eisenstein was a massive observer and paid enormous attention to detail. Highly visual, he was fascinated by colour and the theory of colour, like many with Asperger syndrome. Much like Luis Buñuel, he loved religious rituals, especially that of the Russian Orthodox Church. He also "adored clowns". Throughout his life he was a novelty-seeker, hyperkinetic and distractible, with poor attention for things that failed to interest him.

Eisenstein was essentially a complex, contradictory character with identity diffusion, who always looked for the different sides of characters in his films. Seeing human beings as made up of multiple parts that could be taken apart and put back together was important to him. There were also naive and child-like components to his personality. He drifted easily between fact and fiction and indeed the so-called realist film *Battleship Potemkin* was as much fiction as fact. This is necessary for great artistic creativity, however.

His talents were many and varied: he was a polymath and a polyglot. He learned at an incredibly fast rate, as is typical of people of genius. He knew a vast number of facts and had truly "encyclopaedic knowledge", though often described as arrogant. As a superb linguist, he could move easily between a number of languages and would only use the word or language that was "exact" in each case. James Joyce and his style of writing influenced him profoundly and his own writings were often "set out in the numbered paragraph style of Spinoza or Kant". This is an autistic style, as exemplified by Wittgenstein the philosopher. His humour was described as "robust and Rabelaisian" – and indeed persons with Asperger syndrome can handle humour (Lyons & Fitzgerald, 2005). He was also given to "repetition", which is much loved by persons with Asperger syndrome.

According to Bergan, he had an intellectual desire to be a rationalist and had an "emotional pull towards mysticism". He was very much fascinated by the occult and in what would now be called science fiction – matters that are greatly of interest to the autistic mind, i.e., the "cosmic universal confluence". He was also interested in ecstasy and "prenatal experiences". As an intellectual Eisenstein was drawn to Freud and psychoanalysis, and also to Marx and Pavlov. In a way he saw himself as a "God" similar to them. Hence many of his films appear "formalistic", such as *Battleship Potemkin*. His relationship with Stalin was uncertain – it appears to us that he supported Stalin a great deal and many regarded his films as Soviet propaganda.

Other areas of fascination included perversity, sadism and torture, the Marquis de Sade and the killings of the French Revolution. Much like Buñuel, Hitchcock and DeMille, he was fascinated by sadism and cruelty. There was a great deal of almost mindless violence in his films, demonstrating his "alarming streak of brutality". He also created a good number of perverse sadomasochistic drawings. Some of the drawings were homoerotic like those of musician Kurt Cobain. Bergan states that he drew a number of penises, in different postures, with faces drawn on them: "a giant, fat, bourgeois, sportsman, a dwarf – happy and erect or sad and drooping". Bergan believes that the sadomasochistic streak in Eisenstein's character, and his morbid fascination with martyrdom, especially that of St Sebastian, which is so prevalent in gay iconography, dated back to his childhood reading, and later revealed itself in his drawings, films, and in his memoirs. This mythology "merged with that of the bullfight such as the crucified bull pierced with arrows, and St Sebastian as a dying matador". Lawrence of Arabia also had sadomasochistic elements to his personality and it is hardly surprising that Eisenstein expressed an interest in him. In a way Eisenstein was polymorphously perverse; however, the perverse aspects of his personality were critical to his creativity. The burden of creativity also meant that he suffered considerable depression.

Eisenstein was quite androgynous and interested in "hermaphrodites". He worked in Mexico in the early 1930s and noted the androgyny of Mexican Indians:

> The masculine frenzy of temper, the feminine softness of outline hiding a steel musculature and the outer muscles flowing around it; and the disposition to forgive coupled with a childish naughtiness … Adult men and women seem adolescent in comparison with other races; a race of young people, where the men have not yet lost their early femininity, nor the women abandoned their puerile pranks and both seem charmingly childish … Mexico is tender and lyrical but brutal too.

Bergan describes this correctly as "a composite that found an echo in his own character".

Social Relationships

Eisenstein had problems with reciprocal social relationships. He married to cover up his homosexuality and indeed when he wrote his autobiography he forgot to mention his wife, Vera Atasheva. Their marriage was largely platonic and produced no children. In his dealings with people he was very controlling and dominating, however. Once at a banquet in Hollywood he offered to change places with the butler "on the grounds that he disliked being waited on". He was at times very tactless and unaware of the unreasonable pressures he was putting on people. Clearly, he had an empathy deficit.

Work

According to Bergan, Eisenstein liked to take a plot apart like a machine to see how it worked. This is very much like Hitchcock and constitutes an autistic style of working. Bergan notes that genius is "the infinite capacity for taking pains" and certainly Eisenstein took great pains. He approached his work like a great artist would a painting. Writer Herbert Marshall said of Eisenstein's editing that "the basic method of artistic composition applied to all works of art". Being highly visual, Eisenstein was fascinated in particular with Leonardo da Vinci, who was both an artist and scientist. He said it was da Vinci that influenced him in producing the "montage sequence" in films that became his trademark and was so influential in later filmmaking. For Eisenstein, a montage was “the associative chain between a certain depiction and the image which it should evoke in our minds … a chain of intermediate depictions which coalesce into an image”. In the tradition of da Vinci, Eisenstein became the great engineering visual artist. Logic was very important to him as well as “mathematical precision” – just like it was for Leonardo da Vinci. When mathematical precision was combined with emotional intensity it gave rise to great art. Eisenstein said of da Vinci’s painting *Virgin of the Rocks* that it had the “geometric arrangement of line and form, from the positioning of the figures and setting … Yet this knowledge in no way diminishes the intense emotion, the feeling of ecstasy that overwhelms me. The logic behind it makes everything clearer, but only after the emotional response.” Eisenstein also admired Walt Disney, another Asperger-type filmmaker, and there are strong similarities between them. Eisenstein was also influenced by the work of Francis Bacon, a painter with Asperger syndrome.

Eisenstein believed wholeheartedly in Goethe’s assertion that “in order to be truthful you can risk an occasional defiance of truth itself”. Eisenstein paid attention to this in his films, for example, *Battleship Potemkin*, depicting events that did not always stand up to historical scrutiny. His realist style had tremendous impact, however. He said declared that “I prefer to hit people hard on the nose … I don’t produce films to please the eye but to make a point”. He was said to be “a cold, intellectual artist, uninterested in the ‘human participants’ in his films, but only in the theories behind them”. Others described him as a “calculating, didactic theorist, whose films lack humanity”. These criticisms are valid; however, he was also a courageous director in a communist state. His film *Ivan the Terrible* was a major achievement. Needless to say, Ivan was quite perverse, and it is not surprising that Eisenstein was interested in him.

Film theorist Robert Stam (2000) notes that commentators found Eisenstein’s approach “totalitarian and suffocating”. There was also an enigmatic quality to his work. Stam (2000) quotes Russian filmmaker Andrei Tarkovsky as stating that “Eisenstein makes thought into a despot; it leaves no ‘air,’ nothing of that unspoken elusiveness which is perhaps the most captivating quality of all art”.

Sergei Eisenstein died from a heart attack in Moscow on 11 February 1948, at the age of 50.

Chapter 38

JOHN SCHLESINGER

John Schlesinger (1926–2003) is best known for directing films such as *Midnight Cowboy*, *The Day of the Locust* and *Marathon Man*. He was a rebel and innovator and meets the profile of many highly successful film directors in which identity diffusion is critical. I believe that he had Asperger syndrome.

BACKGROUND

John Schlesinger was born in London on 16 February 1926. His father, Bernard, was a pioneering and innovative paediatrician in the world-renowned Hospital for Sick Children, Great Ormond Street. The eldest of five children, Schlesinger therefore came from a privileged background much disposed towards the arts. Bernard was rather stubborn but courageous and Schlesinger's paternal grandmother was, as often the case with grandparents, more free and playful with the children and particularly with Schlesinger. Schlesinger had a Jewish background but was not very orthodox and attended an Anglican boarding school. His parents believed that too much praise for a child could damage their development: in actual fact, it was the withholding of praise that was somewhat damaging for Schlesinger. Both parents were musical and his mother Winifred in particular was an accomplished violinist; she later developed a malignancy in middle age and died.

Schlesinger had an uncle who was regarded as being very odd and most likely had Asperger syndrome as well. Schlesinger's brother, Roger, remembered this uncle as leaving behind after his death a box filled with little wrapped packets containing blades: "every blade he had ever shaved with, together with a description of what sort of shave it had been".[38] This uncle, like many with Asperger syndrome, got on far better with children than with adults.

From early in life Schlesinger was controlling and dominating, and poor at social interactional play. He began to direct small plays with his siblings from an early age, which is not an untypical beginning for people who later become great artists. Having received the gift of a home movie camera at age 11 he began to shoot movies. He certainly had narrow interests, particularly in this kind of playmaking and filmmaking.

---

[38] Except where otherwise indicated, quotes in this chapter are from Mann (2005).

Schlesinger's childhood–school experience was of a typical Asperger type. Though bullied at school, his parents were not at all sympathetic, expecting him to cope with it himself. It is not surprising then that he became depressed at school. He was "shy and awkward" and had a tendency to be ill at ease. He was not a sportsman in terms of playing team games with other children: "He was the son who was never as good at games as his father wished him to be." Once again he was on the edge, looking in, and wanted to do his own thing. Schlesinger certainly had no wish to do what other children did. At heart he was a negative thinker and had a negative attributional style. Of course, this undermined his self-esteem even more and also drove him to greater efforts in his work. Like most boys with Asperger syndrome, he felt completely tormented by school, and "would wander off on his own, away from the other boys, dreaming up scenarios for the plays and films he'd make during school holidays".

He was the classic odd boy out, seen as eccentric in his behaviour. His growing awareness of his homosexuality also increased his sense of being an outsider. Left to his own devices he indulged his huge imagination and was a daydreamer. He was a huge observer of life and saw more than other boys did and furthermore could pick out greater detail in social situations. Schlesinger was very much a visual thinker: he adored photography and had a massive artistic imagination. He was interested in the odd, the strange, the bizarre and the unknown as well as in musical dramas. This was also part of his novelty-seeking. It also found expression in architecture, but only as an aide to getting into filmmaking.

Schlesinger spent time in the army during the Second World War and, not surprisingly for a person with Asperger syndrome, joined the Royal Engineers. He hated being controlled by the army, however, and showed evidence of oppositional behaviour.

Personality

Schlesinger was highly innovative, novelty-seeking and sensation-seeking. He always pushed things to the limit and worked till his health gave out in the end. Despite being a rather charismatic individual, he was always uncertain of himself. His character was marked with identity diffusion and therefore in his films he moved fluidly from one identity to another, which made it difficult for critics to pigeonhole him. Persons with Asperger syndrome are often interested in the interface between fact and fiction and Schlesinger was no exception. His films were best when they expressed his personal conflicts, or had figures who expressed these conflicts. He was a man in search of self – in search of some resolution to his identity diffusion, which he never achieved. Throughout his life, he retained an immature, child-like element to his personality, which allowed him to see the world through the eyes of a child. His homosexuality and homosexual identity also had a powerful impact on his films. Great creativity is very often carried out by what is considered outsiders. It would be interesting to know how many great directors are homosexual or bisexual, and whether the proportion is greater than in the general population. Casual observation would suggest that this is so, and indeed sexual identity diffusion appears to be quite important for great creativity. Of course, the vast majority of homosexuals and heterosexuals are not creative in the genius sense.

Schlesinger had quite vulnerable self-esteem and was rather narcissistic. Many great creators show these traits, which can often be a motivating force. For him, work was his self-esteem regulator and antidepressant. His self-esteem could sink quickly with obstacles, but he always fought back and was not one to lie down and surrender. He also suffered a good deal of anxiety and depression in his life, offset somewhat by his immersion in work. There was also a rather sadistic, perverse element in Schlesinger's personality. Some of his jokes were tactless and he didn't fully appreciate this because of his empathy difficulties. Temper tantrums occurred throughout the course of his life too.

Social Relationships

Schlesinger was not a joiner of groups and was very independent. As with all persons with Asperger syndrome, there was an isolated, lonely core to his personality. He had problems with superficial chitchat in cocktail party settings. He also at times had a fear of social groups, particularly in earlier life, which was almost a form of social phobia. He was fearful of intimacy and of other human beings. Other times, he had a tendency to try to get "blood from a stone" in seeking to form relationships with people who were unavailable. This is rather perverse, masochistic and self-defeating. Nevertheless, it mirrored his relationship with his father, where it was so difficult for Schlesinger to get praise or attention. He did have close family relationships, however, and never got over the grief of his sister Susan committing suicide in 1963, at the age of 30.

Schlesinger engaged in a certain amount of promiscuity, although by Hollywood standards it was limited. He preferred the masculine gender at any function he organised. Like a number of other homosexual directors, Schlesinger formed a long-term relationship in the latter half of his life, similar to comedian Frankie Howerd. This was hugely important to him, and certainly by midlife Schlesinger showed a capacity to improve his interpersonal relationships and to trust people. This is quite common in Asperger syndrome. In fact the philosopher Wittgenstein did so as well and his long-term partner in later life was HIV positive. Indeed Schlesinger lost many friends to AIDS.

Work

Echoing his own life, Schlesinger was interested in outsiders, people on the edge, and these featured in his films. At his best he was a meticulous filmmaker and enjoyed the preparatory phase of the filmmaking process more than the actual day-to-day shooting. Like most directors, including Hitchcock, his work was not consistently brilliant and he made some rather poor films as well.

One of Schlesinger's major films, *Midnight Cowboy*, was described by biographer William Mann as a "dazzling display of decadence and perversion". A very intense person, Schlesinger concentrated very much on what interested him, such as thrillers, horror movies and the occult. Mann points out that he was interested in making "thrillers, with magic and illusion, and the macabre defining his art", and emphasises that he was a great storyteller. In some films you could say there was a kind of autistic narrative that gave the film an incoherence.

Schlesinger essentially wanted to move his audiences emotionally. Work in some way normalised his conflicted psyche; it also allowed him to get away from his psyche. This did not mean that work could not be tormenting for him, however. Filmmaking is undeniably a very difficult job. In a way he did not differentiate himself from his films – he was a good person if he made a good film. He merged with them. Because of his negative thinking he needed the applause of the audience to feel better about himself; therefore, critics were particularly upsetting to him. During shooting he would have periods of great uncertainty and doubt about his art and his capacity to make a good film. This linked to his negative attributional style. There was also a masochistic, somewhat self-destructive element to him; hence his choice of some very unsatisfactory film projects.

More than likely he had weak central coherence along with his massive "eye for detail". In life he had tremendous determination to achieve his aims and extraordinary visual imagination, which was highly important to him in filmmaking. Like many with Asperger syndrome, he adored television and indeed factual channels. He also produced operas, not surprisingly given his interest in musical dramas and in music generally. And, regardless of the genre he employed, he was always recreating new worlds to move audiences in whatever way he could. According to Mann, the critic and screenwriter Gavin Lambert said that there are those who create the same world with variations in it and "those like Schlesinger, who create a different world with each film yet show the same person behind the different worlds".

Schlesinger was undoubtedly a great creator who was interested in the development of artists, particularly visual artists, and only stopped working when serious illness prevented him. He was a massive observer of the human condition, like another with Asperger syndrome, George Orwell (Fitzgerald, 2005).

John Schlesinger died in California on 25 July 2003, aged 77.

Chapter 39

SAM PECKINPAH

Sam Peckinpah (1925–1984) was the classic psychologically disturbed director of genius – a tormented but significant filmmaker of the more perverse, transgressor type. Among his well-known movies are *The Wild Bunch*, *Straw Dogs* and *Pat Garrett and Billy the Kid*. He had many features of Asperger syndrome.

BACKGROUND

David Samuel "Sam" Peckinpah was born on 21 February 1925 in Fresno, California, into a middle-class family of Frisian heritage. He said that "my people were all crazy, just crazy. And they dominated the valley too".[39] He was spoilt by his mother, Fern, but nonetheless had a deep anger towards her and said that "when she died, he was going to piss on [her] grave". She was a hypochondriac, like himself, and appears to have suffered from paraphrenia in later life. His father, David, was an autodidactic man and a great reader. However, his father was under his mother's thumb and Peckinpah experienced severe corporal punishment at his hand, which engendered a lifelong hostility towards his parents. As a child, Peckinpah was aggressive to other children. He also had several features of attention deficit hyperactivity disorder and in particular was very restless, with huge reserves of energy. The oppositional and defiant aspect of his character led to him being described as "a wild boy". His school progress was less than outstanding, although he showed artistic talent from an early age.

PERSONALITY

Peckinpah was an enigmatic, highly contradictory man, whose personality was marked with identity diffusion. He was very much a myth-maker and tended to "invent the life he needed". He drifted easily between fact and fiction, as many creative people do. In effect, he was like a chameleon with multiple selves and confused people by switching from one persona to the next. He had many sides but, according to biographer Marshall Fine, "that

[39] Except where otherwise indicated, quotes in this chapter are from Fine (1991).

charismatic side – the thoughtful, intuitive, funny, playful Sam – inspired almost fatal loyalty in his friends and could project a powerful magnetism". Identity diffusion was one of the keys to his creativity: the clash of various identities led to his creative outbursts. As previously noted, creative activity is an attempt at healing identity diffusion – it is part of the search for an authentic self, which is never fully achieved. As Fine says, he was always "reinventing himself as an adult". Actor Dustin Hoffman said "don't ask me what the real Sam Peckinpah is like. Because I have no idea." This again suggests identity diffusion. Peckinpah certainly did not verbalise his inner thoughts. Actor Dennis Hopper recalled that Peckinpah "didn't say a hell of a lot. He had an intense kind of energy but he didn't seem to have a great gift for gab."

At heart Peckinpah was a novelty-seeker and sensation-seeker who grew bored quite easily. It often found release in various addictions; alcohol, drugs and gambling, where he was given to "wild hunches and reckless bets". There has always been a group of Hollywood creators with this profile; he was a tormented individual, yet one cannot have great art without tormented individuals providing it.

Peckinpah was a very tense person, a very anxious person, a very conflicted person, a person very uncertain about himself behind the multiple personas that he presented. An acquaintance in his early life described him as an "unpredictable loner with maybe a little chip on his shoulder". The aggressive instinct was highly developed in him. He often showed great lack of empathy, was very controlling and dominating, and found it extremely difficult to see things from others' point of view and be sensitive to other people. He had a kind of narcissistic self-certainty that he was right and indeed was very uncompromising. In terms of creating films he had a high ego ideal and was a perfectionist, working very slowly and meticulously to achieve the right effect. He was poor at collaboration and "never one to take a compliment graciously".

Transgressors are often great creators and with Peckinpah this was the case. He displayed a rather perverse personality and was quite sadomasochistic. Egocentric and selfish, he took pleasure from physical violence, especially towards women, and his most controversial statement was that most women enjoy rape. Actor Charlton Heston remarked that there was a "dangerous instability in Sam. I am not saying he was literally crazy, but he was unstable".

Social Relationships

Peckinpah was a "strangely solitary figure" and saw himself as an outsider. In his dealings with others he was a cantankerous, difficult person and Fine points out that he was "prickly and insulting". Charlton Heston said that "Sam was a driver but a terrible leader … he was good with actors but … lousy with crew people." Peckinpah seemed very poor at reading social situations, yet in the wider social context of the film set people often felt he was very intuitive about them and had an idea of what was going on in their minds even before it was expressed. There is a huge contradiction here again. Although he showed gross empathy deficits, he was also a massive observer of other people and could perceive their feelings if he wished. His daughter Sharon stated that "he had a psychic sense of what was going on with people" and indeed disturbed people not uncommonly have this talent. It often led to disharmony on the film set. According to Fine, Peckinpah rarely told actors what to do, letting them find their moments themselves. He would also manipulate them in ways that would provoke off-screen responses that would alter their performances. Actor James Coburn said that "Sam made a lot of assumptions. That was one of the things that caused problems. He made assumptions and acted on them and created acrimony as a result."

Charlton Heston also said that "Sam is the only person I have ever physically threatened on a set", that he "won't quit until he gets you mad at him", and that "there are directors who seem to function well in an atmosphere of continuing crisis. Sam is one. Personally, I can't stand it."

His personal relationships were fraught with difficulty and characterised by violence and wife beating. His hostility to his parents had endured and he wanted to get married without their presence. Three of his marriages ended in divorce, although he remarried his second wife twice. He was extremely difficult to live with to judge by his first wife, Marie's account: "I was sensitive to anything he told me. If I didn't respond to something immediately, he took it personally. I was fearful of displeasing him." He completed ignored and dismissed her wish to be an actress – they met while she was a drama student. She was there to serve him, to be his slave, and that was all. His once broke her cheekbone in a drunken rage and often beat her up. She said: "He was a very sensitive man … which made him wonderful in some ways and extraordinarily cruel as well." He was a Jekyll and Hyde character and did suffer guilt when he sobered up.

When he had children, four from his first marriage and one from his second, he showed little interest in being a father. Like his own parents he was an equally poor parent to his own children and rather bored by fathering. Sharon Peckinpah once said that her father had his priorities: "his work, his drinking, and then his children came into it. Our welfare was high on his list of priorities but not necessarily seeing us." His first divorce was acrimonious and he sought custody of the children, which was absurd and of course did not happen. After the marriage he became hypersexual for a period and domestic violence became a feature of his intimate relationships.

WORK

Fine quotes an old saying that "a man has to be judged, in the final judgement, not by the depths to which he sinks but by the heights to which he rises". In this respect, Peckinpah was a great filmmaker, though many of his films focus on violence, so much so that he was called "Bloody Sam". He tended to make up films as he went along, despite having a script. His filmmaking was also in the here-and-now mould and his approach was to "destroy the script, break everything down into small pieces, and then reassemble it".

Peckinpah argued with the studio heads and this led to him spending years in the wilderness, during which he wrote incessantly and obsessively. Many studios saw him as "trouble" and he was once described as "the best rewrite man in town". Film producer Daniel Melnick said that one of the great things about Peckinpah, unappreciated by most, was that he was a director who knew everything there was to know about film. Melnick also remarked:

> Sam had an ability to convince you that he was the last person, if not on earth, certainly in the film business, with both guts and integrity. In truth, a lot of that was

Sam's sense of himself. Sam, like most people in a highly competitive business, made all kinds of decisions out of expediency.

The quintessential Peckinpah themes, according to Fine, were loyalty to partners, living up to a code, honour among the amoral, and men caught in a time warp. But Peckinpah will probably be best remembered for the level of violence in his films, most notably the western epic, *The Wild Bunch*. Despite being phobic of blood in real life, Peckinpah gloried in gory movies. The critics quickly seized upon it: the *Los Angeles Times* said that he had "an instinct for both cruelty and compassion", while *Time* magazine described him as a "maverick action-film director whose best work combines an obsession with the ubiquity of violence and a surgeon's skill at blood letting". The critic and academic Judith Crist described *The Wild Bunch* as "two hours of murder and mayhem wherein the innocent are killed by the bad guys who are killed by worse guys. I'd as likely drop in on the local abattoir for entertainment as look to the bloodiest spaghetti western for social significance." Film producer Arnold Laven said that there was a reality and meanness to Peckinpah's violence that bothered him: "It was overt."

Success was a double-edged sword for Peckinpah. After *The Wild Bunch*, according to Fine, "his demons of self-doubt were being kept at bay even as the ones that fuelled his sense of omnipotence were being fed". Success had a huge impact on his personality; though still a workaholic, he was happiest when shooting a film and king of the castle. However, his authority did not wane on the film set. He continued to be extremely controlling and dominating and often sacked people, seeming to get a kick out of abusing people verbally. According to Jules Levy, he was very violent-minded, an angry person for no reason: "He had talent as a writer and director but he was impossible. He would do things the hard way and not be concerned about costs or the problems with the studio."

It is hardly surprising that he became paranoid on cocaine and, in 1979, suffered a heart attack. He had a pacemaker inserted and, according to Paul Peterson, his ex-brother-in-law, he was convinced that the pacemaker was a CIA plant and that it could be detonated at any time.

Sam Peckinpah died in California on 28 December 1984, aged 59.

Chapter 40

FRANK CAPRA

Frank Capra (1897–1991) was a major film director, described by John Ford as "the greatest motion picture director in the world". His films won numerous Academy Awards, among them *It Happened One Night*, *Mr Smith Goes to Washington* and *It's a Wonderful Life*. I believe that he showed traits suggesting Asperger syndrome.

BACKGROUND

Frank Russell Capra was born Francesco Rosario Capra in Sicily on 18 May 1897. His birth was traumatic, a not uncommon event in persons with traits of Asperger syndrome. His father, Salvatore, was a farmer but also "a dreamer, with the poetic soul of troubadour".[40] Clearly, the apple does not fall far from the tree. Salvatore was musical but a "ne'er-do-well" and hence there was constant marital tension and bickering between his mother, Sarah, and father. Capra said that his "mother had a hard head" and was very much a survivor and a practical woman. An Italian childhood friend remembered Capra as being "brazen and pugnacious". In search of a better life, the family emigrated to the USA when Frank was six years old and settled in Los Angeles.

By all accounts Capra always lacked "a family feeling". Indeed he was highly ambivalent about his mother, moving between putting her on a pedestal and remembering the severe corporal punishment she administered to him. In fact, he said his house was "a house of pain" and that his mother was "a witch". He often felt rejected by her. Sarah had some Asperger-type traits herself: she was not one for hugs and affection, had difficulty in expressing herself, and was "a hard woman".

As he grew up Capra was totally uninterested in his place of origin and his relatives; instead he was wholly focused on climbing the professional ladder. He was obsessed with education and rightly saw it as his ticket out of poverty. He was a very bright, intelligent boy with an engineering-type mind. At school he was "jeered at, scorned and even beaten" (Capra, 1971). This is not an uncommon experience for those with Asperger syndrome. A childhood acquaintance, Rory Washington, recalled that he was "different", "studious",

[40] Except where otherwise indicated, quotes in this chapter are from McBride (1992).

"didn't compete in the playground", "wasn't tough", was a "bookworm", and was "aloof". His personality led to him being excluded from gangs.

At the age of 10, while continuing his education, he became a newspaper seller for several years and was "bullied" and "raped" by an older male. He was mathematically minded, as persons with Asperger syndrome often are, and after high school enrolled in the California Institute of Technology to study chemical engineering. His mother was against him continuing in school, but later did support his education. He clearly had talents in this area and soon became an expert on cameras and photography. Persons with Asperger syndrome are often fascinated by language and Capra was no exception. He was a massive observer and a great reader. His superb linguistic skills came to the fore and he benefited from his acting experiences at school. Like his father he was also musically minded and could play the violin, mandolin, guitar and ukulele. In order to make extra money during college he regularly played his guitar in a brothel.

PERSONALITY

Capra was an incredibly fast learner and addicted to filmmaking and this became his narrow interest. Furthermore, he was a novelty-seeker and a sensation-seeker, which helped his film work greatly, as did his extraordinarily persistent and stubborn nature. He was helped on his way to the top by people such as teachers, but liked to play this down, just like Leonard Bernstein. He preferred to see himself as the origin of all his greatness; he viewed himself as unique in comparison to his siblings and said that his family saw him as a maverick (Capra, 1971).

Capra's autobiography is better for his comments on other people than on himself. This is typical of persons with Asperger syndrome, who are better at observing other people than themselves. He probably had identity diffusion, because there is no sense of himself in his autobiography. Indeed he had the wonderment of a child and retained this in his attitude and view of films. His love of nature and the great outdoors ensured his being out of the house often. According to biographer Joseph McBride, he had a "penchant for fanciful storytelling" and a "dreamy peasant mysticism". Later he adored Mussolini and kept an oil painting of him on his bedroom wall. Indeed persons with Asperger syndrome are fascinated by dictators.

Capra was no stranger to melancholia and depression and undeniably work was his antidepressant. Following the death of his young son, he suffered major depression.

SOCIAL RELATIONSHIPS

Capra clearly had difficulty making friends and was a loner. A former classmate, Esther Gleason Schlinger, recalled: "I don't know anybody who really liked him. He was ostracized, people never invited him anywhere. He was just a terrible wop." Arguably, these comments reflect worse on Schlinger than on Capra. She also said that he had his own life, that he didn't care about other people, and that "he went away by himself". According to Schlinger, nobody would go out with him, he dressed untidily, he was uncouth and had no manners. She also described him as "derelict, an outcast". If given half a chance, Capra could be aggressive. By his own admission, Capra was ashamed of himself as a boy and admitted that he found it difficult to socialise. He had one friend, Jimmy Doolittle, later a general in the US Army, which is typical of persons with Asperger syndrome.

In adult life, the film studio gradually became his real home and the workers there his family. This is typical of someone with Asperger syndrome: they can cope with a working family more than a real family. Capra's first marriage ended in divorce while his second produced four children. He had "sexual problems" in both his marriages. There is no doubt that his second son John had autism. This boy died after a routine tonsillectomy but had delayed speech development, poor eye contact, and was happy in his own company. He was a very isolated child who was fascinated by the sun.

Work

Given his addiction to filmmaking, Capra was always a workaholic and described as "brash". At the start of his career he worked at absolutely everything in relation to making a film from the bottom up. For him, his own vision of what a film should be was paramount. He believed that it was one man's singular vision for each movie that could work: it couldn't be done by committee. He wrote that "there are no rules in filmmaking, only sins. And the cardinal sin is dullness" (Capra, 1971).

Clearly, filmmaking was everything to him and went to enormous lengths to realise his vision. He recalled that no human can ever forget the thrill of their first accomplishment, their first film and that "I picked the creative brains of others, stole ideas, made energy count where talent failed" (Capra, 1971). He points out that no two motion pictures are alike in the making: "Each film is a living piece of your life in a small unreal world with its own character and integrity; its own new set of memorable experiences and incredible happenings. You wish it would never end. But the film does end" (Capra, 1971).

His advice at the end of his autobiography was "so hang in there". He certainly did. Frank Capra died in California on 3 September 1991, aged 94.

Chapter 41

GEORGE CUKOR

George Cukor (1899–1983) was a major film director whose films included *The Philadelphia Story*, *A Star Is Born* and *My Fair Lady*. He was a highly enigmatic and contradictory figure, with a very strong feminine self and showed evidence of identity diffusion. In his work he was fascinated by outsiders and by the effect of chance on the affairs of men and women.

BACKGROUND

George Dewey Cukor was born in New York City on 7 July 1899 to Hungarian Jewish parents. His father, Victor, was a shadowy, "colourless" figure more interested in the internal than the external world and lived in a world of his own.[41] He tended to merge with the background, loved to watch life passing by, and was an almost invisible man. Psychoanalysts suggest that fathers of this kind often have homosexual sons, while Cukor's close relationship with his mother, Helen, also supports psychoanalytic theories. Nevertheless, sexuality is more complicated than this factor alone. Cukor was myopic, did not have an impressive academic record, and truanted from school. As a boy, he was fascinated by "popular mechanics" but bored by sports. As an adolescent he was not interested in girls. This type of background is not uncommon in creative personalities. Cukor's genuine interest in the theatre began in childhood and his show-business career was formally launched in 1919 on becoming stage manager of a theatre troupe in Chicago.

PERSONALITY

Cukor was a massive observer, much like his father. He had many ideas and was enormously energetic, fun loving and extravagant – a novelty-seeker in essence. Throughout his life he was a massive collector of everything that interested him: programmes, letters, photographs, paintings, etc. and threw out very little as a result. He also had a photographic memory and was a prolific letter-writer. All this suggests Asperger syndrome traits; however,

[41] Except where otherwise indicated, quotes in this chapter are from McGilligan (1991).

he was enormously social at the same time and a good listener. Physically, Cukor had an unattractive appearance, described as "a lack of physical beauty" and that "ugly is the word that frequently cropped up, unprompted" when people were asked about him. Throughout life he was obsessed with cleanliness.

Cukor was a highly contradictory figure with multiple selves, which was partly responsible for his great creativity. He was rather mysterious, though far from having a "put-on air". On a film set he would regularly carry round a novel and go "over and over the same page or the same paragraph that he had marked – even after the scenes had been written – as if searching for some elusive significance". In fact, the most elusive thing of all was himself, though he never managed to find himself. According to biographer Patrick McGilligan, he always looked for approval from the big studio father figures such as Jack Warner. While Cukor had only a rather vague identity, he was generally quite secretive and made homophobic comments to cover up the fact that he was homosexual. McGilligan points out that he was always "camping" and making fun of homosexuals. He was also voyeuristic in his wish to know in great detail about people's sex lives. According to actress Ruth Hammond, he had a great empathy for woman characters – this was because of the strong female component to his personality, which was key to his success. He could identify with women and had a deep, insightful understanding of the human personality, particularly the female one.

Cukor had a special talent for language and was often "spewing out foreign phrases". He also had a store of funny stories – "vulgar and otherwise" – for every occasion. In addition, he was a hyperkinetic talker whose vicious side was shown in his jokes about homosexuals and Jews. Given his linguistic talents, he paid huge attention to the language in scripts, word by word. On set he tended to talk too much and overexplain things, at least according to the actresses he worked with. Cukor was an "inveterate gossip", which was probably also linked to his rather "feminine" personality. His letters were full of "chatter about other people but superficial about his own emotions". In fact, he was something of a "frustrated writer" from his youth as well.

There was a "tough resilience and inner determination" to Cukor's character too, which sometimes featured tantrums on his part. He was thus able to pick himself up and dust himself down after a setback. Cukor earned a vast amount of money but had financial problems later in his life. He had quite a lavish lifestyle, but tended to compartmentalise his life because of his homosexuality. For the same reason he could not write an autobiography.

Social Relationships

Cukor did not like to be alone and constantly interacted with people as a way of averting loneliness and avoiding looking at himself. He was highly outgoing and gregarious, the life and soul of the party, and maintained relationships that endured. He was masterful at the dinner table, drawing everyone out. He loved to talk on the phone and had endless parties, on which he spent a considerable fortune. According to McGilligan, Cukor always had been obsessively secretive about himself – "determined to blend in … at the same time that, perversely, he enjoyed throwing out clues". He cultivated important people, including studio bosses, producers, actors, financiers, etc. and was also adept at managing close personal relationships with the wives of powerful men. In fact, both Cole Porter and Cukor gathered around them huge groups of influential and well-known homosexuals at various parties that they regularly hosted. It is possible that homosexuals are more artistic and certainly many artistic people have been homosexuals, for example, Noël Coward.

Cukor led a very active sex life, if somewhat clandestine. Notwithstanding his sociability, he found it very difficult to pick up homosexuals for sex. Usually he paid for sex, despite having a long-term relationship later in life. He liked to have someone else with him in order to engage in the preliminary social interaction. McGilligan notes that he was incessantly curious about whether other people were homosexual or not and always eager to pry into other people's sex lives.

What satisfied him essentially were work, food and sex. A contemporary who knew him well stated that he was always with an entourage and that he was "so totally social that personal relationships seemed non-existent". That said, he could be nasty, sadistic and bullying, for example when ridiculing Joan Crawford in private, yet he was "patient with silliness or vulnerability" and "profusely charming, endless buoyant". He seemed at ease in the intimacy of hotel rooms, in taverns and restaurants. These are not features of Asperger syndrome – quite the opposite, indeed. The actor David Manners stated that Cukor always had quips and funny remarks to make about people and that everybody liked him: "He was like the mother hen, taking care of her chickens; every night he would come to the dressing room to see how you were." He was fond of a saying by songwriter Alan Jay Lerner to "never underestimate the stupidity of actors". Indeed he described actors as insinuating, lazy and undependable, and that they were devoted to bickering and gossiping. He felt that they were "shallow people", yet at the same time he was deeply empathetic with them.

WORK

Endowed with bravery and strength, Cukor very quickly achieved the status of a great director in Hollywood and his films won many and varied Academy Awards. The "gutsy and uncompromising" director was a tremendous collaborator and delegator – again a contrast with John Ford. He is best remembered for his extraordinary skill in working with actors, especially actresses, and his careful attention to detail, paying extreme attention to scripts. *My Fair Lady* was a great success, for which he received his only Academy Award for best director. *Little Women* and *David Copperfield* were notable artistic successes as were *The Philadelphia Story and A Star Is Born*. He was fired from one of the greatest films ever made, *Gone with the Wind*, as it appeared that Clark Gable did not want the film to be directed by a homosexual. Some of the actresses however continued to telephone him for advice during its making.

Cukor was considered a slow director, but could also be quick, tending to rehearse a lot with numerous takes. In this he was precisely the opposite of John Ford. When Cukor directed at a slow pace he became an expensive director for the studio: "He wasted a lot of time on pipe-dream films that never came to pass." Not being a technical man, he left the cinematography to the cameramen.

He essentially confined his work to helping actors, being a tremendous motivator and able to coaxes great performances from them. In directing women, he used various techniques: (1) "flatter her into it", (2) the "lulling technique", (3) the "sane reasoning method", (4) being "hurt, but not angry", (5) "whoever told you you were an actress?", and (6) "my dear child, you must have confidence in me, I know best". That said, he respected women and made them feel very relaxed. Cukor liked strong actresses in particular who could show their weak side. He was marvellous at dealing with very difficult actresses, so much so that he was seen as a "woman's director", just as John Ford was regarded as a man's director. He formed a tremendous actor–director relationship with Katharine Hepburn in particular and she appeared in several of his films. Unusual for the time he also employed a lot of female scriptwriters, and was extremely careful in casting women and in the dialogue he gave them. In effect, he possessed the enhanced capacity for communication which is so often characteristic of females.

Like all good showmen, George Cukor was superb at selling himself. He worked until he was over 80 years of age and died of a heart attack in Los Angeles on 24 January 1983, at the age of 83.

PART III: COMPOSERS AND CONDUCTORS

Chapter 42

LEONARD BERNSTEIN

Leonard Bernstein (1918–1990) was an American composer and conductor for whom "music was a permanent, obsessional necessity" (Burton, 1994). He had a highly contradictory personality and a sometimes tortured personal life.

BACKGROUND

Leonard Bernstein was born Louis Bernstein in Lawrence, Massachusetts on 25 August 1918, into a Ukrainian Jewish family. His parents, Samuel and Jennie, always called him Leonard. His father was a successful businessman and the family lived in considerable comfort, while his mother was a very independent woman. The Bernstein family life was somewhat disharmonious, however. Bernstein felt that there was huge marital conflict between his parents and that they were quite unsuited to each other. His father was "stubborn … and crazy about music", just like Bernstein would become (Burton, 1994). Bernstein, who experienced much childhood illness, was greatly adored by his mother and sister Shirley. (Freud felt this feature was very important for success in later life – it is certainly common in great creators.) As a small child, according to biographer Humphrey Burton (1994), he was caught experimenting sexually with his sister and got into serious trouble.

Bernstein was a hyperkinetic, restless child who ate ravenously. There were certainly elements of the ADHD child in him: he "did virtually no homework" and was easily bored (Burton, 1994). He resisted all discipline at school, being oppositional and defiant, which often goes with ADHD. However, as a child, he was very interested in scientific experiments and had a high IQ. His younger brother Burton said that he was "such a brilliant boy – always the leader of his gang, always the best in school".[42]

Bernstein's interest in music was awakened at a very early age. Even as a toddler he was tremendously drawn to music, according to Humphrey Burton (1994). Though not a musical prodigy, there is no doubt that the seeds of greatness were there. He took to the piano like a duck to water and had an extensive and high-quality musical education. He was an extremely fast learner, as all people with huge musical talent are. From the beginning he was something of a night owl and enjoyed playing the piano at night. From the age of 12, he started

[42] Except where otherwise indicated, quotes in this chapter are from Peyser (1998).

composing and adored having people listening to him. With characteristic independence, he stood apart from the crowd in the sense that people saw him as exceptional and having special talent. After graduating with a music degree from Harvard University in 1939, he enrolled at the Curtis Institute of Music in Philadelphia, where he trained to become a conductor.

PERSONALITY

Some people regard it as sacrilege to analyse genius. They believe that we should simply see geniuses as awesome and admire them. Biographer Joan Peyser points out that many who love Bernstein believe that to analyse is to dissect and to dissect is to destroy. This is an absurd position, as this book attempts to show. Bernstein was undeniably larger than life, a charismatic giant of a man – that was certainly how he came across to me when I once saw him perform at the Royal Albert Hall in London. He had vast energy, the capacity to mesmerise audiences, and was hyperkinetic on the podium.

From early life Bernstein was a novelty-seeker, a sensation-seeker and extremely energetic and egocentric. Hand in hand with that came courage and great determination. Of course these are features of many with great creative talent. He certainly had immense energy and belonged to a group of musically talented people who were described as "a bunch of hyperactive kids". As he progressed in the world of music, Bernstein was always looking for the next mountain to climb in musical terms, always on the go, hyperkinetic, leading life "at a frenetic pace, conducting, lecturing, proselytizing, composing". Naturally with this hyperkinesis, he was a workaholic and drove himself incessantly. He had exceptionally high musical standards in all forms of music, and was extremely demanding of himself and others. In life he was a multitasker and this excited him – and indeed it was part of his hyperkinesis.

Bernstein's character is marked by an extreme independence of mind. As a young adolescent he was an "impressive figure, cocky, dashing, and glamorous". He was naturally rebellious and anti-authority and forged his own path, especially when it came to music. The different genres of music fascinated him wholly because of the novelty element. Despite having a "gut approach to his craft", he was still quite cerebral and an "intellectualised" composer. He had a great musical memory, which is very common in savants in this area: indeed, exceptional memory is critical for great creativity. He had insatiable curiosity as well, and loved to take mechanical structures apart to see how they worked. Bernstein said of Freud that he had "an incredible intellect, a Faustian sense of enquiry", to which the composer could well relate. Throughout his life Bernstein was a voracious reader as well as a talented writer. He loved to teach too, being somewhat charismatic, which was another way of performing, and to wallow in the glow of his pupils' admiration. He spoke in a hyperkinetic fashion and Peyser points out that he had an "affected, orotund" mode of speech that was "idiosyncratic". Indeed hyperkinetic people often are impulsive and talk almost before they engage their mind.

There was a child-like element to his personality and certainly immaturity of this kind is critical to great success. In fact, it is also indicative of identity diffusion. He dismissed, for example, the impact schools had on his talent and success. It is very common for creative artists to present themselves as completely unique, as having done everything themselves and owing nothing to anyone, which is highly narcissistic and egocentric. It fits the myth of heroic creativity. Bernstein was certainly a mythmaker in this regard, like many great men. Peyser quotes Mark Twain as saying that the older he got, the more vividly he remembered things that had not happened. The same could be said of Bernstein. She points out that, although Bernstein came from a very wealthy family, his primary purpose was to convince those at the table, when dining for example, of "his heroic transcendence of his lowly origins". This was fundamentally a lie on his part and towards the end of his life he most likely began to believe his own myths. The identity diffusion also found expression in his being an exhibitionist and self-publicist who adored the roar of the concert audience. It was indeed life-giving for him. The inherent contradictions in his personality were critical to his success, for example, being "both angel and devil" and loving both "home" and being an international wanderer (Burton, 1994).

Bernstein was also bisexual and very promiscuous, which also formed part of his pursuit of novelty and sensation. Sexual identity diffusion was critical to his creativity, as is often the case. This confusion and conflict over it seems to stimulate creativity. However, it is simplistic to attribute all creativity to sexuality, but identity diffusion is a sign of a lack of integration and balance in a personality, a lack that is vital for great creativity. Like many bisexuals, he swung from periods of heterosexuality to periods of homosexuality, which likewise increased the novelty factor. Burton (1994) states that it was revealing to learn that Bernstein had taken "monk-like vows of sexual denial", but that there was something "uncharacteristically hysterical about his self-pitying tone".

All creative artists have major dark sides and Bernstein was no different. He had a strong, overtly aggressive side to his personality, to which many fell foul. Playwright Lillian Hellman described him as a "monster" and indeed Bernstein was tactless and could be quite unempathic. There's no denying his highly narcissistic nature, perverse, controlling and dominating. He called the shots and nobody else was going to tell him what to do. Peyser says that he had a "powerhouse personality" in that he always had to be the centre of attention, like the sun from which all light came. With many talented people he came in contact with, he was massively and unrelenting competitive – an artistic transgressor, and indeed a transgressor in most areas of life. He was even critical of some quite good composers. Creativity often necessitates a great deal of aggression, and indeed a capacity to hate as well as love. It requires an extreme intensity of emotions of both the positive and negative kind. There are no great, happy, nice creators, it must be said.

Music gave Bernstein inexhaustible personal satisfaction, as did composing, but he did suffer considerably from depression, as almost all great artists do. There was a lonely side to his personality that most likely helped his musical composition. Peyser says that he had "canyons of darkness as well as shafts of brilliant light". Psychoanalysis became a lifelong addiction for him but it was more a way of life than a treatment. He also read many psychiatric textbooks in an effort to understand himself. He was certainly very psychologically conflicted and quite puzzled by himself, as many great creators are. He even had some insight into his character and once remarked "I'm not nice".

There was also evidence of considerable obsessive compulsive traits and a "ritualistic" nature, if somewhat sadomasochistic. When his wife Felicia, whom he had neglected and rejected, died, he experienced "obsessive guilt". Throughout his life, he suffered a lot from insomnia and abused alcohol a great deal. He smoked incessantly and was particularly fatalistic and self-destructive in that respect. At times he thought of himself as being immortal, other times he worried about growing old. Though death anxiety can be characteristic of great artists, at the same time Bernstein delighted in challenging fate. He once said: "I smoke, I drink, I stay up all night, and screw around. I'm over-committed on all fronts". The nature of suffering in the service of art also featured in his mindset. Greek conductor and friend, Dimitri Mitropoulos, described the "artistic temperament" in the following way: "There is, behind the soul and the whole life of the artist, perhaps the suffering soul" (Burton, 1994). This certainly described Bernstein, who said he learned "to transform suffering into a form of art". This practice is critical for the alleviation of suffering, and indeed reduces the risk of suicide. Bernstein was aware of the similarities between his career and that of Orson Welles, according to Burton (1994), and indeed Welles was another monumental sadomasochistic genius.

SOCIAL RELATIONSHIPS

Great creativity and excellent interpersonal relationships tend not go together. On the contrary, great creativity and a propensity for poor, non-reciprocal, exploitative interpersonal relationships do go together. From an early age Bernstein was a hyperactive socialiser and socially gregarious. He was magnetic and outgoing, with an abundance of acquaintances from all walks of life, as his fame increased. He loved to mix with the great and the good, including presidents of the United States. He was contradictory in that he talked about the poor but, according to Peyser, he cultivated a "social circle that excluded everyone but the talented, beautiful, and rich". He was very egocentric in truth and cared about few people except himself. In fact, he was intensely competitive and had to be the most admired and most envied.

There is little doubt that he was often abusive in his interpersonal relationships. People were there to be used and abused by him – not unlike Picasso. Hence, in his dealings with people, he was often tactless and cruel. Peyser notes that Bernstein's most important relationships in life were with men. She also states that he used art and sex interchangeably. Despite being homosexual, he married actress Felicia Montealegre in 1951. Engaging in a heterosexual marriage was therefore quite stressful for him and he was serially unfaithful to his wife. A significant homosexual relationship conducted while married was with the writer Tommy Cothran. When Felicia had a mastectomy, this failed to stop him humiliating her in front of his friends. Clearly, there were significant empathic deficits in his personality, as there often are in every great creator. When he left Felicia for Cothran, she pointed her finger at him in fury and predicted, in a harsh whisper: "You're going to die a bitter and lonely old man" (Burton, 1994). In one way she was right: he was plunged into massive grief when she died in 1978 and he blamed himself for her death. This is similar to Thomas Hardy, who showed immense grief at the death of his wife, despite being brutal to her with his extramarital affairs while she was alive. Bernstein continued to hide his private life and lied to his daughter about his homosexuality when confronted. Nevertheless, his wife was a vital anchor for him in his life, and indeed was an important support for his creativity, much like the wife of W. B. Yeats in relation to his poetry.

Interestingly, Peyser notes that Thomas Mann and Oscar Wilde were other artists who went through similar experiences: "It was during their marriages that these artists, sexually ambivalent, did their best work." It appeared that when Bernstein was not acting out sexually he could do his best composing. This was not about sublimation, but about halting the acting out in order to facilitate creative work. His wife Felicia thus allowed him to gather all his creative energies – in the sense of multiple creative genes of small effect, particularly musical ones – together and not dissipate them in acting out. Elements of Bernstein's personal behaviour and sexual promiscuity were similar to Richard Wagner: he was egocentric and narcissistic like Wagner.

WORK

Bernstein was a wholly independent musician and, in his musical life, he was an original. He was noted for his accomplishments both in classical music and popular music: he created chamber music, ballets, symphonies and operas, as well as music for voice, film, dance and Broadway musicals. In fact, he was a major "cross-over" artist and a celebrity, and indeed treated like a film star. His most famous composition today is the Broadway musical and film *West Side Story*.

The conductor Marin Alsop described Bernstein as a "great storyteller" and said that "everything was motivated by storytelling". In a musical work Bernstein was always looking for the "big idea". He was extremely dogmatic and controlling in his work, however. At a concert with pianist Glenn Gould, he once engaged in "renunciation of Gould's ideas", according to Peyser. He was in a way competing with Gould and wanted to "reduce" him. It was cowardly of Bernstein not to support Gould on that particular night, as the latter was a performing genius and highly original. In terms of his own work, Bernstein clearly was less original, but nevertheless had a strong element of originality. He was far too outgoing to focus mainly on composition. In fact, he did not have a sufficient autistic component to his personality to be a great composer.

Leonard Bernstein died of lung disease on 14 October 1990, at the age of 72.

Chapter 43

LEOPOLD STOKOWSKI

Leopold Stokowski (1882–1977) was a hugely influential and successful British-born conductor, who worked with some of the great orchestras of the 20th century, especially in the USA. A driven genius with a contradictory personality, he showed many traits of Asperger syndrome.

BACKGROUND

Leopold Stokowski was born in London on 18 April 1882 to parents of Polish and Irish origin. There is some mystery surrounding his early life, compounded by the fact that he later claimed to be younger than he actually was and he affected a "foreign" accent. In his early years, he trained at the Royal College of Music, London and at Queen's College, Oxford, and worked as an organist before becoming a conductor.

PERSONALITY

Stokowski lived well into old age and had a titanic personality. He was novelty-seeking and sensation-seeking; oppositional, defiant and anti-authority; controlling, dominating, tyrannical, unempathic, moody, perverse and aggressive; narcissistic and vain: and a bully and a genius. He is best described as a musical dictator, seeing that dictators often have long lives when not ended violently. Stokowski rather candidly confessed: "I always want to be first. I'm what's known as egocentric. It is a disease, a mental disease."[43] Clearly a genius, Stokowski could hyperfocus on his musical interests, with great powers of observation and innovation. He was also a tremendous motivator, especially of musicians under his conductorship. In fact, he was a workaholic with massive energy and required less sleep than the average person. Given his novelty-seeking nature, he was quite impulsive and would quit orchestras rather suddenly.

It is beyond doubt that Stokowski had considerable identity diffusion. He was a multifaceted figure, which is typical of genius. Sigmund Freud took a great interest in

---

[43] Except where otherwise indicated, quotes in this chapter are from Chasins (1981).

Stokowski, noting that "the musician is fascinating … but the man is perplexing. He is really two men." Clearly, Freud had identified his identity diffusion and his multiple selves – something extremely important in understanding him. His enigmatic personality made it difficult for people to grasp the nature of the man, which was further hindered by the immature, childlike aspect to his personality. However, the latter is necessary for great creativity. Stokowski created myths about himself and, like many great geniuses, loved the idea of having "mythic origins". He was described as "an awkward and insufferably pretentious character" as a result. Not surprisingly, he was a great self-publicist, as people with Asperger syndrome often are. His eccentricity was widely known and similar to that of Thomas Jefferson, who also had Asperger syndrome (Fitzgerald & O'Brien, 2007). According to biographer Abram Chasins, Stokowski was apt to greet visitors "in lounging pyjamas in some shade of red or yellow set against socks or slippers in vividly contrasting colours".

Stokowski was dictatorial as mentioned and his word had to be law. Not surprisingly, he had trouble with the boards of orchestras, as with him there was only one voice – his. He was "a notoriously unyielding person" and demanded total obedience; everybody else was there to fulfil his wishes and failing that he would quit. In his demand for full control he wanted to be treated as if omnipotent, which included the power to change his mind. Hence he was highly critical and always found fault with whatever orchestra or group he happened to be working with. The reverse he could not tolerate either: his hypersensitivity to criticism certainly did not endear him to colleagues and peers. However, he was most demanding, driving and perfectionistic in relation to himself and was never satisfied. There was always the desire to put on a more perfect performance next time. With his critical, self-righteous and imperious manner, he often alienated people.

There also existed features of a perverse personality, demonstrating the link between creativity and perversion. There was a masochistic as well as a sadistic element to him which was part of his perversity. Furthermore, Stokowski once confessed that he had no conscience, suggesting autistic psychopathy. Nevertheless, as the case with most great artists, there was huge insecurity on his part. The insecurity was associated with being extremely narcissistic – in fact, those with narcissism often have very low self-esteem hidden behind it. It does emerge too that Stokowski was mean-spirited. His solicitor Joseph Sharfsin remarked that the man was stingy. Aside from money, Stokowski was an unforgiving personality with a great capacity to hate – a "dependent and lonely man, always in need of love and assurance".

Social Relationships

Stokowski became something of a celebrity in the modern sense. Despite his charismatic and indeed magnetic nature, however, Stokowski was a "loner" who showed "Olympian detachment" and certainly was not a team player. He got on well with Walt Disney because both were loners "who craved the spotlight" and shared an interest in technical innovation, according to Chasins. Both had Asperger syndrome. The American composer Ned Roren said that Stokowski had a "cool social loftiness" that stood in contrast to his "conductorial fire", where his emotions came to the fore. His relationships with orchestras were often "brutal and insulting" in rehearsal, which showed his lack of empathy. Musicians found him cold, remote, self-centred and unapproachable and he could be "melodramatic in his tantrums".

Most great men tend to use women to climb their career ladder and Stokowski was no different. There was a misogynistic streak to his personality, however. Women initially helped him to get a foothold in the USA after he went there in 1905, for example, pianist Olga Samaroff, who became his first wife. According to Chasins, to women especially, he was "an object of inscrutable mystery and fascination". There was a kind of "harem" of women around him who supported him in the background throughout his life, similar to the life of comedian Spike Milligan. Stokowski made three high-profile marriages, all of which ended in divorce. He was in fact incapable of a stable marital existence. When he grew bored with his first wife Olga, he simply moved on and courted Johnson & Johnson heiress Evangeline Love Brewster Johnson. His third wife, railroad heiress Gloria Vanderbilt, who was 42 years his junior, had to submit to his every whim. He was overcontrolling and obsessed with his two sons. His marriages produced five children: three daughters and two sons, and he got on far better with children than with adults. There was a question of occasional impotence too. According to Chasins, the highly strung Stokowski was "sporadically impotent". He rejuvenated himself however by using women and once had an affair with Greta Garbo.

WORK

For Stokowski music was everything and during his lifetime worked with several orchestras, such as the Philadelphia Orchestra, All-American Youth Orchestra, NBC Symphony Orchestra, the New York Philharmonic, and the New York City Symphony Orchestra. He also founded the American Symphony Orchestra in 1962. In Hollywood he conducted music for films, such as Walt Disney's *Fantasia* in 1940, and raised the standard of music in that genre. In fact, he wanted to become "a movie star and to make musical history in Hollywood" and guest-appeared in several films. Indeed he was something of a flamboyant musical showman, highly independent and conducted orchestras in his own unique way. He gave up using the baton at the end of the first quarter of the twentieth century, believing it to be unnecessary, which was novel at the time. His style was also invested with great emotion. "He allowed himself to react emotionally and intuitively to the music as it went along and then attempted to bring out his personal feelings in the performance." He frequently saw himself as greater than the composer in the way in which he changed musical scores.

Stokowski found recording difficult because he could not understand all the modern technology, which was difficult for someone who demanded to know everything and be in control of everything. Nevertheless, he was fascinated by electronics. Stokowski was often tremendously successful with the music produced from orchestras, and indeed orchestras that he created from scratch. In fact, he controlled the audience as much as he controlled the orchestra. For him the sound an orchestra produced and the audience reaction were far more important than anything else in a concert. Much of the time was spent analysing and observing. He was "compulsively concerned with the difference between abstract sounds as they spring up in the composer's imagination". Stokowski earned a reputation as an inspirational conductor. He conducted a great number of new works and would search the world for performers to make his orchestras the best. Orchestral members were in fact "astounded by the Maestro's omniscient or psychical ability to draw superhuman powers from his players". He did give his best individual players some leeway, however, and allowed them "individual freedoms of expression in the inspiration of the moment". This was to the greater purpose of producing a great sound from his orchestra.

Leopold Stokowski died in England of a heart attack on 13 September 1977, at the age of 95.

PART IV: WRITERS

Chapter 44

ANTON CHEKHOV

Anton Chekhov (1860–1904) was one of the greatest Russian playwrights of the late 19th century. He also produced a huge amount of other writing, including short stories. According to biographer Ronald Hingley, he introduced his own special brand of "elusiveness into literature" and was himself a "most elusive man".[44] He also had traits suggestive of Asperger syndrome.

BACKGROUND

Anton Chekhov was born on 29 January 1860 in Taganrog, a Russian harbour town, where there existed a great deal of poverty. His father, Pavel, was an autocratic and dictatorial shopkeeper who ran the home with military precision and often beat the young Chekhov. Though Chekhov had an unhappy childhood, he later was able to transform this experience into great writing and it did not subdue him. According to Hingley, in his childhood there was a "tragi-comic, truly Chekhovian failure of communication between the generations". Religion was very important in his upbringing, especially during his schooling. The headmaster of his school was a harsh disciplinarian where one punishment involved a form of crucifixion, being lashed to a window shutter. Then there was "running the gauntlet", which meant, according to Hingley, being spat at in turn by the entire pupil body as it paraded past the culprit in single file. The curriculum at that time was strictly regulated to eliminate any revolutionary ideas. Chekhov was never a revolutionary as such and generally paid little attention to politics. He was a reserved boy, in fact, known for "inventing comic nicknames" and telling funny stories. It appears that at this time he related better to adults than his peers.

As a child, he loved fishing and swimming, and snaring goldfinches, which he would sometimes sell. He also "enjoyed rough shooting" and "rode wild ponies". He always suffered from physical complaints, such as headaches and migraines, and there was evidence of psychosomatic problems in childhood and tuberculosis as an adult. Though Chekhov was a mediocre pupil, he was a massive reader and very much an autodidact. He later studied medicine and became a medical doctor, but made very little money from medicine.

---

[44] Except where otherwise indicated, quotes in this chapter are from Hingley (1976).

PERSONALITY

Chekhov was a complex character and not easy to pin down. He certainly had multiple selves: the private writing self and the more public self. This divided self was the source of his great creativity. The psychologist D. W. Winnicott has emphasised façades and false selves in people and certainly Chekhov had a false self in Winnicottian terms. He tried to heal this identity diffusion with creativity throughout his life and in one way he was a wounded writer. There certainly was a split in his personality: a schizoid element. He did not have a cohesive, mature or integrated personality and, accordingly to Hingley (1976), he lacked the element of male sexual aggressiveness. Indeed there were naive and child-like elements to his personality. Asperger traits can overlap with creativity and this probably did apply to him. His identity diffusion also helped him to be a talented mimic.

Chekhov liked routine and there was an element of preservation of sameness in him in the sense that it was difficult for him to "write at a strange desk". He certainly had a tremendous eye for detail and was a great observer. His medical work gave him opportunities for observation of the human condition and of human relationships. He demonstrated a scientific and systematising kind of mind and was always very careful regarding the scientific accuracy of his stories. He wrote that "as a doctor I think I've described mental illness correctly and in terms of all psychiatric canons". He confessed that medicine was his wife and writing – he also wrote a number of works about medicine – a mere mistress.

What is extraordinary is how much of Chekhov's life was given to the practice of medicine. To achieve all he did, he most certainly had to be hyperkinetic. He gave of himself unstintingly in his medical career and was very generous with his medical services to poor people. He wrote that "an author must be humane to his fingertips", and that "the serious novelist must stand aloof from everything ephemeral".

One of his favourite forms of communication was letter writing; in fact, he wrote "over 4,000 private letters". He was more comfortable with this mode than with face-to-face communication. During much of his creative life he experienced ill-health and wrote a great deal in letters about his illnesses, often denying their seriousness. Nevertheless, it was hardly wise for him to travel to Siberia when suffering from tuberculosis. He also complained of piles and suffered depressive episodes. In a way he was able to live in two worlds: the world of a sick man and that of a creative genius. It was another split in his psyche.

Chekhov had many contradictory features, which Asperger syndrome covers. He was very self-critical, but then most great artists are. He was as often distressed by excessive praise as by criticism. Both unsettled him. In fact, he hated critics, as most writers do. Publicising his works brought little enjoyment either. This can be compared to what is called "fear of open spaces" and he was most likely in a claustro-agoraphobic position. There was a huge amount of "sadness and alienation" in him as well, often found in great writers. Because of his identity diffusion he had no unifying philosophy of life and in his work he showed just how puzzling and contradictory human beings could be. He was also obsessional and compulsive, and emphasised the dirt of the town of Taganrog where he was born and many other places he visited throughout his life. Cleanliness was highly important to him, not least because of his profession but also his personality.

Social Relationships

The greatness of Chekhov clearly set him apart from humankind. Chekhov's fellow writer Maxim Gorky once said to him: "I think you are the first free man I've ever seen" but noted "how lonely Chekhov is, how little he's understood". Chekhov was indeed something of an autistic wanderer and loner. According to Hingley, on Easter nights he loved to stroll around Moscow from one church to another, listening to the bells. He was always interested in church ritual, although he rejected formal religion. He was more an intellectual than a socialite – effectively a one-person writer whose massive creativity originated within his head.

There was a shy, somewhat withdrawn side to his personality. He was a private and secretive person, who rarely engaged in outgoing behaviour and had little capacity for small talk. Hingley notes that when he had guests he would repeatedly slip away to his study, write two or three lines in private, and then rejoin the company a few minutes later. This is typical Asperger-type behaviour. Hingley also describes him as having an absent air: "A distant, withdrawn look would come over him. Lost in thought, he would sit by himself on the bottom step of the porch, preferring in such moods to be left alone with his thoughts." This is similar to Ibsen. Chekhov was generally happy in his own company and introverted. One woman that was attracted to him noted his egocentricity and self-absorption. The writer Ignaty Potapenko saw Chekhov as "so outwardly cold that he seemed encased in armour". Even those closest to him were always conscious of a certain distance and Potapenko admits that Chekhov had no friends, "though many sincerely believed themselves his friends." For his part Chekhov once confessed that he could not "show fondness for others". But that is not to say that he was incapable of feelings. On the contrary, he was profoundly upset and grieved deeply for his brother Nikolai, who died of tuberculosis aged 31.

For Chekhov, like Franz Kafka, marriage was a claustrophobic thing which he always feared. In fact, married couples in his plays are more often dissatisfied than satisfied. He had a negative view of women and saw them as inferior to men, writing that "women rob men of their youth", "the sexual instinct is a greater hindrance to work than vodka" and "in the field of [artistic] creativity woman is a goose". Many great writers have felt that their creativity would be sapped if they got married and Chekhov was no exception. Deep down, he feared women. According to Hingley, women seemed particularly hateful to him when their misdemeanours were amorous. Despite in general not being critical of his writing peers, Chekhov did tend to patronise all female writers. He often said of literature he admired that it "doesn't think like a woman". More than likely Chekhov preferred more masculine, tomboyish girls, not driven by romantic notions. Androgyny is in fact central to Asperger syndrome creativity. Women therefore had to be kept at a distance and Chekhov had to keep himself under control. This detachment from women made him more attractive to them, however.

According to Hingley, Chekhov tended throughout his life to speak as if men and women would greatly benefit if they could avoid making love altogether, or at least to reduce that activity to a minimum. By all accounts Chekhov had a low sex drive and probably a great fear of sexuality. His sexual relations throughout life were minimal: the only person apart from his wife that he might have had a sexual relationship with was with actress Lydia Yavorsky, and briefly at that. In fact, he was "almost ascetic" with "a harsh, puritanical, censorious streak" and a harsh superego. For all his aversion to marriage, however, Chekhov did get married at the age of 41, three years before his death. He had met his future wife, the actress Olga Knipper, when she performed in his play *The Seagull* some years earlier. After the wedding ceremony, he arranged to stay away from his wife because of his intense claustrophobia in intimate relationships; she worked in Moscow, while he lived far away in Yalta. Such was his indifference to the marriage that he failed to even turn up for a dinner to celebrate his marriage. He spent so much time away from his wife that it was a more a legal marriage than a real day-to-day marriage. His idea of a "separate" marriage of course was not marriage at all, but all that he could cope with. Soon afterwards Olga became pregnant but miscarried. She wrote to him: "We are so much apart anyway, and you have to engineer an unnecessary separation." You could say that he had to engineer this kind of marriage to survive psychically, as he could not bear the endless intimacy of marriage. It was suffocating for him.

Chekhov not only was uncompromising about artistic matters, but also in family and other relationships, showing the extent of his controlling and dominating personality. His sister, Maria, was quite upset when he married. Indeed Chekhov showed a "casual despotism" towards her, wanting her to dedicate her life to him, which she did. He took her for granted, echoing Kafka in his last years. In fact, Chekhov did not allow Maria to marry when she had a suitor because he had no wish to lose her services in caring for him. This is possibly one of the few cruel acts he was guilty of in his entire life: Maria devoted herself to Chekhov rather than having a life of her own.

Though Chekhov clearly had difficulties in intimate communication, he used these difficulties in his fiction. His conflicts and his problems fuelled his tremendous plays. Of course one could say that at some level all communication between human beings has an element of failure and impossibility.

Work

Hingley notes that freedom was the one abstract idea that the pragmatic Chekhov returned to again and again, "the ideal which he pursued and seemed to seek in vain throughout his life". For a period he was highly influenced by Tolstoy before finding his own voice as a writer. In his earlier writing, he could be "appallingly verbose and repetitive" but improved over time. In some ways he was also a realist writer, particularly in terms of his short story "Peasants", depicting the harsh conditions under which peasants lived. Chekhov always has the ability to surprise the reader and that is one of his secrets. He could express a massive amount in a short story. He also wrote prolifically for newspapers and magazines. Some of this can be seen in his collected works, although he excluded much that he had written from these volumes. In later years he made a contract with a publisher that led to him losing a great deal of money; clearly he was exploited and could be naive on occasions.

As a medical doctor he was a man of action and of great help to people. When he became a landowner near Moscow he generously treated the local peasants medically. His trip to Sakhalin – Russia's Devil's Island – in 1890 to conduct a survey of the medical and living conditions of prisoners at the Siberian penal colony there was a massive undertaking, particularly for a man with tuberculosis. It was a journey of thousands of miles under the most uncomfortable conditions, but an antidote to boredom for Chekhov. He also travelled to

Singapore and Ceylon as well as around Europe. It is likely these trips were detrimental to his health and to his long-term survival. Siberia was probably about the worst possible place on earth for a sick man to visit. In a way Chekhov was both a literary and a geographical explorer, who could be quite impulsive. He was very interested in evolutionary theory as espoused by Darwin and was "a gardening addict" and "delighted in novelties of subtropical horticulture". He also championed Alfred Dreyfus, a Jewish officer in the French army charged with treason because of anti-Semitism. He approached this defence as a scientific problem, examining the situation on a factual basis.

Chekov's sister Maria reported that she could always tell from Chekhov's mood when he was in the throes of creation. She stated that:

> His way of walking and his voice changed, a sort of absent-mindedness appeared and he often answered questions at random. He looked a bit odd at these times. This continued into the moment he began writing, when he became his old self again ... obviously the theme and images now fully matured, and his creative tension was ending.

This is very much like W. B. Yeats who went into the same kind of detached position when great creativity overcame him (Fitzgerald, 2004). Yeats used to move his arms about wildly in the throes of poetic creativity. These writers were essentially digging down into the depths of their personality to mine their unconscious for great creative work. In a way, this creative work was done before they ever put pen to paper. The physical act of writing was almost a transcription of this detached phase of their existence. Similarly, Chekhov once spent a winter in Nice, where it was noted that he was liable to disappear for days on end "when pregnant with a story". He failed to show up for meals and when at last he reappeared, "after parturition", his face was pale and thin. During walks he appeared silent and pensive, brooding on his creation. Again, this is typical of great creativity and also seen in the sciences, for example, with Isaac Newton.

Accordingly to Hingley, Chekhov saw the creative process as "independent of his volition" and compared it to the voyage of a steamer, governed by external and unpredictable factors such as wind and weather. This is certainly what separates the genius or great creator from the run-of-the-mill writer. Hingley asks: "Was writing such a terrible burden? It was and it was not. Which was the true Chekhov? The man who found the creative process inseparable from gnashing his teeth? Who repeatedly cursed the obligation to write, finding it incompatible with the urge to live?" While writing was an extremely painful process at times, there was also huge private satisfaction when Chekhov got it right. He metabolised a lifetime of experiences and kept them in his memory for long periods before he might use them in his writing. A great memory is indeed critical to creativity. Chekhov revealed that it was only from memory that he could write: "I have never done live portraits from nature. I need my memory to sieve the subject, filtering out just what is essential and typical."

Throughout Chekhov's mature period, according to Hingley, his creativity as a whole was governed by instinctive timing, which he could "neither analyze nor consciously regulate". This in fact relates to the biology of creativity – to genetic factors underlying his creativity. It is what separates the greater writer from the ordinary "scribbler". Bad reviews of his plays, often due to inept acting, hurt him severely. Indeed he was so hurt by one bad review and failed production of *The Seagull* that he thought about giving up completely. Clearly, his work was breaking new ground at the time. Hingley writes that with *Uncle Vanya* we "realize that we have entered a strange anti-climactic, anti-romantic, anti-dramatic world such as has never existed on the stage before Chekhov … a world with its own laws, its own dimensions, its own brand of humour". This is true creativity, true originality, and a true surprise for audiences at the time.

For all its trials, it was writing that kept him alive: work was his antidepressant and he suffered depression when a piece of work was finished. He held a mirror up to the society he lived in for better or for worse. Hingley concludes by talking about the "incongruity in this careful, pragmatic, down-to-earth scientifically trained yet elusive observer whose straightforward prose could hauntingly flick at the unknowable … and who, while capturing on paper the inspired fantasies of his creative genius, was so often simultaneously cursing his lost galoshes, his piles, his diarrhoea, his reviewers". Ordinary life cannot be totally avoided, even for a genius.

Anton Chekhov died on 15 July 1904, at the age of 44, while on holiday with his wife in the Black Forest.

Chapter 45

HENRIK IBSEN

Henrik Ibsen (1828–1906) was a Norwegian playwright and considered one of the greatest ever. According to biographer Michael Meyer (1971), his contribution to the theatre was threefold and drama owes more to him than to any other dramatist since Shakespeare. Firstly, he broke down the social barriers that had previously bounded it and showed that high tragedy could be written about ordinary people in everyday prose; secondly, he threw out the old artificialities of plot; and thirdly he developed the art of prose dialogue: "The importance of that seemingly simple achievement can hardly be exaggerated." Ibsen also had traits suggestive of Asperger syndrome.

BACKGROUND

Henrik Ibsen was born in Skien, Norway, on 20 March 1828 to Knud and Marichen Ibsen. Ibsen became the eldest of five children, after his older brother died at an early age. Initially a wealthy merchant from a long line of sea captains, Knud was "a good raconteur with a large stock of funny stories and a quickly inventive tongue" (Meyer, 1971), but had a harsh superego, like Ibsen would have. Major family turmoil and upheaval occurred, however, given that Knud was a poor financial manager and ultimately unsuccessful, which led to a number of house moves. Later, alcoholism and poverty greatly debilitated him and "he became combative, sarcastic and bitter towards those who were not his friends, and also very litigious" (Meyer, 1971). The family slid down the social scale, which had a traumatic effect on Ibsen that he would later turn creatively into artistic work (Meyer, 1971). There was a rumour that Knud was not his real father, though it was probably unfounded; however, economic failure and illegitimacy are themes that feature in his work (Meyer, 1971). His mother, Marichen, was keen on drawing and painting, had a theatrical mind and was musical. She became depressed and deeply wounded by her husband's economic failure and indeed Ibsen was aware of her "unexpressed dreams, her longing to flee the harsher realities of life, her need for a world of poetry and make-believe".[45] He later achieved this for himself in his own work.

[45] Except where otherwise indicated, quotes in this chapter are from Koht (1971).

Ibsen was a massive reader and, like his mother, liked to paint and draw caricatures and had a lifelong fascination for colour. There was also an obsession with clothes and dolls in childhood.

> Henrik Ibsen as a child would lock himself in with his books, dolls, and drawings. Soon he started his own puppet theatre. He also learned some skills as a conjuror … how to make a watch disappear from someone's pocket and replace it there unseen, or pound a watch in a mortar and restore it whole; and other tricks including ventriloquism. (Meyer, 1971)

This kind of talent is not rare in persons with Asperger syndrome, for example, Harry Houdini. Ibsen had a great many interests, including classical antiquity, religion, German and Latin. He had no interest in games and showed preservation of sameness. Nevertheless, his companions saw him as somewhat narcissistic and grandiose. A typical Asperger feature was that he gave his companions money so that they would not accompany him to school. Children regarded him as an "ugly mug" (Meyer, 1971) and, in appearance, he had rather piercing, dramatic eyes. There was also evidence of dyspraxia and poor eye contact; he was a not a good dancer and fared badly at school.

Restless and oppositional, Ibsen had numerous temper tantrums. He was also aloof and peculiar – the classic outsider and a massive observer – and could hyper-focus on what interested him. He found books far better companions than people and was fascinated by the theatre from early childhood, gradually becoming a poet. At the age of 15, due to the family circumstances, he was forced to leave school and get a job. Initially he worked as a pharmacy apprentice on low wages and became a workaholic. He had a good deal of deep-down aggression and regarded his boss in the pharmacy as an "animal" (Meyer, 1971). All the while he was "taciturn and withdrawn, didn't say much, but wrote short poems with extraordinary facility". He also had empathy difficulties and was "rough with girls". Despite being a loner and eccentric, he impregnated a local servant girl in 1846 but acknowledged paternity and was compelled to support the child until he reached 18. Ibsen later experienced guilt in relation to the son he had abandoned. Undoubtedly, Ibsen was somewhat emotionally naive and immature, though intellectually advanced. He continued to be obsessed with reading books and painting and often walked alone (Meyer, 1971) – something that is typical of people with Asperger syndrome. Overall, it was a rather traumatic childhood for Ibsen, the pain of which never left him.

PERSONALITY

Ibsen was without doubt highly intelligent and had a massive memory, which is critical for great creativity. Extremely persistent and extremely determined, he had huge energy levels and could do the work of two or three people. Given to impulsivity, he was also a sensation-seeker and a novelty-seeker where art was concerned. Aside from writing, he had odd interests, typical of persons with Asperger syndrome, such as hypnotism and telepathy, and was obsessed with the sea. This was all necessary in order to become a pure artist in his creative work – a singular man – where his characters are often "bound to a single path". He also had a macabre sense of humour and was hugely amused on one occasion by describing the way somebody completed suicide (Meyer, 1971).

There is evidence that Ibsen had identity diffusion. A desire to resolve his identity diffusion, to work out who he really was, and to find a sense of self is central to many of his plays. One of the chapters in Halvdan Koht's biography on Ibsen is called "A Mind Divided". This points to his identity diffusion, but of course he had more than two identities, in fact multiple ones. Certainly, he was contradictory and enigmatic, dubbed the "sphinx of the north", and his plays were littered with "riddles and ambiguities". A student, Fr G. Knudtzon, said that there were so many conflicting minds in him that he could not possibly strike one as a harmonious personality. This is very perceptive, and of course what is described here is creative genius. Ibsen was also quite narcissistic and interested in honours, which could partly heal previous hurts and rejections. For much of his life he suffered from an inferiority complex and felt himself an outsider excluded by the upper Norwegian classes. After being awarded an honorary doctorate he insisted on being described as "Doctor Ibsen". Perhaps, not wishing to repeat the mistakes of his father, he was an extremely careful financial manager. Ibsen was in fact obsessed with his legacy and wanted to be remembered in more than a thousand years. Indeed it is likely that he will achieve this aim. He once declared: "Zola is a democrat, I am an aristocrat." An aristocrat is clearly a more domineering figure and an Asperger-type figure. Interestingly, Ibsen was attracted to the phrase "the tyranny of the majority" coined by French historian Alexis de Tocqueville, and was somewhat authoritarian and fascist in person, which are often features seen in persons with Asperger syndrome.

His love–hate relationship with Norway and indeed with himself was important in his work. He was a kind of autistic wanderer, and spent time collecting ballads and folktales, which is a typical Asperger-type activity. While in exile, Ibsen had a very negative image in his mind of Norway. This was largely inaccurate and based on the hurts he experienced in childhood. He often thought of returning and eventually did. The Norwegian explorer Fridtjof Nansen once wrote to him, saying: "To the man who put his stamp on my youth, determined the course of my development, the man who proclaimed the necessity of obeying one's calling and the nobility of the will." This is another view of Ibsen from the Norwegian side.

Chekhov, according to Stanislavsky (1924), thought of Ibsen as "dry, cold, a man of reason". Ibsen was essentially a truth-seeker, for whom "guilt is the agent of man's defeat and only death can bring expiation". He had a harsh autistic superego, was extremely egocentric and focused on work to the exclusion of other activities. His conscience could never be satisfied with anything less than absolute personal truth, according to Koht. Koht states that his biography emphasises Ibsen's ethical drive on behalf of human creativity, which even went beyond the ethical to a potentially religious conviction. Hence Ibsen was highly moralistic, as people with Asperger syndrome often are, and was very demanding and intolerant with actors, as he was with the Norwegian people. In fact, he was Norway's greatest critic of itself. Ibsen was also besieged with guilt, harshest on himself, and wanted to make the world a better place. However, revealing and disclosing the truth has consequences too. Ibsen wrote in *The Wild Duck* that to "take the life-lie away from the average man and straight away you take away his happiness".

Being such a man of reason, Ibsen thought a great deal about issues and was interested in fundamental things, such as freedom and what made people tick. Like Freud, Ibsen was also interested in evolutionary theories and the unconscious. Danish philosopher Søren Kierkegaard's struggle for personal honesty and freedom of soul was also a source of fascination for him. Freedom and liberation took many forms, personal and political. Ibsen was a highly alienated man, particularly from his family and indeed his country. During his lifetime Norway was governed by Sweden and he desired an independent, pure Norway. According to Koht, Ibsen also showed a profound understanding of human psychology before and during Freud's time. Ibsen himself declared: "I look into myself; there is my battle ground". Of course, the same could be said of Freud. Meyer (1971) likewise points out that Ibsen knew what Freud and Jung were later to assert, "that liberation can only come from within". Ibsen described his poetry as "self-anatomizing" and it would appear that when he used this phrase he meant self-analysis, like Freud's. For Ibsen, self-realisation was all-important, especially given his identity diffusion: "I think that to realise oneself in one's life is the highest goal man can attain". According to Koht, Ibsen longed for inner freedom, which was the kind that made a man "refuse to be chained by social conventions or anything else that is not of his own choosing". In his mind Ibsen had many internal chains that he tried to break. His personal conflicts were transmuted into plays and poems to the point where he was "an emancipator of man's mind". As he struggled with his feeling that "all mankind is a failure" and had "gone astray", he asked himself was it possible to rid man of all "the phantoms from the past that rode him like nightmares". Later Freud and psychoanalysis would pay great attention to these phantoms or memories from the past. Ibsen analysed himself, like Freud later, and this was very important to his art. At the age of 40, his self-discipline was greater than ever, "the inevitable stamp on his character placed there by years of testing soul and conscience. His experiences would be instruments of his ethical will."

Ibsen was a man of great regularity and "lived like a clock" (Meyer, 1971). He showed preservation of sameness and wanted his "usual room" when staying at hotels. He had rituals on the street every day, similar to the philosopher Immanuel Kant. Like W. B. Yeats and Anton Chekhov, he went into a particular physical mode during a bout of creativity, which was almost like a pseudo-pregnancy. Success and prosperity ushered in a different set of rituals for Ibsen. Knudtzon stated that there was now a certain precision in his personality as in his dress – "a long, buttoned frock coat, a proper neckerchief – the whole thing faultless". The previous year, before the success of his play *Brand*, Ibsen had gone around with holes in his sleeves, "as if indifferent to such mundane matters". In terms of his eating habits, these were ritualised and he was a slow and selective eater.

There was a good deal of aggression in Ibsen and he was somewhat paranoid, combative, oppositional and defiant. He still showed temper tantrums as an adult and was rather hypersensitive. For all his bravery, he over-reacted to criticism, showing the typical paranoid traits of persons with Asperger syndrome. Mental distress was a motive force for Ibsen's art and an understanding of it was critical to him. He suffered considerably from depression in his life and experienced a good deal of death anxiety. He was in constant fear of anything that might stop his writing, such as an illness or an accident. Such anxiety is common in great creative writers and in persons with Asperger syndrome. Of course the two often overlap.

SOCIAL RELATIONSHIPS

Ibsen was at heart a loner. As a boy, he was somewhat shy, lonely and had poor social know-how. In adolescence, like many people with Asperger syndrome, he had problems in sharing his thoughts. These features did not alter dramatically in adulthood. A character in *The Wild Duck*, Gregers Werle, is a "lonely brooder who bears so much resemblance to Ibsen himself", according to Koht. When Ibsen left his home region of Skien to go out into the world, he cut off the people from his early life, including family. It was a clean break. He could not tolerate them, especially their pietism, and always felt misunderstood, just like the philosopher Wittgenstein who also had Asperger syndrome (Fitzgerald, 2004). Even when his sister Hedvig informed him of their mother's death 20 years later he did not bother to write to her for four months. This is almost unbelievable and shows huge anger towards his family.

Ibsen loved to sit in cafés alone, watching people pass by, and did not like to be interrupted. His mother-in-law once described him as a "shy little marmot". He certainly preferred to be by himself both at meals and on his daily walks. Cocktail party small-talk was difficult for him and he did not enjoy these type of gatherings. In fact, persons with Asperger syndrome rarely like such social events.

Like many with Asperger syndrome, he got on far better with females than with males. According to Koht, Ibsen on his solitary daily walks made an exception to chat to ladies only, especially young ones. In fact, he had semi-infatuations with some young girls, with whom he was able to be open and frank and did not feel threatened; they were immature in personality just like himself. This is reminiscent of Lewis Carroll who also had Asperger syndrome (Fitzgerald, 2004). One or two of these girls were deeply hurt when he broke off the relationship, as they became burdensome to him. Ibsen said: "I for one always have to keep something back for myself." These were not physical relationships as such. In fact, physical relationships between men and women were always distasteful to him. As a young man, he said that if he ever got married he and his wife would have to live on separate floors, see each other at mealtimes, and not address each other informally (Meyer, 1971). This in effect is a typical Asperger-style marriage. Nonetheless, Ibsen married a strong, cultured woman, Suzannah Thoresen, in 1858 and she bore him his only child, a daughter Sigurd. The independent-minded Suzannah protected him from unwelcome visitors and was a supportive wife. Men like Ibsen need this kind of strong "wife–mother".

In most relationships Ibsen was controlling and dominating and would not take advice. As a theatre director he still showed many difficulties in social relationships. He found it challenging to direct the actors and stuck rigidly to the playwright's script. In this regard, he felt very alone and was unable to make social connections to share his theatrical problems and interests. At times he was in considerable personal distress. Rather tellingly, he conveyed it in his play *Brand* in the line "to be mad, to be alone; it is all the same". He wanted the character Brand to be a warning against unreasonable hardness, according to Koht. Brand shows a "tragic guilt" and never understood "the gentleness of merciful love". Much of this was a self-portrait of Ibsen.

Ibsen also did not wish to waste time in social relationships when he could be doing creative literary work. He felt that they would suppress his creativity. Like James Joyce, Samuel Beckett and Sean O'Casey, he thought that his creativity would be stifled if he remained in his country of birth. Hence he went to Sorrento, Italy with his family and continued to write. Year after year he felt that he would be misunderstood if he went back and feared this conflict. When he did return after 27 years abroad, he felt socially and personally suffocated, and very paranoid about the Norwegians he met in the street and elsewhere.

Work

It took Ibsen quite a long time to find his *metier* and be able to use his inner struggle, which was the great material for his work. Initially he used literature and history to inform his work, but of course this was rather dead and not very effective. However, he learned to transmute Norwegian stories into great plays. Ibsen was very much an organic writer, where there was a great deal of trial and error in his work. He started a play at the "ending" which was the anchor for the rest of the writing. While obviously characters were based on life, Ibsen remarked that there is a great difference between a model and the finished portrait. Because of his great visual memory and massive powers of observation he was able to create his characters in detail in his mind long before he ever put pen to paper. He wanted to convert daily life into art. According to Koht, he had lived himself through everything of value he had ever created and "his greatest works are those wherein he gives himself fully". His confused, contradictory self is expressed in his work, which has a huge autobiographical element.

For Ibsen, writing, including poetry, was "a profound ethical imperative". He hated ornamentation, like Wittgenstein, and was highly aware of all the intellectual and social currents in society at the time. His writing showed a "fierce moral indignation and his hatred of all betrayal and deception". In fact, he was very harsh with characters that showed cowardice and deceit; for him truth and freedom were fundamental, as mentioned previously. All his life he loved to make provocative statements in his work. He was essentially a great provocateur in society; his writings were subversive and caused conflict. He did not soothe but instead held a mirror up to society and thus characters in his plays reflected the conflicts of the day.

In *A Doll's House*, the question arose of whether or not it was morally right for the character Nora to abandon her husband and children for the sake of her own intellectual freedom: "She was being judged as an actual person, not as a character in a play." The idea of a woman doing her own thing was revolutionary and scandalous at the time. Ibsen gave Nora yearnings that were not acceptable to society. A wife was supposed to obey her husband and not think or act independently. Writers with Asperger syndrome are able to break the mould, however, and Ibsen "succeeded in capturing the elusive, hidden movements of the human soul more fully than any modern playwright had ever done".

An Enemy of the People, a damning indictment of bourgeois complacency, was partly a response to criticism of Ibsen's 1881 play *Ghosts*, which had scandalised contemporaries with its portrayal of a case of congenital syphilis in a well-to-do family. The subject matter was an attempted cover-up of pollution of local baths in a town in Norway, against which a doctor stood up. A phrase in *Ghosts* – "mother, give me the sun" – has echoes of Egyptian gods. *Peer Gynt*, the Norwegian fairy tale mixed with social satire, contains the lines: "what ought a man to be? Well, my short answer is himself." The desire for a sense of self is never far from Ibsen's mind.

Ibsen was an innovator and gradually became attuned and in touch with the creative processes in his mind, and began to flow with these processes. He started to realise that creativity cannot be rushed and has a considerable unconscious component. He searched for an understanding of man similar to what Freud would do later. In so doing, he had a massive capacity to understand the human mind and to portray its "depths and nuances" (Meyer, 1971). He became more attuned to human conflicts in men and women and was better able to describe them in his plays. A great characteriser of women, he developed an enormous capacity to describe the feminine psyche and was extremely aware of the societal restrictions placed on women. In his work, as we have seen, he anticipated Freud by probing the uncharted waters of the unconscious mind (Meyer, 1971). Indeed Freud discussed Ibsen's play *Rosmersholm*, the political tragedy, in his writing on character types. *Chambers Biographical Dictionary* (1997) notes that Ibsen's last plays, such as *The Master Builder*, had a strong emphasis on symbolism and the unconscious. He wrote in *Ghosts*, Act II:

> I almost think we're all of us ghosts ... It is not only what we have invited from our father and mother that "walks" in us. It is all sorts of dead ideas, and lifeless old beliefs, and so forth. They have no vitality, but they cling to us all the same, and we can't get rid of them. Whenever I take up a newspaper, I seem to seek ghosts gliding between the lines. There must be ghosts all the country over, as thick as the sand of the sea. And then we are, one and all, so pitifully afraid of the light.

Ibsen is basically referring to the human fear of self-knowledge and the fear of dealing with the past. This is brilliant psychoanalysis long before Freud. He was a man that strove for the truth people were afraid of, whereby his life was a search for a true, authentic personal self. Perhaps the desire to resolve his own identity diffusion and to find a sense of self channelled his work and "his greatest battles were fought only in his imagination". Drama critic Desmond MacCarthy said that "Ibsen's theatre is the theatre of the soul" (Meyer, 1971). Success came late to Ibsen, but perhaps it was a good thing as he did not have to cope with the damaging effects of celebrity.

Henrik Ibsen died in Oslo on 23 May 1906, at the age of 78.

Chapter 46

LUIGI PIRANDELLO

The Italian dramatist Luigi Pirandello (1867–1936) was one of the great theatrical figures of the 19th and 20th centuries. He was awarded the Nobel Prize for Literature in 1934. Pirandello was a mould-breaker who subverted old theatrical ideas, a rebel and a radical man of the stage. He described the world as through a glass darkly, seeing it as full of inauthentic and false people playing social games. He struggled to get behind people's façades to reach the real, authentic person. He was enigmatic and unique – an autistic intellectual.

BACKGROUND

Luigi Pirandello was born in Agrigento, Sicily on 28 June 1867, into a wealthy family that was involved in the sulphur industry. His father, Stefano, was authoritarian, as Pirandello himself turned out to be. Pirandello became involved in Stefano's business before going on to university in Palermo to study law. There he became involved in proto-fascist politics.

PERSONALITY

Clearly Pirandello exhibited considerable identity diffusion and was a restless man. He was also a courageous man and a workaholic. For him, the meaning of his life and people's lives in general was a constant search and – like Ludwig Wittgenstein, who also had Asperger syndrome (Fitzgerald, 2004) – he wanted to clarify people's thinking. Moreover, he wanted to tear away the mask from society. He searched for clarity and personal healing, and felt that chance was critical in the affairs of men. He saw a great deal of meaninglessness in life, writing that "my mind is completely alienated. I can no longer make contact with anything or anyone."[46] According to biographer Renate Matthaei, Pirandello wrote in 1908 that "each one must arrange his mask as best he can – his outer mask. For inside of it there is then the inner mask, which often fails to square with the other. And nothing is true!" The phrase "nothing is true" is one Picasso could indeed have used at a personal level. Pirandello was essentially trying to put the disconnected bits of his own personality together through his work. What he

---

[46] Except where otherwise indicated, quotes in this chapter are from Matthaei (1973).

was concerned with was nothing but the constant assembling and dismantling of the personality in the struggle for life, which is not unlike psychoanalysis.

Pirandello was a very fearful person, who, according to Matthaei, felt the demands made by society and fear of isolation, fear of the "bewildered emptiness of a mind that comes to know the fragility of all accepted norms and categories". He was moreover preoccupied with the impossibility of communication in an absurdly organised world. The struggle was always to lead an authentic, meaningful life – to get away from existential *angst*. There was something of a hollowness in his personality too, much like W. B. Yeats and T. S. Eliot. Because of his identity diffusion he often changed his mind about things – in common with Einstein, who said to him "we are kindred souls" (Büdel, 1966).

Pirandello was misogynistic and indeed eulogised Mussolini and fascism. Persons with Asperger syndrome are highly attracted to the "strong man" – the dictator who would put order on human beings and who would straighten everything out. There was also an element of the fascist dictator in Pirandello himself. Despite the complexity of his thoughts, he had a wish for a very clear, black-and-white world with no ambiguity. This is in effect the autistic world. He wrote: "I am fascist and not only from today. I have been a fascist for 30 years." He showed himself strongly anti-democratic, demanded the abolition of the freedom of the press, the abolition of parliament, and in general "the speedy liquidation of everything". He was a man of contradictory emotions and even contradicted himself when he said: "I am apolitical … I consider myself to be only a man on earth" (Büdel, 1966).

Clearly, Pirandello was complex, being a paranoid, reserved and hostile figure with a rather bizarre sense of humour. He saw himself as "a humorist who is suspended between laughter and tears, a humorist who cannot give himself to an emotion without perceiving something that makes faces at him that fill him with anxiety, bewilderment and rage". Büdel (1966) notes that Pirandello wanted to reaffirm the truth of art to life by making fun of art as art. He was certainly conflicted by feeling and thinking, and had most of the negative personality characteristics he attributed to others.

Social Relationships

Pirandello was a schizoid intellectual who loved intellectual human interactions – what Büdel (1966) calls "arguing and reasoning". There was also a deep quest in him for authentic human contact. He wanted to reduce his sense of personal alienation, yet at times he nevertheless sounded more like a man from Mars and his characters like aliens. This embodies a rather pessimistic, hopeless view of the world. The ideas of alienation and inauthenticity were central to him and his view of people and he saw much of people's behaviour as strange or false. This is the "Asperger" position. He wanted humans to be clear and honest about themselves and who they were; he wanted them to be authentic, open and virtuous; he wanted things to be fixed and not relative. Instead he found that people's emotions were confused, ambiguous and mixed. Human beings behaved in a chaotic, two-faced and selfish way, which he found all very puzzling. It was because of his confused internal world that he was able to hold the mirror up to the chaotic human world that he observed – from individuals to the family and to the wider society.

In 1894, in his late twenties, Pirandello married Antonietta Portulano, who bore him three children in the following years. She became severely mentally ill in 1903 and Pirandello looked after her for many years. This had a huge effect on his writing. Later she resided in a psychiatric institution.

WORK

Pirandello was a true genius of the theatre. He subverted the theatrical conventions of the day, breaking them into pieces and putting them together in a new and novel way. He was truly original, and changed both the forms and the content of theatre, turning it upside down and inside out. In his work, human beings are a kind of automaton – a bit like painter L.S. Lowry's matchstick men. One is also reminded of W. B. Yeats's phrase "the centre cannot hold" in thinking of Pirandello's work. His bleak view is also not unlike T.S. Eliot's poem *The Waste Land*. Indeed Pirandello saw human existence as a trap that imprisons and immobilises humankind: "Thus, man is indeed dead as long as he lives by his illusions and fictions, until he returns again to the stream of true life" (Büdel, 1966).

A great deal of Pirandello's stage work and writing was a struggle to find his personal authentic self. He was very much the intellectual, questioning playwright. Indeed, his life's work was a kind of self-psychoanalysis – an effort to sort himself out. Boundaries for Pirandello were very blurred; for example, the boundary between actors and audience was fluid. The process was almost like the free association of ideas.

Pirandello, as mentioned, wanted to hold a mirror up to the audience so that they could see themselves, see through their masks, and see the pointlessness of it all. Furthermore, he wanted to shock the audience to its senses – to become aware of the essential existential despair of their lives. He was preoccupied with the contradictory aspects of human beings. He struggled hugely with the separation of fact from fiction and his work constantly drifts between the two. The people in his plays have fragmented identities, like himself, where the mask, the false façade, is critical. For Pirandello, the dramatic intensity of his work was more important than ostentatious staging:

> Pirandello shunned scenic extravagance, allure, display. His aim was always to bring the play to life from within, to obtain his effects not by means of elaborate staging but from his own direct experience, which he wanted to transfer onto the stage in the most direct way possible … He himself was a natural actor. When he read the text aloud he changed with startling rapidity and intensity into the different characters.

In his play *It Is So! (If You Think So)*, the characters "make no visits, live only by themselves, but they do not live together". This for Pirandello is his ideal family. It is an innovative dramatisation of the meaninglessness of private experience, according to Matthaei. In the stage directions for *Six Characters in Search of an Author*, Pirandello wrote that this play had no acts or scenes and no plot in the ordinary sense of the word. It is a play that has to be constructed by the players' six stage characters – father, mother, son, stepdaughter, little boy, little girl. They appear before the director, who is on the point of rehearsing a Pirandello play, and beg him to let them perform their own tragedy. Their drama is on two levels: "the melodramatic family story, which they act out in their roles, and the tortured awareness that their story is incomplete".

Pirandello's preoccupation with masks has echoes of the psychologist D.W. Winnicott's false self – indeed the former's ideas may have influenced Winnicott. "By refusing to wear the mask, Pirandellian characters in the eyes of this world chose death. Thus they may die the symbolical death of insanity" (Büdel, 1966). There are also echoes here of R. D. Lang and the divided self. For Pirandello, even a name is "something fixed, a fiction, a mask" (Büdel, 1966). He saw language as imprisoning: once it is spoken it takes on a power of its own.

Luigi Pirandello died in Rome on 10 December 1936, at the age of 69.

Chapter 47

JOHN OSBORNE

John Osborne (1929–1994) was an English playwright, actor and screenwriter who won an Academy Award for scriptwriting the film *Tom Jones*. With his most famous play *Look Back in Anger*, he became the leading exponent of "British social drama" and one of a group known as the "angry young men". A Jekyll-and-Hyde figure, Osborne was brutally honest. According to biographer John Heilpern, "though he appeared outwardly reserved, taking life's measure through a watchful, studious gaze, his instinct was animal. By temperament, he proceeded uncensored from the gut and his unstoppable animosity towards his mother was unyieldingly cruel, comic, and devastating."[47] I believe that he may have had Asperger syndrome.

BACKGROUND

John Osborne was born in London on 12 December 1929. His father, Thomas, was an artist who worked in advertising and who died of tuberculosis at the age of 39, when Osborne was 10 years old. His mother, Nelly, was a barmaid, who was obsessive–compulsive. There was much marital disharmony between his parents and indeed Osborne had a difficult relationship with his mother. She frequently embarrassed and mocked him, which upset him greatly. He declined to attend her funeral in adulthood and later wrote that "my mother for years kept me away from school as often as she dared on the pretext of poor health; in reality, it was because she was bored with being on her own and needed even my childish company" (Osborne, 1981). Growing up, Osborne suffered from fainting fits that seemed to happen in public places such as cinemas or restaurants "or where they would create the maximum of irritation and embarrassment for my mother" (Osborne, 1981). He later vindictively wrote that "a year in which my mother died can't be all bad". Nevertheless, he supported his mother financially and was in many ways "dutiful" to her.

According to Heilpern, Osborne was often ill as a child and fearful of crowds and noise. Boisterous children's parties upset him in particular, "even Punch and Judy shows". This could indicate that he had sensory integration problems. According to Osborne in his autobiography, he was also a "finicky eater" (1981) – a characteristic of Asperger syndrome.

[47] Except where otherwise indicated, quotes in this chapter are from Heilpern (2006).

As a child, in addition to fainting, he suffered from rheumatic fever and recurrent migraines and bedwetting. He was also controlling and dominating and suffered a great deal of childhood psychological symptoms and conflict, especially death anxiety, feeling he would die young.

Osborne had a difficult, troubled time at school and recalled: "[When] one of the boys spoke, 'd'you want a fight?' I knew that there was only one answer to this question. Refusal was impossible and would lead to unending torment instead of isolated bouts of pain." He did manage to fight a boy, unsuccessfully, that established his "lowly place in the herd" (Osborne, 1981). At school, scarcely anyone spoke to him directly, staff or boys (Osborne, 1981). A schoolfriend of his however was Mickey Wall, described by Osborne as "an eccentric boy" (1999). Persons with Asperger syndrome indeed often mix with other eccentric young people. Osborne's passion quickly became the cinema. He states that "the cinema was my church and academy" and from the age of four he went at least twice a week and, given it was the era of double features, he would see over 200 films a year (Osborne, 1981).

Osborne's alternative ways did not go unnoticed. He was accused of being a "sissy", which he declared was "a heinous tag in those ungay days", and became accustomed to his grandmother telling him that he looked like "a street-corner Nancy boy". However, he took this to be part of her general puritanism and disapproval of his "fugitive flamboyance". For example, he recalled being once jeered at for wearing a new yellow pullover, a gift for his 12th birthday (Osborne, 1981). George Walden, reviewing the Osborne biography by Heilpern in the *New Statesman* (2006), points out that when Osborne was sent to private school he "got his characters mixed, turning up in the kind of loud-checked suit favoured by Max Wall, his hero at that time, instead of uniform. He was later expelled for hitting the headmaster." Osborne confessed that apart from physical timidity he was also rather "girlishly fastidious": "I was, and am still, almost spinsterish in my distaste for noise and personal disorder, although I am capable of initiating both" (Osborne, 1981). These are all typical features of boys with Asperger syndrome and identity diffusion. Despite his difficulties at school, Osborne was a tremendous reader and largely self-educated. He did not attend university, however, and chose to become an actor instead.

PERSONALITY

At the beginning of his biography of Osborne, John Heilpern quotes from Turgenev's *Fathers and Sons*: "What aim do you wish to achieve, where are you going, what is in your soul? In a word, who are you? What are you?" These would be good questions for Osborne, who had identity diffusion, essentially multiple identities. His life was a search for a sense of an authentic, integrated self, which was unsuccessful, much like critic Kenneth Tynan's. He existed by moving from one sensation to another and in fact was a novelty-seeker, though he could never achieve internal harmony. Osborne always remained an immature, impulsive, somewhat child-like personality. He essentially fused with his mother and his identity became more confused when with her.

According to Heilpern, Osborne was "a Cavalier and a Roundhead, a traditionalist and revolutionary, a radical who hated change, a protector of certain musty old English values, a born dissenter who wasn't nice". Not surprisingly for a man with multiple identities, he could at times present a gentle façade and show autistic charm, another one of his identities. Lynda Lee-Potter wrote in the *Daily Mail* that he was "prickly and truculent on the outside, but inside the sweetest and kindest of men". In later life, when a successful playwright, Osborne tried to play the country squire, which of course was a new identity too. Walden (2006) says that Osborne and writer Kingsley Amis were playing a similar game, cultivating new identities, although "Osborne was a far greater talent than Amis".

Throughout his life Osborne was oppositional, defiant and combative – very much a rebel. His tormented childhood partly explained his adult anger and frustration. It was said that his hatred of himself was greater than anyone else's hatred of him. Given there was considerable psychological disturbance in the family, he was extremely self-destructive – a vengeful man who seemed to thrive on conflict and argument. For him it was "I shout, I argue, therefore I exist". The psychological torment of his personality is highly evident and indeed the misery of his life is its strongest feature. No wonder alcohol was used to dampen down this torment, as well as amphetamines, codeine and sleeping pills. Nothing could cure the wounds and the conflicts inside him. Probably not all of these were due to the psychological trauma of childhood; some may have arisen from temperamental or more biological elements. Moreover, Osborne was often paralysed with depression and had massive self-loathing and guilt. He had a harsh superego, needless to say, but at the same time was often sadistic, abusive and masochistic. In fact, he was paranoid and saw betrayal everywhere.

Like many a great artist, he had poor life management skills and was a poor financial manager – he earned a great deal of money but squandered it.

SOCIAL RELATIONSHIPS

Male relationships were important to Osborne. One man claimed to have had a homosexual relationship with him but later denied it. What is certain is that Osborne had sexual identity diffusion. There was a significant homosexual side that was one of his multiple personalities. Nonetheless, Osborne married five times and had numerous affairs with women. In his autobiography he writes that he "dispatched ex-wives like unwanted footnotes". He was particularly vicious towards his fourth wife, actress Jill Bennett, whom he came to loathe, even after her death by suicide. His relationship with his only child, daughter Nolan, from his third marriage, was particularly abusive. According to Heilpern, he abandoned his daughter via a cruelly abusive letter when she was 16 and never spoke to her again, while he reached for "his poison pen to damn Jill Bennett [ex-wife] in print when he learned of her suicide". Similarly, in a review of Heilpern's biography in *The Independent*, John Arditti (2006) states that his treatment of his first four wives and his rejection of his only child, Nolan, was "callous, brutal and egotistical", and that his unconscionable attack on Jill Bennett after her suicide was, according to his editor, Robert McCrum, "gratuitously cruel and tasteless and even silly".

Osborne revealed that he found it hard to recall faces: "I forget faces quickly, often alarmingly so. The images of people with whom I have spent long, intimate months, years even, become easily blurred, almost as if a deliberate act of censoring evasion takes place either through me or by some strange agency" (Osborne, 1981). This is also typical of persons with Asperger syndrome.

WORK

Osborne started out as an actor and ended up signing himself "John Osborne, ex-playwright", reflecting his hyper self-criticism and identity diffusion. His celebrated play, *Look Back in Anger*, is partly drawn from his own life. Walden (2006) notes that Osborne pulled off the angry young man character in the first part of his life brilliantly: "Jimmy Porter/Osborne is not just some youthful lefty, all anti-Suez and social resentment: he is a man of no fixed qualities, ill at ease in his skin and not knowing what skin he should be in." This describes multiple selves or identity diffusion. Walden also describes Osborne as an "alienated young man". What marks Osborne's work today is largely invective and self-pity. Stokes (2006) writes that "self-pity" was what Osborne had to offer and that this was his metier and his means, though "to what end wasn't always clear". Director Peter Hall in the Stokes article says that "I don't think we've had a writer who has been better at invective since Swift".

Yet behind the talent, there is a sense of Osborne not reaching his full potential or being overrated. Banville (2006) notes that "probably his talent was not so great as his successes would make it seem". Reviewing Heilpern in the *London Review of Books*, David Edgar (2006) quotes David Hare as saying that Osborne's career provides "all too convenient a parable of squandered promise". Nevertheless, Osborne (1981) was correct when he wrote: "On the 8th of May 1956, my first play to be produced in London, *Look Back in Anger*, had its opening at the Royal Court Theatre. This last particular date seems to have become fixed in the memories of theatrical historians." Stage history will certainly not forget him.

John Osborne died of diabetes at his home in Shropshire on 24 December 1994, at the age of 65.

Chapter 48

T. S. Eliot

T. S. Eliot (1888–1965) was an American/British poet and playwright, who became one of the major poets and literary critics of the 20th century. He is best known for his epic work, *The Waste Land* (1922), and was awarded the Nobel Prize for Literature in 1948. His personal traits indicate that he had Asperger syndrome.

Background

Thomas Stearns Eliot (1888–1965) was born on 26 September 1888 into a middle-class family in St Louis, Missouri. His mother, Charlotte, was a social worker, while his father, Henry, was a businessman. As a child, in some ways he was intellectually adult but emotionally immature, which was something that remained with him throughout his life. He spent his childhood more in the company of books than with other children and was fascinated by objects on the shoreline of New England. Like many people of genius, he had a sense in childhood that there was great work in store for him in life. His paternal grandfather was obsessed with "self-denial and public service", according to biographer Lyndall Gordon.[48] Indeed Eliot himself showed similar traits. Eliot's mother was a highly intelligent woman who wrote poetry; more than likely she had some identity diffusion in that she had fewer feminine traits than one would expect in a woman. She was in fact rather androgynous, like Eliot himself, and didactic. There is a suggestion that his father may also have had Asperger syndrome, as he had the "acute sense of smell", so common in persons with the syndrome. One might say that Eliot was born a century too late and would have been more at home in earlier times. This is typical of persons with Asperger syndrome.

Personality

Eliot was an odd, eccentric figure – the teacher/banker and great poet; the man with multiple selves. He was recognised by Virginia Woolf as quite odd and eccentric, while English writer Osbert Sitwell said he was "like an Aztec carving". His wife described him as

[48] Except where otherwise indicated, quotes in this chapter are from Gordon (1977).

having "deep, hawk-like eyes" and indeed persons with Asperger syndrome typically have piercing eyes.

Like William Blake, Eliot shifted a lot between fact and fiction in his thinking – in his mind there was no sharp division between the two. This is very important for artistic creativity. Indeed Eliot wrote that "I have lived with shadows for my company". Again like Blake and W. B. Yeats, he had unusual perceptual experiences. These out-of-body experiences or depersonalised moments fascinated him greatly. While at Harvard, according to Gordon, one day in Boston, he saw the streets "suddenly shrink and divide". He had a few moments like this in life, which he valued highly, claiming that "you may call it communion with the Divine or you may call it temporary crystallization of the mind". Such experience occurs more in those who can move easily between fact and fiction and is not linked to psychosis. Gordon notes that in his Harvard classes he kept suggesting that "illusion", "hallucination", or "superstition" might be more worthy of serious philosophical attention than social or material objects. Eliot read a great deal in the area of mysticism too, which persons with Asperger syndrome are very interested in – like W. B. Yeats, another poet with Asperger syndrome (Fitzgerald, 2004).

Eliot was obsessed by his private experience and determined to guard it, according to Gordon. He tried to find an understanding of himself in philosophy and became something of an autistic systematizer. This was effectively an intellectual effort at sorting out his identity diffusion. He trained to be a philosopher but failed to complete his studies; in the course of them he indulged in "solipsistic speculation". At one point he became an "almost demented philosopher, keeping all-night vigils in his room". Gordon notes that Eliot wrote his own biography:

> Enlarging in poem after poem on the character of a man who conceives of his life as a religious quest despite the anti-religious mood of his age … as more is generally known of Eliot's life, the clearer it seems that the impersonal façade of his poetry – the multiple faces and voices – masks an often quite literal working of personal experience.

Eliot himself wrote that "there is transfusion of the personality or, in a deeper sense, the life of the author into the character". According to Gordon, his poetry and life were complementary. In one sense his working self was who he was and, similar to Franz Kafka, who had Asperger syndrome, he longed for "metamorphosis". At night Eliot would wander the streets and behaved like "a kind of scavenger, turning over his observations to find some clue to the meaning of life". He also got voyeuristic satisfaction from observing rundown areas with prostitutes and the like. This voyeurism was part of the perverse side of his personality, yet it was also relating at a safe distance.

Eliot used religion to try to give meaning to his existence and to give himself an identity. In "The Love Song of J. Alfred Prufrock", according to Gordon, Eliot said that J. Alfred Prufrock was partly a man of about 40 and partly himself, though Eliot was younger at the time: "The demarcation between fiction and autobiography fits neatly along the lines of Prufrock's divided self." There is no doubt that Eliot had a divided self. This was something that distressed him greatly, but it was also hugely important in his creativity. Throughout his career he was interested in the motives, the behaviour, and the achievement of saints. For example, St Ignatius Loyola, founder of the Jesuits, was a favourite. Furthermore, Eliot was also fascinated by sadomasochism and wrote "martyr poems". His period of teaching in London, which bored him, probably satisfied some of his masochistic yearnings.

With his obsessive–compulsive personality, cleanliness was highly important for Eliot. He also engaged in a lot of obsessional ruminations. In the process he suffered massively from anxiety and depression, and was very indecisive. Throughout his life he had an extremely harsh autistic superego or conscience and was often trying to purify himself. When he became a doctrinaire Anglican, he wanted to purify that religion as well and set higher standards for it. You could say he had the zeal of the convert. Yet it was always extremely difficult for him to reach his ego ideal, in Freudian terms. He once stated that "the recognition of the reality of Sin is a New Life". According to Gordon, "he hunted down decadence, and allowed lust and drunkenness to circle round him, so that he might contemplate with horror a life bereft of morale or dignity". Of course, his observation of the environment was also important to his poetry, and particularly to *The Waste Land*.

Social Relationships

Eliot was something of a tormented, introverted, unhappy creative genius. An ascetic figure, he has often been described as shy, solitary and reclusive. His library and books were genuinely "home" to him and often he felt more friendship with books than with people. It is interesting that there was a period in later life when Eliot had not seen his mother for six years. This shows extraordinary detachment. Yet after she went home from a visit to him he collapsed with "psychological troubles", which suggests a highly ambivalent attitude to his mother. He found women very difficult to understand and was in some ways a misogynist. The latter often comes from an inability to understand women. Indeed, he had what Simon Baron-Cohen (2003) calls the extreme form of the male brain. Letter-writing was another way of relating at a safe distance and Eliot wrote a couple of thousand letters to the literary critic Helen Gardner.

In *The Waste Land*, he discusses women in terms of their "unreal emotions and real appetite". In an impulsive move, he married Vivienne Haigh-Wood in 1915; however, the marriage was full of turmoil, causing him considerable pain and distress but which also fuelled his creativity. Vivienne was a very intelligent woman, also poetic, but highly disturbed, with tremendous fluctuations of mood and long periods of severe mental illness. This is similar to F. Scott Fitzgerald who was also married to a severely mentally ill woman. It is likely that Eliot had erectile dysfunction and there were certainly many "sexual failures" in the marriage. In this context, Gordon notes that Eliot seemed to suffer from "an inability to empathize with suffering outside his own experience". The intimacy of a difficult and mentally ill wife further stressed him and depressed him. It also fed his masochism. Though she was committed to a psychiatric hospital, guilt did not permit him to leave her for many years, until 1933, when he accepted a Harvard professorship. She later died in 1947.

His second marriage, to Esmé Valerie Fletcher, towards the end of his life was quite successful. But of course he had mellowed by then and his much younger wife knew how to mother him and look after him. She was in the typical mould of the Asperger man's wife.

WORK

In the literary world Eliot casts a very long shadow and is a canonical poet of the 20th century. He was a critic of modern life – of extreme poverty in parts of the city – and of the commercial classes. A long-time friend, Mary Hutchinson, who knew him well, described *The Waste Land* as his "autobiography". In *The Waste Land*, "one way of proclaiming sainthood is by abandoning civilization for the solitary vigil; another is by discerning in one's civilization the moral counters of a waste land – lust and avarice, mindless workers bound upon the wheel of fortune, and betrayed and wretched women". This has echoes of George Orwell, who also had Asperger syndrome (Fitzgerald, 2005). Eliot projected a lot of his inner conflicts and feelings onto the world: *The Waste Land* is "about a psychological hell in which someone is quite alone". Eliot's identity diffusion and inner emptiness are seen there.

By and large Eliot's poetry was influenced by his "horror of time and decay"; Gordon notes that his poems showed an "exaggerated hopelessness". (This also brings to mind Walt Whitman, who wrote about the "hollowness at heart" – indeed Whitman also had Asperger syndrome and who appeared to be from another age as well.) Eliot's poems also have a "confessional element", which of course satisfied his superego (conscience) and mopped up some guilt. Some of *The Waste Land* certainly emerged from his unconscious: he described it as coming from "unknown psychic material". Of course, a good deal of creativity does emerge from unconscious mental processing (Fitzgerald & James, 2007). In terms of language Eliot showed some evidence of an autistic narrative: this is suggested by Ezra Pound's comment that Eliot's work was "too given to hesitation, drifting, 'maudlin confession', and aerial fantasy – the phantasmal sea surge and the precipitation of 'insubstantial manna' from heaven".

T. S. Eliot died in London on 4 January 1965, at the age of 76.

Chapter 49

F. SCOTT FITZGERALD

F. Scott Fitzgerald (1896–1940) was one of the most famous 20th-century novelists and a Hollywood screenwriter. Nowadays, according to biographer André Le Vot, he is remembered for his "extravagant gestures, the dandyish silhouette, his tumultuous love affair with Zelda, his debts, his alcoholism, his meteoric passage through American letters".[49] His most famous book, *The Great Gatsby*, was made into a film, as was *Tender is the Night*.

BACKGROUND

Francis Scott Key Fitzgerald was born on 24 September 1896 in St Paul, Minnesota, into a middle-class Irish-American family, to whom he was known as "Scott". His father, Edward, worked for Procter & Gamble, but was sacked when Fitzgerald was 10, and abused alcohol. His mother, Mary (Mollie), was overprotective, overindulgent, and enmeshed her life with her son's. Fitzgerald was, according to Le Vot, "a coddled child deprived of a father's authority, dominated by women". In the Catholic schools he attended he was seen as "a poor boy in a rich world". Like many highly creative people, Fitzgerald wondered whether his father was his real father or not. He thought of himself as a "foundling", declaring "my father is a moron and my mother a neurotic, half insane with pathological nervous worry".

As regards his education, Fitzgerald showed poor school progress, but was a good athlete. He was also a novelty-seeker and sensation-seeker and at school began smoking in secret. He was also quite narcissistic and highly unpopular at school – other boys hated his "insolent ingenuousness". In his narcissism, he always wanted to be admired and famous. After leaving school he attended Princeton University in 1913, where he began to show evidence that he could write well. However, he found it hard to concentrate on a third-level career and dropped out of college.

---

[49] Except where otherwise indicated, quotes in this chapter are from Le Vot (1985).

PERSONALITY

Fitzgerald was always fascinated by books and had great imagination and wit. He loved history and the theatre and could hyperfocus on what interested him, especially writing. He was fundamentally a thinker and an intellectual, notwithstanding the superficiality of some of his work. He also showed evidence of identity diffusion and had an immature, child-like personality throughout his life. He once considered becoming a Catholic priest – this religious, moral side was part of his identity diffusion – and he always retained "a latent religiosity". Nevertheless, the other side – the opposite – was more powerful. Fitzgerald himself wrote: "I guess I am too much a moralist at heart and really want to preach at people in some acceptable form rather than entertain them."

At Princeton he was moody, narcissistic, and craved admiration. In his early life he had wanted to be a sports star, given his athletic prowess, and be adored and worshipped, a goal which he did not achieve. Interestingly, he was concerned about his feet, which caused him a sort of "shame and revulsion".

Despite the huge charisma and charm he exhibited, Fitzgerald was very masochistic. In later life alcoholism began to take over, with large debts and trips to jail. He ended up as a rather pathetic, self-destructive and addicted man, who attempted suicide with opiates. He was regarded as being "disorientated and scatter-brained", and spent way beyond his financial resources. This would fit with attention deficit hyperactivity disorder.

SOCIAL RELATIONSHIPS

Fitzgerald clearly had empathy deficits. His "autocratic tendencies" came to the fore when he joined the US Army in 1917. He was very harsh with the men he commanded and his "irresponsibility was legendary" in camp. With women, it was a different case. He had a very good understanding of the female psyche, even from adolescence, and his "sensitivity was infinitely closer to that of Europeans". His identity diffusion certainly helped him to write better about the female psyche. From his Princeton days, he became fascinated by unavailable women, some of whom were desired by others, which made them all the more desirable to him.. In 1920, he married Zelda Sayre, a society girl and the daughter of an Alabama Supreme Court judge. She was a woman who "craved action, the clash of rivalries, and the heat of competition. She could not be satisfied to remain within the bounds convention set around proper young ladies." In fact, she was a novelty-seeker and a sensation-seeker, like Fitzgerald, who lived dangerously. There was a blend of courage and fearlessness in her, yet she was always anti-authority. Their relationship was tumultuous, with much disharmony, and they engaged in rather immature behaviour, trying to shock people. Zelda was diagnosed with schizophrenia in 1930 and spent the remainder of her life in and out of psychiatric hospitals.

WORK

Like most writers, for all his talent, Fitzgerald had to struggle to get established. A very poor financial manager he often had difficulties meeting deadlines. To finance the extravagant lifestyle he and Zelda led, he supplemented his income from novels by writing short stories for magazines and screenwriting in Hollywood. His "moral conscience would be stronger than his artistic conscience. He would prostitute his talent and kill himself doing it to pay the bills for Zelda and himself." On reading *The Great Gatsby*, I found it rather lightweight, frivolous, empty and pointless. It certainly put emphasis on characters with identity diffusion. Le Vot notes that Fitzgerald, like his character Gatsby, knew that experience always fell short of the dream: "Fitzgerald put his stamp on this new age: henceforth it would be known as the Jazz Age."

Fitzgerald ended up with an "Irish-style suicide by gin" – the not uncommon price of creative greatness and died in Hollywood on 21 December 1940, at the age of 44.

Chapter 50

FRIEDRICH SCHILLER

Friedrich Schiller (1759–1805) was a major German dramatist and poet – a writer of the first order in German literature. His plays include *Don Carlos*, *Maria Stuart* and *Wallenstein*. He showed some, though not all, of the criteria for Asperger syndrome.

BACKGROUND

Johann Christoph Friedrich von Schiller was born on 10 November 1759 in Marbach am Neckar, Germany. His father, Johann, was "a farm labourer, barber's apprentice, and wound-dresser", who became a medical orderly in the army and later, on retirement from military service, a "head nursery man" in a demesne belonging to the Duke of Württemberg.[50] Schiller, an only son, also had five sisters. His mother, Elisabeth, was very interested in reading biographies and writing poetry, and was a good storyteller to her children.

A solitary figure, Schiller was fascinated by thunder and lightning and became transfixed by the theatre and literature from the age of eight. He was certainly very intelligent, as well as impulsive, impatient and a hyperkinetic thinker. In 1773, aged 13, he started to attend the Karlsschule – a military academy established and governed by the Duke of Württemberg – in Stuttgart to study law but performed poorly and later transferred to medicine. He was bored by standard education and frequently felt awkward and out of place. Neither did it help that he was shy, shabbily dressed and unable to dance – indeed he may have had some dyspraxia. He would show classic school refusal behaviour by complaining of illness so that he could stay home and read books that interested him. In fact, he could be quite oppositional and indeed defiant. While at the Karlsschule, he expressed the wish to become a professor of physiology and medicine, and wrote that "I have simply no other ambition in the world than work on my chosen subjects". However, his real interest was drama, though his early forays into the world of acting were not remarkable. He tried acting in a play "but made himself a laughing stock with his appallingly over-emotional acting style". Nonetheless, he wrote his first play, *The Robbers*, in 1781 at the tender age of 22. He wished to explore, to break new ground, to be original – all of which he achieved.

[50] Except where otherwise indicated, quotes in this chapter are from Pilling, Schilling and Springer (2005).

PERSONALITY

Schiller had a massive imagination and an extremely analytical mind. Interestingly, he possessed a very large head, which is something that occurs in about half of people with Asperger syndrome. With his phenomenal capacity to hyper-focus for long periods on what interested him, especially the theatre, he worked late into the night and early morning and was a late riser. Schiller was also extremely determined, ambitious, persistent, and brave, breaking out of the cultural straitjacket in which he found himself. Adventurous and a risk-taker, he loved playing cards and was a novelty-seeker and sensation-seeker. And being hyperkinetic he loathed revising a play, once it was finished, always wishing to get on to the next one. It's not hard to imagine that he grew bored easily and had concentration problems in terms of what did not interest him. These features are typical of creative characters.

For all his intelligence, Schiller was naive and immature, for example, in the way he approached prospective patrons. He showed some identity diffusion and some of his work was a search for an authentic identity. He often tended to confuse fact and fiction – a very helpful trait when working in the artistic arena. Biographers Pilling, Schilling and Springer state that Schiller had not had much experience of life; "hence he aspired to live it through literature. His disjunction from reality gave rise to comic episodes." In response to criticism, he once wrote in a letter: "Did you not always say that I lacked the true feelings of the heart, that everything was fantasy, poetry which I had picked up through reading Klopstock ... and that I had no friendship in my innermost soul!" This suggests features of Asperger syndrome, although he did not meet all the criteria for it.

In the early years it was difficult for him to meet his basic needs: lack of money was a constant problem and he had large debts. Wishing to stage his play, *The Robbers*, in Mannheim, Schiller left the regiment without permission from the Duke of Württemberg and without completing his medical education, which resulted in a loss of patronage. At times Schiller could be quite a negative thinker and suffered from depression, sometimes driven to thoughts of suicide. He wrote: "I have carried around in my heart the choice of whether to depart this world." He also began to drink alcohol excessively as a young man.

SOCIAL RELATIONSHIPS

There was an innate desire for isolation in Schiller. Early in his life he wrote: "I still sustain myself with my favourite idea of retreating from the outside world, to live in a philosophical tranquillity, to live for myself." At the same time he was far from being asocial. He understood that his "genius" needed social contact to flourish, but social awkwardness remained with him, although at times he could be quite social. He wrote letters to a trustworthy friend called Johann Andreas Streicher that were "distant and condescending", however, and failed to see that this was unempathic and insulting.

Schiller formed an intellectual relationship with Goethe, but "was incapable of living in a state of unbroken friendship" with his fellow writer. In fact, his relationship with Goethe was based on "common work" and rather distant. At times Schiller did not have much faith in human beings, who he felt operated purely from self-interest and not for the good of other people. In 1790, aged 30, Schiller married Charlotte von Lengefeld, who was highly educated and cultured. She bore him two sons and two daughters.

WORK

Writing for Schiller was his *raison d'être* and he wrote that "I must live from writing". He was essentially an independent creative thinker and an "analytical" playwright, who felt that his plays should educate the audience and that audiences were very concrete in their thinking. His first play, *The Robbers*, written in 1781, received critical acclaim almost immediately. The play was anti-authority and somewhat subversive, but he evaded censure and it was successful. As a critique of society at the time, it was innovative and mould-breaking.

In common with many people with Asperger traits, Schiller was very attracted to history and ideas. In 1788, he became a professor of history and philosophy at Jena University and achieved further fame for his work entitled *A History of the Thirty Years' War*. He was well aware that "chance and historical circumstances made heroes". In essence, he desired for history to be literature. This was an attempt to unite fact and fiction. He wanted various strands of study to be united, which makes no sense unless he wished to create a more cohesive sense of self. Some of his work was indeed a search for an authentic identity. For example, in his only novel, *The Man Who Sees Ghosts*, fact and fiction were blurred and the "identity of figures uncertain".

In his narcissistic way Schiller had huge ideas about his talents and was very conscious of his legacy, wanting his complete works published in a single volume. However, he was correct to regard himself as an "original genius".

Friedrich Schiller died of tuberculosis in Weimar on 9 May 1805, at the age of 45.

Chapter 51

VOLTAIRE

François-Marie Arouet de Voltaire (1694–1778), usually known by his pen name, Voltaire, was a French writer and philosopher, and one of the most creative and fascinating literary men of the Age of Enlightenment. Thomas Carlyle wrote of him: "Innumerable high-dressed gentlemen, gods of this lower world, are gone all to inorganic powder, no comfortable or profitable memory to be held of them more; and this poor Voltaire, without implement except the tongue and brain of him, he is still a shining object to all the populations; and they say and symbol to me, 'Tell us of him! He is the man!'" (Mitford, 1957/1976).

BACKGROUND

François-Marie Arouet was born in Paris on 21 November 1694, the youngest of five children – two of whom died. His father, François, was a notary and minor treasury official. However, he "found his younger son a constant trial" and felt he was "a ne'er-do-well".[51] In fact, he had such little faith in Voltaire that he would not allow him to have his inheritance until he was 35. His mother, Marie, died when Voltaire was seven years old. A hyperkinetic, novelty-seeking, sensation-seeking type of personality was evident from an early age. According to biographer Nancy Mitford (1957/1976), he was "the bad boy of the Jesuits at their school" and the "black sheep of the family". He was temperamentally difficult as a child, and in later life was oppositional to the Catholic Church and authority. He also claimed to have been sexually abused at school. As a young man he was constantly getting "into scrapes with the kind of friends who do a young man no good" (Mitford, 1957/1976). He trained in law but it bored him, preferring to spend his time writing essays and reading Classical literature and histories.

Voltaire's early life was not unlike Oscar Wilde's in that they were both celebrities and greatly admired by people of influence. He had piercing eyes – everybody talked about his eyes. It was said that "his appearance was delightful, a droll, impertinent, inquisitive look, dancing black eyes, a turned up nose, elegant little figure", according to Mitford (1957/1976). "His conversation matched his looks, droll, impertinent, inquisitive, dancing, elegant, and

[51] Except where otherwise indicated, quotes in this chapter are from Mason (1981).

brittle. He was the greatest amuser of his age and all history does not record a greater" (Mitford, 1957/1976). In my view this was so until Oscar Wilde came to the fore and certainly his witticism most likely outdid that of Voltaire's.

PERSONALITY

Even as a young man, Voltaire was a great observer and could hyper-focus on what interested him. He had tremendous verbal fluency and was quite humorous – "Humour bubbled up out of him, as aphorism, satire, repartee". The critic Matthieu Marais said that from youth he showed "the genius of an accomplished man". He demonstrated enormous restless dynamism as well and from childhood onwards had a high capacity for impetuous indiscretions. According to Mitford (1957/1976), he seemed to be "one of those people who would get into trouble even in a Trappist monastery". He was a hyperkinetic wanderer – basically a night owl who got up late in the day and socialised extensively in the evenings. Fame came at a price, however; he was obsessed with being a celebrity – with being a famous man and having people talk about himself.

Despite his courage in speaking out, he was constantly getting into trouble with the authorities because of his critiques and attacks on them. It is hardly surprising that he spent a few periods in the Bastille as a result, though fearful of prison. He nonetheless adored the commotion that he created and everybody talking about him, from the highest in the land downwards. He took great enjoyment from provoking people, particularly the clergy. According to Mitford, "his intolerance of stupidity and superstition, his hatred of cruelty, his love of teasing, and his desire to be read combined to make him intensely rash".

During theatre performances he was a terrible fidget, jumping up and down the entire time. And at any adverse demonstration, "even little whispers or giggles", he would be on his feet screaming, according to Mitford (1957/1976). This would suggest ADHD (Fitzgerald, 2008). Voltaire was clearly quite sensitive and indeed paranoid, and prone to anger outbursts or temper tantrums. He often showed the tactlessness and poor empathy characteristic of creative people and could not resist the "wounding jibe": "Voltaire sincerely felt that, while he himself was at liberty to stamp on other people's feelings, his own must be spared."

The official view of Voltaire was of an *enfant terrible* and that it was time he grew up, according to Mitford (1957/1976). But had he grown up he would no longer have been a genius – no longer Voltaire. Mitford also writes that he engaged in endless, rather ridiculous quarrels, partly due to his immaturity. For example, he was quite jealous of Jean-Baptiste Rousseau and used to refer to him as "the late Rousseau", even when he was still alive. Mitford also notes that Voltaire said that everybody has "a good angel and a bad", and was energised by conflict and crisis and emotional turbulence (Mitford, 1957/1976).

Voltaire was quite a contradictory figure, which is often characteristic of creative people. There was always a childlike, immature side to his personality, even in later life. He found it easy to cry and liked other people's children, having had none of his own. This persistent immaturity is often required for great creativity, that is, to be able to see the world as through the eyes of a child. Scottish philosopher Adam Ferguson, after visiting his house, remarked that Voltaire's tongue became "as frolicsome as that of a boy of 18". The child-like behaviour also reflected his identity diffusion, which is critical for creativity. Certainly part of his work was motivated by his search for an identity. He therefore had a "chameleon-like adaptability" and could merge or fuse with his plays on the stage. Rather tellingly he once said of himself: "I have become English in London, I am German in Germany." He also lacked self-awareness, which was observed by his physician friend, Théodore Tronchin: "Of all men living in the world together, the one he knows the least is himself."

Voltaire had access to a variety of feelings, being highly independent, with massive energy and charisma. He loved role-playing and acted, though not a consummate actor. Nevertheless, he grew bored easily and showed mercurial moods. There was also a depressive core to his personality and he was quite hypochondriacal. Reflecting his mood at the time, he once said that "there is no more happiness for me, there has indeed never been any". There were Byronic elements to his personality too, but he was not as self-destructive as Lord Byron was.

Voltaire made quite a lot of money by managing to outwit the lottery in Paris with the aid of his mathematician friend Charles Marie de La Condamine. In fact, he was quite a good financial manager and traded commodities on the stock market.

Social Relationships

Voltaire was also a contradictory figure in that he loved both isolation and social interaction. He had many conflictual social relationships and was often naive in these. He quarrelled a great deal with people and was impatient with aristocratic figures; indeed he was once beaten up at the instigation of a member of the aristocracy that he had insulted. He had even considered a duel with this particular aristocrat, though people saw him as behaving stupidly and overreacting grossly. Voltaire also had much conflict with Frederick the Great – a psychopathic warmonger but also an intellectual and an extremely perverse individual – who became his patron and erstwhile friend. Frederick said of him: "It is a great pity that such a despicable soul should be joined to such a beautiful genius. He has all the charming ways and all the malice of a monkey" (Mitford, 1957/1976). This referred to the relationship of Voltaire and his mistress, Émilie du Châtelet, who was also a gifted mathematician and an intellectual in her own right.

In relation to women, Voltaire was somewhat impulsive and liked them tempestuous, according to Mitford (1957/1976). Émilie du Châtelet was certainly that, in addition to being tactless, a novelty-seeker, a gambler, and a self-destructive genius. For the duration of his 16-year affair with Émilie, she was married to an aristocrat and had children. Voltaire lived a very luxurious life with her and was inconsolable when she died in 1749, and even considered becoming a monk. He confessed: "It is not a mistress that I have lost but half of myself, a soul for which my soul seems to have been made" (Mitford, 1957/1976). He seemed to have "merged" with her; she was Ada Byron to his Lord Byron. In later life Voltaire formed a long-term relationship with Madame Denis, a widowed lady, who was also his niece.

WORK

Voltaire mainly argued for religious toleration and freedom of thought and many of his ideas foreshadowed the French Revolution. In England he met all the great figures of the day, including Jonathan Swift and Alexander Pope. It was Voltaire that put out the story about the apple falling from the tree and Isaac Newton observing it. Voltaire was certainly Newtonian in thinking, wanting to keep science and facts separate from the arts and religion. According to biographer Haydn Mason, he showed an interdependent relationship between commercial success, social equality, intellectual liberty, and political freedom. These were at the centre of his life. A great admirer of English freedom, Voltaire most admired Englishmen such as John Locke and Newton.

Throughout his life, Voltaire showed massive creativity, but especially towards the latter end. He is reputed to have written 15 million words. "Voltaire was sober and moderate, said his secretary, in everything except work". Work was certainly his antidepressant and he had a vast range of interests and was extraordinarily versatile. In the theatre he dominated the Comédie Française during his lifetime, according to Mason. Every genre – "epic, tragedy, life poetry, mock-epic, history and narrative" – benefited from his contribution and tremendous skill and he is also credited with introducing both Shakespeare and William Congreve to France.

According to Mason, "with boundless ambition, not to say supreme arrogance, he laid early claim to pre-eminence in two of the most exalted domains of letters … tragedy and the epic". This was not grandiosity, because that was precisely what he achieved with his inimitable and supreme self-confidence. Mason notes that he said death will come "too soon or too late". Some people live too long; others die too young. On that score, Voltaire certainly got it right.

Voltaire died in Paris on 30 May 1778, at the age of 83.

Chapter 52

TRUMAN CAPOTE

Truman Capote (1924–1984), a writer of novels, short stories, non-fiction and plays, was a major figure on the American literary scene in the 20th century. Some of his books were made into films, notably *Breakfast at Tiffany's* and *In Cold Blood*. He was a strange and troubled person and always remained emotionally immature. In terms of talent and personality he bore similarities to Oscar Wilde.

BACKGROUND

Capote was born Truman Streckfus Persons in New Orleans on 30 September 1924. His mother, Lillie Mae Faulk, was just 17 years old when he was born. She was a very important but highly ambivalent figure in his life. According to biographer George Plimpton, she was irresponsible and childlike, with arrested development in the sense that she behaved as an adolescent well into her thirties. She married the first man she met who had money, salesman Archulus Persons, and abandoned their baby Truman, aged about two, and "went off hoping to live the high life with her husband."[52] Capote's father, Archulus, was shadowy and feckless, to judge by his son's account: "You would think that every word rolling out of his mouth was the gospel, but most of it was just some scheme to get money out of you. He even conned me into flying him over the south one time in an aeroplane. He never paid the gas bill, the hotel bill, or anything. I picked up the tab."

Capote was left in the care of Jenny Faulk, a relative of his mother's who was "a hard-nosed businesswoman" living in Monroeville, Alabama. There he was pampered and encouraged "to dress up in ladies' clothes" and indeed was often attired like "Little Lord Fauntleroy". At school he wanted to relate to people who were interesting and found it intolerable for the spotlight not to be on him. He was an unpopular boy, disregarding those he could not be bothered with. His small stature as well as his personality made him a target for bullies as well. Nonetheless, he hyper-focused on what interested him, steering clear of team sports, but he was also easily bored and skipped classes he did not like. Not surprisingly, he showed poor school progress and failed a number of language exams.

---

[52] Except where otherwise indicated, quotes in this chapter are from Plimpton (1998).

Capote was clearly highly intelligent. In literary matters he was very talented from the beginning, helped by a few insightful schoolteachers who appreciated his gifts. He could also perform unusual physical feats and may have had a high pain threshold. A risk-taker, he drove a car as a very young boy not even able to see over the steering wheel. This behaviour is typical of a hyperkinetic child.

In 1933, he moved to New York to join his mother and her new husband, Joseph "Joe" Capote. She had divorced his father Persons some years before. Joe Capote was a wealthy Cuban businessman who adopted Capote as his stepson and gave him his surname. Capote adored his mother, despite the fact that she had neglected him over the years. She also showed massive emotional lability and swung from positivity to negativity in an instant. Emotionally immature at heart, she really never grew up and, not surprisingly, could relate to Capote's adolescent friends. As erratic as Capote's own father Archulus, Joe was a gambler and liked the high life, like Lillie Mae, and the couple both engaged in other relationships. Joe later went to prison for embezzlement.

According to Plimpton, Lillie Mae was "lovely" to Truman at one point and terrible the next, so he was constantly ricocheting: "She'd insult him in front of people … You never knew what she was going to do next and that is not fun to live with." Capote's high school performance was also very poor at the Franklin School in New York. Described as "an odd fish out of water" in the all-Jewish boys' school, he dressed oddly and presented a superiority complex as a defence against his insecurity.

PERSONALITY

It is often from harsh, unsympathetic, rejecting environments like Capote's that great creators come. Great creativity can sometimes arise from chaos, but of course there has to be a genetic predisposition. This was so for Capote. He was a tremendous reader and hyper-focused on books that interested him and had excellent observational skills of people. Highly creative, he was extremely imaginative and good at making up and telling stories. By all accounts he had an unusual tone of voice. Literary critic Diane Trilling, in conversation with Plimpton (1998), described him as "this little creature, odd looking, and with his extraordinary squeaky voice, very high-pitched and very resonant".

Capote clearly had identity diffusion and lacked a cohesive sense of self. It is hardly surprising that people generally found him very hard to understand, given his many false selves and that he was so egocentric, narcissistic, and masochistic. On occasion, like Picasso and William Golding, his creative activity seemed "outer willed and effortless", according to himself (Clarke, 2006). Another side of his personality was painting, though he had no artistic talent. A fellow filmgoer, Andrew Lyndon, recalled that he was an "insane combination of sophistication and naiveté" (Clarke, 2006). All these characteristics are critical to great creativity and were part of his multiple selves and identity diffusion. In person, Capote also had "a tremendous natural ebullience", according to Plimpton. It was still very important for him to be the centre of attention and he certainly was a show-off and an exhibitionist. Biographer Gerald Clarke (2006) notes that he had a tremendous power to be "seductive" with the camera.

Capote's personality was also marked by obsession and superstition: he was "notoriously obsessed with the placing of a comma, the weight of a semicolon". The ruptures that occurred in his parenting left him with anxiety and insecurity for much of his life. His entire life was haunted by "abandonment", according to Plimpton, because of his childhood experiences. For her part, his mother found him baffling. When she found out about Capote's homosexuality, she called him a "fairy" and revealed it to everybody, saying that he would end up in prison. More than likely she was a borderline personality who had identity diffusion and no real sense of her true self. She was undoubtedly psychologically disturbed and committed suicide in 1954.

The stresses of life and fame took their toll on Capote too. He suffered from alcohol and cocaine abuse and great depressions. He was massively self-destructive and abused drugs far more than alcohol. Certainly, the highly persistent man of his early career waned with his later addiction to drugs when unable to cope with celebrity. His drug addiction led to hallucinations, which can be associated with stimulant use.

Social Relationships

Like many great creators, Capote had a huge capacity to use people for his own benefit and the advancement of his career. This happened with teachers at school and many others later on, whereby he was able to learn from what they knew. He was also intensely competitive with other literary lions. A great conversationalist, Capote evidently had social know-how and a capacity for friendship with those he liked. He especially adored the smart set and yearned to be one of them, going so far as to organise some of the greatest New York parties of the 20th century. But there were contradictions too: despite a fondness for extreme luxury, he often lived a "Spartan" life, like a "Trappist monk" (Clarke, 2006).

At the same time, as Clarke points out, loneliness was nothing new to him: "from earliest childhood he felt isolated and unwanted". However, his hatred and contempt for people are evident in his letters (Clarke, 2004). Writer Colm Tóibín (2005) notes that his letters "are far superior to the stories … more nuanced and realised" and that Capote lived as a "predator" and was "narcissistic to the bone", with a mixture of "innocence and ruthlessness". In a perverse and self-destructive manner, he would disclose intimate confidences and wrote an article attacking the celebrities he loved to mix with. People therefore felt he was a traitor to friendship.

Though Capote related well to rich and famous women, it was men whom he sought out. According to Clarke (2006), he was attracted to straight, ordinary-looking men: "It thrilled him to think that he had such appeal that he could take a man away from his wife and family. And he did! Jack Dunphy was one of those married men." Capote and Dunphy had an enduring relationship, which did not always find favour with Capote's friends. Jack was described as a rough diamond by editor Pearl Bell: "I stopped inviting him to dinner parties after a while because at some point he would always stand up and insult someone at the table in resounding terms and stalk out. This got too much." The break-up of more than one homosexual relationship brought massive grief to Capote and at times he would engage in petty revenge (Clarke, 2006). Indeed he was someone who suffered a lot of anxiety and needed to be hospitalised after a psychological collapse.

Work

Capote's first job as a copyboy at *The New Yorker* exposed him to the world of publishing. As more and more of his short stories were published, for example in The Atlantic Monthly, Harper's Bazaar and The New Yorker, he gained popularity. His debut novel *Other Voices, Other Rooms*, based on his Alabama childhood, became a bestseller. His true crime novel *In Cold Blood* was original and innovating non-fiction and became a huge success. On the subject of writing, Capote confessed:

> Writing was always an obsession with me, quite simply something I had to do, and I don't understand exactly why this should have been true. It was as if I were an oyster and somebody forced a grain of sand into my shell – a grain of sand that I didn't know was there and didn't particularly welcome. Then a pearl started forming around the grain, and it irritated me, made me angry, tortured me sometimes. But the oyster can't help becoming obsessed with the pearl.

This is an excellent description of the power of creativity and how it grips the person. Capote also wanted to give the idea here that he owed all his creativity to himself. According to writer John Knowles, Capote was tremendously disciplined up to the writing of *In Cold Blood* and had been one of the most disciplined writers he had have ever met: "But he couldn't sustain it after that. A lot of motivation was lost. That is when he began to unravel." Capote finished up as a kind of talk-show parody of himself. Like many great creators, his ending was pitiful and rather sad; among his last words were "mama, mama" (Clarke, 2006). His life was nonetheless featured in various films, such as *Capote* (2005) and *Infamous* (2006).

Truman Capote died in Los Angeles from liver cancer on 25 August 1984, at the age of 59.

Chapter 53

OLIVER ST JOHN GOGARTY

Oliver St John Gogarty (1878–1957) was an Irish playwright, poet, sportsman, politician and wit, described by W. B. Yeats as "one of the great lyric poets of the age".[53] He was also a medical doctor, like Chekhov and Schiller, although it took him a decade to pass his examinations. He was an excellent athlete, a risk-taker and a novelty-seeker.

BACKGROUND

Oliver St John Gogarty was born on 17 August 1878 into a middle-class Dublin family. His father, Henry, was a doctor while his mother, Margaret, was the daughter of an industrialist. He seemingly inherited his "gift of the gab" and inexhaustible energy from his mother. At school he was "the most popular boy" and noted for his "soft voice, witty tongue, and pallid, handsome face". He trained as a medical doctor at Trinity College Dublin.

PERSONALITY

Gogarty "was a gifted mimic" who had a massive memory and tremendous capacity to quote poetry. In fact, he was an incessant talker with a "reckless imagination". In appearance, he was something of a dandy and was meticulous in his attire. From his early days he excelled at a variety of sports, including cricket and soccer. He also had a passion for fast cars and aeroplanes and loved danger. This also reflected his hyperkinetic and novelty-seeker nature with the constant need for new sensations. In his endeavours he had phenomenal energy and did not seem to require much sleep. There was also evidence of his being a hypochondriac.

[53] Except where otherwise indicated, quotes in this chapter are from O'Connor (2000).

Social Relationships

Clearly Gogarty had a gregarious nature and socialised much in Dublin, which was the second city of the British Empire at the time. He dined with all the top echelons of Irish and London society and was a popular guest in the mode of Oscar Wilde – only his conversation was probably a little less scintillating than Wilde's. He lived briefly with James Joyce in a Martello tower in Sandycove, Dublin, and figured as Buck Mulligan in Joyce's novel *Ulysses*. Joyce may indeed have been somewhat jealous of him, which would explain why he portrayed him somewhat negatively.

Gogarty was a close friend of Arthur Griffith, a future president of the Irish Free State, and sided with the pro-Treaty government at the end of the Irish War of Independence. He despised the anti-Treaty leader Éamon de Valera, who many years later would become president of the Republic of Ireland. Gogarty was lucky to escape assassination during the Irish Civil War and managed to jump into the River Liffey and escape. He wrote a poem about the short-sightedness of de Valera, both physical and political: "We rose to get Ireland a utopia and all we got was Dev's myopia" (Jeffares, 2001).

Work

Owing to his medical work, Gogarty was in touch with all layers of society; he had a large private practice and was an excellent surgeon – "he was like lightning with his hands". Gogarty was an outstanding poet while attending Trinity College and his talent as a playwright also came to the fore. He had a very strong social conscience and was appalled by the ghastly poverty, tuberculosis and starving children he witnessed in Dublin. He hence wrote a play called *Blight* on the topic, which was performed in the Abbey Theatre in 1917. Biographer Ulick O'Connor says that it shows that Gogarty possessed a flair for dramatic dialogue and comedy and that he also had a gift for character creation. Other plays followed: *A Serious Thing* mocked the "English inability to understand Ireland", while *Incurables* was "an attack on charitable institutions" (Jeffares, 2001).

Gogarty engaged in many different activities and completed an enormous amount of work in his lifetime. He was a man of tremendous courage and larger than life; he learned to fly an aeroplane and did so very often; he also saved several people from drowning in the River Liffey. Later Gogarty became a member of the Irish senate along with W. B. Yeats.

Though highly talented, Gogarty's work never reached supreme heights, possibly because nothing was sacrificed, unlike with Joyce: "Joyce sacrificed race, religion, and friends in his unswerving devotion to the cause of art": The writer and artist AE (George Russell) considered that it was Gogarty's refusal to separate art from life that brought a fresh, joyous note into his work, according to O'Connor. This may have been so, but his work did not endure in the same way that Joyce's has. That said, biographer A. Norman Jeffares (2001) is correct to point out that Gogarty has been "unreasonably neglected since his death". He lived in the USA from 1939 onwards and died on 22 September 1957, at the age of 79.

Chapter 54

IAN FLEMING

The British author Ian Fleming (1908–1964) is famous for creating the amazingly successful James Bond books. Both Fleming and the "Bond" character were simple-minded in that they saw things in black and white, without the complications of human interpersonal relations. James Bond was essentially Ian Fleming's alter ego. Fleming met the criteria for Asperger syndrome and secondary attention deficit hyperactivity disorder, which is a common profile in creative people.

BACKGROUND

Ian Fleming was born in London on 28 May 1908 into a wealthy upper-class family. His father, Valentine, became a Member of Parliament (MP) and was "one of those rare, slightly baffling Edwardian figures".[54] His mother, Evelyn, was passionate and extravagant but found her son disappointing because of his childhood behaviour. In contrast, his older brother Peter was far more successful for much of his life. Fleming was a hyperkinetic, rebellious and mischievous child – unpredictable, oppositional and defiant. He received a privileged education at Durnford School, Dorset and at Eton College. It is hardly surprising that he showed poor school progress and was regarded by his mother as the "black sheep" of the family. Indeed, biographer John Pearson describes him as "rude, resentful, and determined to make the most of his disgrace". Nevertheless, he could always hyper-focus on what interested him, such as athletics and reading. While he certainly grabbed the attention of his peers as he grew up, many found his behaviour somewhat tiresome. This type of boy almost always truants from school and Fleming was no exception.

PERSONALITY

Fleming was an enigmatic, immature personality and a highly contradictory figure. A schoolfriend at Eton said that he was "odd with everyone – terribly unpredictable". When people in general described him, the most common word they used was "eccentric". The

[54] Except where otherwise indicated, quotes in this chapter are from Pearson (2003).

reason was partly because Fleming was so tremendously novelty-seeking and sensation-seeking and adored risk-taking (Fitzgerald, 2008) – from mountain climbing to shark fishing to living dangerously. Intensely competitive, he found excitement at the limits of behaviour and loved pleasure and luxury. Bored by the minutiae of money, however, he was always fairly reckless financially. He was well able to take on people in authority, being confident, fearless and impatient, and liked outsiders. He particularly enjoyed the world that Captain Nemo inhabited in the books of Jules Verne. Interestingly, the fictional character Captain Nemo can be seen as having had Asperger syndrome, as can Verne.

However, most of Fleming's action took place in his imagination and he was a phenomenal reader. He lived in a somewhat one-person world where his own needs, wishes and rituals took priority. Considerably narcissistic, he was utterly the centre of his own world. He was also very much a fantasist, given to "flights of fancy", and often moved easily between fact and fiction, as of course do people who work in the Secret Service. Not surprisingly, he loved mystification and indeed the cave paintings in Lascaux, France held particular fascination for him. Like many people with Asperger traits, he had mathematical interests and was fascinated by gadgets.

Despite his love of sensation-seeking and novelty, he also had a very strong sense of preserving sameness. He led a very ritualistic life and was a ritualistic writer, obsessed with symmetry in all aspects of his life. This is a compulsive Asperger-type trait. When he wrote in his Spartan house in Jamaica he appeared as a kind of "self-absorbed 18th century original". This kind of statement is often made about people with Asperger traits.

Other aspects of Fleming's life were chaotic, however. His living quarters for example were disorganised. He was very much like the poet Lord Byron who had attention deficit hyperactivity disorder (Fitzgerald, 2001). Both were described as rakes, although Fleming was far less a rake than Lord Byron and his family. Certainly there was something of the frenzied romantic about him. A teacher who knew Fleming well in early adulthood, Ernan Forbes Dennis, described him as "half Faust, half Byron". There was also a rather cyclothymic side to Fleming, with moods swinging up and down. "Solitariness and despair" were part of his picture as well, not least because Fleming was a sensitive person in general and also sensitive to pain. He also feared public humiliation and always had a sense of insecurity. Of course, this is critical to creativity. Like many a creative person, he found solace in various addictions. He had similar features to theatre critic Kenneth Tynan, who likewise abused alcohol and cigarettes and had Asperger syndrome. It is hardly surprising that Fleming died of heart disease in middle age. Despite all the evidence for attention deficit hyperactivity disorder, Asperger syndrome most likely is his primary psychopathological diagnosis.

Social Relationships

Fleming was something of a loner and was aloof, with a "shell of toughness to keep potential intruders at bay". He had a compartmentalised personality and kept people in separate compartments in his mind. For this reason, he was an "eccentric" host. Throughout his life he was a very secretive and private person, traits incompatible with real intimacy. Not surprisingly, he had a fear of genuine intimacy and found it hard to share his intimate thoughts with others, particularly women. He was also fearful of being engulfed by women and had an "almost Swiftian abhorrence of physical female defects". (Indeed, Swift also had Asperger syndrome (Fitzgerald, 2000)). Hence Fleming found it hard to have meaningful relationships with women. Nevertheless, he wanted to be mothered by them, which was contradictory, and despite having little regard for affectionate, caring women.

From early adulthood he was a womaniser and preferred more perverse relationships with women as these were more exciting. In this he shared many features with Lord Byron. One girlfriend claimed that Fleming was quite ruthless about girls, while another said he was "totally amoral in sex". Sex for him was rather mechanical and without much relationship. Indeed the satisfaction he got from women was purely momentary and superficial. Given that he had the extreme male brain himself, he was baffled by the female mind and refused to accept that "a mistress could have a mind". This was a way of distancing himself, but was also due to genuine puzzlement about the female mind. He simply felt that women were not intellectual enough: he had a "part–object" relationship with them, whereby he simply used them for his own purposes as objects rather than as human beings. In a way James Bond was his ideal for himself – it was his better kind of alter ego.

Fleming was equally unsettled by being alone and being "the odd man out": there was no safe place for him, with or without a woman. You could say that he was in a no man's land. This is all part of his Asperger syndrome. There were unempathic psychopathic elements to his personality and his wife remarked that his "capacity for human beings was extremely limited". Certainly, Fleming was very controlling of people; they were there to amuse him and to be used by him. He often made tactless remarks that upset people and could be rather hurtful, rude, and "sinister".

Typical of persons with Asperger syndrome, marriage came late in life for Fleming. His wife Ann, a socialite, said that he was "totally unlike anyone else I had ever met", which is a typical comment about people with Asperger syndrome or Asperger traits. Ann was a kind of Asperger wife who looked after him and make no "real demands" on him: "He rather enjoyed presenting himself as a sort of simple-minded martyr on the pyre of his wife's burning sociability." Inept at communicating his personal emotions, his marriage caused him a great deal of anxiety and he worried how it would fare. He certainly knew he had no natural talent for marriage.

WORK

During the Second World War Fleming served in the Secret Service as a naval intelligence officer and was very successful. He formed a unit of commandos composed of specialist intelligence troops that seized enemy documents, which he directed from the rear. Using his wartime experiences, he produced his first book, *Casino Royale*, at the age of 43. It was written quickly and an immediate success. According to Pearson, *Casino Royale* "came straight from his memory and imagination". At the same time it was a rather humourless book and lacked genuine human characterisation, as did many of his James Bond novels:

> Because he was fundamentally isolated from people Fleming never succeeded in introducing a single really credible character into the dream world disclosed in his novels. He was never a man to get really close to other human beings, and he had none of the real

> novelist's interest in human character – his curiosity was reserved for material objects and practical techniques, and he no more invited profound confidences from people than he bestowed them. The result of this isolation was that everything had to come from within himself. While this provides much of the uniqueness of the James Bond books, it also limits them drastically. It accounts for their oddly claustrophobic atmosphere.

This is a description of typical Asperger writing. Fleming put arcane information into his books, according to Pearson, and the Bond girls were objects to be used. In the character of James Bond, there is a kind of "zombie" to perform the dreams of violence and daring that fascinated his creator: "It is only because Fleming holds so little of himself back, because he talks and dreams so freely through the device of James Bond, that the book has such readability." Pearson believes that *Casino Royale* is really an experiment in the autobiography of dreams. You could say that it sits in the very common genre of autobiographical fiction. The Bond character also lived in a one-person world in the sense that "there was only one person to praise or blame. Oneself." Furthermore, there is a good deal of perversity and sadism in the Bond films and books. Pearson suggests that Fleming possibly had a masochistic infatuation and was obsessed by pain. Over time, James Bond gained ascendancy over the man who created him, according to Pearson, which is a fascinating new perspective, looking at the effect of a character on the creator.

Ian Fleming died of a heart attack on 12 August 1964 in Kent, at the age of 56.

Chapter 55

PHILIP K. DICK

Philip K. Dick (1928–1982) was one of the great science fiction writers, whose work was turned into highly successful films such as *Blade Runner*, *Minority Report* and *Total Recall*. He was also perhaps one of the strangest human beings that ever lived – a complete original. He had major identity diffusion associated with Asperger syndrome.

BACKGROUND

Philip Kindred Dick was born in Chicago on 16 December 1928, to Dorothy and Joseph Edgar Dick, who worked for the U.S. Department of Agriculture. Both Dick and his twin sister, Jane, were born prematurely and were of low birth weight. Jane died six weeks later and her death would affect Dick for the rest of his life. In fact, difficulties around childbirth are not uncommon in persons with Asperger syndrome. His mother, Dorothy, a massive reader with literary aspirations, was a highly independent, forward-thinking woman. She separated from Dick's father, Joseph, when Dick was five years old and moved to Washington DC and later to California. Like many persons with Asperger syndrome, Dick was clingy to his mother and they were rather enmeshed. She was obsessed with the functioning of his physical body, just like Howard Hughes's mother. In later life Dick wanted women to mother him in a similar way. On the other hand, his relationship with his father was strained. As a young child, Dick utterly panicked when his father put on a gas mask. For a long time afterwards, he "kept scanning his father's face for signs of the substitution".[55] Separating fact from fiction was a constant problem for Dick, which was also the secret of his success. He was a lonely boy and a classic person with Asperger syndrome. As a child, he found peace hiding in old boxes, silent and safe from the world, according to biographer Emmanuel Carrère.

Dick disliked the usual social interactions of children his age. He hated sports and any physical contact activities, and lacked macho, masculine traits. However, he adored reading, like his mother, as well as music and typing. His early life was quite similar to that of Nabokov's Luzhin or Glenn Gould (his contemporary and in some respects his spiritual cousin), according to Carrère. In fact, Glenn Gould (Fitzgerald, 2005) and Vladimir Nabokov

[55] Except where otherwise indicated, quotes in this chapter are from Carrère (2005).

had Asperger syndrome too. Carrère notes that Dick was like his mother in being "an artistic soul, an albatross with an enormous wingspan that prevented him from walking on the earth". This is probably the best description of him and gets to the core of his personality.

Given his massively creative imagination, Dick founded a "magazine" as an adolescent that focused on intergalactic adventures, "the fruit of the feverish daydreams of the prolix adolescent who was the magazine's sole contributor". This is the typical autistic position. Showing poor school progress, he dropped out of school and stayed at home reading books, often esoteric material, and listening to music.

PERSONALITY

There were many features of Asperger syndrome to Dick's personality: highly intelligent, charismatic, hyperkinetic and hypersensitive as well as the awkward gait and the sensory integration issues in relation to noise. He was also extremely egocentric, narcissistic, introverted, and a loner.

The most remarkable aspect of Dick's personality, however, is his identity diffusion, multiple selves and problems with experience of time. Essentially, he had a very unusual, unintegrated brain and lived in a fragmentary, disconnected world. Carrère's biography focuses on a man who regarded even his craziest books "not as works of imagination but as factual reports". This is a typical Asperger position, where fact and fiction are the same. It represents an autistic world, wherein Dick lived. Internally his psychological world constantly drifted between fact and fiction, which was the secret of his creativity. For Dick, "the world is not what it seems to be" and he was like a man from another world – a non-human world such as Mars. No wonder then that he would find Planet Earth unusual if he felt he was from another planet. Being a science fiction writer however was "the best possible disguise for an android". Whereas other people claim to remember past lives, he claimed "to remember a different, very different, present life". Although he was a *Homo sapiens*, he had little of the thinking of the so-called average *Homo sapiens* in the twentieth century. He was not burdened with standard thinking or basic presuppositions of average, so-called normal human beings. Such presuppositions or perceptions of the world are disastrous for great creativity. The great creators have to be confused, unique and enigmatic. In fact, Dick was a very naive and immature boy, and remained so all his life, seeing himself as a "loser and oddball". According to Carrère, Dick was a chameleon, "an actor, adept at reading his audience and figuring out their expectations". This certainly relates to his false selves and identity diffusion, where he could change personas often. For Dick, words meant "whatever he wanted them to mean"; often getting them to mean the exact opposite. He showed an autistic narrative in that, as Carrère points out, he was not content merely to contradict himself, but would sometimes in the course of a conversation deny having said what the person had heard him to say only minutes earlier. Indeed, one of his wives talked about him in terms of being another Goebbels!

Dick particularly liked C.G. Jung, whose writings drifted between fact and fiction a great deal and indeed were often quite imaginative and literary. For Dick, the Jungians were the *crème de la crème* as they specialised in the creative personality. He also liked the Jungian idea of a collective unconscious and phylogenic memories, and was very much into the "mind-blowing example of Jungian synchronicity". Interestingly, Jung also had Asperger syndrome. Carrère points out that in straddling the line between autobiography and fiction, Dick's novels and stories provide "the best window into a man who, in a far more radical way than any of his contemporaries, effectively abolished the difference between life and literature". This is a reflection of his identity diffusion. As a young man he also feared homosexuality. Seeing that he was androgynous, as persons with Asperger syndrome often are, he had sexual identity diffusion. Nevertheless, he was mostly heterosexual.

Dick suffered a good deal of depersonalisation and derealisation, particularly associated with panic attacks, which aggravated his identity diffusion. He did not feel particularly real and neither did the world around him, which is a very frightening world to live in. He noted a 1641 quotation from Descartes: "How do I know that I am not being deceived by an infinitely powerful evil demon who wants me to believe in the existence of the external world – and in my own body?" He was endlessly into conspiracies and autistic paranoid thinking, which paradoxically was also the source of his great creativity. He felt that "the universe spins around me, without any other purpose than to torture me". Moreover, he felt that the inner psychic mechanism whose function it was to filter reality had shut down. In this respect, there is reduced repression in persons with Asperger syndrome and probably more access to unconscious material. There is evidence that he had the autistic fear of engulfment and annihilation, whereby he always dreaded merging with somebody and being taken over. He lived on the edge of annihilation, which is a common enough position for Asperger people.

Dick was fascinated by religion, where of course fact and fiction are intertwined and indeed where fiction is more or less treated as fact. In his desire to become a Christian, he did however encounter one particular problem, which is hardly surprising given his treatment of fact and fiction: it concerned the Catholic belief in the Eucharist, where "whoever eats my flesh and drinks my blood has eternal life". Furthermore, Dick was deeply esoteric and, according to Carrère, was convinced that beneath the visible there lay a "Hidden Secret". In this respect Dick was following in the footsteps of William Blake, who once said: "If the doors of perception were cleansed, everything would appear to man as it is, infinite". Isaac Newton searched in much the same way for that kind of knowledge when not carrying out scientific work. Like Blake, Newton too had Asperger syndrome (Fitzgerald and O'Brien, 2007). Dick looked for this ultimate knowledge and ultimate secrets from culture, psychoanalysis, and even religion. He wanted "the passport that would permit him to escape from the cave wherein we are shown not the real world but only its shadows". But this Platonic cave was his autistic brain in fact.

There was also a fascination for horror films in keeping with many with Asperger syndrome because that is the kind of world in which they live and with which they empathise. Carrère notes that similar to Sherlock Holmes, Dick could date a file by the thickness of the dust covering it and "relish being the only one who can make sense of the reigning chaos". His weak central coherence and massive eye for detail made this possible. Both Arthur Conan Doyle and his fictional detective Sherlock Holmes had personality features suggestive of Asperger syndrome.

Dick did not have schizophrenia, although adult psychiatrists might have been tempted to diagnose him as such. He suffered from generalised anxiety disorder and was under psychiatric treatment on and off for most of his life. He also abused drugs a good deal. He was essentially an autistic hypochondriac with a history of suicide attempts. Many of his psychoanalytic sessions went round in circles and classical Freudian or Jungian analysis was inappropriate for him. Nonetheless, Dick was interested in creativity and the value of schizophrenia, although he was wrong about it, as it is people on the edge of schizophrenia that are creative, not those with schizophrenia itself. At times he was thought-disordered and this kind of phenomenon can be present in Asperger syndrome and is not solely associated with schizophrenia. It is also fair to say that he had a schizotypal personality. While Asperger syndrome is clearly the best diagnosis, persons with schizotypal personality disorder do have ideas of reference, odd beliefs or magical thinking, superstitiousness, bizarre fantasies or preoccupations, unusual perceptual experiences, odd thinking and speech, suspiciousness, paranoid ideation, inappropriate and constricted affect, behaviour or appearance that is odd, eccentric or peculiar, and excessive social anxiety. Judging by the evidence, there is no doubt that he had so-called schizotypal personality disorder, but a great many of those with this disorder would be better seen as being part of Asperger syndrome. It is very common for psychiatrists to diagnose somebody with schizophrenia if they have poor abstract thinking and are very concrete, but clearly they have to have some other symptoms as well.

Social Relationships

Dick was an eccentric loner with major problems in reciprocal social relationships and empathy. He was quite incapable of sustained, meaningful intimate relations. Furthermore, he could not stand to be with people, yet could not stand to be alone either. He was therefore in no man's land. From the very beginning he was very much into power, control and domination, which also reflected his fascination for dictators. Indeed persons with Asperger syndrome are often fixated with dictators such as Hitler and Napoleon.

Dick's adult life was one of serial monogamy – he was married five times – and he had three children in total. Persons with Asperger syndrome often need a "wife–mother" when they marry and Dick was no exception. Many of his wives mothered him and were one hundred per cent devoted to him and his needs. It is hardly surprising that the marriages were unhappy and brief in some cases. It was quite hard for Dick to keep up pseudo-normal interaction over a long period, though he did try various false selves. There was evidence of misogyny as well, described as "raging misogyny" by Carrère, which is very common in males with Asperger syndrome. When one of his wives, Anne Williams Rubinstein, was having a baby he developed a kind of couvade syndrome, also called sympathetic pregnancy: "He was having chest pains – his way of participating in Anne's labour pains." He developed paranoid delusions about Anne and had her briefly committed to a psychiatric hospital. Later he went to the hospital to say that he was the one who needed to be locked up: "He had schizoid tendencies".

Work

As a science fiction writer Dick was a genius and highly regarded. Science fiction is a kind of quasi-delusional world of the imagination, which is where he lived and flourished. In fact, he was one of the greatest travellers of all time in his imagination. There is nothing ordinary about science fiction and it takes an extraordinary as opposed to an average person to produce it. It requires a mind that is chaotic, suspicious and paranoid, full of fears about the ordinary world that is seen as malevolent. For such people, a minor misperception can set off a massive conspiracy theory. For example, Dick wrote about conspiracies where everybody except the person he was writing about knew a "great secret". Science fiction writers are fascinated with gadgets and indeed more at home in a futuristic, mechanical world. The computer world is often more real and more interesting for them than the ordinary human world. A great science fiction writer like Dick possessed few balanced human traits, and had little internal or external harmony.

His writing was a kind of autistic narrative due to his pragmatic language difficulties and he engaged in a great deal of autistic paranoid thinking, as we have seen. In his book *Do Androids Dream of Electric Sheep?*, he invented the word "kipple" to designate "an entropic state of decomposition and chaos towards which all things naturally tend". This is quite close to Freud's death drive. Overall, Dick got lost in his stories, which became like a maze for him and hard to find his way out. It is not surprising that he was interested in director Stanley Kubrick, who directed the iconic *2001: A Space Odyssey* – another with Asperger person.

Philip K. Dick died in California of a brain haemorrhage on 2 March 1982, at the age of 53.

Chapter 56

William Shakespeare

The English playwright and poet William Shakespeare (1564–1616) was, and is, the greatest of all playwrights. It is doubtful if anyone will ever supersede him. Facts about Shakespeare are thin on the ground and speculations about him make world libraries groan. Dealing with Shakespeare, one often has to go on gut instinct or on the balance of probabilities, after accumulating as much indirect or hearsay evidence as possible. Some would argue that silence is the best way. However, everyone agrees that he was a genius of the first order.

A somewhat recent speculation on Shakespeare (Kenny & Fitzgerald, 2006) suggests that he had Asperger syndrome – this idea emerged during discussions with academic Zehanne Kenny at Trinity College Dublin. It would appear that to produce such a colossal volume of work one would need to be massively persistent, extremely intelligent, a huge observer of detail, and a workaholic. The kind of person that tends to possess these traits is the person with Asperger syndrome (Fitzgerald, 2004).

Background

William Shakespeare was born in Stratford-upon-Avon, England, and baptised there on 26 April 1564. His father, John, was a "skilled craftsman" – a glover – and became an alderman.[56] This suggests a man of some substance and intelligence. Later he suffered a financial collapse for reasons unknown, but it would appear that he was a novelty-seeker, ambitious and rather reckless. Shakespeare's mother, Mary Arden, gave birth to four sons, only one of whom, William, married. Many believe the surname Shakespeare to be of French origin and indeed Sigmund Freud felt that Shakespeare was of French stock – a Freudian "fantasy".

[56] Except where otherwise indicated, quotes in this chapter are from Bryson (2008).

PERSONALITY

Clearly Shakespeare was fascinated by the theatre and writing plays. He had the genetic profile for this, however, we have as yet not unravelled what this profile looks like. He certainly had the capacity to hyper-focus and worked assiduously. The material for his plays came from himself and from any other source to which he had access. He had some narrow interests, for example, in plants, military matters, medical matters and legal terms. This would be typical of a person with Asperger syndrome. You could say he was a kind of magpie in that he rewrote existing material. Persons with Asperger syndrome are often fascinated with language and Shakespeare was no different. He used fantastic language in the process of rewriting other material. He put hundreds of new words into the English language, many of which have survived in general use. He also originated countless phrases that we still use today, such as "one fell swoop", "vanish into thin air", "bag and baggage", "play fast and loose", "in a pickle", "budge an inch", "milk of human kindness", "more sinned against than sinning", "remembrance of things past", "beggar all description", "cold comfort", "to thine own self be true", "more in sorrow than in anger", "salad days", "blinking idiot", "pomp and circumstance", and "foregone conclusion". We are lucky that he did not have vast amounts of ancient learning, as this would have clogged up his mind and his plays. It would have left him less free, and he might have used ancient words rather than the many new words he introduced into the language.

He was also hyperkinetic writer, as can even be seen in *Hamlet*, where there is evidence of haste. In terms of output, a number of playwrights wrote a great deal more than he did, but he by far produced the best body of work. It seems at times that he would get fascinated by an idea and keep following it endlessly, despite adding little to the play and indeed unbalancing it. He was massively curious and excited by the pleasure he got from following the associations in his brilliant mind. Moreover, he had a tremendous knack of seeing bits and putting them together in wholes. This is sometimes described as weak central coherence, common in Asperger syndrome.

Like many great writers, he confused fact and fiction and was cavalier with facts. The great playwrights mix fact and fiction, seeing that a play is entertainment and not a scientific experiment. There is strong indirect evidence too that Shakespeare had identity diffusion, including sexual identity diffusion, which helped him to write so convincingly about women. Some of his sonnets are homoerotic and focus on a "lovely boy". He was quite adept, particularly in the sonnets, at expressing the feelings of males for other males, which is part of his identity diffusion. It is not a question of male or female, but of the two together or a strong intertwining. The sonnets – probably his greatest work – show a more feminine side of himself. In biographies of today, sexual identity diffusion is often confused with homosexuality: biographers see some evidence of homoeroticism in prose or poetry and immediately jump to the conclusion that the person was a homosexual. This is far from the truth, even though it is evidence of identity diffusion.

Shakespeare was fascinated by novelty and lost interest in plays once they were performed: he wanted to go on to the next play. As he got older he withdrew more into himself and his plays become more introspective. This is a natural part of the ageing process.

Social Relationships

Shakespeare married Anne Hathaway at the age of 18, when she was 26, and she bore him three children. There is no evidence of any warmth between Shakespeare and his wife, or indeed any other person. Was this autistic disconnection? When Shakespeare worked in London they were separated for long periods, which is not an uncommon Asperger-type marriage. In 1596, the death of his 11-year-old son Hamnet from unknown causes plunged him into grief. In a biographical touch, Shakespeare wrote in *King John* that "grief fills the room up of my absent child".

Work

Shakespeare, otherwise known as the Bard of Avon, was the English national poet and considered by many to be the greatest dramatist of all time. His works include 38 plays, 154 sonnets and two long narrative poems, and are studied by students all over the world. Mystery surrounds the identity of the subjects of some sonnets, for example, the Lovely Boy and the Dark Lady. Shakespearian scholar A.L. Rowse, who had Asperger syndrome, became obsessed with the idea that the Dark Lady was Emilia Bassano, daughter of one of the musicians at the court of Elizabeth I. In typical Asperger fashion, he would not admit that he could be wrong and this did untold damage to his academic reputation. Academics are still torturing themselves as to the identity of the Dark Lady.

Speculation on the authorship of the works attributed to William Shakespeare has raged for some time. Names suggested in the academic game entitled "Who Wrote Shakespeare?" include Francis Bacon; Edward de Vere, 17th Earl of Oxford; and Mary Sidney. Anyone can play and large numbers of people have done so. It may have advanced their academic careers but it has shed no new light on Shakespeare. This game is somewhat akin to the conspiracy game "Who Killed Kennedy?" Some suggest that Christopher Marlowe, another dramatist of the time, "wrote Shakespeare". This is absurd, as Marlowe died young, probably had attention deficit hyperactivity disorder, was impulsive and tactless, and killed in a fight in a tavern. At the time of his death he may have been equal to Shakespeare, but the Bard subsequently went far beyond him.

William Shakespeare died of unknown causes on 23 April 1616, aged 52.

PART V: PRODUCERS/FINANCIERS

Chapter 57

SAM SPIEGEL

Sam Spiegel (1901–1985) was a hugely successful film producer who worked on films such as *Lawrence of Arabia*, *The Bridge on the River Kwai* and *On the Waterfront*, winning Academy Awards for all three. He was a charming criminal-type figure, ideally suited to Hollywood and the film business. I believe the autistic psychopathy form of Asperger syndrome would best suit the profile of his behaviour.

BACKGROUND

Samuel Spiegel was born on 11 November 1901 in Jarosław, Galicia, in present-day Poland, into a Jewish family. His father, Simon, was in the tobacco business, while his mother, Regina, was a dominant figure in his life and educated him well. The boss of the family, she was rather narcissistic and grandiose and, like Oscar Wilde's mother, lied about her age. She presented a false self and trained him to have false selves as well. For her, appearance was everything and indeed there are echoes of Truman Capote's background here. Spiegel was very fearful of illness and took after his mother who was quite hypochondriacal. His father, who travelled widely, was a more peripheral figure in his life. Spiegel witnessed a great deal of anti-Semitism in Poland during his childhood. A superb linguist, he could speak nine languages and enrolled in the University of Vienna in 1920 and spent some time studying political science. Having joined a youth Zionist movement years earlier, around the same time he travelled to Palestine and worked in a kibbutz, where he showed his strong physical physique. He arrived in New York in November 1927 and in Hollywood a few months later.

PERSONALITY

Spiegel was an extraordinary character who had the capacity to hyper-focus on what interested him. Given his novelty-seeking and sensation-seeking nature, being a showman was what he enjoyed most and he was perfectly suited to the entertainment industry. As a young man, he said "I'll either become a very rich and famous man or I will die like a dog in the gutter". In a way he became both rich and famous and lived in the gutter. He was a driven, persistent man and a wanderer across Europe, America, Palestine and later Israel.

With Spiegel, there is evidence of identity diffusion, given how enigmatic he was and a classic mythmaker. As with many others in this book, there was a split personality and multiple selves. His third wife, Betty, once remarked: "Remember Churchill's line about Russia? A riddle wrapped in a mystery inside an enigma … hmm, that was Sam."[57] Spiegel was constantly reinventing himself, living in the here-and-now, so much so that he was a tremendous conman. Because he had "exquisite manners", he was able to con people relatively easily, was quite good at buying gifts and flowers, and could lie with a straight face. He went to America without papers in the late 1920s and was arrested months later but pretended to be a diplomat. After his period in custody there, he went to Berlin to work in the film industry but allegedly escaped from the Nazis before the borders were closed. However, there is some doubt as to the veracity of that story, as he was a mythmaker. Admittedly, there were some positive attributes like courage but it was dwarfed by his misdemeanours.

From the beginning, Spiegel was a man whom "many liked, but few trusted". An extremely controlling, dominating figure, the whole world was there to serve him and be abused by him. He was guilty of "shark-like behaviour and an appalling ruthlessness", according to biographer Natasha Fraser-Cavassoni. Director Billy Wilder, his fellow émigré from Galicia, said that Spiegel was a modern-day Robin Hood, "who steals from the rich and steals from the poor". Yet there was always "a certain panache to him, like being in the presence of a nobleman and a gangster." Lacking any moral compass whatsoever, he was free to do what he wanted and was "a hardened wheeler-dealer", who believed there were no rules for his profession. In fact, he made his own rules from early life, like not paying his bills in restaurants, hotels, etc., and was a born survivor. You could say he was a "maverick and wheeler-dealer" like Robert Maxwell, the Czech-born English media tycoon (Fitzgerald, 2008). Spiegel was certainly a gambler – he did love playing cards after all – who lived on his wits and possessed a kind of *pseudologia fantastica* or compulsive lying. He genuinely enjoyed conflict and adored lies yet was not sure what was true and what was false, but he was certainly far more attracted to telling fibs. Again, it was like *Alice in Wonderland*: language meant whatever he wanted it to mean. An acquaintance and Fox executive, Max Youngstein, said that financially speaking Spiegel was always one step ahead of the sheriff. However, he did serve terms in a number of prisons in several countries, including Brixton Prison in London, for non-payment of rent and fraud.

Spiegel was quite a visual person and a great collector of art. He did have good taste and was generally appreciative of paintings. In addition, he adored good food and fine wines and lived a luxurious, hedonistic lifestyle.

Social Relationships

Everybody was there to be used by Spiegel for his own selfish purposes in what psychoanalysts call a "part–object relationship". This is highly characteristic behaviour of creative figures. Actress Katherine Hepburn was very accurate when she remarked that Spiegel was "just a pig in a silk suit who sends flowers". For all that, Spiegel was massively

[57] Except where otherwise indicated, quotes in this chapter are from Fraser-Cavassoni (2004).

socially energetic and successful. He hosted amazing parties attended by the who's who of society.

A Don Juan and good dancer, Spiegel used women and they certainly helped him on his upward climb. Possibly his feminine side showed in the fact that he was very appreciative in his comments about women and noticed any changes or differences in their attire. While he had "a rhino-like hide" himself, he was extremely shrewd about human nature, as psychopaths often are. He had a rare cunning in dealing with people and was incapable of feeling guilty, but nonetheless had a capacity to make others feel guilty. Clearly, he had the gift of the gab. American screenwriter Bud Schulberg stated that "Sam really knew how to play on other people's weaknesses ... He was an inspired pimp. He could create those very high-class mosh-pits. Women were looking for acting jobs and it was a knee up the ladder."

Spiegel had problems maintaining social relationships, however, and showed a "customary detachment" from his family. He kept people in compartments, which reflected his fragmented, compartmentalised sense of self. Emotionally detached, he failed to attend the funeral of his father in Haifa, Palestine in 1936. According to Fraser-Cavassoni, he used to confuse the circumstances of his father's death with that of his younger brother. Spiegel once told Harold Pinter that "the secret of happiness is whores". Here he could have the detached, controlling type of relationship he wanted and certainly intimacy was "the one commodity Spiegel was incapable of providing". Spiegel met and married Rachel "Ray" Agranovich in Palestine in 1920, but after five years he quickly abandoned her and their baby daughter Alisa. As a father, he tended to relate very poorly to Alisa – after her first year, he didn't see her again until her adolescence. Neither did he attend her wedding. He certainly was far too narcissistic, egocentric and self-centred to have time for his daughter. There is a kind of autistic detachment in this scenario. Another marriage followed in 1948, this time to actress Lynne Baggett, which was beset by infidelity and reckless behaviour and ended in divorce in 1955.

Lynne subsequently committed suicide. Spiegel was indifferent to this event and did not attend her funeral, so emotionally "switched off was he". In fact, Spiegel never discussed personal matters with anyone and was a "lone wolf". In this respect, he was like the director David Lean, with whom he worked on *Lawrence of Arabia,* and who also had Asperger's syndrome. His third marriage was to Betty Benson in 1957 and it was deeply unconventional in that they lived apart shortly afterwards. His relationship with Ann E. Pennington produced a son, Adam, in 1968. As a highly unreliable father, Spiegel still tended to ignore his children. It is hardly surprising that his son described him as "peculiar" and that his last will and testament had "no personal touch".

WORK

Spiegel was a highly successful producer, who was perfectionistic in wanting the highest possible standards for his films. Some are considered epics, such as *The African Queen, On the Waterfront, The Bridge on the River Kwai* and *Lawrence of Arabia.* It is no wonder that he won 25 Academy Awards in all for many of his films. An entertaining figure for all his shortcomings, he could never be accused of being boring.

Despite Spiegel's extreme deviousness, the producer Norman Spencer said that he had this ability to put his finger on what was wrong in relation to a film. The same could be said for Sam Goldwyn.

Sam Spiegel died in Guernsey on 31 December 1985, at the age of 84.

Chapter 58

William Randolph Hearst

William Randolph Hearst (1863–1951) was an American newspaper magnate and film producer, who also dabbled in politics. He briefly served as a Democratic member in the U.S. House of Representatives. He was an enigmatic individual and showed traits suggestive of Asperger syndrome.

Background

William Randolph Hearst was born on 29 April 1863 in San Francisco into a rich family. It would appear that his father, George – a mining engineer – had Asperger syndrome. George had little education and spoke poorly; he loved whiskey, playing cards and chewing tobacco, and dressed in stained clothes. Nonetheless, he was brave, intelligent and novelty-seeking – a socially awkward gruff man. Hearst's mother, Phoebe, was a determined woman who spoilt and indulged him but ensured he got the best education possible. In typical Asperger fashion he was clingy to his mother and showed anxiety when separated from her.

As a child and in later life Hearst showed evidence of attention deficit hyperactivity disorder and was oppositional and defiant. Hyperactive and easily bored, he always had phenomenal energy and loved to work at whatever interested him. Like many Asperger children, Hearst was bookish and collected stamps. People noticed that he had leadership qualities as he grew up and was especially brave. However, he was extremely dictatorial and fascinated by dictators, exhibiting a "Napoleonic complex". As a child, he had adult autistic interests, whereas as an adult he was emotionally immature and somewhat naive. He also spoke in an adult fashion as a child, which is characteristic of persons with Asperger syndrome. After his expulsion from Harvard University for misconduct, where he excelled in journalism, he went into business, taking over the management of the *San Francisco Examiner* on behalf of his father in 1887.

Personality

To the world Hearst was a bewildering, unfathomable individual. He possessed a massive memory, something not uncommon in Asperger syndrome, and had an immense capacity to hyper-focus on his narrow interests, such as journalism. He had the "penetrating gaze" of persons with Asperger syndrome, while his voice was unusual and high-pitched, with a "girlish timbre". There was also evidence of pragmatic language difficulties and he spoke with a kind of autistic narrative. According to biographer W. A. Swanberg, he had an "inability to make a speech" and this problem with communication seriously damaged his political ambitions.

A novelty-seeker and sensation-seeker, Hearst was always impatiently searching for new novelties and new stimuli. In this regard, according to Swanberg, he had a "juvenile worship of size, noise, and display. He wanted to be the biggest, the showiest. Quiet quality bored him." At one level he remained the eternally immature boy with his toys in his castle. There was also evidence of repetitive behaviour. Indirectly Hearst liked to show off and shock, much like a little boy – a "braggart" and a "maverick" who engaged in silly practical jokes.[58] This type of behaviour is not uncommon in persons with Asperger syndrome (Lyons & Fitzgerald, 2004). The novelties also extended to collecting art. He was an indiscriminate art collector later in life, like Freud, though lacking in any aesthetic taste. I found his art collection an unbelievable mishmash, highly offputting, when I visited Hearst Castle in San Simeon, California. Because of his very naive, immature personality art dealers commonly took advantage of him. He was in fact a spendthrift and highly irresponsible about money, eventually almost bankrupting his business. Like many people with Asperger syndrome, for example, Ludwig Wittgenstein (Fitzgerald, 2000), money meant very little to him.

Nevertheless, Hearst was obsessed with power and control. He loved to wield influence unseen through his newspapers and, in business, was aggressive and extremely competitive. Typically persons with Asperger syndrome show these traits, with suspicious, paranoid elements. In Hearst's case, he was obsessed with ultimate power, including becoming President of the United States. His display of extraordinary grandiosity was rooted in believing himself to be "a guardian of American interests" and having the right to act for the people of the United States. In addition, he had an "imperial sense of righteousness", and while he showed his aggression in political speeches, his general verbal communication was restricted, as noted earlier. He also saw himself as a Christ-like figure – the saviour of the world and "a lone warrior against injustice and outmoded tradition". He was similar to another Asperger-type political aficionado, Éamon de Valera (Fitzgerald, 2004), who saw himself in the same position in Ireland. These are not uncommon features of highly talented people with Asperger syndrome. That said, for all his grandiose ways, Hearst was sensitive to the extreme poverty he witnessed on a visit to Ireland.

To understand Hearst you have to understand his identity diffusion. He moved easily between fact and fiction and was a great fantasist – a kind of Don Quixote figure. (Indeed the fictional character Don Quixote and his creator, Cervantes, can both be seen as having had Asperger syndrome.) In Hearst's eyes, everything was in black and white – a typical Asperger view: "He lived in a child-like dream world, imagining wonderful stories and then going out and creating them, so that the line between fact and fantasy was apt to be fuzzy." This Asperger position features a blur between the world of the imagination and the real world. Hearst had a considerable creative imagination in his own idiosyncratic way, and was able to abandon reality and "accept his own fantasies as facts", which absolved him from any obligation towards the truth and "led him into wild bypaths of error." Not surprisingly, he was

[58] Except where otherwise indicated, quotes in this chapter are from Swanberg (1996).

narcissistic, egocentric, and a great self-publicist. He was also a Jekyll-and-Hyde figure where his employees were concerned and was extremely demanding of himself and all those who worked for him: he could be sadistic with some workers and then tolerant with alcoholic workers. Employees noticed that he could be both brutal and generous to them. One worker said of him: "If you should put Hearst in a monastery, he would become abbot or die". He always had to be "top dog".

Hearst measured success by the profits of his companies while at the same time he was personally careless with money: profits were there to show how powerful and how much of a genius he was. Swanberg correctly summarises him as a "jungle of contradictions". There were always two contradictory sides to him in everything; for example, "the dictator and the democrat". He displayed a joint fascination for Thomas Jefferson, the democrat, and Mussolini, the dictator. At times he behaved like a king from another age and also identified with Julius Caesar and Napoleon: indeed persons with Asperger syndrome are very often fascinated by Napoleon. Interestingly, Hearst had a construction/architectural-type mind: he did a great deal of building and spent considerable time with his architect. This has echoes of Hitler, who also had Asperger syndrome (Fitzgerald, 2004).

Hearst was psychopathic and indeed had autistic psychopathy, which was how Hans Asperger (1944) described his syndrome originally. Utterly ruthless and, in the run-up to the Spanish–American War in 1898, he allegedly told a photographer "you make the pictures and I'll make the war" (Davies, 1975). Hearst was also sadomasochistic and had a strong perverse side. He recognised no limits and thought only of his self-interest. Theodore Roosevelt said that "Hearst is an unspeakable blackguard [who combines] with exquisite nicety all the worst faults of the conscienceless, corrupt and dissolute money man, and of the conscienceless, corrupt and dissolute demagogue". Essentially, Hearst had an autistic superego in one of his selves and a psychopathic superego in another self.

Social Relationships

Hearst was really an outsider, highly independent and self-reliant, but a loner-type figure living in the autistic world of his mind: a one-person world. There are many accounts of how socially awkward he was in addition to his oddness and eccentricity. He was very poor at conducting ordinary conversation with people, at social chit-chat or small talk. Over the years, according to Swanberg, he showed "a built-in failure of communication, an aloofness of temperament, an air of secrecy and loneliness, an inability to unbend into the true, easy spontaneity and exchange of confidences that bring men together". It is also noted just how tactless, dismissive and hurtful he was to people.

He had many acquaintances but few close friends and generally did not like people. People with similar personalities to himself were hired by him, which is a common feature in persons with Asperger syndrome. Lincoln Steffens, a journalist, wrote that Hearst was elusive and had no warmth: "And the reason there is no warmth seems to be that there is no sense of his need for friends. Mr Hearst is not only a silent, he is a lonely soul." Steffens also wrote that Hearst had no storytelling, no entertainment, "no relief of any sort".

Hearst occasionally had temper tantrums and expressed autistic aggression when frustrated. With his seriously diminished capacity for empathy, he was often callous and indifferent to people. People were there to be used for his personal purposes. He had a surprisingly dependent element to his personality, which was seen in his relationships with older women. However, in 1903, at the age of 40, he married 21-year-old Millicent Willson, a chorus girl. The marriage produced five sons but failed like most of his social relationships. As a father Hearst was considerably neglectful. Remarkably repetitive, in 1917, Hearst fell in love with another showgirl, 21-year-old Marion Davies of the *Ziegfeld Follies.* Since his wife Millicent refused to grant him a divorce, he lived openly with Marion until his death. He had a part–object relationship with Marion and simply saw her as an extension of himself and not as a human being in her own right. Wielding total omnipotent control over the subservient Marion, he was like a puppeteer with her. He was also rather paranoid about her and watched her carefully. Her considerable youth was attractive to him, and of course persons with Asperger syndrome tend to get on better with younger people. In later life she became addicted to alcohol.

WORK

Hearst built up an enormous media empire and dominated journalism for nearly half a century. He became notorious for his sensational type of reporting known as "yellow journalism". This featured large eye-catching banner headlines, exaggerated stories – many of them focusing on crime, political corruption and negligence – cartoons and illustrations. Talented writers were employed in his many publications across America and circulations soared. He also diversified into movie newsreels, a comic strip syndication business, King Features Syndicate, and produced over 100 films.

Many of the films featured his companion, Marion Davies, whose career he managed. Orson Welles remarked that she would have been a star if Hearst had never happened (Pfau and Marx, 1975). This was said most likely because of Welles's hatred of Hearst and because of the latter's damaging intervention in the launch of Welles's film *Citizen Kane*. The film was largely based on Hearst's life, portraying him as a fool who was only interested in collecting statues. In many ways Hearst and Welles were similar: they were equally exhibitionistic, megalomaniacal and self-destructive. However, the depiction of Hearst in *Citizen Kane* was an accurate one.

As regards his political career, Hearst served for two terms as a Democratic member for New York in the U.S. House of Representatives. Having been elected to Congress in 1903, he was an outsider – a "political maverick" who did his own thing. In the mould of British media tycoon Robert Maxwell, who was elected to the House of Common, Hearst was only interested in himself and incapable of cooperating with political allies. Not being clubbable he lacked political charisma and hated the day-to-day work of politics. Hearst was unable to empathise with people, probably because of theory of mind deficits. He failed politically because of his lack of capacity for social reciprocity, his dictatorial attitudes and an inability to compromise or cooperate. Lacking the skills of a conversationalist, he continually alienated political colleagues.

In fact, he became "the most hated man in the country", according to Swanberg because of his behaviour, namely because he did not want America to go into the First World War. In a way he was like Charles Lindbergh in the Second World War in pushing for pacifism and non-engagement (Fitzgerald & O'Brien, 2007). Hearst was despised in the way Lindbergh was hated at the same time. Both had Asperger syndrome and difficulties with empathy.

In Hearst's life there could only be one voice – his voice. He made his own laws and rules and everyone had to obey them with dispensations from normal behaviour given to him. He was special and had to be given special treatment; hence everyone was there for his greater glory.

William Randolph Hearst died in California on 14 August 1951, at the age of 88.

Chapter 59

SAMUEL GOLDWYN

The Polish-born American film producer Samuel Goldwyn (1879–1974), though not a creative person, had a massive impact on the film industry. On his way to America as an illiterate immigrant, he scavenged the famous streets of London, "hungry and penniless", and years later went on to build up Paramount Pictures and Metro-Goldwyn-Mayer (MGM). A great film producer, he won an Academy Award for *The Best Years of Our Lives* in 1946. Goldwyn was an disagreeable man in his interpersonal relationships, however, and showed traits suggestive of Asperger syndrome.

BACKGROUND

Goldwyn was born Schmuel Gelbfisz in the Jewish quarter of Warsaw around July 1879, the exact date of his birth unknown. He was the eldest of six children in the impoverished family of Hannah and Aaron Gelbfisz. His mother had "piercing eyes and squashed features" and tended to "shout rather than speak".[59] In fact, she was an extremely controlling woman and ruled the household. His father was a pedlar, though well-educated and a former rabbinical student. As a child, Goldwyn was "indifferent, often bitter" and when his sickly father died he blamed his mother for killing him. For the rest of his life he was very hostile towards her. A restless and extremely determined child, he had a rather hypersensitive personality. Like his father, he was a great reader and a superb linguist. Realising he was unlikely to rise above his straitened circumstances, Goldwyn looked to America for his salvation. At the age of 16, he left Warsaw and eventually made his way to Birmingham, England, where his mother's married sister lived, and changed his name to Samuel Goldfish at the instigation of relatives. By the age of 19 he had reached the USA, where he worked in a glove factory in Upstate New York.

---

[59] Except where otherwise indicated, quotes in this chapter are from Berg (1989).

PERSONALITY

Goldwyn was hyper-focused on his work and a highly driven man. This was evident from his early days as a glove maker. At lunchtime, according to biographer A. Scott Berg, he would "eat out of a brown paper sack, speaking to practically nobody, and then hasten back to the cutting room because time was money". He also worked during the day and attended classes at night. In his work, quality was a huge issue for the perfectionistic Goldwyn. Later, when producing films, he always worried that his next film would not be quite good enough. Hyperkinetic features are commonly associated with Asperger syndrome, as are workaholism and a major capacity to persist.

In terms of physical traits, Goldwyn had associated dyspraxia and "never learned to hold a pen properly – he rested it between the second and third fingers of his right hand". He also had "peculiarities of speech" and a "high-pitched voice". There were also pragmatic language difficulties and an inability to express himself not to mention malapropisms, paradoxes and other speech errors that came to be known as 'Goldwynisms'.

A highly intelligent man, nonetheless, Goldwyn had extremely narrow interests and was novelty-seeking and sensation-seeking. He became a gambler once he had money and this continued throughout his life. With these features it is hardly surprising that he was a great publicist of his films. He also had "boundless enthusiasm – fuelled by supreme self-confidence", which has echoes of the conman. Nevertheless, he was more complex than this. He certainly showed evidence of identity diffusion and was indeed a chameleon. During his life he struggled "to be somebody", so much so that he once got somebody to write semi-fictional memoirs for him, as he liked to "rewrite his history". He also contributed to charities, especially Jewish ones, as a way to perpetuate his name.

Goldwyn had a ritualistic working day: he was very precise about his dress, took a nap regularly for an hour in the afternoon, and was obsessed with keeping the temperature at a steady 70 degrees. These obsessive–compulsive personality traits also stretched to "a fear of germs and an obsession about cleanliness". He was in fact obsessed with getting an Academy Award and "lusted for the public approval and professional acknowledgement", which fed his narcissism. When he got the Oscar, his wife said that he was like a child who had got absolutely everything he wanted at Christmas. There was an extraordinary controlling and dominating aspect to Goldwyn's personality too and he engaged in endless lawsuits. Berg points out that Walt Disney left United Artists (UA) because of him. As he grew older Goldwyn became even more controlling and dominating. With his "brash, uncouth manner", he was fundamentally an anti-authority figure and had to be number one himself. On one occasion, he uttered the famous phrase "Include me out!" when storming out of a business meeting. This was part of his autistic narrative. He could also show courage and determination in confronting authority. For example, when Hollywood became obsessed with the hunt for "communists" during the McCarthy era, Goldwyn spoke out saying: "I have been astounded and outraged at the manner in which the committee has permitted our industry to be vilified by gossip, innuendo and hearsay."

Goldwyn was a monster in many ways and a charming psychopath in others. Founder of Paramount Pictures, Adolph Zukor stated of him that "as far as his honesty and integrity are concerned, there is none". By all accounts Goldwyn engaged in huge stakes in card games and "cheated shamelessly". Composer Irving Berlin was wary of him because he had been "cheated at Goldwyn's card table enough times to know better than to get involved with him". Indeed Goldwyn's work was a form of gambling and he was also quite capable of lying. Sometimes fact and fantasy merged in his mind, again indicative of identity diffusion. And a fact was only a fact when Goldwyn said it was. Writer *Garson Kanin* asked him hundreds of times to be a director only for him to refuse. When the man became a director elsewhere, Goldwyn said to him that he had never asked him to be a director. This can be a feature of persons with Asperger syndrome, whereby the person is never wrong in their own eyes.

After experiencing trouble in one of his companies, Goldwyn once collapsed with "nervous exhaustion". Nevertheless, he was a man who triumphed in adversity and seemed to get a kick out of trouble. As a self-made man, with steel in his personality, he ultimately sorted out his problems by himself. Nonetheless, he did suffer from depression and "self-despair", where he had periods of great hopelessness and futility.

Social Relationships

Essentially a loner, Goldwyn lived in a one-person world inside his head with little capacity for reciprocal social relationships. He found the social chit-chat of a cocktail party extremely difficult. Newspaper magnate W. R. Hearst had a similar personality and indeed the two often met. For Goldwyn, family life was always quite tortured and he displayed a gross lack of empathy and callousness towards them. When his own sister was dying close to Los Angeles he did not bother to go to see her, and when the time came for her funeral, he said: "I don't go to funerals." This shows his cruel and unemotional side, which was a very significant part of his personality. Given his excessively controlling nature and poor relationships with women, he did not know how to interact with them and tended to manhandle them clumsily, using the "casting couch" more than most. As far as he was concerned, females were there to be used and abused by him; they were his harem.

Goldwyn was lonely for quite a very long time before he married. His first marriage at the age of 31, to Blanche Lasky, was unsuccessful as they had nothing in common. According to Berg, he was uncompromising in his ways and expected his wife to "surrender to his demands". For her part, Blanche craved affection, which he was totally unprepared to give. Clearly, his inability to give emotionally was an innate biological lack, resulting from Asperger syndrome. After five years the marriage broke up but not before his wife gave birth to a daughter, Ruth. Goldwyn was equally unempathic to his second wife, actress Frances Howard. Their marriage produced a son, Sammy. Once again, Goldwyn could not create a warm family home, though the marriage endured for nearly 50 years. Being somewhat paranoid and masochistic, Frances tolerated his abuse, his sadism, and indeed helped him, smoothing over his tactlessness. She sought refuge in alcohol and later became an alcoholic.

Not only did Goldwyn fail as a husband but also as a father. He had to be "in absolute control, an undisputed paterfamilias", according to Berg. He was grossly insensitive in meetings with his daughter, Ruth, whom he neglected and rarely visited. On one occasion he threw the 12-year-old girl out of the Astor Hotel and resolved never to see or speak to her again: "From that moment … his support payments ceased, their correspondence ended." This was rather cruel and sadistic, and showed his lack of empathy. Ruth remarked that her father "always did what he wanted. Once he saw what he wanted to have next, he went in an absolutely straight line to get it." Goldwyn's son, Sammy, fared no better and could not recall eating a single dinner with his parents. They made "almost no time for him at home", sending him to school in a limousine, which led him to being bullied. As far as Sammy was concerned, his parents subjected him to their constant criticism and even when he moved into his own apartment, they still quarrelled with everything he did. Goldwyn even failed to turn up for his son's graduation, which was something that upset Sammy enormously. Goldwyn also changed his will and took back properties that he had bequeathed to his son. Like the great inventor Edison, Goldwyn became obsessed with his son doing anything that reflected badly on himself. When Sammy joined the U.S. Army at the outbreak of the Second World War, his father for once was able to admire him. For Sammy's part, it was a relief get away from his father to Europe, particularly England, for a few years. Sammy pointed out that, despite all his success, Goldwyn was still "an outsider". From a psychological point of view, the only place for a person with Asperger's syndrome is as an outsider, locked into their own personal worlds.

People were there to be used by Goldwyn as he saw fit and he engaged in extremely aggressive interpersonal relationships. He seemed to be stimulated by the endless rows that he had with people and often fell out with business partners. A friend of his said "you fight even when people agree with you". A colleague recalled: "Goldwyn is the kind of man who, if he understands what you tell him, thinks he thought of it himself." There was a significantly unpleasant side to his personality as a movie mogul. He could be vicious and nasty and undermining to his employees, instituting a "reign of terror" in his studios. He would needle people endlessly and once subjected the director William Wyler to "emotional tyranny". In his dealings with his chauffeur – Goldwyn was unable to drive – he was vicious, especially on one occasion when the chauffeur left him in an isolated place with his car. The chauffeur was unable to take any more abuse from him. Goldwyn could also be quite paranoid at times and indeed felt that his wife was out to poison him.

Work

In the early part of his life when glove making, Goldwyn became aware of the importance of quality and soon progressed to glove salesman, becoming a financial success in the process. The notion of quality was also transferred to producing films, where he set high standards; quality was far more important to him than quantity. Goldwyn was a genius, as seen in some of the films he produced, for example, Wuthering Heights (1939), The Little Foxes (1941) and The Best Years of Our Lives (1948). Part of his success was in signing and discovering successful stars and the publicity he generated. He was also highly intuitive about films when they were not working successfully. Despite not being able to explain his intuition, he was often right and pressed other people to explain what was wrong with a film or the way it was developing. His genius did not however have a creative aspect. Nonetheless, according to Berg, Goldwyn made up for any artistic inferiority with advertising superiority. In terms of creative input, William Wyler, who directed many of his most-lauded films, said: "I don't recall his contributing anything other than buying good material and talent. It was all an attempt to make a name for himself as an artist. But as far as being creative, he was zero."

His son Sammy stated that his father got compulsive about producing each picture as though it were his last: "That was the one he would go out on, the one he'd be remembered for." Goldwyn also had a huge fear of growing old and indeed death anxiety is very common in persons with Asperger syndrome. As a result, Goldwyn went on working hard past his 80th year, declaring he was "never going to retire". *Life* magazine said he was the last of "the one-man gang".

Samuel Goldwyn died in Los Angeles from a stroke on 31 January 1974, aged 94.

Chapter 60

HOWARD HUGHES

Howard Hughes (1905–1976) was an American business tycoon, aviator and filmmaker during the 20th century. Possessing an engineering mind and enormous wealth, he was a disturbed and disturbing man. He also showed significant features of Asperger syndrome.

BACKGROUND

Howard Robert Hughes Jnr was born in Texas on 24 December 1905. His father, Howard, was a "wildcatter" in the oil exploration industry who invented a bedrock-piercing drill that made him incredibly rich. Hughes had an extremely close relationship to his mother, Allene. Like the mother of Sam Spiegel, she was obsessed with the cleanliness of his body. According to biographers Brown and Broeske, the family's wealth provided her with the means to mould her son into a Little Lord Fauntleroy, "a misfit among the brash, hell-raising sons of most oil barons".[60] He was clingy to her and she exerted "iron-willed control" over him. This type of mother–son relationship is quite common in persons of high creativity. The Martin Scorsese film *The Aviator* (2004) seems to attribute Hughes's later problems to an overprotective mother very fearful of disease. This is rather simplistic: the genes that Allene gave Hughes were far more important than the nurturing. The fact that he was an only child greatly enhanced her malign influence. When he was 16 years old, she died, followed by his father 22 months later.

Hughes was bullied at school, as persons with Asperger syndrome usually are. He was mechanically and mathematically minded and hyper-focused on his narrow interests: in fact he obsessed about engineering topics. Even as a child he always wanted to know how things worked and loved taking mechanical objects apart. From an early age he was hypochondriacal and obsessed with his body and any malfunctions, real or imaginary. Persons with Asperger syndrome can be quite psychosomatic and indeed Hughes certainly was. As a child he had a poor appetite and was regarded as being rather weak, which led to his mother overprotecting him even more. Germs were a worry to both mother and child and, under this excessive anxiety, he had an episode of hysterical paralysis.

---

[60] Except where otherwise indicated, quotes in this chapter are from Brown and Broeske (1998).

Growing up, Hughes was always a social misfit and found it hugely difficult to forge social relationships, to have social reciprocity, and to see things from other boys' perspective. He was essentially a loner. Seeing that he was obsessed with films as an adolescent, he spent long periods watching them alone. Howard Hughes Snr probably had hyperkinetic syndrome and had a sensation-seeking personality like his son. Therefore, it is most likely that the novelty-seeking genes were passed on to his son. There is considerable similarity between the Kennedy political dynasty in the USA and the Hughes family in terms of sensation-seeking genes and hyperkinetic syndrome, which were key to their success. The result is an extremely driven and somewhat miserable lifestyle, however. Hughes Snr was also promiscuous, like many of the Kennedys. Nevertheless, many individuals with this condition have made great contributions to society while being a failure in interpersonal terms.

PERSONALITY

Hughes was an amazing man, highly intelligent and charismatic, with a commanding personality. Hyperkinetic and always on the go, he was a workaholic who recognised no limits either for himself or for other people. In pursuing his narrow interests of engineering and filmmaking, he was a novelty-seeker who adored "powerful machines". His long-time business executive Noah Dietrich said that Hughes showed his brilliance by providing the inspiration for hundreds of electronic advances: "And he was brilliant at finding the greatest scientists and convincing them to fulfil his dreams. He cast a spell over them." Hughes approached filmmaking in a similarly mechanical way; it was basically an engineering problem for him.

Hiscock (2004) notes that Hughes remained oddly unattached even to his most celebrated projects, such as films. It was the act of doing that was important for Hughes rather than the finished product. At the closure of each project and the challenge met, he typically grew bored. It was no matter that he set international records in aviation or commanded powerful performances from actors. In some ways he was like Charles Lindbergh, who also had Asperger syndrome, and shared the same kind of fame.

There is clear evidence of identity diffusion in Hughes. Described as a "chameleon", he didn't know himself and other people didn't know him either. In fact, he was unknowable, unless viewed through the lens of Asperger syndrome. Throughout his life he was extremely egocentric and engaged in "fantastic flirtations with masquerades and false identities". He liked working with the CIA, supplying military electronics and espionage equipment, because of the buzz it gave him. Obviously, the CIA world is a paranoid world, anyway, where fact and fiction easily mix and he was therefore very much at home in this milieu. Hughes was a Jekyll-and-Hyde figure who had many problems with reality testing. His split personality, which was very often cold and callous, could also at other times be generous. Another major interest was his self-aggrandisement and concern about leaving his mark on the world. He certainly did succeed at things that he set out to do. *Time* magazine described his disordered self as follows in 1948:

> This tall, gangling, aging and sick looking man of 42 whose life and eccentricities have become a lurid legend … the private life of Howard Hughes might be described as a complete and carefully protected disorder. He has no interest in clothes, only the barest

> minimum of interest in food and sleep. He owns five suits, of which the newest is five years old; he is rumpled and dishevelled most of the time, gets dressed up only for special occasions. He postpones haircuts as long as possible. Since he sleeps only when he is sleepy, he calls up his lieutenants at all hours of the night. Sometimes he identifies himself as Mr Hoyt. He also has a number of other aliases … he likes to make business appointments in out-of-the-way spots, usually at night, and he is always 30 minutes to two hours late, if he shows up at all.

Hughes was psychopathic and indeed had autistic psychopathy (Asperger syndrome). He was self-destructive and masochistic, involved in a number of serious accidents and possibly suffered brain damage. Granted Hughes had hearing difficulties and suffered from otosclerosis, a bone disease of the ear. Not all of his behaviour can be explained on this basis, however, as he had shown most of his characteristics before the accidents. Quinn (2004) describes Hughes as "a movie maverick" and "a classic megalomaniac … the Citizen Kane of the skies, with ambitions and flaws the size of Xanadu". He is presented as being "addicted to drama and danger – both real and manufactured – whether it came from staring at death behind the wheel of an untested aeroplane or from romancing several incendiary women at the same time". Hughes did indeed think a good deal about death, but that never stopped him from taking risks. Nonetheless, he did suffer from depression and grief, and indulged in self-pity. Dietrich described his home as one of "universal gloom where the sun never shone".

One of the most widely portrayed features of Hughes's personality is his obsessive–compulsive disorder (OCD). There is little doubt that his mother also had the same disorder. Hughes had many motor rituals and got other people to do things in a ritualistic fashion in relation to him. He liked to eat the same food repetitively and had it cooked to exact specifications. He washed his hands to the point of bleeding. Similar to many with Asperger syndrome, he carried notebooks and filled them with mechanical details. Salzman (1968) points out that obsessive–compulsive behaviour is an attempt to maintain the illusion of control over functioning and to avoid decision-making and commitment. He believes that it protects the individual from feelings of failure, imperfection and human fallibility. If ever this protection fails then the ritual – with its magical possibilities of overcoming human limitation – attempts to guarantee control. If that fails too, the individual can develop phobias, thereby avoiding any encounter with threatening situations, which is exactly what happened with Hughes in later life. Hughes suffered from doubting, ambivalence, avoidance of involvement and intolerance of observation. Those with obsessive–compulsive disorder and Asperger syndrome are often inveterate collectors: in the case of Hughes, he collected rare South American butterflies.

Hughes's OCD got worse as he got older and there were certainly no serotonin reuptake inhibitors at that time for him. In the past people with OCD were given brain leucotomies or helped with electroconvulsive therapy (ECT), but as far as can be deduced he did not get such treatment. It's unclear why he was not prescribed tricyclic antidepressants, which were available. The drug Ritalin is not effective for depression, however, Hughes took too much of it and began hallucinating. He also abused barbiturates. Some of the drugs he was taking had the ability to make him paranoid or increase his paranoia.

Social Relationships

Hughes was an alienated individual who at times liked to be in alienated environments, although he did interact with people like himself, for example, Gary Grant. He had massive difficulty in social relationships and was a somewhat pathetic figure – a "lone wolf". His penchant for control and domination was particularly seen in his relationships with women. An extreme user of people, particularly women, he had no capacity for intimacy – he failed to realise that women needed human relationships too. As the rich playboy, his girlfriends and wives were objects to be manipulated by him rather than human beings – trophies for his greater glory. In his search for the perfect woman he failed time and time again. A reciprocal marriage, or indeed a reciprocal ordinary social relationship, was clearly beyond his capacities. His relationship with a woman was a part–object relationship, which meant that her feelings were not taken into account. He also feared becoming dependent on one woman and therefore had a large number of girlfriends simultaneously instead. He was extremely immature emotionally and very often attracted to "teenage Lolitas". He married three times but all ended in divorce; first to Ella Rice in 1925 followed by Terry Moore in 1949, allegedly conducted in secret, and finally to actress Jean Peters in 1957. In between he dated and proposed to a long line of famous women, including Katharine Hepburn, Ava Gardner and Joan Fontaine.

Salzman (1968) notes that dependency on people is even more difficult for people like Hughes than dependency on objects. Hughes depreciated people's usefulness to minimise his need for them. Marriage is difficult for the obsessional not only because of the commitment required but also because of the inevitable dependencies:

> He may tyrannise his partner in order to maintain an illusion of power and independence. Thus he may appear to be the boss or in control when he is the one that is more dependent. This dependence–independency struggle manifests itself in the tug of war for domination and control that is regularly present in obsessional households. It is not long before the obsessional begins to feel that those he depended on, whether a marital partner or colleague – are malevolent and exploitative while he is the generous benefactor. (Salzman, 1968)

Some of his girlfriends and wives behaved like mothers and had a calming influence on him. Like everything else for Hughes, women were "possessions" and it was not unusual for him to spy on those with whom he was involved. He once proposed to teenage starlet Faith Domergue, by saying: "Remember, you belong to me now, so don't even look at another man". He was also interested in the women for what he could get out of them. He once beat up his girlfriend, actress Ava Gardner, because of her infidelity, although she retaliated in kind. In all of this, there was a rather desperate quality to his womanising.

Byrne (2005) quotes the actor Leonardo DiCaprio, who depicted him in *The Aviator*, as saying of Hughes: "You can never truly know the man." The best way to know him is to understand his Asperger syndrome. Hughes was a genius and it is important to realise that geniuses do not put out milk bottles at night, they do not put out the bin, they do not bring people tea in bed, and they do not switch on the electric blanket. Happiness is not a general feature of genius, but the work of geniuses often keeps them from ending their lives. Not so for Howard Hughes.

WORK

There was no limit to Hughes's talents as a business tycoon, an aviator, aerospace engineer, inventor, filmmaker, investor, and philanthropist, amassing a billionaire fortune in the process. Cohen (2005) describes Hughes as having "enormous energy and visionary drive". She notes that he built the fastest plane of its time, set a record for flying around the world, and purchased *Trans World Airlines* (TWA). Moreover, she points out that Hughes was drawn to movies and aeroplanes because "he was himself a kind of machine of ambition and innovation". His obsession with making films resulted in him putting enormous resources into them. Financial success followed his first two films, *Everybody's Acting* (1927) and Two Arabian Knights (1928). So much so that the latter, a comedy, won him an Academy Award for Best Director. Many of his other films were memorable if somewhat controversial, such as The Racket (1928), Hell's Angels (1930), Scarface (1932) and The Outlaw (1943). Philanthropy was another aspect of his work that perpetuates his aims. After his death, he bequeathed money to the Howard Hughes Medical Institute, which, since 1984, has pumped more than 500 million dollars per year into the laboratories of more than 300 investigators, including 10 Nobel Laureates.

As he grew older, Hughes became malnourished and in the end was killed by a single lethal injection of codeine, to which he was addicted. Howard Hughes died from kidney failure on board an aircraft on 5 April 1976, at the age of 70.

REFERENCES

THE PSYCHOLOGY OF STAGE AND SCREEN

Abrahms, M. H. (1993). The Mirror and the Lap: Romantic Theory and the Critical Tradition. Oxford: Oxford University Press.

Andreasen, N. (2005). The Creating Brain. New York: Dana Press.

Asperger, H. (1938). Das psychisch abnormale Kind. Wiener Klinische Wochenschrift, 51, 1314–1317.

Asperger, H. (1944). Die "Autistischen Psychopathen" im Kindesalter. Archiv für Psychiatrie und Nervenkrankheiten, 117, 76–136.

Atkinson, R. C. (1993). The origins and development of high ability. Ciba Foundation Symposium, 178, Chichester: Wiley.

Baron-Cohen, S. (2009). Autism test 'could hit maths skills'. BBC website, 7 January. Retrieved from http://news.bbc.co.uk/2/hi/health/7736196.stm.

Bazin, A. (1967). What is Cinema? Berkeley: University of California Press.

Broad, J. H. (1977). Schizotypy. Oxford: Oxford University Press.

Bronowski, J. (1972). Science and Human Values. New York: Harper and Row.

Calaprice, A. (Ed.) (2005). The New Quotable Einstein. Princeton, NJ: Princeton University Press.

Carlyle, T. (1825). Life of Friedrich Schiller. Facsimile edition with New Introduction by J. L. Sammons (1992). Columbia, SC: Camden House Publishing.

Collins (2000). English Dictionary and Thesaurus. London: Harper Collins.

Darwin, C. (1995). The Descent of Man and Selection in Relation to Sex. London: The Folio Society.

Fitzgerald, M. (2004). Autism and Creativity: Is There a Link between Autism in Men and Exceptional Ability? New York: Brunner-Routledge.

Fitzgerald, M. (2005). The Genesis of Artistic Creativity. London: Jessica Kingsley.

Fitzgerald, M. (2008). Attention Deficit Hyperactivity Disorder, Creativity, Novelty Seeking and Risk. New York: Nova Scientific.

Fitzgerald, M., & O'Brien, B. (2007). Genius Genes: How Asperger Talents Changed the World. Lenexa, KS: Autism Asperger Publishing Company.

Frith, U., & Houston, R. (2000). Autism in History. Oxford: Blackwell.

Gregory, R. (1987) (Ed.). Oxford Companion to the Mind. Oxford: Oxford University Press.

Heilman, K. (2005). Creativity and the Brain. Hove, UK: Psychology Press.

Howe, M. A. (1999). Genius Explained. Cambridge: Cambridge University Press.
Hudson, L. (1987). Creativity. In R. Gregory (Ed.), Oxford Companion to the Mind. Oxford: Oxford University Press.
Hyman, R. (1993). The Pan Dictionary of Famous Quotations. London: Grange Books.
Julius, A. (2002). Transgressions: The Offences of Art. London: Thames and Hudson.
Jung, C. (1952). Psychology in literature. In B. Ghisclin (Ed.), The Creative Process. New York: Mentor/New American Library.
Livingstone, M. (2002). Vision and Art: The Biology of Seeing. New York: Abrahams.
Lykken, D. (1998). The genetics of genius. In A. Steptoe (Ed.), *Genius and the Mind*: *Studies of* Creativity and Temperament in the Historical Record. New York: Oxford University Press.
Lyons, V., & Fitzgerald, M. (2007). Asperger (1906–1980) and Kanner (1894–1981), the two pioneers of autism. Journal of Autism and Developmental Disorders, 37, 2022–2023.
Lyotard, J. F. (1984). The Postmodern Condition: A Report on Knowledge. Trans. Geoff Bennington & Brian Massumi. Minneapolis, MN: University of Minnesota Press.
Monk, R. (1990). Ludwig Wittgenstein: The Duty of Genius. London: Jonathan Cape.
Monk, R. (1996). Private lives. The Times Magazine, 30 November.
Pramaggiore, M. (2008). Neil Jordan. Urbana, IL: University of Illinois Press.
Porter, R. (1998). Forward. In A. Steptoe (Ed.). Genius and the Mind: *Studies of* Creativity and Temperament in the Historical Record. Oxford: Oxford University Press.
Rausch, J., Johnson, M., & Casanova, M. (2008). Asperger's Disorder. New York: Informa.
Robertson, I. (2002). The Mind's Eye. London: Bantam.
Rodriquez-Fernandez, J. L. (1996). Is "sudden illumination" the result of activation of a creative centre at the human brain? Perspectives in Biology and Medicine, 39, 2, 287–307.
Roscoe, T. (1841). Thoughts on various subjects. In The Works of Jonathan Swift, vol. 2, London: Clowes.
Roth, I. (Ed). (2007). Imaginative Minds. Oxford: Oxford University Press.
Sabbadini, A. (2003). The Couch and the Screen. Hove, UK: Brunner-Routledge.
Simon, N. (1998). Rewrites: A Memoir. New York: Touchstone.
Simonton, D. K. (1994). Greatness: Who Makes History and Why? New York: Guildford Press.
Singer, I. B. (2007). Ingmar Bergman: Cinematic Philosopher. London: MIT Press.
Snyder, A., Bossomatier, T., & Mitchell, D. J. (2004). Concept formation: "object" attributes dynamically inhibited from conscious awareness. Journal of Integrative Neuroscience, 3, 1, 31–46.
Stam, R. (2000). Film Theory. Oxford: Blackwell Publishing.
Steptoe, A. (Ed.) (1998). *Genius and the Mind*: *Studies of* Creativity and Temperament in the Historical Record. New York: Oxford University Press.
Tredell, N. (2002). Cinemas of the Mind. Cambridge, U.K: Icon Books.
Wolff, S. (1995). Loners: The Life Paths of Unusual Children. London: Routledge.

Creativity and Actors

APA (2007). *APA Dictionary of Psychology*. Washington, DC: American Psychology Association.

Baron-Cohen, S. (2000). Autism: deficits in folk psychology exist along superiority in folk physics. In S. Baron-Cohen, H. Tager-Flusberg & D. Cohen (Eds). *Understanding Other Minds*. Oxford: Oxford University Press.

Carroll, J. (2007). Evolutionary approaches to literature and drama. In R. Dunbar & L. Barrett (Eds.), *The Oxford Handbook of Evolutionary Psychology*. Oxford: Oxford University Press, 637–48.

Coe, K. (2003). *The Ancestress Hypothesis: Visual Arts as Adaptation*. New Brunswick: Rutgers University Press.

Cross, I. (2007). Music and cognitive evolution. In R. Dunbar & L. Barrett (Eds.), *The Oxford Handbook of Evolutionary Psychology*. Oxford: Oxford University Press.

Dunbar R., & Barrett, L. (Eds.) (2007). *The Oxford Handbook of Evolutionary Psychology*. Oxford: Oxford University Press.

Fitzgerald, M. (2004). Autism and Creativity: Is There a Link between Autism in Men and Exceptional Ability? New York: Brunner-Routledge.

Fitzgerald, M. (2008). Attention Deficit Hyperactivity Disorder, Creativity, Novelty Seeking and Risk. New York: Nova Scientific.

Gazzaniga M., & Heatherton, T. (2003). *Psychological Science: Mind, Brain, Behaviour*. New York: Norton.

Pinker, S. (1997). *How the Mind Works*. New York: Norton.

Plotkin, H. (2007). The power of culture. In R. Dunbar & L. Barrett (Eds.), *The Oxford Handbook of Evolutionary Psychology*. Oxford: Oxford University Press.

Rizzolatti, G., & Fogassi, L. (2007). Mirror neurons and social cognition. In R. Dunbar & L. Barrett (Eds.), *The Oxford Handbook of Evolutionary Psychology*. Oxford: Oxford University Press.

Roberts, L. W., Hoop, J., Dunn, L. B. (2008). Ethical aspects of psychiatry. In R. Hales, S. Yudofsky & G. Gabbard (Eds.), *Textbook of Psychiatry*. Washington DC: American Psychiatric Publishing.

Wilson, E. O. (1998). *Consilience: The Unity of Knowledge*. New York: Vintage Books.

Identity, Diffusion, Postmodernism and Creativity

Andreasen, N. (2005). *The Creating Brain*. New York: Dana Press.

Asperger, H. (1944). Die "Autistischen Psychopathen" im Kindesalter. *Archiv für Psychiatrie und Nervenkrankheiten*, 117, 76–136.

Austin, J. H. (2003). Chase, Chance and Creativity. The Lucky Art of Novelty. Cambridge, MA: MIT Press.

Baron-Cohen, S. (2000). Autism: deficits in folk psychology exist along superiority in folk physics. In S. Baron-Cohen, H. Tager-Flusberg & D. Cohen (Eds), *Understanding Other Minds*. Oxford: Oxford University Press.

Beard, M. (2006). Men who have fat feminine faces are far more likely to be hit comedians. *Irish Independent*, November, p. 17.

Bergson, H. L. (1911). Laughter: An Essay on the Meaning of the Comic. New York: Macmillan.

Brownell, H., & Gardner, H. (1988). Neuropsychological insights into humour. In J. Durant & J. Miller (Eds.), *Laughing Matters: A Serious Look at Humour* (pp. 17–34). New York: Longman.

Casanova, M., Switala, A., Trippe, J., & Fitzgerald, M. (2007). Comparative minicolumnar morphometry of three distinguished scientists. *Autism: International Journal of Research and Practice*, 11, 6, 557 – 569.

Charke, C. (1999). *A Narrative of the Life of Mrs Charlotte Charke*. Ed. and with introduction and notes by Robert Rehder. London: Pickering and Chatto.

Fields, F. S. (1991). Charlotte Charke and the liminality of bi-genderings: A study of her canonical works. In S. King (Ed.), *Pilgrimage for Love: Essays in Early Modern Literature in Honour of Josephine A. Roberts* (pp.221–248). Tempe, AZ: Arizona Centre for Medieval and Renaissance Studies.

Fitzgerald, M. (2002). John Nash: Asperger's syndrome and schizophrenia. *Irish Psychiatrist*, 3, 3, 90–96.

Fitzgerald, M. (2004). Autism and Creativity: Is There a Link between Autism in Men and Exceptional Ability? New York: Brunner-Routledge.

Fitzgerald, M. (2005). *The Genesis of Artistic Creativity*. London: Jessica Kingsley.

Fitzgerald, M. (2008). Attention Deficit Hyperactivity Disorder, Creativity, Novelty Seeking and Risk. New York: Nova Scientific.

Fitzgerald, M., Bellgrove, M., Gill, M. (2007). *Handbook of Attention Deficit Hyperactivity Disorder*. Chichester, UK: John Wiley & Sons.

Freud, S. (1905). *Jokes and Their Relation to the Unconscious*. Harmondsworth, UK: Penguin.

Frith, U. (1991). *Autism and Asperger's Syndrome*. Cambridge: Cambridge University Press.

Fry, W. (2002). Humour and the brain: a selective review. *Humour: International Journal of Humour Research*, 3, 305–333.

Gardner, H. (1997). *Extraordinary Minds*. New York: Basic Books.

Gladwell, M. (2008). *Outliers: The Story of Success*. London: Allen Lane.

Goel, F., & Dolan, R. (2001). The functional anatomy of humour: segregating cognitive and affective components. *Nature Neuroscience*, 4, 237–238.

Hamer, D., & Copeland, P. (1998). *Living with Our Genes*. London: Macmillan.

Harpur, J., Lawlor, M., & Fitzgerald, M. (2004). *Succeeding in College with Asperger's Syndrome*. London: Jessica Kingsley.

Hartman, T. (1999). Attention Deficit Hyperactivity Disorder. Dublin: New Leaf.

Heilman, K. (2005). *Creativity and the Brain*. Hove, UK: Psychology Press.

Honos-Webb, L. (2005). The Gift of ADHD: How to Transform Your Child's Problems into Strengths. Oakland, CA: New Harbinger Publications.

Howe, M. A. (1999). *Genius Explained*. Cambridge: Cambridge University Press.

Jamison, K. (2004). *Exuberance*. New York: Knopf.

Kanner, L. (1946). Irrelevant and metaphorical language in early childhood autism. *American Journal of Psychiatry*, 103, 242–246.

Koestler, A. (1964). *The Act of Creation*. New York: Dell.

Konner, M. (1990). Why the Reckless Survive and Other Secrets of Human Behaviour. London: Viking.

Korn, E. (2007). Barrels of laughs. *Times Literary Supplement*, 23 February.

Lampert, M. D., & Ervin-Tripp, S. M. (1998). Exploring paradigms: the study of gender and sense of humour near the end of the 20th century. In W. Ruch (Ed.), *The Sense of Humour: Explorations of a Personality Characteristic* (pp. 231–270). New York: Mouton de Gruyter.

Lefcourt, H. M., & Martin, R. A. (1986). *Humour and Life Stress: Antidote to Adversity*. New York: Springer Verlag.

Lykken, D. (1998). The genetics of genius. In A. Steptoe (Ed.), *Genius and the Mind: Studies of Creativity and Temperament in the Historical Record*. New York: Oxford University Press.

Lyons V., & Fitzgerald M. (2004). Humour in autism and Asperger's syndrome. *Journal of Autism and Developmental Disorders*, 34, 5, 521–531.

Lyons V., & Fitzgerald M. (2005). *Asperger's Syndrome Gift or Curse?* New York: Nova Scientific.

Mackie, E. (1991). Desperate measures: the narratives of the life of Mrs Charlotte Charke. *ELH*, 58, 84 –865.

Martindale, C. (1999). Genetics. In M. Runco & S. Pritzer (Eds.), *Encyclopaedia of Creativity*, vol. 1. London: Academic Press.

McGhee, P. (1979). *Humour: Its Origin and Development*. San Francisco: W. H. Freeman and Company.

Moore, L. (1991). She was too fond of her mistaken bargain: the scandalous relations of gender and sexuality in feminist theory. *Diacritics*, 21, 2–3, 89–101.

Morreall, J. (1989). Enjoying incongruity. *Humour: International Journal of Humour Research*, 2, 1–18.

Murray, P. (1989). *Genius: The History of an Idea*. Oxford, UK: Basil Blackwell.

Murray, S. (2008). Hollywood and the fascination with autism. In M. Osteen (Ed.), *Autism and Representation*. London: Routledge.

Nahemow, L. (1986). Humour as a data base for the study of aging. In L. Nahemow, K. A. McCluskey-Fawcett & P. E. McGhee (Eds.), *Humour and Aging* (pp. 3–26). Orlando, FL: Academic Press.

O'Hagan, A. (2005). Why we'd be lost without comedians. *The Telegraph Arts*,16 July, 9.

Pasachoff, J. M. (2009). When winning a Nobel Prize seems to run in the family. *Nature*, 457, 379.

Paulos, J. A. (1980). *Mathematics and Humour*. Chicago, IL: University of Chicago Press.

Phillips, H. (2008). Beautiful minds. *New Scientist*, October, 29–33.

Pramaggiore, M. (2008). *Neil Jordan*. Urbana, IL: University of Illinois Press.

Prentky, R. A. (1980). *Creativity and Psychopathology*. New York: Praeger.

Pullen, K. (2005). *Actresses and Whores: On Stage and in Society*. Cambridge: Cambridge University Press.

Rampton, J. (2008). Tither ye not: Frankie had a dark side. *Telegraph Review*, 29 March, 5.

Raskin, V. (1985). *Semantic Mechanisms of Humour*. Boston, MA: Reidel.

Reddy, V., Williams, E., & Vaughan, A. (2002). Sharing humour and laughter in autism and Down's syndrome. *British Journal of Psychology*, 93, 219–242.

Ruch, W., McGhee, P., & Hehl, F. J. (1990). Age differences in the enjoyment of incongruity-resolution and nonsense humour during adulthood. *Psychology and Aging*, 5, 348–355.

Simonton, D. K. (1994). *Greatness: Who Makes History and Why?* New York: Guildford Press.

Stam, R. (2000). *Film Theory*. Oxford, UK: Blackwell Publishing.

Suls, J. M. (1972). A two-stage model for the appreciation of jokes and cartoons: an information-processing analysis. In J. H. Goldstein & P. E. McGhee (Eds.), *The Psychology of Humour: Theoretical Perspectives and Empirical Issues* (pp. 81–100). New York: Academic Press.

Waller, N. G., Bouchard, T., Lykken, D. T., Tellegen, A., & Blacker, D. M. (1993). Why creativity does not run in families: A study of twins reared apart. *Psychological Enquiry*, 4, 235–237.

Wilson, J. H. (1958). *All the King's Ladies: Actresses of the Restoration*. Chicago, IL: University of Chicago Press.

Zeki, S. (2001). Artistic creativity and the brain. *Science*, 293, 5527, 51–52. doi: 10.1126/science.1062331

Zuckerman, M. (2007). *Sensation Seeking and Risky Behaviour*. Washington, DC: American Psychological Association.

CHAPTER 1

Irving, Laurence (1951). Henry Irving, the Actor and His World, by His Grandson. London: Faber & Faber.

CHAPTER 2

Benedetti, Jean (2001). David *Garrick* and the Birth of Modern Theatre. London: Methuen.

Davies, Thomas (1780). Memoirs of the Life of David Garrick. London: Davies.

CHAPTER 3

Atkinson, Brooks (1936). 'The Play'. *The New York Times*, 3 November.

Callow, Simon (1996). *The Road to Xanadu*. London: Jonathan Cape.

Clay, Jean (1962). Interview with Orson Welles. *Réalités* (Paris), no. 201.

Fitzgerald, Michael (2004). Autism and Creativity: Is There a Link between Autism in Men and Exceptional Ability? Hove, UK: Brunner-Routledge.

Fitzgerald, Michael (2005). The Genesis of Artistic Creativity: Asperger's Syndrome and the Arts. London: Jessica Kingsley.

Houseman, John (1972). *Run-Through: A Memoir*. New York: Simon & Schuster.

Noble, Peter (1956). *The Fabulous Orson Welles*. London: Hutchinson.

Rosenthal, Jean & Wertenbaker, Lael (1972). The Magic of Light: The Craft and Career of Jean Rosenthal, Pioneer in Lighting for the Modern Stage. New York: Little, Brown.

Tynan, Kenneth (1967). *The World of Orson Welles*. London: Weidenfeld.

Wullschlager, Jackie (2000). *Hans Christian Andersen: The Life of a Storyteller*. London: Allen Lane.

Woititz, G. Janet (1983). *Adult Children of Alcoholics*. New York: Health Communications, Inc.

CHAPTER 4

Croall, Jonathan (2001). *Gielgud: A Theatrical Life, 1904–2000*. London: Methuen.

CHAPTER 5

Botham, Noel (2002). *Valentino: The First Superstar*. London: Metro.

Fitzgerald, Michael (2004). Autism and Creativity: Is There a Link between Autism in Men and Exceptional Ability? Hove, UK: Brunner-Routledge.

Leider, Emily (2004). *Dark Lover: The Life and Death of Rudolph Valentino*. New York: Farrar Straus & Giroux.

CHAPTER 6

Strachan, Alan (2005). *Secret Dreams: The Biography of Michael Redgrave*. London: Weidenfeld & Nicolson.

CHAPTER 7

Callow, Simon (1988). *Charles Laughton: A Difficult Actor*. London: Vintage.

CHAPTER 8

Brown, C. (2005). Frankly, he was a thug. *Ireland on Sunday*, 5 June, pp54–55.

Fitzgerald, Michael (2004). *Autism and Creativity: Is There a Link between Autism in Men and Exceptional Ability?* Hove, UK: Brunner-Routledge.

Galvin, Tom (2005). All or nothing at all. *Village Magazine,* 10 June, pp53–54.

Morton, Brian (2005). Frankie's family. *Sunday Tribune*, 29 May, p40.

Paton, Maureen (2004). How could men match up to my father? *The Daily Telegraph*, 8 November.

Sinatra, Tina & Coplon, Jeff (2006). *My Father's Daughter: A Memoir*. New York: Simon & Schuster.

Summers, Anthony & Swan, Robbyn (2005). *Sinatra: The Life.* New York: Vintage.
Taraborrelli, J. Randall (1998). *Sinatra: The Man Behind the Myth*. Edinburgh: Mainstream.

CHAPTER 9

Bragg, Melvyn (1988). *Richard Burton: A Life*. New York: Warner Books.
Estrin, M. & McCarthy, J. (1997). *International Dictionary of Films and Filmmakers: Actors and Actresses*. 3rd edn. A. E. Unterburger (Ed). Detroit, MI: St James Press.
Thomas, David. (2003). I never felt I was doing anything wrong. *Sunday Telegraph Review*, July 6, pp.1–2.

CHAPTER 10

Eliot, Marc (2007). *Jimmy Stewart: A Biography*. New York: Harmony.
Fitzgerald, Michael (2004). *Autism and Creativity: Is There a Link between Autism in Men and Exceptional Ability?* Hove, UK: Brunner-Routledge.
Fitzgerald, M. & O'Brien, B. (2007). *Genius Genes: How Asperger Talents Changed the World.* Shawnee Mission, KS: Autism Asperger Publishing Company.
Spoto, Donald (1983). *The Dark Side of Genius: The Life of Alfred Hitchcock*. New York: Little, Brown.

CHAPTER 11

Read, Piers Paul (2005). *Alec Guinness: The Authorised Biography*. London: Simon & Schuster.

CHAPTER 12

Fitzgerald, Michael (2004). Autism and Creativity*: Is There a Link between Autism in Men and Exceptional Ability?* Hove, UK: Brunner-Routledge.
Morley, Sheridan (1990). *Odd Man Out.* London: Coronet Books.

CHAPTER 13

Fitz-Simon, Christopher (1994). The Boys: A Biography of Micheál *Mac Liammóir* and Hilton Edwards. London: Nick Hern.
Ó hAodha, Micheál (1990). *The Importance of Being Micheál: A Portrait of Mac Liammóir.* Dingle, Ireland: Brandon Press.

CHAPTER 14

Kalush, William & Sloman, Larry (2007). The Secret Life of Houdini: The Making of America's First Superhero. New York: Atria Books.

CHAPTER 15

Goodwin, Cliff (2004). Behaving Badly: *The Life of Richard Harris 1930–2002.* London: Virgin.

CHAPTER 16

Lord, Graham (2004). *Niv: The Authorised Biography of David Niven*. London: Orion.

Norman, Barry (1985). *The Film Greats.* London: Hodder & Stoughton.

CHAPTER 17

Holroyd, Michael (2008). *A Strange Eventful History: The Dramatic Lives of Ellen Terry, Henry Irving, and Their Remarkable Families*. New York: Picador.

Terry, Ellen (1982). *The Story of My Life.* New York: Schocken Books. First published 1908.

CHAPTER 18

Gronowicz, Antoni (1990). *Garbo: Her Story*. New York: Simon & Schuster.

CHAPTER 19

Birdwell, Michael E. (1999). *Celluloid Soldiers: Warner Bros.'s Campaign against Nazism.* New York: New York University Press.

Trimborn, Jürgen (2008). *Leni Riefenstahl: A Life*. New York: Faber & Faber.

CHAPTER 20

Clarke, Gerald (2003). *Get Happy: The Life of Judy Garland*. New York: Random House.

Chapter 21

Shipman, Pat (2007). *Femme Fatale: Love, Lies and the Unknown Life of Mata Hari.* London: Weidenfeld & Nicolson.
Keay, Julia (1987). *The Spy Who Never Was: Life and Loves of Mata Hari.* London: Michael Joseph.

Chapter 22

Chandler, Charlotte (2007). *Hello, I Must Be Going: Groucho and His Friends*. New York: Simon & Schuster.
FitzGerald, Michael & James, Ioan (2007). *The Mind of the Mathematician*. Baltimore, MD: Johns Hopkins University Press.
Marx, Groucho (2008). *Groucho and Me*. Cambridge, MA: Da Capo Press.
Thompson, J. W. (2002). He dwelt apart. *Literary Review*, July, pp.5–6.

Chapter 23

Lewis, Roger (2004). *The Life and Death of Peter Sellers.* London: Arrow Books.
Daily Telegraph (2006). Obituary of Michael Sellers. 5 August. Retrieved from http://www.telegraph.co.uk

Chapter 24

Fitzgerald, Michael (2005). T*he Genesis of Artistic Creativity: Asperger's Syndrome and the Arts.* London: Jessica Kingsley.
Fitzgerald, M. & O'Brien, B. (2007). *Genius Genes: How Asperger Talents Changed the World.* Shawnee Mission, KS: Autism Asperger Publishing Company.
Goodwin, Cliff. (2000). *When the Wind Changed: The Life and Death* of *Tony Hancock.* London: Century.
Lyons, Viktoria & Fitzgerald, Michael (2005). *Asperger Syndrome: A Gift or a Curse?* New York: Nova Science.
Oakes, Philip (1975). *The Entertainers: Tony Hancock.* London: Woburn.

Chapter 25

Davies, Russell (1993). *The Kenneth Williams Diaries*. London: HarperCollins.
Fitzgerald, Michael (2004). *Autism and Creativity: Is There a Link between Autism in Men and Exceptional Ability?* Hove, UK: Brunner-Routledge.
Williams, Kenneth (1985).*Just Williams: An Autobiography*. London: J.M. Dent & Sons.

CHAPTER 26

Curtis, James (2003). *W.C. Fields: A Biography.* New York: Alfred A. Knopf.
Chambers Biographical Dictionary (1990). Edinburgh: W & R Chambers.

CHAPTER 27

Carpenter, Humphrey (2003). *Spike Milligan: The Biography.* London: Hodder and Stoughton.
Farnes, Norma (2004). *Spike: An Intimate Memoir.* London: Harper Perennial.

CHAPTER 28

Ryan, Philip B. (1990). *Jimmy O'Dea: The Pride of the Coombe.* Dublin: Poolbeg Press.

CHAPTER 29

Louvish, Simon (2007). *Cecil B. DeMille and the Golden Calf.* London: Faber & Faber.
de Mille, Agnes (1973). *Speak to Me, Dance with Me.* New York: Little, Brown.

CHAPTER 30

Benedetti, Jean (1990). *Stanislavski: An Introduction.* London: Methuen.
Fitzgerald, Michael (2004). *Autism and Creativity: Is There a Link between Autism in Men and Exceptional Ability?* Hove, UK: Brunner-Routledge.

CHAPTER 31

Kezich, Tullio (2006). *Fellini: His Life and Work.* London: Hamish Hamilton.

CHAPTER 32

Fitzgerald, M. & O'Brien, B. (2007). *Genius Genes: How Asperger Talents Changed the World.* Shawnee Mission, KS: Autism Asperger Publishing Company.
Forsyth, James (1976). *Tyrone Guthrie.* London: Hamish Hamilton.
Lyons, Viktoria & Fitzgerald, Michael (2005). *Asperger Syndrome: A Gift or a Curse?* New York: Nova Science.

CHAPTER 33

Chandler, Charlotte (2005). *It's Only a Movie: Alfred Hitchcock – A Personal Biography*. London: Simon & Schuster.

CHAPTER 34

Baxter, John (1994). *Buñuel*. London: Fourth Estate.
de Buñuel, Jeanne Rucar (2010). *Memoirs of a Woman Without a Piano: My Life with Luis Buñuel*. Brooklyn, NY: Five Ties Publishing.

CHAPTER 35

Carpenter, Edmund. (1968). Very, Very Happy; Very Happy. *New York Times Book Review*, 5 May.
Fitzgerald, Michael (2004). *Autism and Creativity: Is There a Link between Autism in Men and Exceptional Ability?* Hove, UK: Brunner-Routledge.
Fitzgerald, Michael (2005). *The Genesis of Artistic Creativity: Asperger's Syndrome and the Arts*. London: Jessica Kingsley.
Fitzgerald, M. & O'Brien, B. (2007). *Genius Genes: How Asperger Talents Changed the World*. Shawnee Mission, KS: Autism Asperger Publishing Company.
Gabler, Neal (2007). *Walt Disney: The Triumph of the American Imagination*. New York: Random House.
Gould, Stephen Jay (1979). Perpetual Youth. *New Scientist*, 7 June, pp.832–834.

CHAPTER 36

Frischauer, Willi (1973). *Behind the Scenes of Otto Preminger: An Unauthorised Biography*. London: Joseph.
Preminger, Otto (1977). *Preminger: An Autobiography*. Garden City, NY: Doubleday.

CHAPTER 37

Bergan, Ronald (1999). *Eisenstein: A Life in Conflict*. London: Little, Brown.
Lyons, Viktoria & Fitzgerald, Michael (2005). *Asperger Syndrome: A Gift or a Curse?* New York: Nova Science.
Stam, Robert (2000). *Film Theory: An Introduction*. Malden, MA: Blackwell.

CHAPTER 38

Fitzgerald, Michael (2005). The Genesis of Artistic Creativity: Asperger's Syndrome and the Arts. London: Jessica Kingsley.

Mann, William J. (2005). *Edge of Midnight: The Life of John Schlesinger*. London: Arrow Books.

CHAPTER 39

Fine, Marshall (1991). *Bloody Sam: The Life and Films of Sam Peckinpah.* New York: Donald I. Fine.

CHAPTER 40

McBride, Joseph (1992). *Frank Capra: The Catastrophe of Success*. New York: Touchstone Books.

Capra, Frank (1971). *Frank Capra, the Name above the Title: An Autobiography*. New York: Macmillan.

CHAPTER 41

McGilligan, Patrick (1991). *George Cukor: A Double Life*. New York: St. Martin's Press.

CHAPTER 42

Burton, Humphrey (1994). *Leonard Bernstein*. London: Faber & Faber.

Peyser, Joan (1998). *Bernstein: A Biography*. New York: Billboard Books.

CHAPTER 43

Chasins, Abram. (1981). *Leopold Stokowski*: *A Profile*. London: Robert Hale:

Fitzgerald, M. & O'Brien, B. (2007). *Genius Genes: How Asperger Talents Changed the World*. Shawnee Mission, KS: Autism Asperger Publishing Company.

CHAPTER 44

Fitzgerald, M. (2004). *Autism and Creativity: Is There a Link between Autism in Men and Exceptional Ability?* New York: Brunner-Routledge.

Hingley, R. (1976). *A New Life of Anton Chekhov*. Oxford: Oxford University Press.

Chapter 45

Chambers Biographical Dictionary (1997). Edinburgh: W & R Chambers.
Fitzgerald, Michael (2004). *Autism and Creativity: Is There a Link between Autism in Men and Exceptional Ability?* Hove, UK: Brunner-Routledge.
Koht, Halvdan. (1971). *The Life of Ibsen*. Trans. E. Haugen & A. E. Santaniello. New York: Benjamin Blom.
Meyer, Michael. (1971). *Ibsen: A Biography*. London: Penguin Books.
Stanislavsky, K. (1924). *My Life in Art*. Trans. J. J. Robins. London: Geoffrey Bles.

Chapter 46

Büdel, Oscar. (1966). *Pirandello*. London: Bowes & Bowes.
Fitzgerald, M. (2004). *Autism and Creativity: Is There a Link between Autism in Men and Exceptional Ability?* New York: Brunner-Routledge.
Matthaei, Renate. (1973). *Luigi Pirandello*. Trans. Simon and Erika Young. New York: Frederick Ungar Publishing.

Chapter 47

Arditti, Michael (2006). The hatreds of a has-been. *The Independent*, 5 May, p.23.
Banville, John (2006). A look back at anger. *Irish Times Weekend Review*, 3 June, p.10.
Edgar, David (2006). Stalking out. *London Review of Books*, 20 July, pp.8–10.
Heilpern, John (2006). *John Osborne: A Patriot for Us*. London: Chatto & Windus.
Osborne, John (1981). *John Osborne: A Better Class of Person*. London: Faber & Faber.
Stokes, J. (2006). A voice to fear, *Times Literary Supplement*, 23 June, pp.3–4.
Walden, George (2006). Man of many parts. *New Statesman*, 29 May, pp.50–51.

Chapter 48

Baron-Cohen, S. (2003). *The Essential Difference: The Truth about the Male and Female Brain*. London: Basic Books.
Gordon, L. (1977). *Eliot's Early Years*. Oxford: Oxford University Press.
Fitzgerald, M. (2004). *Autism and Creativity: Is There a Link between Autism in Men and Exceptional Ability?* New York: Brunner-Routledge.
Fitzgerald, M. (2005). *The Genesis of Artistic Creativity: Asperger's Syndrome and the Arts*. London: Jessica Kingsley.
FitzGerald, Michael & James, Ioan (2007). *The Mind of the Mathematician*. Baltimore, MD: Johns Hopkins University Press.

Chapter 49

Le Vot, André (1985). *F. Scott Fitzgerald: A Biography*. Trans. W. Byron. Harmondsworth, UK: Penguin Books.

Chapter 50

Pilling, C., Schilling, D., & Springer, M. (2005). *Schiller*. Trans. A. McGeoch. London: Haus Publishing.

Chapter 51

Fitzgerald, M. (2008). *Attention Deficit Hyperactivity Disorder, Creativity, Novelty Seeking and Risk*. New York: Nova Scientific.
Mason, Haydn. (1981). *Voltaire*. London: Granada Publishing.
Mitford, Nancy. (1957/1976). *Voltaire in Love*. London: Hamish Hamilton.

Chapter 52

Clarke, Gerald (Ed.) (2004). *Too Brief a Treat: The Letters of Truman Capote*. New York: Random House.
Clarke, Gerald (2006). *Capote: A Biography*. London: Abacus.
Plimpton, George (1998). *Truman Capote*. London: Picador.
Tóibín, Colm (2005). In his pink negligee. *London Review of Books*, 21 April, pp.8–10.

Chapter 53

Jeffares Norman, A. (2001). *The Poems and Plays of Oliver St John Gogarty*. Gerrards Cross, England: Colin Smyth.
O'Connor, Ulick (2000). *Oliver St John Gogarty: A Poet and His Times*. Dublin: The O'Brien Press.

Chapter 54

Fitzgerald, M. (2000). Jonathan Swift: victim of Asperger's syndrome. *Canadian Journal of Diagnosis*, May, 31–36.
Fitzgerald, M. (2001). Did Lord Byron have attention deficit hyperactivity disorder? *Journal of Medical Biography*, 9, 31–33.

Fitzgerald, M. (2008). *Attention Deficit Hyperactivity Disorder, Creativity, Novelty Seeking and Risk*. New York: Nova Scientific.

Pearson, John (2003). *The Life of Ian Fleming*. London: Aurum Press.

Chapter 55

Carrère, Emmanuel (2005). *I Am Alive and You Are Dead: A Journey into the Mind of Philip K. Dick. Trans.* T. Bent. London: Bloomsbury.

Fitzgerald, M. (2005). The *Genesis of Artistic Creativity: Asperger's Syndrome and the Arts*. London: Jessica Kingsley.

Fitzgerald, M., & O'Brien, B. (2007). *Genius Genes: How Asperger Talents Changed the World*. Lenexa, KS: Autism Asperger Publishing Company.

Chapter 56

Bryson, Bill (2008). *Shakespeare: The World as Stage*. London: Atlas Books.

Fitzgerald, M. (2004). *Autism and Creativity: Is There a Link between Autism in Men and Exceptional Ability?* New York: Brunner-Routledge.

Kenny Z., & Fitzgerald, M. (2006). *Shakespeare had Asperger's Syndrome*. Unpublished paper.

Chapter 57

Fitzgerald, M. (2008). *Attention Deficit Hyperactivity Disorder, Creativity, Novelty Seeking and Risk.* New York: Nova Scientific.

Fraser-Cavassoni, Natasha. (2004). *Sam Spiegel.* London: Time Warner.

Chapter 58

Asperger, H. (1944). Die "Autistischen Psychopathen" im Kindesalter. *Archiv für Psychiatrie und Nervenkrankheiten*, 117, 76–136.

Davies, Marion (1975). *The Times We Had: Life with William Randolph Hearst*. P. Pfau & K. S. Marx (Eds.) Indianapolis, IN: Bobbs-Merrill Company.

Fitzgerald, M. (2000). Did Ludwig Wittgenstein have Asperger's syndrome? *European Child & Adolescent Psychiatry*, 9, 61–65.

Fitzgerald, M. (2004). *Autism and Creativity: Is There a Link between Autism in Men and Exceptional Ability?* New York: Brunner-Routledge.

Fitzgerald, M., & O'Brien, B. (2007). *Genius Genes: How Asperger Talents Changed the World.* Lenexa, KS: Autism Asperger Publishing Company.

Lyons V., & Fitzgerald M. (2004). *Humour in autism and Asperger's syndrome. Journal of Autism and Developmental Disorders,* 34, 5, 521–531.

Pfau, P., & Marx, K. S. (Eds.) (1975). *The Times We Had: Life with William Randolph Hearst.* Indianapolis, IN: Bobbs-Merrill Company.
Swanberg, W. A. (1996). *Citizen Hearst.* New York: Galahad Books.

CHAPTER 59

Berg, A. Scott (1989). *Goldwyn: A Biography*. London: Sphere Books.

CHAPTER 60

Brown, P. Harry, & Broeske, P.H. (1998). *Howard Hughes: The Untold Story*. Los Angeles, CA: Warner Books.
Byrne, Paul (2005). High-flying DiCaprio has got Hughes under his skin. *Evening Herald*, 13 January, p.26.
Cohen, Marantz P. (2005). Citizen plane. *Times Literary Supplement*, 7 January.
Hiscock, J. (2004). Film review. *The Telegraph Arts*, 4 December, pp.4–5.
Quinn, A. (2004). Leo fails to take off. *The Independent*, 24 December, pp.6–7.
Salzman, L. (1968). *The Obsessional Personality*. New York: Jason Aronson.
Time Magazine (1948). Howard Hughes. 19 July.

INDEX

B

C

F

G

H

I

J

K

L

M

N

O

P

Q

R

S

T

U

V

W

Y